OWEN LOVEJOY: Abolitionist in Congress

OWEN LOVEJOY:

Abolitionist in Congress

EDWARD MAGDOL

Rutgers University Press

New Brunswick, New Jersey

The photograph of Owen Lovejoy is in the collection of the
Office of the Chief Signal Officer, the National Archives
(photograph 111-BA-1128).

Dedicated to the memory
of my teachers
at the University of Michigan:
ALBERT K. STEVENS
MENTOR L. WILLIAMS
RALPH NEAFUS

Foreword

*"the unblemished abolitionist Congressman
Owen Lovejoy, with a curiously steady light
of conscience for a lamp to his feet. . . ."*
                              —*Carl Sandburg*, The War Years.

This is a political biography of Owen Lovejoy, an antislavery hero,
a radical in his time. He came on the stage of history in a minor role
and stayed to play a major part in the struggle for freedom for the
Negro and the white man. What Lovejoy did in his lifetime has
relevance to our own times. He was one of the outstanding abolitionists who insisted that government—political power—should be
the instrument and guarantor of civil rights.

Lovejoy was an Illinois Republican congressman who in the late
1850's was elected to represent the largest constituency of any district in the United States. He was reelected in 1860 and 1862 even
after reapportionment took away from him some of his most faithful
counties. He had labored some twenty years in the antislavery cause
before he was elected to office, first in the Illinois General Assembly,
then in the United States House of Representatives. In the course of
his career his name came to be well known throughout the country.

The antislavery idea was the motor of his life. Slavery's moral,
legal, and physical wrongs aroused him to anger and action. Even
before his eldest brother, the Reverend Elijah Parish Lovejoy, was

murdered by a drunken proslavery mob in Alton, Illinois, in 1837, Owen Lovejoy had become an abolitionist. At first he and his co-workers used only the propaganda of moral suasion directed at slaveowners, but this was done in vain; then they agitated for some vague "immediate emancipation," without immediate results; finally they moved to more effective forms of active liberation. Lovejoy, for one, was always ready to acknowledge openly his efforts on the Underground Railroad. Finally, he rose to the level of *political* abolitionism and led the struggle in the Illinois countryside and in the federal legislature. The cause for which he at first labored in minor parties eventually became the cause of the whole nation. Lovejoy died in 1864, only a few weeks after he had introduced in Congress a bill to declare free all slaves wherever they lived in the jurisdiction of the United States.

His name is directly associated with only one act of Congress—to abolish slavery forever in the territories of the United States. This was the sole unifying issue in Northern American politics in the 1850's and 1860's. On it the most diverse elements—farmers, capitalists, laborers, abolitionists, disgruntled Democrats, Germans, Negroes, and partyless Whigs—united. On almost every other question, most of them of an economic nature, these sectors of the population easily disagreed and stood opposed to each other. Yet the movement to proscribe slavery became the one that brought them together and provided them with a solid base in one of the most fluid and fascinating decades of American politics.

On this issue the Republican party came into being and raised Abraham Lincoln to the Presidency. Yet this party, the party of emancipation, emerged only after an incubation period of at least twenty years. Owen Lovejoy was one of its most prominent and active attendants, and, like some fellow antislavery political leaders, he was a radical outcast until the public caught up to his teachings.

His mature life and activity touched closely on Lincoln's. The two men influenced each other and developed mutual trust and respect over almost ten years of political collaboration. This friendship between the radical abolitionist and the former Whig seriously calls into question estimates of Lincoln's relations with the radical Republicans. Insult, vituperation, disrespect, and a host of other sins have been attributed to the radical Republicans in their dealings with the President, and the cliché of "Lincoln versus the radicals" has persisted until recent years. Rather early in my research for this book, some time ago, I found reason to dispute the cliché. I hope that my story of Lincoln's and Lovejoy's political friendship will prove a useful addition to the literature on the intraparty struggle.[1]

Owen Lovejoy deserves to be remembered as well for his role in enacting the Homestead Act, and for leading in a campaign to give farmers in a farm country a voice in the federal government through the creation of a department of agriculture. He was vocal on the other issues of his time—the money question, the railroads, army expenditures and extravagances, taxation, and land grabbing in the Caribbean. He adamantly opposed the efforts of some slaveowners to put Cuba in their pockets in the name of the United States when they meant the slave states.

Owen Lovejoy was an agitator in the better sense of the word. He was a big genial man from the Illinois farmland, but he could loose thunderbolts of moral indignation over slavery. He had a sharp and homely sense of humor that he turned on slaveowners, but not on the South. He was all for the North, but not for all of the North. He was partisan, sectional, and zealous. Some readers may deem him to be too puritanically one-sided. Lovejoy did over-work rhetoric in stating the case against slavery and in fighting the war against its investors. He was a man with strong feelings and with a capable mind. He used both, the latter sometimes too little, the former sometimes too much. But he used them to affect and improve the human condition.

Owen Lovejoy appeared in the House of Representatives rather shabbily dressed and was considered a parliamentary boob by an Ohio Democrat. But this Northern opponent voted in the minority against Lovejoy's bill to abolish slavery in the territories.

If Lovejoy seemed rural, unkempt, and awkward, his mind was constantly engrossed by the best in urbanity and true cultivation. He had been reared on Jefferson, the Bill of Rights, the Declaration of Independence, the Bible, and militant Protestantism. His readings ranged from the Roman and Greek classical writers through such English masters as Shakespeare, Pope, Dryden, and Cowper. Guizot's *English Revolution*, Macaulay's *England*, and Prescott's works on the Americas found their way to his desk. He borrowed from the Library of Congress Cervantes' *Don Quixote*, Swift's *Gulliver's*

Travels, George Sand's *Consuelo*, George Eliot's *Mill on the Floss* and *Adam Bede;* also Whittier, Irving, Hazlitt, and Goethe.

He was a Congregational minister and a farmer who seriously practiced what he preached about being his brother's keeper. He was devoted to "values, ideals and programs that demanded fundamental changes in society." This was the meaning of his life and the explanation of his actions. In sum, he was a man who took his times seriously and helped to change them for the better. I have chosen to be frankly partisan and agree with Jesse Fell, the Quaker businessman who was Lovejoy's friend and political backer, that "Lovejoy was the real hero of the antislavery cause. . . ." [2]

I owe a large debt of gratitude and appreciation to the men and women who helped to make the source materials available to me, and to those who read the manuscript and made valuable suggestions, criticisms, and recommendations. I am, of course, responsible for the interpretations, judgments, and emphasis it contains. I have continued to hold some beliefs and to place on events certain emphases with which some critics may disagree. For example, I hope that readers will bear with me in my old-fashioned belief in the widespread existence and significance of the Underground Railroad. Notwithstanding a recent skeptical work on this subject, I believe that Lovejoy's activity in the Illinois Underground Railroad supports the original scholarship on this institution by Professor Wilbur H. Siebert. [3]

That there is more in this book of the public Lovejoy than of the private Lovejoy is due in part to the nature of the primary materials available to me. I have offered generous helpings of Lovejoy's own words to illustrate the man's sarcasm, pugnacity, sympathy, and courage, and on the other hand to show him when he was bombastic, intemperate, unfair, and unwise. These may only begin to show what he was really like. At any rate, my research turned up more of the public, political man than of the man in the intimacy of family and friends. To my knowledge, the exciting and important Lovejoy is the public and political Lovejoy.

My search for information on Owen Lovejoy has led to many libraries and repositories of manuscripts, among them the Chicago Historical Society, the Illinois State Historical Society, the Bureau County Historical Society at Princeton, Illinois, the Matson Library of the same city, the Peoria Public Library, the American History Room of the New York Public Library, the Brooklyn Public Library, the Columbia University Library, the Manuscript Division of the Library of Congress, the National Archives, the American Missionary Association Archives at Fisk University, and the State Historical Library of Wisconsin.

Without the Owen Lovejoy Papers at the William L. Clements Library at the University of Michigan, the Wickett-Wiswall Collection of Lovejoy Papers at Texas Technological College, Lubbock, and the Owen Lovejoy collection at the Bureau County Historical Museum, much of this book could not have been written.

Willard L. King of Chicago led me to the prodigious collection of papers he had made for his biography of David Davis, Lincoln's manager. The late Adlai E. Stevenson tried to put me on the track of a private collection of papers of Jesse W. Fell, his great-grandfather and a collaborator of Owen Lovejoy's. Finally some of these papers were supplied by Helen E. Marshall of Illinois State Normal University. I am deeply grateful to them for their many kindnesses.

I wish to acknowledge also the help of Richard N. Current, Allen Professor of History at the University of Wisconsin, and Merton L. Dillon, Professor of History at Texas Technological College and the author of a biography of the Reverend Elijah P. Lovejoy. Both were good enough to read the manuscript at different stages, and both gave me challenging criticisms.

I am also indebted to John O. Killens and The Harlem Writers Guild Workshop for criticism and encouragement.

Throughout my work I have been fortunate to have as my most patient listener and discerning reader my wife Miriam.

EDWARD MAGDOL

Madison, Wisconsin
September, 1966

Contents

O W E N   L O V E J O Y : Abolitionist in Congress

1

The Murder of Elijah P. Lovejoy

*"He who will never turn when trodden on is
deficient in spirit."*

—*Abigail Adams*

On the moonlit night of November 7, 1837, a mob stood hushed
on the cobblestone waterfront of Alton, Illinois, on the Mississippi River. Before them loomed a three-story stone warehouse,
its roof in flames. The ladder propped against one wall suggested
arson.

On the bare floor upstairs a man was bleeding to death. He was
well built, with black hair falling back from a broad, open face
that had been serious and intelligent. He had given his life to
defend his right to print a newspaper, to express his opinions
freely, and to protect an uncrated press in the warehouse. It was
the fourth he had ordered in two years. Each of the others had
been torn from his printing office, smashed, and, with precious
cases of type, sunk in the mud of the Mississippi River just above
St. Louis.

This man, the eldest brother of Owen Lovejoy, was the Reverend Elijah Parish Lovejoy, a Presbyterian minister who had

become an antislavery leader in Illinois. On November 7, two days before his thirty-fifth birthday, he was murdered because he would not retreat from his principles. Anticipating violence from proslavery community leaders and the mob that followed them, Elijah Lovejoy had resolved some weeks earlier to arm his trust in the Almighty with a gun and put up a fight. Being on the frontier of slavery, he had learned that this might be his only hope.

Elijah Lovejoy began his struggle for freedom of the press and against the institution of slavery in 1835 in the columns of the St. Louis *Observer*, a religious newspaper of which he was the editor. When its press was destroyed, he resumed publication in the Alton, Illinois, *Observer*. He had hoped to wage a peaceful campaign against slavery, but vile actions of slaveowners in and around his own city impelled him to turn to pointed criticism of their abuses. When the mildest statement brought scorn and threat and violence, he felt he must probe further into the evil. Each horror perpetrated by the slaveowners dug into his conscience, which had been shaped by his New England heritage.

After a melancholy youth spent first as a brilliant student in Maine, then as a schoolteacher and the editor of the Whig St. Louis *Times*, he had been swept up in a religious revival movement in January, 1832, and decided to become a minister. Following graduation from the Presbyterian Princeton Theological Seminary in New Jersey in 1833 he preached in Newport, Rhode Island, and in the Spring Street Church in New York City. But he preferred to go back west and readily answered a call from fellow churchmen in St. Louis to return and edit a Presbyterian newspaper, the St. Louis *Observer*.

The first issue was dated November 22, 1833, and the thirty-one-year-old minister and editor took a devout Presbyterian stand. Even so, Lovejoy was controversial in the ranks of his own church, and over doctrinal questions. At that time the impact of social reform movements sweeping the land was felt in the churches of all the leading Protestant denominations, and heavily in the Presbyterian, which was split on the issue of slavery. One section—the Old School, as they were called—held fast to conservative doctrine, especially the tenet that man sinned and fell with Adam. The liberals, or New School Presbyterians, were held by the conservatives to be "tainted with lax discipline." This was perhaps so, since the New School preferred to believe that man was capable of saving himself by his own actions. This "New Haven" theology advocated reform of man by his works, by his revival, and by his efforts on behalf of his fellow man. Elijah Lovejoy was such a Presbyterian. It was no simple task to choose a side and yet edit a newspaper for all Presbyterians.

Lovejoy was immersed in good works. He was an agent of the American Home Missionary Society; organized temperance societies and Bible societies; and became an agent of the American Sunday School Union, and treasurer and agent of the Missouri and Illinois Tract Society, whose views were reflected in the pages of the *Observer*.

The newspaper also carried zealous anti-Catholic articles signed by one "Waldo." These were among many outbursts of militant Protestantism in various parts of the country. However, in the St. Louis of the 1830's, one-third of its people Catholics, this was a hazardous and misdirected undertaking. A strong Catholic reaction to Waldo's columns elicited a counterreaction from Lovejoy. Even though he tried to explain that "the cause of Truth" demanded his own writings against the Catholic Church, he made the error of wiping out their effect with intemperate statements. He only earned a reputation for stubbornness and bigotry among Catholics, who increasingly preferred that he leave St. Louis.[1]

The growing danger to Lovejoy did not come mainly from the religious question, for all the white heat it generated. By 1835

Lovejoy's conscience had been deeply touched by the iniquities of slavery. Fellow New School Presbyterians had taken their stand for abolition. These were men Lovejoy respected, but even without their lead he could see for himself the effects of slavery all about him. He tried to understand the system but was troubled by it. He had always been opposed to slavery, as thousands of Americans were, but he had taken no more advanced position than for colonization of slaves in Africa. The degradation of free Negroes in the cities prompted Lovejoy to believe that the solution to their betterment would be to send them back to Africa.

When William Lloyd Garrison, organizer of the New England antislavery movement, denounced the colonization idea in a hard-hitting pamphlet in 1833, Lovejoy was a student at the Princeton Theological Seminary. He reacted strongly and denounced Garrison. Lovejoy considered Garrison's *Thoughts on Colonization* to be the work of "an incendiary fanatic." Although he did not approve of slavery, Lovejoy had lived in a slave state and had formed a less hostile impression of the system than Garrison, the militant editor of *The Liberator* in Boston. Lovejoy was upset enough to ask his brother Joseph C. Lovejoy, then active in the Maine Anti-Slavery Society, in a letter of November 21, 1834: "How can you hold communion with such a foul mouthed fellow?" [2]

Rather, Lovejoy hoped Southerners would, in true New School fashion, do the Christian thing and liberate their slaves. He seems to have been innocent of the knowledge that property, the investment in it in the form of slave labor, and the profit to be derived from its exploitation, was at the bottom of things. Thus when the Missouri *Republican* proposed in April, 1835, that there be gradual emancipation without hurting slaveowner property rights, Lovejoy agreed and began to urge this course in the *Observer*. He had little sympathy for the radical immediate emancipationists.

6

His mind was changed rapidly when a wave of anti-abolitionist hysteria in the summer of 1835 swept through Northern and near-Southern cities. Mobs took over the streets, threatened anyone suspected of being abolitionist, and in the fashion of mobs slung a broad brush of tar at many a person wrongly and carelessly classified. In Boston, rioters dragged Garrison out of a hall and led him through the streets with a rope around him. In Utica, New York, on the same day a mob threatened a meeting of abolitionists and sacked the offices of the Utica *Standard and Democrat*. In St. Louis, threats were made against the *Observer*. Fortunately Lovejoy was away at a religious camp meeting and a Presbyterian Synod.

That fall, when two white men ("one was totally innocent—whipped on suspicion till he confessed") had been flogged by about sixty of the "most respectable" of St. Louisans because of "the abduction of several Negroes from a town [in Missouri] into Illinois, by some persons, it is not certainly known who," Lovejoy's life was placed in peril, for he too was mistakenly believed to be an abolitionist. To his brother Joseph he had written: "I expect it. I expect that I shall be lynched, or tarred and feathered, or it may be hung up. All are threatened." But he would not be silenced. "In the *Observer* of Thursday, I shall come out openly, fearlessly. . . . And yet, my dear brother, I am not an Abolitionist—at least not such a one as you are." [3]

In the newspaper, Elijah Lovejoy declared himself "*not* an Abolitionist" and explained that immediate emancipation would be harmful to master and slave, "but chiefly to the latter." Nevertheless he would till the end of his days be opposed to the system of slavery. Above all he would not be silenced by mobs, and he asserted his "civil" right to discuss any matter. "See the danger," he wrote, "and the natural and inevitable result to which the first step here will lead. To-day a public meeting declares that you shall not discuss the subject of Slavery, in any of its bearings. . . . To-morrow, another meeting decides that it

7

is against the peace of society, that the principles of Popery shall be discussed, and the edict goes forth to muzzle the press." Similarly, a ban on discussion of "distilleries, dram shops or drunkenness" will be imposed next day. "And so to the end of the chapter the truth is, my fellow-citizens, if you give ground a single inch, there is no stopping place. I deem it therefore, my duty to take my stand upon the Constitution. Here is firm ground—I feel it to be such." [4]

Even his opponents were forced to agree with Lovejoy that freedom of speech must be upheld. Readers in Missouri and Illinois wrote in, thanking him for his stand. Dailies in New York, Boston, Cincinnati, and Philadelphia backed his plea for freedom of the press. The *Shepherd of the Valley*, the Catholic weekly newspaper of St. Louis, denied that Catholics agitated against the *Observer*, or that Catholics were intolerant of Protestants. The editors were thus trying to demonstrate that they would not be party to violence against Lovejoy's constitutional rights. Prominent St. Louisans managed to break loose from the mob spirit and offered to uphold the editor's right to discuss slavery despite their own disagreement with his views. [5]

In the midst of that siege of mob hatred the proprietors of the *Observer* had asked Lovejoy to resign. He turned the newspaper back to the proprietors and prepared to leave the city. But a happy accident changed defeat into a personal victory for Lovejoy. The proprietors had been put in a position of financial embarrassment by the *Observer* and had sold it to a wealthy St. Louis financier, who held the mortgage. When he came to the *Observer* office to take possession, he found Lovejoy and offered to pay the note himself rather than have the *Observer* stop publication. "It was as life from the dead," the editor wrote to his brother, "as light out of the thickest darkness." Yet he was not an abolitionist, merely "an *emancipationist*." [6]

In anguish about slavery, Elijah told his mother of "a man here, walking the streets in open day, who, about a year since, actually whipped his Negro woman to death. He was tried for murder, but as Negro evidence was not admitted, he could not be convicted. . . ." Or, when in another letter to his mother in Maine, he wrote: "The man [state's attorney for the district] who headed a public meeting the other night [to halt antislavery publications] whipped his female Negro slave almost to death. Her screams brought a crowd, McGinnis narrowly escaping having his house broken into and himself made the victim of mob violence." [7]

As hysteria was whipped up by slaveowners in St. Louis, Elijah Lovejoy learned to live in the shadow of death. The fever of the mobs who had attacked antislavery papers and public men in Boston, Cincinnati, and New York spread to the banks of the Mississippi. To his brother, Elijah wrote: "But daily . . . my conviction is strengthened, that to give way would be a base desertion of duty." [8]

His immediate duty was to the *Observer*, its circulation showing no sign of dropping as a result of the antislavery discussion in its columns. Rather, the circulation was growing, and no attempt to interfere with its publication occurred through the winter months of 1835 and 1836. But in May he and the *Observer* suffered bitterly because he had protested against an act of lynch justice perpetrated against a free Negro by the name of Francis McIntosh. He was the second steward of the steamboat *Flora*, which plied between Pittsburgh and St. Louis. McIntosh had attempted to take a fellow crew member from the constable, William Mull, after the shipmate had been arrested for fighting. McIntosh himself was arrested and a deputy sheriff, George Hammond, and Mull proceeded to take him to jail. McIntosh seemed calm about the matter, probably having seen many waterfront arrests for just such minor infractions. He walked alongside Hammond taking peanuts from his coat

9

pockets and popping them into his mouth. The boat's steward asked Hammond what punishment he would get. The deputy sheriff said, "jestingly," according to one account: "Perhaps they might hang him."

When they crossed the street, McIntosh tried to break loose, and stabbed Mull. When Hammond tried to get McIntosh away from Mull, he too was stabbed. A crowd of about fifty persons ran after McIntosh, who leaped a fence, ran into a backyard house, barred the door, and threatened to kill the first one who laid a hand on him. But he was captured and jailed by St. Louis county sheriff James Brotherton. Word spread hysterically through town, and soon a mob of five hundred to a thousand gathered in front of the jail demanding to lynch McIntosh. Brotherton refused to give up his prisoner. The mob over-powered him, tied his hands behind his back, took the keys, and rushed McIntosh up Chestnut Street.

Someone in the mob shouted, "Let's burn him." Then the mob tied McIntosh to a honey locust tree with trace chains. Others took some shavings and dry pine boards from a nearby carpenter shop. These they piled around the chained man and set him on fire. McIntosh was instantly enveloped in flames and burned to death in a short time. The whole incident took an hour. The mob left his "cindered corpse to be pelted with stones by a rabble of boys!" [9]

In the grand jury investigation that followed in July, Judge Luke E. Lawless condoned the savage act. Elizur Wright, Jr., writing in the *Quarterly Anti-Slavery Magazine*, said, "The charge . . . is a traitorous surrender of the last shred of legal protection of the colored man. . . . It gives the solemn sanction of law to any and every outrage that a sufficiently large mob may choose to perpetrate, and it points out a class of suitable victims." [10]

Elijah Lovejoy editorialized against the lynching in the May fifth *Observer*. He conceded McIntosh's guilt but wrote: "We must stand by the Constitution and laws, or all is gone." Mob retaliation against him for those opinions was quick. Twice between May 30 and June 6 the *Observer* shop and office was attacked and the press damaged. Only a small issue came out on June 9. In July, Lovejoy protested against the charge to the grand jury in an editorial entitled "The Charge of Judge Lawless." He upheld civil rights, condemned lynch law, and said nothing about the question of slavery. But he attacked Judge Lawless on the narrow ground of the judge's religion. He said that the charge was because Judge Lawless was a "Papist; and in his charge we see the cloven foot of Jesuitism. . . ." But others besides Catholics opposed Lovejoy. About twenty men broke into the *Observer* office the night after the editorial appeared, smashed the press and type, and threw the pieces out the windows. Despite this wrath against him, Lovejoy's argument for civil rights and against mob violence was supported by the Missouri *Republican* and the Alton *Telegraph*.[11]

He had in the meanwhile given notice of his move from St. Louis to the rival city of Alton across the river. It was hoped that in free Illinois he would be able to publish with less molestation. But when the remaining type and the repaired press landed there, another mob demolished the press and type and threw them into the river.

The people of Alton assured him that such mob action had no place in their town. At a meeting in the new Presbyterian church they asked Lovejoy for his plans about publishing in their city and about his antislavery views. "I told them, and told the truth," he reported, "that I did not come here to establish an Abolition newspaper, and that in the sense they understood it, I was no abolitionist, but that I was the uncompromising enemy of Slavery, and so expected to live, and so to die." As his antislavery conviction hardened he told his mother: "The

11

cry of the oppressed has entered not only into my ear, but into my soul, so that while I live I cannot hold my peace." [12]

Soon his youngest brother, John, joined him, and sometime later in 1836 Owen did too, both from the Lovejoy family place in Maine. John knew the printing trade, and worked in the *Observer's* composing room. How Owen earned his living at this time is not clear. Possibly he received a stipend from the American Anti-Slavery Society. With the support and love of his brothers, with the solidarity of the family back East, Elijah carried on publication of the *Observer*. He tried to maintain his particular antislavery position, but edged closer to abolitionism. The newspaper won new readers, and circulation rose to 1,700 in March, 1837, and a few months later to 2,000.[13]

In February, 1837, Elijah Lovejoy took a closer look at colonization and gradual emancipation, and decided that both fell short of doing the necessary task of manumission. He wrote: "As well might a lady think to bail out the Atlantic with her thimble, as the Colonization Society to remove slavery by colonizing the slaves in Africa." He became an open abolitionist in the spring of 1837. In June he published in the *Observer* a letter from the national Anti-Slavery Society seeking the names of people willing to help petition Congress for the abolition of slavery in the District of Columbia.[14]

By the autumn of 1837 the Lovejoy brothers in Illinois had joined some of their fellow citizens to set up a state antislavery society. Local units of the American Anti-Slavery Society, founded in 1833, had multiplied in Northern cities and towns from seventeen to two hundred in 1835, to three hundred in the next year and, by 1840, to two thousand, with a membership of almost two hundred thousand. In the summer of 1837 local societies had been created in some northern Illinois communities. These had been the works of enthusiastic New Englanders of various Protestant faiths then pouring into the old Northwest to

12

lay the foundations of towns and cities. They cleared the land, tilled the soil and planted crops, set up colleges and seminaries, and otherwise transplanted the rich intellectual heritage of Yale and Dartmouth and Harvard, and the traditions of the Vermont hills. Something of the spirit of Ethan Allen's revolt against New York landlordism went with them, as well as that of Shays's captaincy in the Massachusetts farmers' rebellion against debt and poverty. They brought with them not only Bibles, but the secular ideas of Roger Williams and John Woolman with his benevolent strictures against property in man. They also brought keen knowledge of how to bargain and calculate and engineer bridges and houses. Their heritage included concern for the slave's freedom, and now in 1837 some of the forward-looking among them set up the local antislavery groups, one in Bureau County, another in Will County, one each in Adams, Jersey, and Macoupin. But they hoped to unite and organize a state society.[15]

Alton, Illinois, was by its proximity to Kentucky and Missouri a hazardous spot for antislavery men. The city's rapid growth as a commercial center rivaling St. Louis made its leading citizens—its merchants with eyes on profits in geometric progression—fear any action that might hurt the town's reputation, especially the antislavery discussion led by Lovejoy. It was a booming town of three hundred houses, some of brick and stone; fifty stores, one importing directly from Europe; four hotels and nine boardinghouses; a bank and two schools; a lyceum and four newspapers; a temperance society and a lodge of Odd Fellows. Bricklayers and stonemasons could ask and get as much as $2.50 a day; common laborers shared the crumbs that fell from the land-speculation table at the rate of $1.50 a day. Some of the stores grossed half a million dollars a year, others were satisfied with two hundred thousand. The city was surrounded by lush stands of timber and rich coal deposits. Eight

13

steamboats were owned here and floated down the involuted Mississippi all the way to New Orleans. Two railroads, it was hoped, would make Alton their terminal. Business lots commanded a price of four hundred dollars a front foot, and stores rented at from four hundred to fifteen hundred dollars a year. Back of town, land was going for ten dollars to forty dollars an acre, and in general the real estate bubble swelled and swelled by 1,000 per cent in two years, and the end was not in sight.[16] In the race for riches most of the merchants and leaders of Alton society seemed blind to the moral evil of slavery. There was no great outcry from them against the system that persisted across the river. They deplored the agitation of the slavery question as detrimental to Alton's commercial progress. Although they were not slaveholders, in Illinois, their sensitivity to the attitudes of slaveholders in nearby slave states was a factor in their desire to suppress antislavery agitation.

Only the *Observer* and the Lovejoys and handfuls of men from the northern counties called for a state organization to discuss slavery, and they were endangering the status quo—and themselves. For freedom for the slave, for their right to write freely in the press on temperance, on religion, on slavery, or on any other subject, the Lovejoys were prepared to fight and die.

During the hot summer days of 1837 that baked the city on the bluffs overlooking the big river, the Reverend Lovejoy was easily recognized on the streets in his white suit and broad-brimmed hat. This man of medium height with broad muscular body seemed confident of his mission. His black eyes, with a "certain twinkle, betrayed a sense of the humorous." His "full countenance," a friend said, "expressed great kindness and sympathy." [17]

He proposed in his newspaper that there be a study of the slavery question. He even suggested that it might be useful to organize a state antislavery group for that purpose. The verbal

14

attacks on him by men of influence eventually led to physical assaults upon Lovejoy and his wife, Celia Ann. In the first week of October he admitted to Joshua Leavitt of the American Anti-Slavery Society that his life was in constant danger: "We have only members of our family with us. A loaded musket is standing at my bedside while my two brothers in an adjoining room have three others, together with pistols, cartridges, etc. And this is the way we live in the city of Alton!" He was reluctant to resort to firearms for defense, yet what could he do when experience had taught him that there was no protection, "either in the laws or the protecting aegis of public sentiment." Most of the merchants and bankers in town saw to that. Nevertheless he and his brothers joined two hundred and forty-four fellow citizens from all over the state to issue a call for a meeting "of the friends of the slave and of free discussion" at Upper Alton on the last Thursday of October, 1837.[18]

This would be a difficult meeting at best. Rev. Edward Beecher, president of Illinois College, had favored a convention confined to the question of "free discussion," to emphasize protection of the rights of free speech and free press. Lovejoy, knowing that four-fifths of Alton's citizens had by now become fearful of truly free discussion of the slavery question, took a different view. Now a convinced abolitionist, he insisted on inviting only convinced antislavery people to the meeting. His objective was to form the state antislavery society.

If the leading citizens of Alton really meant to live by the Constitution and by the laws guaranteeing freedom of speech and of the press, they would not interfere with the antislavery movement in their city. If they really believed in the principle of civil rights, but not necessarily in antislavery, as Beecher hopefully thought, they should be invited to participate in the meeting. But Lovejoy feared that the "respectable" men of the city would only obstruct such a meeting. Nevertheless Beecher took direction in his hands and invited everyone interested in free speech to the antislavery meeting. He was willing to compromise and delay the formation of a purely abolitionist organization. But even he was forced to recognize only days before the convention that his unrealistic offer fell on closed ears. It was too late for him or Lovejoy to do anything to change the situation.

Meanwhile the abolitionists of Ohio, New York, and Boston gave national importance to the forthcoming Alton meeting. Joshua Leavitt felt that Illinois was the "seat of war." James G. Birney, former slaveowner and editor of the antislavery *Philanthropist* in Cincinnati, was urged to go on a speaking tour in Illinois before the convention and if possible attend it. Small financial contributions were made to Lovejoy's cause by New York and Boston abolitionists.[19]

As Lovejoy had predicted, out-and-out anti-abolitionist men, including some of the wealthiest in town, came into the meeting professing to be friends of free discussion. They jammed the meeting with their supporters, tied up its committees in unworkable sessions, and frustrated genuinely free discussion. In effect they obstructed formation of an abolitionist society. After some provocative diversionary moves by Usher F. Linder, Illinois Attorney General, the real friends of the slave and of free discussion conducted a two-day meeting of their own. They brought forth a state antislavery society with Elijah Lovejoy its first general secretary.

Linder was fit to be tied, and after adjournment he climbed onto a pile of wood in the yard outside the convention house and delivered a tirade against Yankees and their confounded newfangled ideas and their newfangled ways—introducing home missionaries and Sunday schools—their abolitionism, and their damned preachings against liquor in their temperance societies. As the last words were blurted out Linder caught himself and added, "But by the way, gentlemen, temperance is a very good

16

thing." He had just remembered his own signature on the total-abstinence pledge a few days earlier. Then he went back to abusing Yankees, abolitionists, and Lovejoy especially. His buffoon performance was only a curtain-raiser for the mob attack organized for the night of November 7, 1837.[20]

During the next five or six days after the antislavery convention several citizens' meetings were held to attempt a solution of the crisis facing Alton. Men of substance were proposing as a "compromise" that Lovejoy sever his connections with the *Observer*. If they had ever read the first article of the Bill of Rights, they had either abandoned it or, to be charitable, never understood that it was to be effective even in the case of one whose views and opinions they hated.

Sometime before this critical moment in November and before the October convention, Alton's leading men had abandoned the editor's rights not only in theory but also by refusing to halt increasing mob attacks on Lovejoy and his press. A series of violent actions during the summer months seriously threatened Lovejoy's chances of survival. The first of them occurred late on the night of August 21, while Lovejoy was walking into town to get medicine for his ailing wife. A gang stopped him and threatened to tar and feather him if he did not promise to leave town or to be silent on the slavery question. He escaped death that night by standing firm and appealing to the consciences of these men. His lack of fear and great self-discipline saved him.

Two days later a less scrupulous mob broke into his office and destroyed his second press. A public appeal for funds to replace it with a new one brought in the necessary fifteen hundred dollars. Lovejoy asked for the funds not for the antislavery cause but "to sustain the laws and guard the freedom of the press," regardless of the paper's viewpoint. The response to the plea was heartening, since the panic and depression of 1837 had affected Alton.[21]

17

Even though money had been raised for the new press and friends in Alton had rallied to the *Observer*, some supporters weakened. Some returned to reactivate the defunct local Colonization Society, an action which today seems a desertion of the struggle for Lovejoy's rights. This is underscored by the fact that neither nationally nor in any local branches did colonizationists have serious impact. Only three thousand colonists were sent to Africa in the first fifteen years of the society's existence, out of the slave population of about three million. To persist in reviving an ineffective formula like colonization could only divert strength from the abolitionists and evade the responsibility to defend Lovejoy's rights. Others were prepared to see Lovejoy leave town and sacrifice principle. Even Winthrop S. Gilman, the one wealthy businessman in town who had been staunch in support of Lovejoy, advised the editor that he could no longer give aid to the *Observer*. Fewer than a dozen men in the county were now willing to state publicly that they supported Lovejoy's right to publish his newspaper as he wished.

The terror under which he and his wife lived had made of Celia Ann Lovejoy a constantly ill woman. This fact and the mounting opposition and the defection of friends almost persuaded Lovejoy that he too must yield.

Owen Lovejoy took a different approach. He felt that his brother should continue to stand on his rights. He suggested that there might still be a chance to stay in Alton, that Elijah ought not to abandon his fight to continue as editor of the paper. Why not put the question to the supporters of the *Observer*, Owen advised, to those who had stood by it at first but who had drifted away, as well as to the handful of faithful men still backing Elijah? Gilman's position was not necessarily held by everyone, Owen argued. Maybe even the anti-*Observer* people would listen to a plea by Elijah.[22]

He followed the advice and posed the matter in a letter to

"The Friends of the Redeemer in Alton." A few days later a response came, in a meeting with Elijah of fifteen men concerned with the fate of the newspaper. They discussed two points: reestablishment of the *Observer*, and whether Lovejoy should stay on as its editor. There was agreement on the first, but division on the second.

The situation for Lovejoy deteriorated faster than he or Owen had believed possible. Violence and threats against Elijah and the newspaper increased. On September 21 a mob struck again and destroyed the newly arrived third press, which Owen had been sent to purchase in Cincinnati. An appeal for funds for a fourth press met a good response, and the machinery was ordered. Although a flicker of hope was still in the situation, *Observer* supporters began to think about an armed guard to prevent damage to this one on its arrival in October or November.

Tempers ran high among the enemies of Lovejoy in the aftermath of the antislavery convention of October 27–29. They were more adamant than before in seeking the ouster of Lovejoy. They did not speak of violence but of compromise, which they defined as total surrender by Lovejoy. In doing so, the respectable gentlemen of commerce and clergy fired the lynch spirit of less pretentious and less sophisticated souls.

A meeting of Alton's prominent men on November 3 made a last-stand offer to Lovejoy: Leave town. They were unwilling to uphold his constitutional right to publish there. Winthrop S. Gilman rallied to Lovejoy's cause and quite bluntly told his fellow citizens: "The rigid enforcement of the law would prove the only sure protection of the rights of citizens, and the only safe remedy for similar excitements in the future." Lovejoy then stepped forward in his own defense, solemnly delivering one of the eloquent statements for civil rights in American history.

"I know that I have the right freely to speak and publish my sentiments, subject only to the laws of the land for the abuse of

19

that right . . . solemnly guaranteed to me by the Constitution of these United States and of this state. . . .

". . . if by a compromise is meant that I should cease from doing that which duty requires of me, I cannot make it. And the reason is that I fear God more than I fear man. . . . Sir, the very act of retreating will embolden the mob to follow me wherever I go. No sir; there is no way to escape the mob, but to abandon the path of duty; and that, God helping me, I will never do. . . .

"Sir, I dare not flee away from Alton. . . . No, sir, the contest has commenced here; and here it must be finished. Before God and you all, I here pledge myself to continue it, if need be, till death. If I fall, my grave shall be made in Alton." [23]

Tears of emotion showed on his face as he left the room. Usher Linder dominated the meeting and dragged in cheap and mean arguments to becloud the issue. As far as he was concerned, the mob he had helped to arouse and encourage had given the final answer. There was no longer room for compromise. Lovejoy had taken his stand on principle. The leaders of the community had abandoned their responsibility and had put their stamp of approval on the mob, disregarding the laws for which they professed to stand. And the mob acted swiftly.

The skipper of the steamboat *Missouri Fulton* had been good enough to agree to land Lovejoy's fourth press at midnight, Monday, November 6, even if he had to lay by for a while to do so. In the meantime the Lovejoys, having failed to win a measure of protection from the mayor and the city council, organized their own guard of about twenty men and boys. Only three or four of them were abolitionists; the others were citizens who wanted to keep the public order. They posted themselves in Gilman's warehouse alongside the Mississippi River and waited. Inside with them was the press when the attack came on November 7.

The three-story stone structure stood between two vacant lots and was thus open to attack all around. About ten o'clock on Tuesday evening a gang of men armed with pistols, clubs, and stones marched on the warehouse and demanded the press. Gilman spoke to the crowd from the third floor of the building, pleading with them to go away peaceably. He said that the press was in his care and the property would be defended. He assured the angry group that he held no ill will toward them. One of the men in the mob flashed a pistol, forcing Gilman to close the door. The pistol-wielder shouted, "We'll take the damned press at the cost of our lives."

The crowd then went to the other end of the warehouse and smashed the windows there with a volley of stones. Crockery was hurled at the attackers by some of the guard in the building. Then the drunken gang outside found a timber with which they were going to batter down the door. But first they fired shots into the warehouse to drive back any of the defenders who might be at the windows and door. Then the mobsters began to ram the door. Inside, the "aged, mild and courteous" Deacon Enoch Long, commanding the defense group, ordered them to open fire with their muskets. One of the mob, Lyman Bishop, was shot and killed. The mob withdrew for a while.

They returned with plenty of liquor flowing among them. They cursed and shouted that they'd like to kill every damned abolitionist in town. They were better armed and rallied more men to their ranks. Half a mile away church bells were being rung by Mrs. Frederick W. Graves, wife of the pastor of the Presbyterian church, to sound the alarm. At the riot scene crowds of spectators gathered. The brilliant moon, reflecting off the river and the cobblestones in the street, shed a cold light on the frenzied mob. The shrilling of tin horns added to the terror of the night.

Mayor John Krum came on the scene at this time and tried to

disperse the crowds, but he failed. Then he went into the ware-house to persuade the men inside to make a compromise. Gilman tried to get the mayor to call on certain leading citizens to help prevent destruction of the building. The mayor said he could not do this, he had used his authority to no avail. Gilman asked, "Shall we continue to defend this place by arms?" The mayor could do nothing but assent. When he returned to the street, he told the mob that the defenders of the press would not make a compromise.

A surge of the mob, with shouts of "Fire the house! Burn 'em out!" swept past the vacillating mayor to the vacant lot on one side of the warehouse. There were no windows on this side, and the mob hurriedly put a ladder up against the wall. One of them mounted to the roof to set its wooden shingles afire. Five of the press guard, including Elijah Lovejoy, came out to try to get hold of the ladder. They fired a volley, frightened off the arson-ist, and went back into the building to reload. A few moments of silence permitted Lovejoy to think it might be safe to step outside again to see if the mob had dispersed. In the moonlight Lovejoy saw no one near the building. But just at that instant someone opened fire from behind a pile of lumber on a vacant lot. Lovejoy reeled and staggered back into the building. The Reverend Thaddeus Hurlbut at the top of the stairs saw Lovejoy struggling up, both hands on his breast, murmuring only, "I am shot. I am shot." Lovejoy reached the top of the stairs and then fell heavily to the floor.[24]

Hundreds of newspaper editorials, North and South, tens and tens of public meetings, recorded shame and indignation over the tragedy at Alton, and millions of Americans were aroused to the evils of slavery and the threat it posed to free speech and free press in America. The mob attacks on antislavery newspapers and the laws of Southern states suppressing antislavery publications were now seen as proof of that threat. Finally, Lovejoy's murder moved many Americans to take active roles in the antislavery movement. Wendell Phillips, who was to become the great orator of the abolitionist movement, made a brilliant speech in defense of Lovejoy's stand in Boston's Faneuil Hall on December 8, 1837. William H. Herndon, later a law partner of Abraham Lincoln, was a youngster at Illinois College in the border town of Jacksonville, where he imbibed the antislavery doctrine of its New England-reared professors and president. Herndon was stunned by Lovejoy's death and, in spite of a father who had contempt for abolitionists, resolved to do something to rid the land of slavery. John Brown, at a memorial meeting in Hudson, Ohio, rose and pledged to dedicate his life to the destruction of slavery.

Among the mass meetings of protest, one organized by free Negroes in New York City resolved: "That as American citizens, we the people of color of the city of New York, repose the utmost confidence *in* and respect *for* the character and principle of the Abolitionists, whose steady advocacy of our rights as men gives assurance that they rather desire to plead God than man. . . .

"That the blood of the martyred Lovejoy calls upon us, an oppressed people, to become more united in sentiment and efforts, while two and a half millions of our brethren are dragging out a life of misery and degradation in that most detestable system of slavery which not only reduces its victims to brutes, but threatens slavery and death to those who plead their cause. . . .

"That among our rights, we hold none dearer than the freedom of speech and of the press. . . ." [25]

Thursday, November 9, 1837, the day of Elijah's funeral, was disagreeable and gray; rain and cold were driven off the river by moist winds. As the little band of mourners plodded through the downpour to Elijah's grave, his sister Elizabeth, who had come from Maine to spend the winter, went up to the Reverend Mr. Hurlbut and in a low voice pleaded, "Please keep close to Owen; don't leave him; if you do, they will shoot him." [26]

But Owen had already decided his course. Alone in the room with his brother's body a little while earlier, he had knelt and made a vow: "I shall never forsake the cause that has been sprinkled with my brother's blood." [27]

2

"Was I to Bewray the Wanderer?"

> "The best university that can be recommended to a man of ideas is the gauntlet of the mobs."
>
> —Ralph Waldo Emerson

The Lovejoys lost the pride of their family when they lost Elijah. Their bereavement was all the more deep as a result, although they might have consoled themselves with memories of their life on the family farm near Albion in the Kennebec country of Maine. In that almost unbroken wilderness the Revolutionary War veteran Francis Lovejoy carved out a farm in 1790 after moving from Amherst, New Hampshire. His ancestors were among a number of Lovejoys in the English villages of Essex, Buckinghamshire, Berkshire, and Kent. Some of them came to the Massachusetts Bay Colony in the 1630's to start the main line of the American Lovejoys. Francis' son Daniel, born in 1776, inherited the farm that was cut out of the Maine wilderness and, after 1805, worked it while he served as a Congregationalist preacher. He married Elizabeth Gordon Pattee, who was born in 1772 at Winslow, Maine, and whose ancestors came from Scotland. She was a woman of deep and strong religious convictions, who must have inspired her children to be strong and self-less in adhering to their principles, whether in religion or in politics. Her sons Elijah and Owen distinguished themselves by just such stubborn devotion to their beliefs. As children, the Lovejoys were taught by their mother to read from the Bible in the farmhouse kitchen. Owen later told how Elijah learned the alphabet in this way, and how at the age of four he could read in the great book. "Throughout his youth, the ends of the day saved from the axe, the plough, and the scythe, were all employed in the diligent use of books," Owen and Joseph Lovejoy wrote about their martyred brother. Judging by Owen's career, he too must have been an ambitious reader. As he grew up, his big brother Elijah helped him select books from their father's shelves and tutored him from them.[1]

Not only was Elijah a leader in his studies but he was also athletic and a particularly hearty swimmer. As his brothers noted: "Swimming was our weekly and almost daily amusement." In summer he and his brothers ran down the long hill, through the woods of maples, birches, larches, and hemlocks to the Lovejoy Pond. They would strip, and Elijah would dive in, whip his wet black hair out of his eyes, and thrash across the lake three-quarters of a mile and back.[2]

Owen was nine years younger than Elijah, and could not follow him when he went off to the Monmouth Academy and then to Waterville (now Colby) College. When Elijah was at home, Owen would sit at his brother's side and learn from him the Latin classics—Virgil, Cicero, Sallust. From the college youth Owen absorbed a penetrating faith in Jeffersonian democracy and a scorn of the Metternichian system of espionage and censorship. The Lovejoy boys also learned Puritan moral and practical values from their parents and grandfather Francis Lovejoy.

Elijah graduated at the head of his class and carried off all the honors. Then he began to earn his living by teaching school. In

1827 he went west to teach in St. Louis and edit a Whig newspaper that supported Henry Clay in the 1832 presidential election.

At home Owen became a mainstay on the family farm. He enrolled in Bowdoin College in 1830 and supported himself by teaching school, but left in 1833 when his father died. Owen apparently wished to follow in his father's footsteps and become a minister. One student of Maine Congregationalists asserted that Owen went to Alton in 1833 to study for the ministry under his brother Elijah, but this probably is not so since Elijah was at the seminary in New Jersey at this time. Furthermore, he wrote, Owen returned to Maine and became a member of the class of 1836 at Bangor Theological Seminary but did not finish his course there. This was about the time Owen may have gone to Alton. However, there is no firm evidence as to what Owen did in these years when, like many a youth of twenty-two or twenty-three, he was trying to find himself and his life's work. Presumably he became a convert to Theodore D. Weld's brilliant persuasion against slavery, for Weld was at that time abolitionizing the countryside, especially in New York, Ohio, and Pennsylvania. Also, at about this time Owen's brother Joseph, an 1834 graduate of Bangor Theological Seminary and in 1835 principal of the Hallowell Academy in Hallowell, Maine, became a disciple of William Lloyd Garrison, who was stirring up a great intellectual storm against slavery in Boston and New England.[3]

Elijah was the first of eight children born to Elizabeth Gordon Pattee Lovejoy and Daniel B. Lovejoy. Daniel B., Jr., was born in 1804 and lived to 1831. Joseph Cammett came into the world in 1805 and in his sixty-six years was a teacher, antislavery worker, minister, and defender of the poor and the imprisoned, but in 1857 an apologist for proslavery propagandists. The Owen Lovejoy born in 1807 lived only three years. His namesake was born on January 6, 1811. The girls in the family were Sybil Pattee, born in 1809, and Elizabeth Gordon Pattee, born in 1815. The latter became Mrs. Noah Wiswall of Skaneateles, New York, in 1839; later a widow, she became the wife of a noted Chicago theologian, Henry Laurens Hammond. The youngest of Elijah's and Owen's brothers was John Ellingwood Lovejoy, who was born in 1817. He joined them in Illinois, helped with the printing of Elijah's paper, and, after a brief career in the Foreign Service of the United States during the Civil War, became a midwestern railroad agent; he died in Scotch Grove, Iowa, in 1891.[4]

After Elijah's death, a group of faithful antislavery men planned to print the *Observer* in Cincinnati, hoping that perhaps in time they could reestablish it in Alton. Owen pleaded with eastern friends to raise money for a new press. He wrote to James G. Birney, secretary of the executive committee of the American Anti-Slavery Society. Lovejoy was confident that if friends in the East would raise enough money, men in Illinois could guarantee a new *Observer* within six months, "even though a hundred lives be lost." [5] These plans were never realized.

Whatever his sorrow, Owen felt that his brother had "done more by his death than living and unopposed he could have done in a century," and with Joseph's aid he moved rapidly to preserve the memory of Elijah's struggle. They were commissioned by the American Anti-Slavery Society executive committee to prepare a memorial volume, a book that would impress on the American people the kind of man Elijah was, the background he came from, his devotion to his parents, his courageous stand on controversial questions, and the fact that he had died defending the freedom of the press in the antislavery controversy.[6]

Owen made New York City his headquarters while the volume was in preparation in the winter of 1838. There he could be near the offices of the American Anti-Slavery Society and near the printers whose dim shops lined the narrow slips of streets in lower Manhattan. He formed cordial friendships in the "Great City," but the Maine farm boy felt somewhat "cooped up" where shops, stores, and office buildings hid the horizon and seemed to crowd the sky. Moreover, he was pressed by a deep family loyalty. On the one hand, he was anxious to get back to Alton, to his sister Elizabeth and brother John, and to the widow Celia Ann, who was expecting a child. On the other hand, he wanted very much to visit Maine.[7]

It was difficult for the young man to reveal his feelings, and he confessed to his mother: "I always had a sort of horror of telling how I feel." He did not know whether this emotional taciturnity arose from "early education or from the association of hearing so many foolish people tell how they feel." Yet later, as one of the country's leading congressmen, he would display almost unbridled anger over the wrongs of slavery, with reddened face and fists held high in the air. This picture of indignation is softened by another, of a genial man with a generous sense of humor. In eulogizing Lovejoy, Henry Ward Beecher said, "To the end of his life he maintained healthiness. He was not a morbid reformer in any sense." [8]

In the memorial volume to Elijah, the Lovejoy brothers traced Elijah's gradual adoption of antislavery doctrines and the events leading to his death. They appended letters, editorials, and public announcements, and page after page of testimonials to the courage and integrity of Elijah Lovejoy. They quoted resolutions of shock, shame, and indignation over his death, and reprinted opinions that drew the lesson to be learned from Alton —the slaveowner meant to still every voice raised in doubt or question, challenge or criticism, of his "peculiar institution."

By February 10 Owen noted that the printers were "getting on with our book pretty well, a hundred pages finished and going on at the rate of 12 pages per day." The campaign to raise money and to rouse public opinion for the cause was advanced by the Anti-Slavery Society, which had struck bronze profiles of the murdered man and put them on sale at the office. In the days since his death, between five hundred and a thousand dollars, Owen said, had been subscribed in different parts of the country for the benefit of Elijah's widow. She gave birth to a daughter on March 5 in St. Charles, Missouri.

Owen Lovejoy, still in New York on March 22, complained of "a great many little things," which, after he thought all was done, had come up to require his presence there. To these little things was added the necessity of "spurring on the tardy workmen," who had delayed him a week longer than he had expected and the printer had promised. But the work was done at last.[9]

This righteous compilation the brothers called *Memoir of the Rev. Elijah P. Lovejoy; Who Was Murdered in Defence of the Liberty of the Press at Alton, Illinois, Nov. 7, 1837.* The foreword was written by John Quincy Adams, former President and a champion of constitutional liberties. The volume became an important instrument of propaganda of the antislavery cause and for the Bill of Rights.

When the *Memoir* was published and ready for distribution Lovejoy felt he ought to speed west. He had no specific plans but seems to have been drawn, as he wrote, "into a way that I neither thought or dreamed of." Joshua Leavitt wanted Owen to become the agent in Illinois for the American Anti-Slavery Society. The responsibility would have been great, but it would have meant a life spent constantly on the move—calling on farms and villages and towns throughout the state. He would have been involved in meetings and the organization of meetings, in promoting the antislavery cause in church basements and little country schoolrooms, in city auditoriums if he was successful. In 1838, with railroads still in their infancy there, an agent of the society would have lived a life in the saddle or high on the seat of

Owen Lovejoy to his mother, March 22, 1838
Chicago Historical Society

a jouncing buckboard. Lovejoy preferred to settle in one place. Nevertheless, when he returned in 1838 he did serve as the agent of the society for Madison County, in which Alton was located.[10]

"I have at last reached this far distant land of blood," he wrote in April after returning to Alton. But there could be no terror powerful enough to frighten him away from his work. Even while he was preparing the *Memoir* he had made trips away from New York to plead the antislavery cause. One was to Hartford, where he attended the Connecticut state antislavery convention. (There is no evidence that he played a prominent part in it). Out in the Midwest, he quickly returned to antislavery duties. He told Joseph that he had ordered a thousand copies of the *Memoir*, five hundred for sale in Chicago and five hundred in Alton. He estimated that two thousand might be sold in Indiana and Ohio each, and promised to make an effort to sell them there. He was conservative in his hopes, having earlier advised Joseph not to speculate too fast—six or seven thousand copies seemed to him too large a number for his brother to undertake to sell in New England.[11] There seems to be no record of the total number sold.

However committed to voluntary antislavery work, Lovejoy felt obliged to settle in one place, to have regular employment, at least to have a steady income. He had studied for the Episcopal ministry while in Alton and now sought to be ordained. He therefore attended the state convention of the Episcopal Church at Rushville in June, 1838, and then went to Jacksonville, hoping to be ordained there. Lovejoy was the house guest of Julian M. Sturtevant, one of the inspiring teachers at Illinois College. Although Sturtevant was not an Episcopalian, he was happy to be host to Owen Lovejoy, "a young man in the flower and beauty and geniality of youth," who was assigned to his house. Later Sturtevant counted his blessings when he recalled the scriptural injunction: "Be not forgetful to entertain strangers for some have

32

thereby entertained angels unawares." The young guest passed his examinations "with approbation" before the Episcopal convention and was recommended by the standing committee to be ordained at Jacksonville. A public announcement was made that Lovejoy would be ordained to the Christian ministry in the Episcopal Church on the Sabbath following. But that was never to happen. On the day before the scheduled ordination the bishop sent Lovejoy a pledge to sign that he would not discuss the subject of abolition, "which pledge," Lovejoy wrote, "as you may guess I refused to sign." [12]

The bishop deferred the ordination until he could consult his brother bishops, but that body would not make a decision until August. Lovejoy was disappointed, but glad that he had stood firm on his refusal to be silenced. He wondered whether he should remove his name from the Episcopal list and instead accept ordination by the Presbytery in Alton. But Alton had become plainly too unsafe for him, truly a "far distant land of blood."

When he reported the incident with the bishop to Sturtevant at his teatable, Lovejoy came with a downcast look. The great teacher said to him: "Well, what is the matter?"

"I am not to be ordained," Lovejoy replied.

"Why not?" Sturtevant asked with what must have been considerable surprise.

Lovejoy told of the bishop's demand and declared: "On such condition I will not be ordained." He showed no bad temper or resentment, as Sturtevant recalled the incident twenty-six years later. He said that Lovejoy's "manner and spirit was dignified and manly," and wished he could do full justice "to the generous and lovely and beautiful traits of character" that young Lovejoy had demonstrated at that time in his home. He particularly remembered Lovejoy's "ease and grace and pleasant intercourse with my household." [13]

33

Sometime during that summer Owen was again in Jacksonville, this time to attend an antislavery meeting. After the sessions, as Lovejoy was mounting his horse with the intention of riding north to Knox County, to find a church he could serve, Rev. Edward Beecher came out to bid him good-by. He asked Lovejoy where he was going. When Beecher heard his answer, he said: "I hear that Mr. Farnham is out of health and needs some help; I think you had better go to Princeton."

"Very well," Lovejoy replied, "then I will go to Princeton."

When he arrived there, he found a transplanted New England community. It was situated on a table of prairie land one hundred and ten miles southwest of Chicago and seventy-five miles southwest of the Wisconsin Territory. A few miles north of town, however, the countryside dipped away into a stream bed surrounded by wooded hills, possibly a pleasant reminder of Connecticut and New Hampshire valleys. Immigrants from New England states had laid it out in 1833 and named it for "the literary metropolis of New Jersey," [14] upon a suggestion from a former resident of that state. Princeton became the county seat of Bureau County.

Here Lovejoy was to make his home. At first he came up against a flinty opposition. Then, through the years of blow and counterblow, he built the state antislavery movement, laid some of the tracks of the Underground Railroad, and used his own house as shelter and way station for the "cars" of freedom.

Here in Princeton the Illinois abolitionists were to go through their political labor pains as they gave birth to the Liberty party.

Lovejoy was appointed supply minister for one year to the Hampshire Colony Congregational Church. Its regular pastor, the Reverend Lucian Farnum, one of the Yale Band of missionaries who had come out to these fertile central prairies from the Nutmeg State, had become ill in August, 1838, and could not completely serve the congregation. Lovejoy was his replacement at a salary of six hundred dollars for the year. It was what he had asked, and it was one hundred more than the congregation had ever given before. In the first four months of his ministry he found things going "to the perfect satisfaction of the good people." He did, however, find it hard to write two sermons in a week and lecture Sabbath evening. Before the twelve months were up Farnum submitted his resignation and Lovejoy, at twenty-seven, became the regular minister.[15] He led his flock there for seventeen years.

On Sunday mornings Lovejoy preached a vibrant morality inherited from the Puritan fathers. Abstinence from alcoholic beverages was one of his strict tenets. On one of those Sundays Reverend Lovejoy took as his text Ezekiel 8:7–10. The occasion had been the opening of a saloon in the town. The proprietor had hung out a sign: "Hole in the Wall." After reciting the biblical text describing the "wicked abominations" to be seen by the Son of man in the "hole in the wall," Lovejoy congratulated the saloonkeeper on the aptness of his title.[16]

In Princeton Lovejoy found only a handful of antislavery men among the two hundred New Englanders—Yankees from Connecticut, New Hampshire, Maine, and Vermont. These few included the Reverend Mr. Farnum himself, the brothers Cyrus, Arthur, and John Howard Bryant (another brother, the poet William Cullen, had remained in the East). Among other Bureau County antislavery men Lovejoy met were John Cross, the brothers Eli and Elijah Smith, some Holbrooks, a Williams Pinkerton, and others who were active in the Underground Railroad. Even with their support, Lovejoy had to fight for his right to be heard sermonizing against slavery.[17]

Some of his more rockbound neighbors hated Lovejoy's antislavery doctrine enough to threaten him with violence. One of them, shortly after Lovejoy began to lead the Hampshire congregation, told the minister that if he dared show himself on

Princeton's main street he would be mobbed and killed. A donation of feathers from her pillow was offered by one woman, if
tarring and feathering Lovejoy were contemplated. Did they forget that he had been baptized in fire at Alton? Lovejoy replied to
the threat by mounting his horse and with apparent unconcern
let his animal saunter up and down Main Street. After the incident no one dared talk of molesting the man.[18]

One Sunday morning Lovejoy was speaking to the congregation, at first holding them fast to their seats with his denunciation
of the slavery that existed less than two hundred miles away.
Then one person stood up and walked out, then another and
another followed. From the pulpit Lovejoy shot out at their de-
parting backs: "I intend to preach this until you like it and then
because you like it." With a twinkle in his eyes he went right
on with the sermon.[19]

As the years passed, Lovejoy visited other churches to preach
his antislavery message. One occasion arose after a split in the
Third Presbyterian Church of Chicago early in the 1850's. A dis-
senting group, under the leadership of Philo Carpenter, active
conductor of the Underground Railroad in that city, withdrew
from the church and established the First Congregational. Since
the group could not meet in the Presbyterian Church, it made
its place of worship a social hall that belonged to Carpenter.
Hardly ever free from debate, the church soon earned the epithet
"nigger church" from its enemies, and "the turned out, burned
out" church from its friends. Owen Lovejoy preached at the
First Congregational to a Negro and white congregation.[20]

Although the platform and the pulpit were his principal places
of battle for Negro freedom, he occasionally wrote letters to the
leading Illinois antislavery newspaper and joined men like Carpenter in helping fugitive slaves through Illinois.

No one will ever know for certain exactly when and where
the Underground Railroad began, for the success of this mag-

nificent effort for freedom jointly conducted by Negroes and whites depended on secrecy. Beginning perhaps in the 1830's, the Railroad ran sporadically out of the miasmic slave states into the Ohio and Mississippi River valleys, through the swamps and over the bluffs of the Ohio, Indiana, and Illinois shores, then with a burst of speed twisted through countless houses, barns, and churches up to the Great Lakes. Some fugitive slaves of the eastern seaboard went up through the Chesapeake Bay country, through New Jersey, Pennsylvania, and New York and New England. With time out for passengers to breathe the free air and embrace brothers and sisters, mothers and fathers, in the lake ports of Buffalo, Cleveland, and Chicago, the railroad followed the North Star to a haven on Canadian soil. Some fugitives settled in Northern cities, where they carried on the liberation effort despite discrimination and race prejudice and the threats of capture by slaveowners' agents. Free Negroes in Chicago and other Northern cities pulled these trains through, aided by white men and women of many faiths and backgrounds. A farmer would as soon go for freedom as a city doctor, clerk, or lawyer, or a minister of a church.

Among others, Gerrit Smith, a wealthy merchant and landowner of New York, had urged this way of fighting for freedom in his Peterboro Address of 1835. In one blow the slave won his freedom and weakened the base of the master by depriving him of his property. The Underground Railroad's work was also consonant with the teaching that resistance to tyranny is obedience to God. To steal in this sense is not to violate the Commandment, Smith wrote.

All over the Northern states courageous souls concurred, and acted on this principle. Associated in the furtive task in Illinois were such men as Zebina Eastman, Philo Carpenter, and C. V. Dyer. Out on the rich farmland of Bureau County, and in its center, Princeton, the Bryant brothers together with Owen Lovejoy, the widow Eunice Storrs Denham, at whose home

Lovejoy boarded, and at least a dozen others maintained stations. The conductors assumed their duties in this complex undercover operation fully aware of the dangers. Sometimes they had to fight to free a slave in the face of loaded pistols; sometimes they had to hold off hired slave hunters; nearly always they had to conceal the hideaways and invent ruses to throw a gang of pursuers off the track. Even if escapes were achieved peacefully, as most were, the rescuers risked imprisonment and fines. Laws for the return of fugitive slaves stood on the federal statute books and were also detailed in many state codes. In Illinois it was a crime to harbor or hide a slave, punishable by a fine of five hundred dollars. Yet in the face of all hazards, traffic grew and the cars were kept rolling to freedom for the slaves.

On January 18, 1843, Lovejoy married Mrs. Denham, and together they continued to make their farmhouse one of the principal depots on the Underground Railroad. On the farm they continued the stockbreeding and raising pioneered by the late Butler Denham. Mrs. Denham had been widowed in 1841 and left with three small daughters and the farm of some thirteen hundred acres just east of the village of Princeton. Her daughter Lucy, born in 1837, was much attached to her stepfather and later became his faithful secretary.[21]

The first child of Owen and Eunice Lovejoy was Sarah Moody Lovejoy, born in 1844. Owen Glendower Lovejoy lived only seven months after his birth in 1845. Another Owen Glendower, born late in 1846, grew up with his father's nickname, Glenny. Ida Taylor Lovejoy and Charles Perkins Lovejoy joined this large and happy family in 1848 and 1849. A fourth son, born in 1850, was named Elijah Parish Lovejoy, II. Sophia Mappa Lovejoy was born in 1852.[22]

Something of what Owen Lovejoy meant to his children was told by Sophia (Mrs. Charles Dickinson), who remembered: "To walk through an orchard with him was a pleasure, to watch

38

him select seed corn was a valuable lesson, to help him train a horse was instructive and to watch him help a child was heredity; had not his mother done it before him?" When she spoke these words, Mrs. Dickinson was sixty-three years old. Mrs. Dickinson also related that her father had been "a keen observer of nature partly because he loved her and partly because he was a good farmer." She could remember that "while walking through a field of timothy at the same time he observed a ground sparrow or a grass-finch that had built her nest on a stalk of grain. This nest was certain to be marked and the haymaker admonished to leave a bunch of grass to protect the mother and her nestlings." [23]

Ida Lovejoy, who served for a time as postmistress of Princeton, must have been about nine years old when she witnessed the arrival of one of the last companies of fugitive slaves at the Lovejoy home. Her grandmother Lovejoy was living with the family in Princeton and was an active leader in the local but important women's antislavery organization. Ida recalled that one morning a wagonful of men slaves drove up to the gate in something of a hurry. They could not stop for long, only to give their greetings and say that they were hotly pursued. Owen and his mother went out to speak to the men. "Are you armed?" Owen asked. When they said they were not, they had only clubs, Owen told them: "If necessary, do not hesitate to use them." As the family went back into the house her grandmother asked, "Owen, are you *sure* you were right to tell those men to use their clubs?" He replied emphatically, "Yes, I am sure." Grandmother Lovejoy walked on in silence and after a few moments said slowly, "I'm not so sure." [24]

This disagreement between mother and son reflected her sympathy with William Lloyd Garrison's ideas of nonresistance, according to Ida. Yet it was from his mother that Owen inherited a distinctive gesture of determination and defiance. Grandmother Lovejoy was a faithful reader of Garrison's *Libera-*

tor, often reading a copy aloud, with comments like "Right—Mr. Garrison, right!" She would drive her emphasis home with a shake of her left fist. This was the gesture Owen used, and over which Southern congressmen teased him. While speaking in the House of Representatives Congressman Lovejoy was interrupted by a Southerner who asked, "Where did you get that gesture?" Lovejoy replied, "I inherited it from my mother." During the rest of that winter, probably 1859–60, "the sentence 'did you inherit that from your mother' became slang among the Southern[er]s," Ida wrote.[25]

Such harassment failed to discourage Lovejoy from his Underground Railroad work. In 1842 Lovejoy had publicly admitted his adherence to Gerrit Smith's Peterboro Address. Lovejoy asserted: The slave is in enemy territory, he must take any means to get his freedom. In a letter to the *Western Citizen*, unofficial organ of the Illinois antislavery movement, Lovejoy advised the fleeing slave to "take all along your route, so far as is absolutely necessary to your escape, the horse, the boat, the food." [26]

Princeton's importance on the Underground Railroad was later confirmed by the angry charge of Southern fire-eaters that Princeton was the "nigger-stealing" center of Illinois. In May, 1843, the Bureau County Court charged Lovejoy with "keeping in his house, feeding, clothing and comforting the said Nancy" and "harboring, feeding, clothing one said Agnes, a slave." [27]

Apparently backed by proslavery elements, Norman H. Purple of Peoria had pressed the charges and then assisted State Attorney Benjamin F. Fridley in the prosecution of Lovejoy. Purple and his supporters hoped to break the back of the effective Princeton and Bureau County Underground Railroad. They had threatened the Peoria Antislavery Society with force early that year and had driven one editor from the town. They hoped to brand Lovejoy the outspoken and principal agent of the Railroad and have him driven from the community as a law-breaker.

Fridley was approached by one of the angry anti-abolitionists and told, "Fridley, we want you to be sure and convict this preacher and send him to prison."

"Prison!" Fridley snapped back, "Lovejoy to prison! Your prosecution will a damn sight more likely send him to Congress." [28]

Fridley's estimate was for a moment wide of the mark, for a grand jury of Bureau County indicted Lovejoy in the May term of the circuit court. The Lovejoy case was scheduled to come up for trial by jury in the October term of the Bureau County Circuit Court.

In the meantime, though, Lovejoy lost no time in proclaiming his determination to run the Railroad. With a characteristic touch of self-confidence he inserted an advertisement (dated May 24) in the June 1, 1843, *Western Citizen*, assuring all who could read that he was placing the notice to allay fears over "abortive attempts" to break up "our LINE," thus "creating a want of confidence in the permanency of our establishment."

Throughout this prairie land of rich stands of corn, farmers and townsfolk were aroused to a peak of excitement by the coming trial. While Purple and his followers stirred up an angry resentment against Lovejoy and the Underground Railroad, supporters of the abolitionists were marshaling their own strength to win this case. Money had been raised to retain the best legal talent available, Alvan Stewart of Utica, New York. He was a crusty lawyer with strong abolition ideas and had been a pioneer advocate in 1839 and 1840 of political abolitionism. Unfortunately he was unable to come to Princeton to display his legal acumen and his talent for sarcasm, but when the "Agnes-Nancy case" came up for trial, Lovejoy was joined in the defense by another staunch antislavery man, James H. Collins of Chicago, and formerly of New York State. Experienced and precise with

41

ipwaras, 7

163

in the State of Illi-
ylogy he studies has
fact. `Now, as I un-
Presbytery have not
young man. It is
:y of their action in
nto security which
: he may be led to
acceptable minister
efuse to rebuke this
position. Now the
a in their action, or
ɔ act at all upon the
., however much I may
a. They have ever re-
: upon the subject,—they
: do not pretend to op-
·is Presbytery pretend to
id some say they have
.rk. It is indeed wonder-
f men should so stultify
a one thing and the
˄ctly in the teeth
˙˙v, thou art a
ᵖresby-

,m.

,ŋ

CORRECTION.

MR. EASTMAN.—In your remarks of last
week, with regard to the action of the Ottawa Presbytery on the subject of Slavery, in
connection with the case of Mr. Williams,
you unintentionally made some misstatements, which, together with your strictures
on their course, were calculated to make a
wrong impression on the public mind. These
misstatements you will allow me to correct,
as one who was present during the sesᵖ
of Presbytery, and who witᵓ⸗⸗⸗·˙ ˙

anu
cated
may here
justice fror
tor.

A clerk in .
ted for stealing
and then selling .
impudent rogue. ˄

WESTERN

" Truth, crushed to
· The eternal yeˉ
But Error, woun
And dies am

THL

TH

Nominated i
N

JAM.

.

The rigʰ

Advertisement in the *Western Citizen,* June 1, 1843

the law, Collins had once been a law partner of John Dean Caton, the judge in this case. He argued close up to the points of law, never yielding easily. When forced to concede, he would speedily grasp a new point and press it. Lovejoy, although not trained, entered his own motions for dismissal. The two abolitionists, conscious that their legal struggle would for a long time afterward affect the work of the Underground Railroad, hung onto the technicalities. Thus Lovejoy and Collins moved for quashing the indictments on the ground that the "name of the alleged owner [of Agnes or Nancy] was not given, nor the residence of the owner." They argued further that neither count of the indictment charged an offense within the true intent of the statute. Finally they asserted that federal law on the same subject made inoperative section 148 of the Illinois criminal code, which fined a violator five hundred dollars for harboring a Negro without a certificate of freedom.

The motions were overruled by Judge Caton and the case proceeded to trial. It lasted a week, and in the course of it the whole county became aroused to the trial's wide implications. The courtroom was packed to capacity every minute of the proceedings. At first the defense was put in a precarious position by witnesses who had seen Agnes and Nancy freely going about the Lovejoy homestead. Witnesses testified that Nancy had related her experiences as a slave at a public meeting in nearby Greenfield. Others testified that Agnes and Nancy had been fed by the Lovejoy family and given some clothing. Isaac Delano, a farmer, told the court that Lovejoy had stopped at his house and that Nancy was in the vehicle with him. He said that Lovejoy told him she was an escaped slave. Conviction seemed a sure result at this point. But in Collins's sharp cross-examination of Delano it was disclosed that Nancy's owner had been taking her from Kentucky to Missouri through Illinois, where she made her escape. Armed with this morsel of information, Collins and Lovejoy knew that the way to acquittal was clear. They passed hastily scribbled notes to each other, and argued that Illinois law was with them in their contention that since the owner had taken his slave to free territory, she became free when her foot touched Illinois soil.

Lovejoy, enamored of Cowper's verses, quoted that English libertarian in his plea to the jury:

Slaves cannot breathe in England; if their lungs
Receive our air, that moment they are free—
They touch our country and their shackles fall.

"If this is the glory of England, is it not equally true of Illinois," Lovejoy wanted to know, "her soil consecrated to freedom by the Ordinance of 1787 and her own constitution?"

Collins took up the strictly legal argument and painstakingly presented it to the jury for seven hours spread over two days of the trial.

Finally, on October 7, when Judge Caton in his charge to the jury upheld the key point of law pressed by Collins, all knew that acquittal was assured. The judge used simple language: "By the Constitution of this state, slavery cannot exist here. If therefore, a master voluntarily bring his slave within the state, he becomes from that moment free, and if he escape from his master while in this state, it is not an escape from slavery but it is going where a free man has a right to go; and the harboring of such a person is no offense against our law; but the tie which binds a slave to his master can be severed only by the voluntary act of the latter."

A friend in Galesburg sent a note written in "grate hast" and borne to Lovejoy by a fugitive: "I rejoice at your deliverance from the Vengeance & malice of your Enemies in the recent indictments." The decision "must effect the interest of our hevenly cause more than any one thing in Ill. for some time."

The friend went on to discuss the opening up of a new underground route from "Navou [Nauvoo?] through our place to Princeton, or somewhere in that direction, to *Wisconsin. . . .*" He had made up his mind to do it "if the friends do not advise otherwise," for the route from Quincy had become "so public." The parcel of clothing accompanying the letter was to be used by Lovejoy as he wished but, the friend urged, "only let it be found in Canada soon." [29]

Lovejoy and Collins had wrung an important decision from the judge and the jury. But when a similar case involving Dr. Richard Eels came before the State Supreme Court in December, 1843, Judge James Shields delivered a frosty rebuke to the petitions of Eels and by implication to all abolitionists and Underground Railroad operators. His colleague, Judge Walter B. Scates, in a case involving Julius A. Willard, held that "A slaveholder has a perfect right to pass through Illinois with his slaves, and comity between the states will protect him regarding the slaves as such, while within our limits." [30]

The abolitionist *Western Citizen* condemned the state's high court and scornfully charged the judges with proslavery inclinations. The Whig Alton *Telegraph*, commenting on the Willard case, bitterly observed that in "Illinois slavery to a certain extent exists under our Constitution and laws." The Chicago *Express* hailed the decision as "solemn warning to abolitionists to mind their own business." [31]

Despite the State Supreme Court's assault on them, the abolitionists resolved to go on protecting fugitives. As a sign of confidence, Dr. Eels was elected president of the Illinois Anti-Slavery Society. In June, 1844, the society's executive committee praised the actions of Lovejoy, Eels, and Willard; condemned the Supreme Court; and proclaimed the justness of aiding fugitive slaves.

In February, 1845, Lovejoy's victory in the Bureau County

Circuit Court was retrieved to a small extent in the case of *Jarrot* vs. *Jarrot*. In that case the Illinois Supreme Court upheld the freedom of a slave on the principle of his residence in a free state when his master voluntarily settled there.

Once again the tracks were cleared for the cars to roll north to the free states and Canada.

Canada and every other British possession had been rid of slavery since 1833, when Parliament had passed the West Indies Emancipation Act. On the tenth anniversary of that act of manumission Americans celebrated, hopeful that the free republic of the United States would follow the British lead. In the town of La Moille, not far from Princeton, a mass meeting in honor of the West Indies Act was scheduled for August 1, 1843. Owen Lovejoy and his friend Ichabod Codding were on their way to the meeting when they met a well-dressed Negro man on horseback going in their direction, probably to the anniversary rally. After exchanging greetings with the stranger, the two Princeton men heard how he had been cheated of nine dollars by an innkeeper at Princeton. The man told of having spent a night at the inn and in the morning presenting a Kentucky ten-dollar bill in payment for the lodgings. The landlord could not make change, and although the Negro paid in coins when he learned he owed only seventy-five cents, the innkeeper refused to return the bill.[32]

Lovejoy, Codding, and the cheated man swung around and rode back to Princeton and confronted the innkeeper. He claimed he had received only a two-dollar bill. Seeing that they would get no place with the landlord, the three men decided to go on to the La Moille meeting. As soon as they had departed, the landlord gathered a few men and rode to La Moille, obtaining a warrant for the arrest of the Negro for holding counterfeit money.

As they were about to make the arrest, Lovejoy told the

Negro to get on his horse and flee. A man named Davis, hired to trail Lovejoy and his new friend, jumped in front of the horse, with his knife drawn. A quick antislavery man grabbed Davis from behind, pinned his arms back, and threw him to the ground. As Davis struggled to get his knife into action Lovejoy brought his foot down on Davis's arm and held it there until the knife was knocked out of Davis's hand and broken and thrown away. The Negro had in the meantime got on his horse and was safely on his way.[33]

The next day Davis brought charges of assault and battery against Owen Lovejoy, Seth Clapp, Caleb Cook, and Bertram Lockwood. Lovejoy was fined fifty dollars and ten dollars costs. The others received lesser fines.

Abolitionist John Cross of La Moille wrote that the incident "added much to the excitement and interest of the day. Another traveller was also with us, who proceeded by *the evening train of under-ground cars* for Canada." [34]

Six years later the cars were still running through Princeton, as the rescue of John Buckner proved.[35] Buckner had escaped across the big river from Missouri, and friends had aided him northward through western Illinois to Princeton. Hungry and in need of rest, he stayed in the vicinity of the friendly town. Enos Matson, with a farm a short distance from the village, had hired Buckner because he was handy with tools; besides, Buckner could use the money he would earn to continue his race toward Canada. In his conversations it was apparent that he was an intelligent man as well as a skilled one.

On a bright spring day of 1849 Buckner was mowing in the meadow of Matson's farm. With all life bursting free around him, Buckner must have felt a great joy in whacking the tall grass with his scythe. But he had no inkling that at any moment hired slave hunters would try to shackle him and drag him back to Missouri. He did not know that only the day before two strange "villainous

47

looking men" had been seen around town and in the local grog shop, the New York House. These two not only planned to seize him but had also engaged one Milo Kendall to defend them in court if necessary.

Suddenly two swaggering white men came up on the meadow. Then he knew it all. He recognized one of them as his former owner. It was too late to run or fight or swing his scythe down on them. Their guns menaced him as they approached and forced him to surrender. One of them bound his hands with a rope and they started to walk to Princeton, on their way to Hennepin to board a boat for St. Louis. This was the way a horse was led through the farm, but a man. . . . This was too much for the people of Princeton. They had come to respect the work of Lovejoy and his antislavery friends, but they had not been confronted with such a sight as John Buckner trussed up and led like an animal.

Princetonians acted swiftly. Matson's neighbor Hinsdale Phelps sped over a shortcut to Lovejoy's home and informed him of Buckner's capture. Lovejoy thought fast of a way to halt or delay the hunters. First he ran into town to the office of Judson Waldo, justice of the peace, and swore out a warrant for the arrest of Buckner and his captors. He charged them with rioting—with this device he could bring all three into court. Then he would have to devise additional stratagems.

Lovejoy had moved so swiftly that by the time the captors and their quarry arrived in town, Sheriff J. V. Thompson was at the barroom of the New York House to meet them with a warrant of arrest. During the hearing in the courthouse a crowd gathered outside. Some were determined to rescue Buckner; others offered to help return the "stolen property." Inside the courtroom Lovejoy, Levi North, and C. L. Kelsey prepared to win the Negro man's freedom. Milo Kendall appeared to defend the slave hunters.

Lovejoy could not have seriously hoped the rioting charge would be upheld. Probably he hoped Buckner could somehow be separated from the white men, and the two Missourians detained by the court. Then perhaps the Negro could be put aboard the "cars" to freedom. With such a strategy in mind, North presented a motion for the release of Buckner on the ground that he had not been taken legally; besides he was not responsible to the charge of rioting, his captors were.

While this motion was being argued, proslavery men moved a wagon up to the courthouse and prepared to take Buckner by force. One of their number, Tallet, a local tavernkeeper, had procurred a warrant for Buckner's arrest from a sympathetic justice of the peace. Tallet rushed into the courtroom waving the warrant and disturbing the proceedings. Buckner and his defenders raised objections and questioned the legality of the tavernkeeper's action. Sheriff Thompson ordered Tallet from the room. When he refused to obey, the sheriff drew his gun and moved toward Tallet. A near-riot of shouting and scuffling broke out in the courtroom, and in the excitement someone cut the ropes around Buckner's wrists. He was hustled out of the room and, with the Reverend Lovejoy and three other men, ran down the stairs and out of the building.

Upstairs Sheriff Thompson, with gun drawn, backed up to the door, closed it, and barred the way to any other escapes. The Missourians and Kendall and Tallet were trapped, their "property" now running with all his might for the farm. Townsfolk were calling out, "Run, John, run for your life," as he sped down Main Street. He had not run very far when the hired man from Lovejoy's farm met him with a horse. Buckner leaped onto the animal and spurred it on to Lovejoy's house.

Lovejoy and his friends raced on foot after the escaped man and in turn were followed by a crowd. Coatless and in his shirt-sleeves, the minister planted himself in the gateway and allowed his friends to enter and stand on the lawn. All others Lovejoy warned to move away. Tallet had come running and tried to crash the gate. He got halfway through, when Lovejoy shoved the gate shut on him and squeezed so hard the proslavery man jumped away writhing with pain.

By now the news had reached every corner of the community and a large crowd gathered around Lovejoy's board fence. In the house the former slave waited for a chance to get away, while Lovejoy tried to divert the crowd. Drawing his most persuasive weapon, he proceeded to deliver an antislavery speech in his best stump style. After he had spoken a short while, someone in the crowd saw a man on horseback dash out of the Lovejoy barnyard. The rider wore a handkerchief over his face. Someone yelled, "There goes John," and immediately a bunch of proslavery men went chasing after the rider. Lovejoy continued to blare out the antislavery message. He seemed unaffected by the pursuit of the masked rider.

Shortly afterward a horse-drawn wagon rolled away from the Lovejoy barn, hardly noticed by the crowd. On the seat with the driver was a woman, her face shaded by a large sunbonnet. The "lady" was John Buckner, a passenger on a "Fugitive Special" fitted out by Lovejoy's friends while he stood under the broad-branched trees in his front yard holding the townspeople spellbound.

The "cars" continued to roll out of the Lovejoy station on into the 1850's. One day in the late fall of 1854 Lovejoy was reported seen at the nearby Somonauk railroad depot. With him was an aged Negro. The local newspaper reported that Mr. Lovejoy had taken up a collection from among the men present to purchase a ticket to Chicago for the old man. The editor said it was suspected that Owen Lovejoy was running off an escaped slave. In 1859 Lovejoy was attacked by Mississippians in the House of Representatives for "stealing" this old man. Illinois Congressman

Owen Lovejoy, at the close of a lengthy speech on the House floor proclaimed:

"A single word as to this charge of Negro stealing. . . . If the object is to ascertain whether I assist fugitive slaves who come to my door and ask it, the matter is easily disposed of. I march right up to the confessional, and say I do.

"I recollect the case of a young woman, who came to my house, who had not a trace of African descent either in feature or complexion. According to her own story, she was betrothed to a man of her race, though not of her color, and was, before her marriage, sold to a libertine from the South, she being in St. Louis. She escaped, and, in her flight from a life of infamy, and a fate worse than death, she came and implored aid. Was I to refuse it? Was I to bewray the wanderer? Was I to detain her, and give her up a prey to the incarnate fiend who had selected her as a victim to offer up on the altar of sensualism? . . .

"Any one who chooses may transform himself into a blood-hound—snuff and scent and howl along the track of the fugitive —loll out his tongue, and lap up the dirty water that stands in muddy pools by the wayside—overtake the rifle-scarred and lash-excoriated slave . . . thrust his canine teeth into the quivering flesh, brace out his fore feet, and hold the captive till the kidnapper comes with fetters and handcuffs, to load down ankles and wrist, and then receive, as a reward of this brutism, a pat on the head from the slave-catcher, and the plaudit, 'Good dog, Bose.'

"Sir, I will never do this. . . .

"Owen Lovejoy lives at Princeton, Illinois, three quarters of a mile east of the village; and he aids every fugitive that comes to his door and asks it. . . . Thou invisible demon of slavery . . . *I bid you defiance in the name of my God.*" [36]

3

Renovate the State!—1840 to 1844

*"Owen Lovejoy was the greatest stump
speaker I ever listened to."*
—*George Schneider,*
editor of the Illinois Staats-Zeitung

In the two and a half centuries of their enslavement the Negroes
of the United States never fully surrendered to the domination of
the white masters. Slaves revolted repeatedly against the system;
as they chipped the physical bonds they also chipped the white
man's intricate legal, political, moral, religious, social, and ethical
rationalizations for slavery. They ran away from the system, conspired to overthrow it piecemeal if not to eradicate it generally
and unconditionally, and they won the support of white men
and women who understood that their freedom was bound to the
Negro's. In addition, these white people condemned slavery as a
moral, economic, and social evil that must be removed from
society.

Sporadic intellectual sorties had been made against slavery for
more than a century by the time Owen Lovejoy reached prominence as an antislavery leader. Quakers like John Woolman and
Benjamin Lundy, as well as individuals in other sects, indicted

slavery. Thomas Jefferson tried to insert antislavery clauses in the Declaration of Independence, and others of the Founding Fathers groped for a way to put an end to the institution. Some well-meaning souls hoped to erase the problem by sending the slaves back to Africa in a colonization program but little came of the idea. Others spoke in vague generalizations about gradual emancipation or immediate emancipation.

William Lloyd Garrison, Wendell Phillips, James G. Birney, and Theodore D. Weld, to name only a few representative white abolitionists who became active in the 1830's, led a growing number of dedicated white people who allied themselves with the Negro in his struggle for freedom. That they exposed themselves to scorn, curses, beatings, and murder for their efforts mattered little to them personally in the long march.

Although by the 1840's and 1850's the intellectual shaft had penetrated so far as to convert hundreds of white people into active conductors of the Underground Railroad, most Northern white people did not understand the plight of the Southern Negro and did not want to be bothered about him. The free Negro in the North also suffered from discrimination, socially and legally. He was denied voting rights and other civil rights, under a number of proscriptive state laws generally called "Black Codes." All this was the application of a self-serving theory that the Negro was of an inferior race.

Yet when proslavery mobs burned abolitionist newspapers and Southern postmasters censored them, when white Northerners murdered Elijah Lovejoy, when slaveowners pressed for expanding the "peculiar institution" in new states and territories, many white people began to see that their own civil liberties, their self-interest, were in jeopardy. Then they began to worry about what many regarded as the conspiracy of the slave power, that is, of the slaveholding interests. However, only when ideas of emancipation were connected with a political action program to ensure appropriate federal action did the American people begin to support the antislavery movement effectively. One of the most effective programs was the petition campaign of the 1830's.

A steady trickle of antislavery petitions to Congress flowed as early as 1790. In the 1820's the increase in petitions for the abolition of slavery, at least in the nation's capital, aroused fear and suspicion among Southern members of the legislature. Congress buried these pleas year after year in a labyrinth labeled: "referred to committee." After 1833, when the American Anti-Slavery Society was established, petitions swelled to a stream, and in 1837 and 1838 a flood of 412,000 went into the House of Representatives. In 1838 and 1839 two million signatures were gathered. By that time Southern members had thrown up what they hoped would be an impregnable dam—the Pinckney resolution providing that such petitions "be laid upon the table and that no further action whatever be taken thereon." This became the operative gag rule imposed on the House for eight years through 1844, and it fed a growing belief in the slave power conspiracy.

Yet a strong negative response immediately met the gag rule. Former President John Quincy Adams stood in the House as a representative from Massachusetts and denounced it as a "direct violation of the Constitution of the United States." Adams was not an abolitionist, but he felt called upon to lead the fight against the rule in order to "sustain the right of petition in the citizen, and the freedom of speech in this House, and the freedom of the press, and of thought, out of it." [1] Adams was joined in the fray by Ohio's Western Reserve Representative Joshua Reed Giddings. The Ohioan had been elected on the strength of his pledge to focus national attention on abolition.

Theodore D. Weld, the abolitionist who was once called "logic on fire," defined the theoretical base of the petition campaign in a pamphlet, "The Power of Congress over the District of Columbia." If slavery could be legislated into existence, it could be legislated out of existence. Laws made by men could be repealed by other men. Insofar as the District of Columbia was concerned, Congress, which made the laws for it, could abolish slavery there. Petitioning Congress to effect such action was therefore proper, in Weld's mind.

James G. Birney, former Alabama slaveowner and in 1838 executive secretary of the American Anti-Slavery Society, believed that "slavery in the District and territories and the domestic slave trade are under the control of political action. . . ." Birney was convinced that "the slaveholders gain their advantages in national politics and legislation, and should be met in every move they make." [2]

Antislavery thinkers like Gerrit Smith and Myron Holley in upstate New York and John Greenleaf Whittier, the New England poet, had already come to conclusions like Birney's and Weld's. As moral suasion upon slaveholders proved ineffectual and petitions were gagged by Southern representatives, antislavery men increasingly saw the necessity for independent political action. In July, 1839, five hundred delegates in a national antislavery meeting at Albany, New York, approved resolutions urging abolitionists to pledge to vote only for candidates who favored the immediate end of slavery. However, a separate political party of abolitionists was not approved.[3]

Political abolitionists led by Myron Holley made another try at forming a third party at Warsaw, New York, on November 13, 1839. A meeting of abolitionists from several Eastern states gathered in the town but succeeded only in naming candidates to oppose General William Henry Harrison, Whig candidate for the Presidency and a hero of the War of 1812, and Martin Van Buren, the Democratic incumbent. Birney was nominated to lead the antislavery ticket and Dr. Francis J. LeMoyne of Pennsylvania was named to run for Vice-President. The two men declined their nominations and the third party was not established.

However, growing displeasure among antislavery people with the Whig and Democratic candidates kept the third-party idea alive in a number of places in the country. Notable were western New York State, Ohio's Western Reserve district, northern Illinois, and parts of New Hampshire, Vermont, and Massachusetts.

In Illinois, the state antislavery society, of which Lovejoy was a leader, resolved in September, 1839, that "every abolitionist . . . carry his abolitionist principles to the polls." By February, 1840, Lovejoy took a more advanced position on political action. He warmly applauded the stand taken by Dr. Gamaliel Bailey, editor of the Cincinnati *Philanthropist*, and Ohio antislavery people. "The Abolitionists of Ohio are waking up in regard to the political question," Lovejoy wrote. "The *Philanthropist* has almost come out in favor of a third candidate." [4]

On the national scene, Birney's conviction that political action should be the main road of the abolitionists prompted him as executive secretary of the national society to withdraw its agents from organization work and send them into local election contests to campaign for antislavery candidates. Contestants for office were to be asked to state their positions on congressional power over slavery in the District of Columbia and in the territories; on the annexation of Texas; and on the "Black Laws" of Northern states. If a candidate's answers proved unsatisfactory, abolitionists were advised to vote against him. The weakness of this tactic was pointed out by some abolitionists. Where, they asked, was the machinery for carrying before the masses independent abolition candidates? and the clear-cut abolition program?

Birney, Holley, and Gerrit Smith pressed the idea of a party of abolitionists. On April 1, 1840, antislavery men in six northeastern states sent delegates to Albany to organize such a party. Smith suggested that it be called the "Liberty party," and the proposal was adopted. Birney and Thomas Earle of Pennsylvania were nominated for President and Vice-President respectively.[5] The antislavery struggle was thus elevated from the level of mere moral suasion to the decisive plane of political action.

Not all abolitionists were happy with such a departure from accepted forms of agitation. William Lloyd Garrison adamantly rejected the step into politics proposed by Holley, Smith, and Birney. Although he possessed a great urge to universal reform, with abolition of slavery foremost, he adhered to pacifist and nonresistance ideas. He detested the government and denounced the churches, the former because it compromised itself by permitting slavery to exist and the latter because they violated the spirit of Christianity by tolerating slavery and slaveowners in their midst. He appeared to be extreme and radical and was denounced by antislavery as well as by proslavery people. Because he was uncompromising he inspired dedication in his abolitionist followers. His writings in *The Liberator* were respected and carefully read by opponents of slavery of varying views and by Southern slaveowners, who saw in Garrison the devil and the embodiment of the abolition movement.

Since Garrisonians could not see how antislavery people could justify holding public office in a government that included slaveowners, they could not be reconciled with the proponents of political action as the effective means to abolition. The split in the movement became final in the 1840 annual meeting of the American Anti-Slavery Society in New York. At a hectic session the Garrison forces outvoted those favoring a third party. The defeated group withdrew and organized a new national society, the American and Foreign Anti-Slavery Society. Thereafter neither of the rival societies ever recovered leadership of the national antislavery movement. During the 1840's Garrison continued to give idealistic leadership to the New England movement but in other Northern states, principally in the Midwest, the movement turned toward politics.

Although none of the Northwest Ordinance states were represented at the Albany organizing meeting of the Liberty party, abolitionists from those states had already signaled the main trend of their thoughts. Among them, the Illinois Anti-Slavery Society seemed to mirror the national organization. At its meeting in Princeton, on July 4, 1840, probably at the Hampshire Colony church, Lovejoy was one of a five-man committee that submitted a resolution for withholding votes from proslavery candidates in the Whig and Democratic parties. The majority, holding fast to political neutrality and refusing to take a definite stand on voting, adopted a milder substitute. Some of the Prairie State abolitionists, dissatisfied with the outcome, voted to cease being auxiliary to the American Anti-Slavery Society.[6]

But this group of Illinois Liberty party sympathizers lost no time and reassembled the next day. They proclaimed themselves for Birney and Earle, yet they did not actually place a Liberty party slate on the Illinois ballot. Their first knock on the door of politics gave the Illinois abolitionists a total response of 157 votes in the state, 42 of them from Adams County on the Mississippi River, on the very front line of the struggle. Against the Democrats' 47,000 and the Whigs' 45,000, the poll of the Liberty candidates was a drop in the ocean.[7]

In the nation as a whole, the new party gathered 7,000 votes in the course of one of the most emotional presidential contests. In eleven Northern states the vote was 801,449 for the Whigs, 727,329 for the Democrats, and only 6,784 for the abolitionists. The humble origin of William Henry Harrison and his military record were parlayed in a hoopla of great rolling balls, torchlight processions, blaring bands, all signifying nothing but "Tippecanoe and Tyler Too." Any serious debate the abolitionists might have hoped to stimulate on slavery was drowned in a razzle-dazzle empty of challenge.

The force of Harrison's sweep enticed hard-headed, otherwise principled Illinois antislavery men. Many who had not been shaken by "the threats and howling mob fury" when Elijah Lovejoy was under siege were sucked into the wake of the "Tip and Tyler" and "Hard Cider" campaign. Leading members of the state antislavery society and "men in the garb of the Christian ministry," one writer complained, lost their footing and their perspective and voted for Harrison.[8]

When the cool dawn of self-appraisal woke them, the abolitionists saw their error. In Illinois, their repentance was voiced on February 24, 1841, at Lowell, home of Zebina Eastman, a journeyman printer and editor from the East. He had been a protégé of the Quaker editor Benjamin Lundy and had come to this tiny village on the Vermilion River to help Lundy print the *Genius of Universal Emancipation*. The town was only a few miles from Princeton. On that February day the first *political* antislavery convention in the state brought together some of the pioneering 157 Birney voters. Now that "the rallying cry of 'Hard Cider' [had] lost its power and a log cabin no longer [had] the charm of novelty" abolitionists were thinking in terms of independent nominations. In 1841, a movement for reorganization of the antislavery party on a national and local basis spread from the Atlantic seaboard to the Mississippi. Abolitionists proposed that they should no longer be tied to either of the leading parties. Both ignored the crucial slavery issue and neither deserved their votes. As far as Illinois was concerned, the third-party men there resolved that (1) abolitionists make nominations of abolitionists for Congress, and (2) a call be issued for a national Liberty presidential nominating convention in 1844. These measures were pressed on the ground that "efficient political action can be produced only by independent and united [antislavery] effort." They denounced the gag rule in Congress and went away from the convention to spend the rest of the year gathering signatures on antislavery petitions. During the year they also agitated for repeal of the state's odious "Black Laws." [9]

Illinois antislavery men had already begun to test in action their new guiding principle. In January a Third Congressional District convention had nominated Fred Collins of Adams County for the office of representative. Realistically, Collins was not expected to win. In this local contest the Democrats won over the Whigs by only 354 votes. The total for Collins was 527. The lesson was clear—their independent stand had elevated the political abolitionists to a balance-of-power position.[10]

A year later, in February, 1842, a committee of correspondence including Owen Lovejoy issued a call for a state Liberty convention in Chicago on May 27.[11] It was a strong indication that the leaders of the state Anti-Slavery Society were prepared to give up their old methods, yielding to their de facto successor, the Liberty party. The society had just undergone two difficult years in which members and funds did not increase at a satisfactory pace, and a new policy and a new direction were necessary to move the antislavery cause toward victory. Lovejoy joined many other pioneering abolitionists and gave up "with some reluctance" the state society created just before his brother's martyrdom. But his enthusiasm for the new party developed quickly, for he undertook a number of duties important to its establishment. Not only did he help write the call but he served on the convention's business and press committees.[12]

The one duty that conclusively classed Lovejoy as a leader of the party was his service on the committee of three charged with preparing "An Address of the Liberty Party to the Voters of Illinois." The other two members were John Cross and James H. Collins. Immersed in Jeffersonian ideology, the three agents of emancipation and civil liberties reasserted the seed idea of revolutionary America—all men are created equal, they are endowed by their Creator with inalienable rights. Yet they conceded to the Southern states: We do not propose to infringe on the constitutional rights of others. "Our warfare," they announced to the voters, "is defensive as much so as was that of the Revolution, albeit we use different methods." [13]

Lovejoy, Cross, and Collins listed their grievances under "The Usurpations of Slavery." First of all the slave power was insatiable; instead of being *local*, slavery was becoming *national*; instead of being *peculiar*, it was becoming *general*. Therefore the men of Illinois felt "called upon to sound the alarm and take the field for a political campaign." Furthermore, the committee claimed, all the high offices of the United States government were held by slaveholders or "Northern men with Southern principles." In the third place the South was charged with warring upon "the great interests of the North—Free Labor." In addition, the whole country was suffering a pecuniary loss because of slavery—the Florida War, the manifesto charged, was a slave hunt at the expense of the United States. Lovejoy's committee referred to the campaign by the United States against the Seminole Indians from 1836 to 1843. Free Negroes and fugitive slaves who lived among the Indians in the swamp country found themselves, as much as the resisting Seminoles, the victims of bloodhound hunts and armed attacks. Abolitionists led the objection to this war and estimated the cost to the United States at twenty million dollars. Furthermore, the state of "depression, insecurity, and scarcity" of the country was attributed to the loss of capital "entombed at the South." The fruits of free labor go into a "bag with holes," wrote Lovejoy and his committee, and neither of the two political parties does anything except for the slaveholders. The document deplored the violation of civil liberties by the South—the suppression of the right to petition and freedom of speech and press.

In conclusion, the "Address to the Voters" proclaimed: "We wish to identify ourselves with the oppressed—with the slaves." The abolitionists sang out in a grand finale: "We are an Anti-Slavery Association, leagued together to vote against Slavery and all its influences, North and South, in a word, we are a Liberty Party."

The work of Lovejoy, Cross, and Collins received the unanimous approval of the convention. The meeting also approved the establishment of an antislavery newspaper in Chicago as a means of communication with the people—the *Western Citizen*. Zebina Eastman became the editor of this successor to the *Genius of Liberty*, which he had edited and published since the demise of Lundy's paper in 1839.

Back at their stores and farms and shops, and from their pulpits, Liberty party men spelled out the message written at Chicago. Opponents charged the abolitionists with expounding alien ideas and being the enemies of their country. Lovejoy picked up this accusation and flung it back at the accusers. He replied caustically in a sermon on the eve of local elections. Drawing on Cowper, he compressed his thoughts into a line by that poet: "England, with all thy faults, I love thee still." Next day the people went to the polls. Again the Liberty candidates drew an insignificant vote, but they did advance over their showing in 1840. Charles W. Hunter of Alton, running for governor, received 909 votes, a tiny fraction of the total cast, but almost six times as many as Birney for the Presidency in 1840.[14]

Lovejoy and his comrades had to content themselves for several years with minor achievements. They had to face the fact that in politics their fellow citizens were reluctant to leave the major parties. Although the Whigs and Democrats agreed with each other in effect by their silence on the slavery issue, they did offer to the voters differing positions on the national bank and tariff issues, and on federal assistance to river and harbor improvements. In the early 1840's the country was witnessing the final phase of the struggle begun by Andrew Jackson against the powerful Bank of the United States. At the same time powerful interests of the North and the South clashed over the protective tariff question. These matters, rather than the abolition of slavery, claimed the attention of the American people.[15]

For Illinoisans, and Chicagoans in particular, opening the Great Lakes to commerce by improving the lake ports was a most important immediate and practical issue. The abolition of slavery, or even its limitation, was not preeminent for the vast majority of voters. But even at the risk of political isolation, which was real and agonizing, the political abolitionists believed that theirs was the paramount issue of the time. They fought for their one-idea party for almost a decade and, after heartbreaking failures, factious internal debate, reorganization after reorganization, and reevaluations of principles and tactics, they emerged victorious under a new name. Lovejoy and the voters of his Fourth Congressional District forged this area into a powerful antislavery magnet that eventually helped in building statewide majorities. The district began to rival Ohio's Western Reserve as a dependable source of impressively large antislavery votes.

The thirty-two-year-old Lovejoy enthusiastically took up a leading role in the new party. In June, 1843, he was named to the party's district central committee, and in August he was sent as a delegate to the Liberty national convention in Buffalo, New York. There he was named one of five secretaries. The convention was remarkable in that Negro delegates played a prominent part. This was an innovation that neither of the larger parties had conceived of. One of the leading spokesmen of the Negro people and a New York minister, author, and editor, Henry Highland Garnett, served with Lovejoy on the committee to nominate officers of the convention. At the 1843 Convention of Colored Citizens in Buffalo he had thrilled the meeting with the cry: "Arise! Strike for your lives and liberty. . . . Rather die free men than live to be slaves." Samuel R. Ward and Charles B. Ray were other leading Negroes from New York in the meetings. Ward was the pastor of a New York Presbyterian church and Ray was a leader of the politically oriented American and Foreign Anti-Slavery Society. Together at Buffalo, white and Negro delegates reaffirmed their principles and solidified their national organization.[16] It set an exciting precedent for Negro and white joint action.

Lovejoy returned to Princeton full of the fervor generated at Buffalo. As the steamboat *Madison* churned her way westward, Lovejoy wrote to Zebina Eastman that it had been "a great, grand and most glorious convention." Enraptured by the spirit of the participants and their actions, he said: "Never has there been such a political gathering since the Convention that met in Congress Hall in Philadelphia in 1776. The Resolution was undoubtedly correct which declared we are not the *third* but the *first* party. . . . Abolitionists, ho! to the rescue. . . . Pray, toil, give, distribute tracts, lecture, preach, get subscribers to the *Citizen*, move, renovate the state." [17]

Lovejoy at home pitched into the congressional campaign of 1843 by stumping the midstate prairies for John H. Henderson, the Liberty candidate. The ardor he put into his speaking tour of the back-country towns, and his good-humored chats with neighbors won some Liberty votes. Lovejoy's performance in the Agnes–Nancy affair was not forgotten. But the Liberty campaigners could not match the magic spelled by "Long John" Wentworth on a platform of Democratic regularity. Backed by a seasoned and entrenched Democratic machine, the Chicago Giant won with more than 7,000 votes, while Henderson ran third with a surprising 1,167 Liberty votes. The party was inching ahead. Moreover, Lovejoy's sermons and speeches reached the eyes of people in the East, and one young man, C. L. Kelsey, a student in New England in 1843, told his tutor he would emigrate to Princeton. "I want to go where I can hear such preachings as the people there hear from Owen Lovejoy." Kelsey soon afterward settled in Princeton, where he became an active Liberty party worker and local businessman and lawyer.[18]

64

Complementing their political work, Illinois antislavery ministers advanced their cause in their religious organizations. Lovejoy and Cross carried the antislavery struggle into the ranks of their ministerial colleagues, especially in the Rock River Congregational Association. They apparently succeeded in affecting the organization. Their Underground Railroad work, together with the attitudes adopted by other Illinois Congregationalists in the forefront of the abolitionist crusade, earned a "bad" reputation for the Rock River Association with the American Home Missionary Society. One writer said that the association's doom was sealed in 1844 and 1845 because the political activities of the abolitionist ministers "disturbed ecclesiastical peace." [19]

Yet Lovejoy performed his assigned duties as association clerk in Princeton for the Missionary Society. The number of new churches he helped to organize in northern Illinois attested to his devotion; the applications for entrance into the general church membership in this period are in Lovejoy's handwriting at the Presbyterian Theological Seminary at Chicago. Lovejoy was also one of the signers to a call upon some eighty-five Illinois and Iowa Congregational churches to unite in a general association. It bound, among others, the Rock River Association, the Fox River Congregational Union, and the Quincy Association— covering a broad area on both sides of the Illinois and Wisconsin border. The convention of the General Association of Illinois met on November 15, 1843, at Princeton, probably in the church "served by the Reverend Owen Lovejoy." The proposed articles of organization contained some that were strongly abolitionist. When the association was formally organized in June, 1844, at Farmington, even more stringent abolitionist sections than in the draft were adopted, according to a later writer. [20]

Moving along the same antislavery lines, a number of Lovejoy's fellow Congregationalists led the effort to bar slaveholders from all Christian institutions. One of their principal targets was the American Home Missionary Society because it permitted proslavery members. In 1846, the antislavery ministers organized the American Missionary Association. Although there is no record of Lovejoy's formal affiliation, his letters reveal that he actively supported the new organization.

The letters also indicate that his church was used for purposes other than worship. In addition to its use as a house for his anti-slavery work, the church served as a place in which he raised money for missionary work. Thus in 1841, at a "regular monthly concert for the slaves," the sum of five dollars was raised for the "Mendian Mission." This was undoubtedly in aid of the slaves who in 1839 under their leader Cinque, had mutinied against their Spanish captors and swung the ship on which they were prisoners, the *Amistad*, back toward Africa. Betrayed by the white navigators, the Negroes were delivered into New London, Connecticut, where their fight for freedom became a cause célèbre in the courts, on the streets, and in the churches. Aboli-tionists led the defense, roused the American conscience, and collected money to win freedom for the African prisoners. Finally, in 1841, the expensive legal defense came to a successful conclusion when the United States Supreme Court reversed the lower courts.[21]

Lovejoy had used the events to preach from the text: "Ethi-opia shall soon stretch forth her hands unto God." Then a collec-tion and a concert followed. The money raised was "but a mite I know," Lovejoy wrote, but it was sent to the defense commit-tee for Cinque and his comrades. He would have made a thou-sandfold more if he could. Little as it was, he sent it "with our prayers for the Mendians—for the Missionaries—for yourself [Lewis Tappan] and others of the Com.[mittee] and for John Quincy Adams," the successful defense attorney for the *Amistad* Negroes in the final arguments before the Supreme Court.[22]

The Princeton minister had been deeply affected by accounts of the ordeal of the *Amistad* prisoners while on board ship. What particularly struck him, however, was "Cinque's treatment of the Spaniards—his noble generosity in regard to the use of the fresh water on board when it became reduced." Lovejoy had read the account in *The Evangelist* several times, and "yet I believe not without tears." He was moved to see the whole affair with indignation—the cruelty toward Cinque and the other Negroes: "And this is the man on whose neck we are required to set our foot! This is the race doomed to everlasting inferiority!" [23]

Six years later, Lovejoy, still thinking in terms of "Ethiopia stretching forth her hands unto God," commented on a proposal to send missions among the slaves. Such men who go, Lovejoy wrote, "must really be men of God, prepared to die for its [the mission's] sake. It would require a baptism far beyond what's required for Anti-S[lavery] men generally." Lovejoy was not so sure that "a man ought to be urged to go," but if any volunteered he ought to be sent by the committee. Such volunteers, Lovejoy felt, should go "without disguise or concealment, with God's word and nothing else in his hands, claiming a right to preach to the slaves . . . we shall then see if the Slaveholders will dare stand between God and his creatures to prohibit them from receiving his message. If they have a right to the *written* so have they a right to the *preached* word." [24]

A few months later the Hampshire Colony Congregational Church sent twenty-five dollars through their minister to the American Missionary Association.

Among other missionary matters Lovejoy wrote about the dissatisfaction of antislavery men with the Home Department of the older Missionary Society: "Were it not for the A. S. ministers connected with it, it could hardly sustain itself." The Lovejoy church continued nevertheless to feed the Missionary Association dribs and drabs of five- and ten-dollar amounts, reaching a high point in 1854 of $109 in April and $115 in

August, at a time when Lovejoy was also very actively engaged in helping to build the footings in Illinois for the future Republican party. A year earlier, while out in the fields on an August day "looking upon the shocks of the abundant harvests," Lovejoy thought, "It would be pleasant to make a small offering to the Lord." He invited the congregation to join him in raising fifty dollars, which went to the American Missionary Association with fifty dollars collected earlier. The money supported the organization of new churches in frontier communities and aided in antislavery church work.[25]

Whether it was a collection for the missions, "stealing" a fugitive slave for freedom, or campaigning for office in the prairie towns, these Illinois Congregationalists were in the forefront of the abolitionist crusade. And because such leaders as Cross and Lovejoy raised a tumult in the ministerial associations, they were eventually effective in reversing the general hands-off policy of the American Home Missionary Society with respect to slavery. It was due, according to the church historian Frederick I. Kuhns, largely because "western Congregationalists were becoming increasingly insurgent as a group." Lovejoy contributed much to this process as well as to the birth of a political party pledged to abolish slavery.[26]

He persistently led the struggling Liberty party in his district, despite a lack of support from the voters. In the state convention at Aurora in 1844, he and Ichabod Codding, an accomplished organizer who had moved to Illinois from Connecticut, played leading roles; Lovejoy served on several committees and as temporary chairman, and Codding's talent for clear analysis furthered the proceedings enormously. The convention designated Lovejoy a Liberty presidential elector for the campaign later that year. But he could not cast a ballot for Birney in the electoral college with only 3,469 popular votes in Illinois. Yet in the Fourth District alone, where Lovejoy had helped the campaign for Birney, 1,882 Liberty votes were counted. Heartwarming though it was, the increased vote was not enough to break through the established two-party front. However, the Liberty party vote in New York State had proved to be a balance-of-power vote, causing Henry Clay to lose the state and the election. Polk, the first "dark horse" candidate, won by a slim popular margin. Liberty party men were encouraged by Birney's national vote of 62,000, almost nine times greater than in 1840.[27]

4

From a One-Idea Party
to Free-Soilism

> *"Anti-slavery thus far had only been sheet-lightning; the Buffalo convention sought to make it a thunderbolt."*
> —Frederick Douglass

Although many a voter might be sympathetic to antislavery ideas, the Liberty party's one-idea platform was not enough to attract him. Moreover, its unusually controversial nature complicated the problem of finding a way to break through the entrenched two-party system. Within the party, voices had been raised against a single platform since its inception, but Owen Lovejoy's was not among them. Questionings among the mass of Liberty faithfuls broke to the surface, and efforts to broaden the platform came in rapid succession after the elections of 1844. Salmon P. Chase of Ohio and other leaders sensitive to a drift toward stagnation called a Southwest Liberty convention at Cincinnati in June, 1845. About two thousand delegates came from the Great Lakes states and the territories of Wisconsin and Iowa, and a sprinkling deputation from New York, Rhode Island, Massachusetts, Virginia, and Kentucky. Ostensibly a congregation of all opposed to slavery, it failed to draw large numbers of

Whigs and Democrats. It remained a narrow affair despite Chase's nods toward the Democrats, and ended by reaffirming the Liberty party platform.[1]

Lovejoy played a minor role in these proceedings, for that spring he had suffered a severe illness, at first expected to be fatal. On the way back to Princeton he stopped in Alton for the Liberty state convention. It was the first antislavery meeting of any consequence in this city of unhappy memory since the murder of Elijah Lovejoy. A monument in honor of the martyred editor had been erected under the supervision of Colonel Charles W. Hunter, a supporter of free discussion and of the Lovejoys. He accompanied Owen Lovejoy and a friend to Elijah's grave, where they stood a few minutes in silent reflection and recollection.[2]

In the state convention Lovejoy made some brief and moderate remarks. But even these stirred infuriated remnants of the mobs of 1837 to pursue him through the streets of Alton. On the Illinois River, as Lovejoy was returning to Princeton, the persistent hatred of the name of Lovejoy was again demonstrated. The boat on which he and C. L. Kelsey, Reverend James H. Dickey, an aged veteran of the state antislavery movement, and a young lady in the old man's charge were traveling was stopped by a bar in the river. They were able to take another boat by "clubbing" their money but could pay for only one cabin, for the young woman. On the open deck the men were exposed not only to the night air but to the wrath of some of the other passengers. When the antislavery men revealed their sentiments and defended them, some passengers stormed to the captain and demanded that he turn the boat ashore "that they might hang us despised abolitionists on the neighboring trees." Kelsey wondered if the river had been mistakenly named by the Indians—"the river of men." [3]

Another call for a broadened Liberty platform soon came from

Michigan, where Birney now lived. Illinois leaders, including Lovejoy, Codding, and Eastman, took an emphatically opposite stand. The two state delegations met in debate at a Northwestern convention in Chicago in June, 1846. Ohio, prominent in anti-slavery politics, was significantly not represented among the six thousand persons who gathered at the meeting under the management of the Illinois radicals. Ohio's absence possibly was due to the influence of Chase, who was disappointed by his failure to swing the Cincinnati convention to his way of thinking.[4]

Guy Beckley, editor of the Ann Arbor, Michigan, *Signal of Liberty*, made the first move toward a more liberal platform by introducing a resolution that said in part that "while the question of slavery was meant to be paramount to all others, still its consideration was not the exclusive business of antislavery men." Michigan delegates S. B. Treadwell and Theodore Foster gave unstinting support to Beckley.[5]

The Reverend Lucian Farnum replied for the one-idea side, asserting that the slavery question was more important than any others, whether the bank or the tariff. Farnum's amendment to Beckley's resolution contradicted it completely. Codding joined the debate to support Farnum, and Lovejoy soon added his backing for the one-idea platform. As the candidate for congressman from his district in the 1846 elections, he received an attentive hearing. Quickly establishing rapport with his listeners, he said, "I'm not afraid of carrying out a principle, no matter where it may lead. To speak in a military phrase, I've drawn the sword and cast away the scabbard." Lovejoy felt that there was some ambiguity about Beckley's resolution, that the idea of it was to pledge the party to "free trade." Lovejoy asked provocatively, "Should we not also bring in the woman question, and assert their right to vote?" For his part he went for the one idea and meant to stick to it. He said he had no objection to free trade, but first and foremost was the one grand idea.

"I'm afraid you'll go to Congress," someone in the crowd shouted.

"If I do, I want to go on the one idea," Lovejoy replied. "I want to look those frowning slaveholders in the face." Noisy approval foretold the outcome of the debate. Beckley's resolution went down to defeat and Farnum's opposition amendment was adopted.[6]

Was the position too narrow? Did it unnecessarily proscribe the growth of the Liberty party at a time when the party's power to attract votes was weakening? Perhaps the Illinois campaign of 1846 could be a proving ground for Farnum's resolution, with Lovejoy as candidate from the Fourth Congressional District and main protagonist of the position.

The state convention of the party at Princeton that spring had resolved to make Lovejoy's district a point of concentration. Detailed plans of organization had been made, from the state committee down to committees in each school district. The *Western Citizen,* in the throes of a daily contest against Post Office hectoring, entered the campaign with 2,600 subscribers and towering enthusiasm. Its editorial of May 6 had been devoted to "Our Candidates," and declared it fitting that the brother of Elijah Parish Lovejoy should be nominated. "When Owen Lovejoy shall fill a seat in Congress by the votes of the people of Illinois," the editor proclaimed, "then let it be said that Illinois has repented. . . ." But standing on his own merits, Owen Lovejoy was the best candidate, he continued. "He has talents of a superior order, and will exert a powerful influence. He has integrity and will command respect. He is actuated by right principles, and can be trusted. He has energy of character, and nerve to stand up and defend the right in the face of its enemies, and he is, therefore, just the man to confront the opponents of Liberty in the Hall of Congress."

It had been no small triumph for Lovejoy to win the nomina-

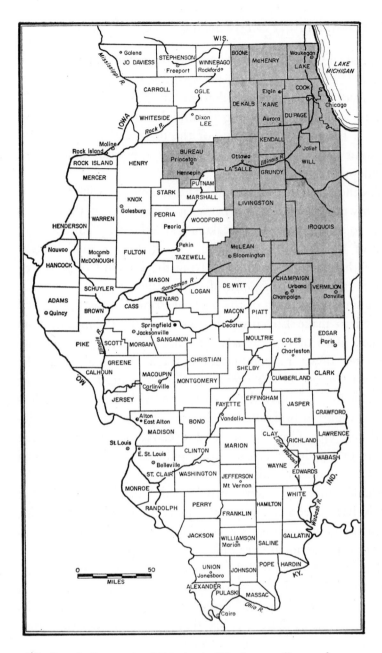

The Fourth Congressional District in Illinois according to the apportionment of 1843

tion. Although his brother's name was revered by Illinois abolitionists, his own was not so easily recognized when submitted.
The Fourth Congressional District was a huge one sprawling
across more than a quarter of the state, from the Indiana line
along the Wabash almost to the Mississippi, and from the southern boundary of Bureau County all the way to the state line, with
Wisconsin on the north. Lovejoy was not generally known
through this vast area, and in the nominating contest, said a fellow delegate from Princeton, "there were others who were
thought to be less obnoxious and the most determined opposition
was manifested." Not until after a two-day struggle in the nominating committee did Lovejoy win its approval. Even then some
Liberty men spoke in opposition to him on the floor of the
convention.[7]

The 1846 campaign marked Lovejoy's first attempt to win a
seat in the federal House of Representatives. It was an unusually
challenging one in the face of the Mexican War hysteria. Southern leaders, fearing that the Republic of Texas might be induced
to abolish slavery so close to the slave states and thus provide a
refuge for fugitive slaves, began to urge annexation of Texas in
the early 1840's. They hoped to bring it into the Union with
slavery intact. They drummed up a demand for annexation,
drove hard to elect Polk in 1844 on an expansionist platform
pledged to "reannex" Texas, and made it evident that the United
States should take a bellicose stand against Mexico, which was
sure to be aggrieved and to object. The Manifest Destiny slogan
was favored not only in the South but also won the approval of
voters in the Mississippi Valley. This imperialist doctrine driven
on by an unreasoning superpatriotism led to a clash with Mexico.
President Polk commanded military advances against the neighbor to the south early in 1846. The war excitement raged and in
the face of it Lovejoy went into his campaign for Congress.
Taking the stump in May, at about the time the United States

declared war against Mexico, the farmer-minister sweated out the summer in one speech after another in every corner of the congressional district. Lovejoy was met in some places by hotheaded egg-throwers or by opponents extremely hostile to him and his antislavery views. Nor was the campaign easy to launch in the face of Whig and Democratic predictions that the Liberty party would be dissolved at the polls.

A fighting song was devised to cheer on the partisans:

We will vote for Lovejoy,
We will vote for Lovejoy
We're for Liberty and Lovejoy,
And for Freedom through the land.[8]

This was one of a handful in the repertoire of the antislavery singer George W. Clark, who joined Lovejoy on the campaign tour for a week in July. Clark had also been an entertainer at the Northwest convention in Chicago.

Lovejoy's brand of humor came out in the course of the contest, notably when he was egged at Bloomington on May 30. In a letter to the *Western Citizen* published as "First Letter from the Stump," Lovejoy observed, "These egg-throwers have such irrepressible yearnings after glory, they are going I believe to win some roosters feathers in the Texan wars. Every egg these *leetle* ones throw, hatches a Liberty chicken, which will be full grown by the time of the election." [9]

Along the campaign route some of Lovejoy's troubles were induced by local speakers who preceded him. "A rash, violent, ranting denunciatory preacher," he said, had spoiled everything at Lowell. "I wish our ministers," Lovejoy complained, "would learn to be a little more prudent, use a little more oil and not so much of the fire and hammer." [10]

Lovejoy reported in the June 17 *Western Citizen* that he continued to encounter the most difficult kind of hostility—from those who would not even listen. At Bloomington Lovejoy was forced to speak to a meeting in a wagon shop cluttered with wheels, springs, harnesses, and shafts, because the courthouse had been denied him. A mob threw eggs before and after Lovejoy spoke.

In another letter from the stump Lovejoy reported that at Danville it was impossible to get a hearing because of the noise and hubbub at an enlistment. The war fever was raging, he wrote, as recruits were being exhorted to join in the war against Mexico. "Even Christian ministers urge on the people to join in the slaughter. . . . They adopt and advocate current phrases—'Our country, may she be right, but our country right or wrong. Go it blind, boys.' 'However unjustifiable the war, now it has begun we must fight it through.' . . . The President involves us in war—an unjust and unjustifiable war—yet we sustain him, right or wrong. Have not the people a right to judge? . . . Why, how much short does this come of the doctrine that the king can do no wrong? . . . The President says that our country has been invaded. Now, if I can understand the matter, that is just a plain, plump lie." [11]

The successful candidate in the Springfield Seventh District, Whig Abraham Lincoln, in his own way challenged the "plain, plump lie" when he took his seat in the House of Representatives. Lincoln demanded of President Polk that he name the spot on which Mexican troops had allegedly intruded and shed the blood of United States citizens.

Despite the similarity in Lincoln's and Lovejoy's views of the Mexican War, the Whig party line in the state and in Lovejoy's district was to predict and encourage dissolution of the Liberty party. But to the Whigs' consternation the farmers out on the plains doubled the Liberty party vote in the Fourth District. For the abolition candidate, 4,276 votes were cast; Democrat "Long

John" Wentworth was reelected with 12,126. Whig John Kerr received 5,523 votes. Lovejoy's defeat was happily balanced by the growth in Liberty votes. Had he predicted that by election day the newly hatched Liberty chickens would be full-grown? There had simply not been enough of them. Yet Lovejoy had received as many votes as the party received in the rest of the state.[12]

In the Fourth District, at least, it could be said that the one-idea party was the "true" one for abolitionists. But it could only be said in this district. Heartening as were the election figures to Liberty men, Lovejoy's achievement was untypical. The Illinois abolitionists had opposed the Mexican War and the acquisition of Texas. They had steadfastly opposed discrimination against Negroes and advocated repeal of the state's "Black Laws." But they had not injected into the campaign their views on homesteads, free trade, or the development of lake cities into harbors for the shipment of wheat and corn to the eastern markets. The electorate wanted to know about these things and, failing to hear from the Liberty party, remained with the Democrats.

Nevertheless, as a result of the election Lovejoy emerged as a definite asset for the national Liberty party. He was promptly called to Massachusetts to participate in the Liberty campaign there. From Cambridge Lovejoy wrote in November that he had been in "labors abundant." He had spoken fifty-five times in forty-one days, on three of which he did not speak at all. "I have a very pleasant time of it indeed," he wrote, "although laborious." All had not been labor, however. On the lake steamer voyage eastward he had relaxed in such diversions as "musical concerts, dancing, recitations, antislavery talking and physiological lecturing." [13]

Lovejoy noted enthusiastically that all eyes were on "Our Fourth Congressional District" in Illinois. His home bailiwick had become, with Giddings's district in the Ohio Western Reserve, one of the best Liberty-voting places in the country. Lovejoy exhorted from afar: "You must rouse up the sons and daughters of Liberty." Between the Bay State's sons and daughters of Liberty and the Illinois farmer there was mutual admiration. While they looked on Lovejoy as the "lion of the West," he was glowing in his praise of the Eastern friends. "This old Bay State," he wrote, "*is* one of the most glorious States in the Union, albeit most of its citizens have found it out." The *Western Citizen* editors were warmed to their hearts to reprint the letter from "our *standing candidate*, Owen Lovejoy. . . . His off-hand, western style of speaking has a wonderful taking way with our down-east friends." And for its devoted band of readers the *Citizen* was pleased to have Lovejoy's assessment of a local Massachusetts campaign: "In the Fourth Congressional District the Whigs and democrats put up men who are well known for their anti-slavery sentiment. . . . The Whigs sail just as close to the Liberty Bark as they can, to suck the wind out of our sails. . . . But the Liberty party here [in Massachusetts] has shown that it cannot be induced to go and worship the idols that the Whigs have set up." [14]

"Mr. Lovejoy's fame had preceded him," was the Boston *Emancipator's* proud opinion, "but his lecture surpassed even our high raised expectations." [15]

The *Emancipator* could be expected to extend such a warm welcome to Lovejoy, for its editor Joshua Leavitt was an early promoter of the Liberty party. He thus stood opposed to his fellow Bostonian William Lloyd Garrison. Lovejoy's presence emphasized the position of the New England political abolitionists and underscored the fact that the two viewpoints were far apart. Within a few months after Lovejoy's return from Massachusetts, Zebina Eastman in the *Western Citizen* resumed the attack on Garrison's anti-political position.

Speaking for the Illinois Liberty party, the *Western Citizen* in February, 1847, denounced Garrisonian abolitionism as destructive of government, church, and society as they existed. A most important concept was at issue: Was the Constitution of the United States a proslavery document or an antislavery one? Garrison, Phillips, and Edmund Quincy, New England antislavery leaders, maintained that the framers of the basic law had yielded to slaveowning interests when it was written, to permit representation based on population including slaves. As late as 1855 Garrison maintained that "the people of the country never did make an anti-slavery constitution." On the contrary, he insisted, the Constitution with its proslavery clause thus became "A Covenant with Death and An Agreement with Hell." It followed that Garrison could not recognize the government of the United States, nor truly swear allegiance to it. The logic of their position led the Garrisonians to assert that the Union ought to be dissolved, for it would be a matter of time before slavery, triumphant in the South, would engulf the North. In order to cleanse itself of the evil, the North ought to sever its connections with the South. Hence, they said, abolitionists could not participate in a proslavery government under a proslavery Constitution, and could not hope to win their battle through political action.

The political abolitionists argued that the Constitution was directly connected with the Declaration of Independence, which had declared that all men are created equal. The Constitution protected the rights of the people and provided a starting point from which to go on to win freedom for the slaves and to guarantee the civil rights of all. Granted the possibility of change under the Constitution, it followed that men should attempt to change the laws under the Constitution. To do so, men would have to win power in the government.

Zebina Eastman admitted to readers of the *Western Citizen* in an editorial of February 23, 1847, that "Liberty partyism is based upon the conclusion that slavery is created by law and sustained by the political power of the nation." This was at least what the

Garrisonians asserted. But Eastman proceeded in an opposite direction from this starting point. Eastman believed that rather than allow a failure to be written on the record of the democratic form of government, the Liberty party had to fulfill its destiny by reforming that government and society as well. He would "purify them from existing evils and abuses."

Garrison's perfectionism led him to reject the compromised Constitution and an imperfect society. He believed that the churches, by failing openly to support abolition of slavery, were in fact aiding slavery, and for that he scorned them. In turn, for that position he was denounced by more conservative men.

Taking a glance at the real state of society, Eastman lectured the anti-politicals: "Wherever Garrisonism places its hand, there it finds work to destroy. It forgets the fact that all things human partake of the imperfections of human nature—that an immediate eradication of every imperfection in mankind, is the destruction of humanity itself."

Under the strains of a falling Liberty vote in the North, the general lethargy that sent party members back to the Whigs and Democrats, and the rough debate among politicals like the Illinois radicals, the Garrisonians, and the broad platform men, the Illinoisans began to make significant concessions. They became more receptive to a broadened platform, and Lovejoy himself was among the first to reveal an inclination away from the one-idea party.

Lovejoy's defender in the Agnes-Nancy case, James H. Collins, at this time told him his prescription for a broad platform: "Free trade, direct taxation as a consequence, the abolition of the army, the dismantling of the navy and the 'Murder School at West Point' and a dozen other things as further consequences must receive our attention. . . . White oppression must receive our attention as well as black." [16] Lovejoy's immediate response, if any, is not known.

As the pressure mounted for a more liberal platform, the debate continued. It was a major issue at the Liberty national convention at Buffalo in October, 1847, but one-ideaism was reaffirmed there. A strong contingent of Gerrit Smith supporters had come from Midwestern cities. On the voyage from Cleveland to Buffalo the steamer's salon was crowded with a caucus over which Lovejoy presided. A heated discussion of one evening was carried over to the next morning, and the general drift was toward "a diversity of planks in the party platform," with land reform a prominent one. "Nor did the Western mind shrink from anticipating that woman suffrage might ultimately be another," one participant recalled. In the convention, Smith had proposed an enlarged platform, and having failed to sway his comrades, withdrew and issued a call for another convention in Buffalo in 1848. He proposed a rump National Liberty party platform devoted to abolishing slavery, advocating free trade, favoring universal suffrage regardless of color, issuing a general statement on social equality, and opposing land monopoly.[17]

Lovejoy agreed with Smith but continued also to concur with the party's main resolution that the "paramount object" of the party was the abolition of slavery by constitutional acts of the federal and state governments. Lovejoy, torn between sympathy with Smith and party regularity, stood by the latter.

John P. Hale, the Democratic senator from New Hampshire, was nominated presidential candidate of the regular Liberty party. In the balloting for the vice-presidential nomination Lovejoy received 76 votes on the first count. Leicester King of Ohio received 72. Since there was no majority for him on the second ballot, Lovejoy broke the impasse by withdrawing in favor of King. It was nevertheless gratifying to have earned this esteem among abolitionists. At the close of the convention Lovejoy was elected as the Illinois representative on the national committee.[18]

So acrimonious was inner party dissension that the contenders lost sight of a lesson taught by the voters. In a local election of

1847 for delegates to the state constitutional convention of Illinois, Lovejoy had come within forty votes of victory. The *Citizen* conceded Lovejoy's vote was larger than the Liberty men should have expected, "some having voted for him who are not Liberty men." His defeat was due only to a local Whig-Democratic coalition, and in the same election a Liberty candidate, Hurlburt Swan, was elected with the aid of Whig votes. Yet the *Citizen* failed to point out that a tactic of coalition could win future elections for the Liberty men.[19]

Finally the Illinois leaders had to yield to the pressure for a break with one-ideaism. Lovejoy was nominated without opposition as candidate for Congress in 1848, and during the contest he and his coworkers were forced to state their views on "mooted questions when called for." [20]

Farmers received special appeals to leave their work, "put their horses into their wagons, and take their families" to Owen Lovejoy's meetings. James Perry, a popular singer of Liberty songs, became a familiar part of the Lovejoy campaign, and afforded an opposition paper the opportunity for a sarcastic dig. The Ottawa *Free Trader* observed: "Mr. Lovejoy will contribute the argumentative and solid part of the entertainment, and Mr. Perry the recreative and harmonious." The editor suggested that the program would be complete if the Liberty party would adopt the barrel of hard cider used by the Whigs in 1840. The *Western Citizen* retorted in behalf of Lovejoy by insisting that instead of the hard cider its candidates would offer hard arguments—"No doubt you'd prefer to discuss the cider, but this you cannot have from us." [21] Abolitionists had not forgotten the diversion of the people from realities by the 1840 "Hard Cider" thumpings.

Lovejoy spoke twice in Chicago, where he was warmly and enthusiastically received. When he spoke from the steps of the courthouse on a beautiful spring evening, his audience was "a large multitude assembled in the streets." Lovejoy came out for exempting the homestead from seizure for debt, "and inalienability of the land without the consent of the wife." [22] The crowd loudly signaled its approval. This was a bread-and-butter issue they wanted to hear about, and they seemed to accept the antislavery message that was tied to it.

At Ottawa, however, Lovejoy was pointedly insulted by leading citizens. A correspondent reported that although two hundred were present to hear Lovejoy, "most of the business men and leading members of the church were not there—some that were solicited say that they had business of more importance, but these men can go to the polls and vote for Taylor or Cass." [23]

When its readers received the July 18, 1848, *Western Citizen*, they encountered something entirely new. The editor protested that many pople did not really understand the one-idea party. He declared that a Liberty man could have more than one idea. As a relevant example, the editor pointed to Mr. Owen Lovejoy, whose political opinions were presented in that issue: Lovejoy's answers to a series of questions propounded by the Liberty party managers.

Their first questions concerned the condition of the United States territories: (1) Will you use your influence to secure freedom of the public lands? (a question about Lovejoy's thoughts on free homesteads); (2) Are you in favor of the Wilmot proviso? And does said proviso cover the whole of the Liberty party ground? (3) To what extent in your opinion has Congress power over the institution of slavery?

Yes, Lovejoy believed Congress ought to open up the public lands in limited quantities, at no charge to actual settlers. States should stop disposing of public land except to actual settlers—this would "foster and multiply what is called the middling class" —the backbone of every country, in Lovejoy's estimation. Lincoln similarly saw this class as the backbone of America. Furthermore, as he had often declared, Lovejoy said, "I am in favor

of the exemption and inalienability of the homestead"—to free it
from seizure for debt and to free the homesteader from eviction
from the land.

Lovejoy reaffirmed his stand on the Declaration of Independence and the preamble to the Constitution, which in his view imposed an obligation upon Congress "utterly and forever" to prohibit slavery in all territories belonging to the United States, including, of course, territories acquired in the Mexican War. Second, he asserted that Congress had the clear right to abolish
slavery in the District of Columbia, and that power should be
used without delay. Third, he demanded that an immediate inter-
dict be put upon interstate and coastwise "traffic in human beings," meaning, of course, the slave trade.

Lovejoy wrote that he believed a slave could be freed if
brought to a free state, a reiteration of the principle in the Agnes-
Nancy case.

Here was the true Liberty party doctrine, as Lovejoy saw it,
straight from the heart.

Having made clear his stand on slavery, Lovejoy addressed
himself to the interests of a belt of free farmers scattered across
the northern prairies, and to the shippers and merchants of Chicago and the towns of central Illinois. The second group of
questions was concerned with those broader matters: What are
your views in regard to a tariff? Are you in favor of, or opposed
to, the appropriation of public money for the improvement of
harbors and rivers?

On the tariff, Lovejoy explained his belief in free trade and
"direct taxation for the necessary expenses of government." He
thought that free trade ought to be a matter of negotiation between governments. But "as a permanent policy of government a
protective tariff was preferable to one for mere purposes of revenue, inasmuch as the latter involves all the expenses and evils
without any of the benefits of the former." (Later, during the

Civil War, sectional and class interests would make him reverse his position.)

He was definite in advocating congressional appropriations for river and harbor improvements on the Great Lakes. He could see no reason why a distinction should be made in favor of salt-water ports. "Our lakes are inland seas—they bear upon their bosom the commerce of the seas, and like those of other seas, their harbors should be improved."

Also as part of the platform Lovejoy advocated a reduction in postage rates to two cents on letters; free delivery of newspapers within thirty miles (possibly the costliness of mailing the *Western Citizen* may have been in mind); and the entire abolition of the franking privilege of members of Congress. He was in favor of direct election of the President without the electoral college.

At last Lovejoy and those who had stood shoulder to shoulder with him at Alton, and those who in 1846 had upheld the one-idea resolution at Chicago, embraced the broadened platform. With Lovejoy as their candidate they looked hopefully toward his election in August, and a break through the two-party system.

On the national scene, however, there was no indication of a sizable departure from the major parties. The Democrats chose as their presidential candidate Lewis Cass of Michigan, a "Northern man with Southern principles." The Whigs bet their all on a Mexican War hero, General Zachary Taylor of Louisiana. Both men could be expected to attract the lion's share of votes, with a small fraction going to antislavery candidates. Those voters who were concerned over the growing evil of slavery found that the Cass and Taylor contest offered them Hobson's choice. The options were so unacceptable as to work discontent within both parties, and encouraged a striving for new alignments.

One sign of such discontent was shown in Lovejoy's home county early in 1847, when his neighbor John H. Bryant, a long-standing Democrat, said he hoped his party would nominate a Northerner, presumably one not sympathetic to slavery. "I do think that defeat with a good northern man would be preferable to victory with a southern slaveholder," he wrote to his brother in New York. Almost a year later Bryant hoped the "Wilmot Proviso Democrats will not recede from the ground they have taken—why do they not take the name *Free Democrats*." [24]

This striving by Northerners for a realignment of parties grew out of their alarm over the expansionist pressure of the slave power. Although they had accepted the Missouri Compromise of 1820, which partially limited the domain of slavery, antislavery people feared the consequences of Southern imperialist proposals to control or take possession of the Caribbean islands, Mexico, and the Sandwich Islands. These and other lands might be used as a base for the slave and cotton markets, they believed. The war against Mexico and the subsequent acquisition of new territories from which slave states might be formed, particularly disturbed the antislavery movement. The Manifest Destiny doctrine that justified such an enlargement of slave territory and of Southern domination over the national government became increasingly unacceptable. As a result, millions of Americans were aroused to the dangers of slavery expansion.

By February, 1848, when peace had been made with Mexico, the question of freedom or slavery in the vast new Territory—the present Southwest, and parts of Colorado and Wyoming—was on the minds of the people. Demands were heard for halting the expansion of the slave power, and they came from Whigs, Democrats, and Liberty men who perceived the need for a new party to achieve that objective. The debate over the status of the newly acquired Territory broke into acrimony in Congress and out. In Congress Democratic Representative David Wilmot of Pennsylvania introduced an amending proviso to a territorial purchase bill of 1846 to prohibit slavery in any territory that might be gained from Mexico. Although his proviso failed of adoption as law or policy, it succeeded in adoption as principle for hosts of nonextensionists of slavery—for example, for a majority of

87

Northern legislatures, which passed resolutions of approval and in the process cut across established party lines. When the Whig national convention defeated a motion to approve the proviso, Henry Wilson of Massachusetts walked out with a considerable following of "Conscience Whigs." In New York State, Martin Van Buren's adherents collaborated with the Whigs to put through the legislature a resolution approving Wilmot's proviso. When President Polk in retaliation threw the federal patronage to William L. Marcy, the Van Buren men, or Barnburners as they were called, cut themselves off from the party. Marcy led the Hunkers, or conservatives, of the Democratic party, who "hunkered" for offices and who tried to avoid a stand on the slavery issue. In contrast the dissident Van Buren Democrats joined a mass meeting at Buffalo in August, 1848, to organize the Free Soil party.

In Illinois the Liberty party's one-ideaism and aloofness from other parties began to disappear when local meetings studied the question. One gathering at Bristol was willing to "lay aside all party preference." At Hennepin a few days later another meeting agreed that "Party names [are] of no importance, principles and objects alone [are] to be tenaciously adhered to." [25] Out of the ideological struggle came a decision to send delegates to the national Free Soil convention. The Illinois Liberty party protested its devotion to abolitionist principles as it pushed out into the main political stream.

Owen Lovejoy, his campaign for congressional election complete, went to Buffalo as a delegate, forgathering with Barnburners, Conscience Whigs, Liberty men, Negro abolitionists, and others opposed to the extension of slavery. In the Illinois contingent also were three Underground Railroad operators, James H. Collins, C. V. Dyer, and John Cross. In the convention, Lovejoy was reported to have served on several committees.[26]

Hale was proposed as a presidential standardbearer by Henry B. Stanton and Joshua Leavitt. But Van Buren led the field in the balloting, and Leavitt and Stanton, having pledged themselves to the Barnburner choice, persuaded Lovejoy and other Liberty party leaders to make the nomination unanimous for Van Buren.[27]

Lovejoy hailed the new Free Soil party that organized in Buffalo on August 9, 1848. For him it contained the soul of Liberty partyism. In a letter of approval to the *Western Citizen* he wrote: "The principle of Liberty is in this movement, undergird and surround it—the immediate object aimed at is one which we cordially approve, and the ultimate object is identical—the extinction of slavery." [28] The Free Soil platform called for the abolition of slavery by the federal government where it had the power to do so; the prohibition of slavery extension; internal improvements; a homestead law; a tariff for revenue; and other planks under the slogan: "Free Soil, Free Speech, Free Labor, and Free Men." The platform was enthusiastically adopted by the various elements present, and Lovejoy's enthusiasm might have been a hint that he was far beyond the one-idea positions of 1845 and 1846. Back home the congressional election results of August 7 gave evidence of the voters' decisive shift away from the radical antislavery party. Despite Lovejoy's answers to the broad platform questions and the seeming departure from one-ideaism, the voters still drifted to the two major parties. The efforts of the Liberty party were insufficient to overcome the effects of its narrow approaches of earlier years. In the Fourth District of Illinois Democrats and Whigs had shrewdly pronounced themselves for Free Soil. The election returns rewarded them: Wentworth won reelection to the House of Representatives with 11,857 votes. J. Young Scammon received 8,302 for the Whigs, and Lovejoy's poll was only 3,159.[29]

The new Free Soil party failed to win state positions in Illinois in the November, 1848, presidential election and failed to carry the state for Van Buren. Instead the electorate chose Cass, while in the nation as a whole the Presidency was won by Taylor. Even so, Illinois free soil and antislavery men helped to run up a higher total than ever before for an antislavery candidate, in this case for one opposed to the extension of slavery. Out of this election the Thirty-First Congress was organized and opened in December, 1849, with 112 Democrats, 109 Whigs, and 9 Free Soilers in the House; and 35 Democrats, 25 Whigs, and 2 designated as Free Soil in the Senate. One of the two third-party senators was Hale, whose seat was not contested; and the other was Chase, who was elected by the Ohio legislature in January, 1849. Giddings was returned to the House of Representatives in the 1848 election and his future son-in-law, George W. Julian of Indiana, was also elected. Lovejoy might have been in this advance contingent of antislavery and anti-extensionist men had his contest been in November rather than in August. Van Buren received 6,400 more votes than Lovejoy had won earlier in the Fourth Congressional District, while Cass received 2,000 less than Wentworth in August in the same district. The Whigs gained only 800 votes for Taylor between August and November. If Wentworth had run at the same time as Cass, he might have suffered by a shift of 2,000 votes toward Van Buren and Lovejoy.[30]

Disappointment and disillusion were rife among Liberty and Free Soil men. When it was apparent that they had failed, many left the Liberty party. The hastily organized Free Soil party seemed to have insufficient political cement to hold its various elements together. No wonder that the exultant cry of Lovejoy that the Liberty party was "not the *third* but the *first* party" resounded instead in 1848 and 1849 almost as a cry of despair.

90

5

A More Certain Sound
in Antislavery Politics

> *"Wherever there are men, there will be parties; and wherever there are free men they will make themselves heard."*
> —*Thomas Jefferson*

Lovejoy and most Illinois Liberty party leaders were left stranded after the 1848 campaign. The defeat was followed by disorganization of the Free Soil party and by almost complete dissolution of the Liberty party in the nation and in Illinois. Yet Free Soil principles were not defeated, as the January, 1849, meeting of the state legislature proved. Whigs joined Democrats, who were in the majority in both houses, to instruct Illinois federal senators and representatives to vote for Wilmot's proviso. The *Western Citizen* immediately claimed credit for Free Soil principles, but the Chicago *Journal* injected its claim for "good Whig doctrine." Now voters could very well ask: If Democrats and Whigs now support the Proviso, then why the need for the Free Soil party, however laudable and victorious its policy? It was an old story—the voters feared to throw away votes.[1]

Lovejoy and other leaders of the Illinois Liberty men discerned this trend among the electorate so well that they refused to attempt reorganization in 1849. Some rank-and-file members in Kane County called for meetings to revive the old organization, however, and Lovejoy, as the leading public figure of the party in Illinois and its "standing candidate," was invited to speak. Lovejoy replied that he was not convinced the Liberty party needed reorganization. In his estimation such a move at this time was not desirable. The new co-editor of the *Western Citizen*, James McClellan, Jr., deemed it "unwise to agitate the question." He agreed fully with Lovejoy but promised his readers that if a new emergency should arise and a new organization be needed, then surely antislavery men would unite again.[2]

Hardly had these apathetic sentiments been published than an emergency did arise in the shape of the Compromise of 1850. The compromise represented an attempt to solve by a "deal" the clash of the slaveholding, expansionist South against a burgeoning free-labor, free-farmer, and free-capitalist North and West. Under its terms, California was to be admitted to the Union with a constitution which prohibited slavery; New Mexico and Utah were to be permitted to decide for themselves about slavery (a concession to states' rights advocates and a surrender of the Wilmot proviso); the Texas borders were established, with a payment of ten million dollars to the state for its concessions. This was in effect a subsidy to holders of depreciated Texas securities. The compromise also included a more stringent Fugitive Slave Law than the one of 1793. This was an attempt to break up the Underground Railroad by allowing slaveowners to chase runaway slaves into free states, by instructing United States marshals to apprehend fugitives, and by giving the marshals the power to organize posses. In addition anyone who gave shelter or aid to fugitive slaves or who stood in the way of enforcing this act faced heavy penalties. Finally, the slave trade was abolished in the District of Columbia but slavery was not touched. Historian Roy F. Nichols observes that the slave trade bill was meaningless, as "slaves could be purchased nearby."[3]

92

Abolitionists were incensed especially by the new Fugitive Slave Act, which protected slaveowners' property and was considered to be an unwarranted concession to slaveowning interests. In addition they denounced the act because it would make informers and slave-catchers of the American people.

The pages of the *Citizen* leaped into life with readers' calls for action, for regrouping and reassembling—to square off and fight back the newest menace of an unbridled slave power. Owen Lovejoy urged that abolitionists quickly move the Free Soil party into action. We must have a large convention, he wrote. "The Democrats are returning like a dog to his vomit," he remarked scornfully in noting that the Michigan legislature had rescinded its vote in favor of the Wilmot proviso. "It is high time we were up, and organizing and doing," Lovejoy said in the spirit of the early forties.[4]

Finally on June 5, 1850, a Free Soil district reorganizing convention met at Joliet to hear Lovejoy make a major speech summoning the stalwarts for new campaigns. The Buffalo platform of Free Soil, Free Speech, Free Labor, and Free Men was reaffirmed; the Compromise of 1850 being contrived in Congress was condemned; and Daniel Webster was singled out for denunciation as a traitor to the cause of Union and Liberty because he was willing to make the compromise, and because he had bitterly attacked the abolitionists. Before they adjourned, the delegates decided to hold a nominating convention at Elgin late in August.[5]

In the meantime, the Chicago *Tribune* hastened to recommend William B. Ogden as the congressional candidate of the Free Soilers in the Fourth District. Ogden had been a Democrat who had opposed Cass and Stephen A. Douglas in his own state. Douglas defended the compromise, denounced the Wilmot proviso, and advocated popular sovereignty or states' rights on the slavery issue. Ogden had favored Van Buren as the true choice of his party in 1848 and had approved of the Wilmot proviso.

93

(The *Citizen* had referred to it as the "Jeffersonian Proviso.") Ogden seemed to be an excellent choice, able to appeal to broad groups beyond the ranks of the abolitionists. Still, a radical vanguard devoted to Lovejoy challenged Ogden's nomination. The Elgin convention thus became the scene of heated struggle between Lovejoy and Ogden forces.[6]

Ogden gained an early lead, and in the end was nominated by a vote of 59 to 38. Having scored this victory early in the afternoon, the Ogden group made a hasty exit to trains waiting to pull out for Chicago at 3 P.M. The Lovejoy supporters, knowing the trains had steam up for departure, had tried in vain to prolong debate and postpone the balloting. After the contest was over it seemed as if there would be a hopeless split hobbling the Free Soilers even before they launched their campaign. However, the *Citizen* and the Bureau County *Advocate*, edited by John H. Bryant, put brave faces on the situation and spoke unflinchingly of party unity at the polls. To support their desire for unity, the *Citizen*'s editors quoted with comforting approval a report of coalition on a county basis between regular and Free Democrats of Free Soil persuasion in Bureau County. Lovejoy and Bryant were prominent in a Bureau County Union Convention of Democrats. A statement of principles almost duplicated Lovejoy's answers to the queries of 1848. All these Democrats had readily applauded a preface to the statement upholding Jefferson's ideals in general and the Northwest Ordinance of 1787 in particular.[7]

During the campaign, even the regular Democrats of the Wentworth and Douglas machine pledged opposition to the extension of slavery into free territories. Their candidate, Dr. Richard Molony, went so far as to write to Ogden, declaring himself for repeal of the Fugitive Slave Law. Ogden immediately announced his withdrawal from the race, declaring that two Free Soil candidates were unnecessary. To complicate matters for the old Liberty men, the Whigs had also come into the election campaign with Churchill Coffing as their candidate and with a platform based on the Free Soil slogan.[8]

Ogden's withdrawal seemed to be a prearranged maneuver. Radical abolitionists were angered. "We are disappointed, grieved, indignant," complained the *Western Citizen*. It accused Ogden of not consulting with Free Democratic leaders before his action. The editors then aired their disappointment by asserting that Molony had been a Cass supporter and could not possibly stand on the Free Soil platform.[9]

The Liberty men reconvened on October 23 at Aurora and nominated James H. Collins as the Free Soil candidate. They rolled up their sleeves for an old-fashioned partisan fight and hurled into the campaign the oratorical talents of Ichabod Codding and Owen Lovejoy. The old enthusiasm was displayed, but it proved to be another case of too little too late. Molony won with 11,231 votes to Coffing's 10,587. Collins ran a poor third with votes variously recorded as 804, 1,213, and 1,076, amid charges of failure to count the minority party's votes. The Fourth Congressional District was the only one in the state in which there were third-party votes. The remainder of the state followed the trend of the North, in which Barnburner Democrats returned to the regular party. The hopes for a vital and successful Free Soil party faded out.[10]

Far more gratifying results of the abolitionists' efforts were the numerous mass meetings of protest against the Fugitive Slave Law. When the Chicago Common Council declared the law unconstitutional, Collins, Lovejoy, Codding, Eastman, and McClellan could be proud. Their labors had influenced sentiment for a resolution by the city's governing body whose language and intent were almost their own. Unfortunately for them, Senator Douglas had great influence and power over the Democrats. He was able to sway the Common Council to rescind its disapproval of the compromise and the Fugitive Slave Law. Douglas had spoken on October 23 to a hostile audience gathered in front of Chicago's North Market. This was one of a series of meetings running from October 22 to October 26, the tenor of which was strongly opposed to Douglas's position. But Douglas prevailed in the council room even if he did meet a new coolness among the people in the streets. The council's rescinding vote was 12 to 1; and the next session of the state legislature repealed its instructions to Senators Douglas and James Shields to oppose the compromise bill in the Senate.[11]

The *Western Citizen,* estimating what was new and vibrant in the situation, pressed on the offensive. Not only was the Fugitive Slave Act an odious one, not only was it unconstitutional, but it must be resisted, it must be ignored to death. Resolutions, meetings, yes! But more than that—resistance, defiance—these must become the guides to radical abolitionist action. The direction was clear—and the response was equally clear. The Lovejoys, the Philo Carpenters and C. V. Dyers, and hundreds of others redoubled their efforts to bring the trains of the Underground Railroad to havens of freedom in northern Illinois—at Princeton, Galesburg, Ottawa, Chicago, Joliet.

New forces for liberty were coming into the state to swell the population and strengthen the abolitionists. German settlers, refugees from economic hardship and from the reactionary aftermath of the 1848 democratic revolutions, swarmed into the old Northwest states at the rate of two hundred thousand annually between 1850 and 1860. They settled in the lake cities of Milwaukee, Chicago, and Cleveland, in St. Louis and southern and central Illinois, and out on the lush prairie farmlands. In their ranks were several varieties of political and social theoreticians—democrats, utopians, Marxists, agrarian reformers, and trade unionists. Their common ground was a desire for freedom—for themselves and for their fellow men of all colors and races and national origins. In the decade of their settlement they played a vital part in the antislavery and homestead movements and in the formation of the Republican party. The German settlers offered hope for victory over slavery in their numbers and in their advanced political thinking, and the abolitionists warmly welcomed them.

Lovejoy provided another source of hope. When finally convinced that the time was ripe for a revival of an antislavery party, Lovejoy introduced a resolution at a meeting of the Illinois Anti-Slavery Society at Princeton on January 21, 1852, recommending a national convention to name presidential and vice-presidential candidates. He reaffirmed the Free Soil slogan and observed that no party then existed which upheld its principles. It was necessary, therefore, to organize such a party of freedom.[12]

Immediate applause came from Frederick Douglass, who wrote in his newspaper *Frederick Douglass' Paper*, published in Rochester, New York, that he welcomed the action of the Illinois radicals and urged other states to follow their leadership. The Negro leader had been bitterly disappointed by the near dissolution of the Free Soil party in the nation, but more so by the dissipation of strict Liberty party doctrine that had been effected by the unity movement of 1848. He feared that instead of seeking eradication of slavery a Free Soil party would be content merely with limiting slavery to one section of the country. Douglass had held aloof from the original Free Soil party, but when he saw signs of hope, such as the move of the Illinois abolitionists, he became enthusiastic for a new party. Recognizing that only in a broad movement like the Free Soilers' could abolitionism advance politically, Douglass by the summer of 1852 swung over. He embraced the movement so warmly as to urge his political collaborator and friend Gerrit Smith to accompany him to the national Free Democratic convention at Pittsburgh in August. Douglass saw an opportunity to influence the policies of the convention toward a stronger abolitionist stand. "Mere *Free Soil*," he wrote, "I am sure, will not satisfy the masses who will attend that convention. The abolitionists of the West are in advance of their leaders. They are ready for a more certain sound than that which has of late called them out to battle." He urged Smith to supply that sound.[13]

Douglass and Smith, ready for action, were among the two thousand delegates and observers who jammed Pittsburgh's Lafayette Hall on August 11. George W. Julian of Indiana and dozens of prominent Old Northwest abolitionists attended. Eastern antislavery people also were amply represented. Joshua R. Giddings headed the platform committee and Henry Wilson of Massachusetts was the convention chairman. Zebina Eastman, C. L. Kelsey, and Owen Lovejoy of the Illinois radicals were present. Their aim was to create a new party, broader than the Liberty but more tightly organized and better devoted to antislavery principles than the Free Soil party. In addition to the principal planks of the 1848 Buffalo platform, this new party condemned the Compromise of 1850 and the Fugitive Slave Law, demanded recognition of the independence of Haiti, inserted a peace plank calling for international arbitration of international disputes, and called for American protests against European monarchs intervening to prevent establishment of republics on the Continent. The last was in response to a plea of Louis Kossuth then touring the United States to win support for the Hungarian republican revolution. But the heaviest emphasis was placed on demands for the immediate repeal of the Fugitive Slave Law and on the assertion that nobody was bound to observe the law since it was "repugnant to the Constitution." A sharp difference arose over two other resolutions in the platform. Giddings's majority report avoided the question of equal rights for the free Negro, but Gerrit Smith, speaking for the minority on the platform committee, provoked angry debate when he proposed resolutions declaring first that slavery was a violation of human rights and that it could not be subject to legislation, and second that the party should try to secure equal political rights for all persons regardless of color or sex. Lovejoy was among those who supported the majority report and he strongly opposed Smith's resolutions. On the first, Lovejoy said that he was not going to declare that slavery was of no binding force when he knew "it was of crushing force," and therefore requiring legislation to limit it. On the second, Lovejoy reacted with considerable impatience. He was unprepared to take so radical a step in public, in spite of his private beliefs, as to declare for equal rights for women in particular. He made an unpleasant reference to Smith's insistence on this point and said he was "not willing to make fools of ourselves to gain a few votes." Giddings said the platform should not be embarrassed by taking "indefensible positions," although both men supported equal rights in their states. Lovejoy had spoken for such rights many times while upholding the Liberty cause, and continued to do so in 1853 in efforts to repeal Illinois' Black Code of Negro restrictions. Giddings pointed out that the Free Soilers had been instrumental in repealing Ohio's Black Laws. However, Giddings and Lovejoy were trying to bring out a platform for a party that could win votes. The demand for equal rights was too strong a prescription for a populace that still discriminated against Negroes and women and proscribed their rights. As Frederick Douglass said later, "what is morally right is not at all times politically possible." The convention voted to table Smith's resolutions, 197 to 14.[14]

The new organization formed at Pittsburgh was named the Free Democratic party, a title suggested four years earlier by John H. Bryant of Princeton in a letter to his brother William Cullen Bryant. Senator John P. Hale of New Hampshire was chosen as presidential candidate, and Julian was nominated as his running mate for the Vice-Presidency.

The election of Frederick Douglass as a secretary of the convention placed the new party on an exalted plane of political action. His choice by acclamation, after nomination by Lewis Tappan, only underscored the earnestness of the delegates. From across the Atlantic the London *Anti-Slavery Reporter* applauded: "That a colored man should be called upon to act as an officer in a large political meeting [is] a sign of progress in that country, where to belong to the enslaved race has been to be proscribed and neglected." [15]

The Illinois delegation returned home and immediately convened ratifying meetings. In Chicago Lovejoy reported on the national sessions, putting special emphasis on the unity achieved: "all grades of the Independent opponents of the Compromise [of 1850], from Gerrit Smith of the higher platform to the many unmentionable ones of the lowest order of Barnburnerism." With great feeling Lovejoy reported that when he entered the hall at Pittsburgh, Douglass was making a speech in defiance of the Fugitive Slave Law. This was as much a highlight for the Princeton minister as it was for the London newspaper.[16]

The *Citizen* wrote about "The People Moving—Meetings in the Country." When a state convention of Free Democrats met in Granville August 25 and 26, 1852, the newspaper cited it as "the largest, most enthusiastic, respectable and telling Convention ever held in this state." At that gathering Bryant presided, and the "old Liberty guard, led on by Lovejoy, were the moving spirits of the convention." [17]

A list of state candidates was drawn up, with Bryant as the standardbearer in the Third Congressional District. This was basically the same area as the Fourth before a redrawing of the district lines—the same abolitionist stronghold that had rallied to Lovejoy in 1846 and 1848. Now, in a national election year, enthusiasm and new confidence gripped the antislavery people. With Lovejoy busy in policy-making and organization, his followers in this district again did their utmost to promote the new party. As in election after election, the faithful cast their votes and brought friends and sympathizers to the polls with them. Even though Free Democratic contestants were defeated, their increased total vote gave them good cause for hope. By comparison with 4,748 votes for the Free Soil gubernatorial candidate in 1848, the Free Democrats rolled up 8,809 for his counterpart four years later.[18]

Hale polled a little more than 156,000 votes in the presidential contest, a considerable decline from 1848. Pierce won, but a large body of Northern Whigs led by William H. Seward and Thurlow Weed of New York were unhappy with the party's support of the Compromise of 1850. The Whigs were split on the issue and suffered irreparable damage, carrying only four states. Evidently a considerable portion of the people were ready for a party strong enough to be elected on a nonextensionist platform at least.

Even so, in the following year the *Western Citizen*, its mail subscriptions falling, was forced to suspend publication. The farm and financial depression had at last confounded the task of sustaining a valiant partisan newspaper. It was Illinois' singular tribune of the antislavery cause. For many years during the forties and early fifties the *Citizen* served as the central organ of the movement in Illinois, northern Indiana, Wisconsin, and Iowa. It was considered to be the leading antislavery paper west of Ohio.[19] Although the subscription list stood between fifteen hundred and two thousand names, the paper folded on October 18, 1853, after a lapse in publication since June.

A successor was published on December 1, 1853, under the auspices of the Illinois Free Democratic party's board of directors in Chicago. Eastman, Hooper Warren, and E. Goodman were named the editors. The pages were made more attractive to the general public. The new paper was called *Free West*, as if to

sum up in this expansive phrase the whole position of Free Soil-
ism. The motto on its masthead quoted the Northwest Ordinance
of 1787: "There shall be neither slavery nor involuntary servitude in the said Territory," of which Illinois had been a part. In
the two years it circulated, the weekly journal recorded revolutionary changes in the state's and the nation's political alignments.
It related the story of Owen Lovejoy's first electoral victory, and
it played a part in the first moves toward the creation of the
grand alliance of progressive forces in its time—the Republican
party.

To set the tone of the *Free West* as a militant antislavery newspaper, the first number devoted considerable space to the news of
Frederick Douglass's appearance on the platform in Princeton
and in Chicago. The prominent place given the text of the Negro
leader's speech in Princeton on October 26, 1853, signified the
editor's concurrence in this attack on the Illinois Black Code. Of
the federal Fugitive Slave Law, Douglass declared: "No one
talks now about repealing the Fugitive Slave Law. It is too
awfully wicked to repeal. It should be spit upon, despised, hated
and disregarded. . . . Let it be hinted that it would not be safe
for the slave hunter to come here." [20]

This speech may have recalled Owen Lovejoy's assertion in
the *Western Citizen* ten years earlier that it was no sin to aid the
escape of Negro slaves on the Underground Railroad, for Douglass's attack was directed at a measure passed by the Illinois legislature on February 12, 1853, designed to prevent the immigration
of free Negroes into the state. The law made it a crime for anyone to bring in a Negro, and arrest and a fine of fifty dollars
faced any Negro who appeared in Illinois and remained ten days.
Passage of the law signified a fearful counter to the success of the
Underground Railroad. Yet the law was openly opposed, not
only by veteran abolitionists but by almost every Whig and
Democratic newspaper in the state, and by eleven Whigs and

eleven Democrats in the House of Representatives at Springfield. The repeal of this law and all the Black laws was made "the point of contests on which we are to fight the battle of our principles and platforms," the *Free West* declared on December 1.

During 1853, while the Underground trains kept rolling north, abolitionist leaders moved toward fresh political action. Their efforts were rewarded in the spring of 1854, when sixteen Free Democratic associations were formed in the state. The Free Democratic party had not gained in New England in the 1852 elections, but in the Northwest states a revival of interest in the new party encouraged efforts to expand it in 1853. In Illinois, that year, Lovejoy, Eastman, and Codding took to the field; Cassius M. Clay came up from Lexington, Kentucky, to campaign and help organize; and Frederick Douglass headed out from Rochester to hurl defiance at the slave hunters. The antislavery men had rallied just in time, for the next blow of the slaveowning interests and their political allies was about to be delivered.

In the spring of 1854 Senator Stephen A. Douglas of Illinois had pushed through the United States Senate the Kansas–Nebraska Act. The boldness of the plan in the bill seemed to prove deliberate aggressiveness on the part of the slave power. The bill as introduced by Douglas and reported to the Senate on January 23, 1854, and enacted on May 30, repealed the Missouri Compromise of 1820. For more than thirty years that compromise between free and slave states had come to be accepted as a principle underlying the government of the territories of the Louisiana Purchase, or the formation of new states out of them. The Nebraska Act set out to organize into territories the vast lands of the Platte country, an area stretching from Missouri to Utah and from Texas to Minnesota. This expanse had been considered free of slavery forever under the Missouri Compromise. The senator's bill proposed that the territories of Kansas and

103

Nebraska be created, and that states formed in them come into the Union "with or without slavery, as their constitution may prescribe at the time of their admission." Douglas enjoyed the support of railroad interests and Southern slaveholders in contending that the 1820 compromise line of 36° 30' was invalid, that a geographic line restricting slavery was no longer tenable. But Douglas himself had told an audience in 1849 that the Missouri Compromise had been an inviolable act "canonized in the hearts of the American people as a sacred thing." And millions had agreed and placed their trust in men like Douglas.

By his reversal in 1854 Douglas was left open to the charge of his opponents that he had betrayed that trust and was playing the game of the slaveholders. That class of men banked on his scheme to open the rich agricultural regions of the huge territory to slavery—some even envisioned slavery in association with the industrial giant growing in the great cities and towns of the East. Proslavery ideologists had been propounding a theory that slavery ought not to be restricted to Negroes—they would integrate slavery. Although offered in all seriousness, this perverse attempt to justify the slave system did not receive wide acceptance, even among Southern leaders. Nevertheless, to discerning minds it forecast what might be in store for all the land if appeasement of the slaveowners became the rule.

Lovejoy and the Illinois Free Democrats reacted without hesitation, defining the issue: "Either Slavery or Liberty must fall." Moreover, thoughtful nonradicals began to realize that they must resist not only the specific aggression imbedded in the Nebraska Act but the whole "peculiar institution." If not arrested and overthrown, slavery could conceivably be extended to all the United States and its virgin territories. The *Free West* held that the North could decide the issue at the ballot box—but, "Neglect to resist slaveholding encroachments a little longer, and the cartridge box will be the only power that can recover lost liberties." [21] In practical politics, however, there were less extreme steps to be taken.

The Germans in Chicago were the first to react against the Nebraska Bill with a demonstration organized by George Schneider, editor of the Illinois *Staats-Zeitung*, and one of the forty-eighters. He was joined by the Quincy *Tribune* and the Alton *Vorwärts*. In February, 1854, many German-American anti-Nebraska meetings were held throughout the North, some organized by the Arbeiterbund led by Joseph Weydemeyer, a close friend of Karl Marx. The Chicagoans organized a petition campaign, and at a meeting in March called for a new organization of the "liberty loving German element" to prevent the Democratic party from "continuing to be an instrument in the hands of the slave power." [22]

Many Northern Democrats were so disgusted with Douglas's act that they gave notice of disaffiliation from the party. Foremost among them in Illinois was Lyman Trumbull, judge and former Illinois secretary of state. Whig politicians also rose up to condemn Douglas and his bill. Richard Yates of Springfield in the United States House of Representatives expressed the economic fears of his farmer constituents over the extension of slavery northward and westward. What would happen to farmers' demands for a homestead law if the slave power dominated the government and ruled the Western prairies, opening them up to the expansion of slavery? Not so different were the sentiments of the German Marxists in New York, who saw "capitalism and land speculation . . . favored at the expense of the mass of the people." [23]

The *Free West* lost no time in pressing abolitionist advantages during the political thaw. The June 8 editorial instructed the old guard of the Free Democrats to close ranks and prepare for the new order of things in anticipation of the general movement of the people against slavery. Free Democrats were asked to keep the flag flying "that bewildered people may see that there is a point to rally to. Let them hold their meetings—bring out their speakers, pass their resolutions, combine themselves into bands of voters. . . ."

At Ripon, Wisconsin, Whigs, Free Soilers, and Democrats united under the leadership of Alvin E. Bovay and voted to discard their old affiliations and assume a new political name and a new organization, a people's or Republican party. They pledged themselves to the sole aim of halting the extension of slavery.[24]

On May 9 thirty members of the House of Representatives met in Washington and after soberly sounding out their views, concurred with Dr. Gamaliel Bailey, editor of the respected antislavery *National Era*, that a new party was needed. What a moment of gratification it must have been for Lovejoy and the Liberty old guard!

At Jackson, Michigan, on July 16, Free Democrats united with former Whigs and Democrats to organize a state Republican party. Wisconsin and Michigan were followed rapidly by Maine, Vermont, Massachusetts, Indiana, and New York. Everywhere the old guard of radical abolitionists stood firm on basic principles and yet were flexible enough to practice fusion. The watchwords became "fusion" and "new party." Such was the tidal wave thrust up by the senator from Illinois.[25]

Yet Douglas's opponents in his home state were slower in meeting the demands of the hour. When Republican parties were already a reality in half a dozen states, the Illinois political abolitionists deferred releasing their call for a state convention. This would have been the normal next step to organize a fusion party. Nevertheless on August 24 the *Free West* could report that the people in various parts of the state were holding preliminary county meetings. At Ottawa, for example, earlier in the month at the height of the harvest season, between five hundred and one thousand wheat and corn farmers and others assembled for such a convention. Even two downstate papers, the Whig Morgan *Journal* and the conservative Alton *Telegraph*, had expressed themselves in favor of the rising Republican party. The radicals were pleased and encouraged by this development. Eastman noted editorially that "we are a little surprised at the earnestness of tone of these papers on the subject. They spurn party trammels and ask for immediate action." [26]

A step toward unity was taken on August 1. The Du Page County Free Democratic convention at Wheaton offered to drop its name and be known "by the name of Republican, as suggested by the friends of fusion in Wisconsin, Vermont and other States." On the same day at Ottawa the First Congressional District Free Democrats, Whigs, and regular Democrats, without using the word Republican, united in an anti-Nebraska convention and adopted the principles of the Wisconsin Republican convention. They also called for a county anti-Nebraska convention on August 30. At that convention at Rockford on August 30, on an independent Republican basis, the Republican name was adopted and Free Democrats were joined by Whigs in approving the following platform: (1) Bring the government back to first principles; (2) restore Kansas and Nebraska as free territories; (3) repeal the Fugitive Slave Law; (4) restrict slavery to the states where it exists; (5) prohibit the admission of additional slave states; (6) exclude slavery from the territories under the exclusive jurisdiction of the government of the United States; and (7) restrict the acquisition of any new territories unless slavery is specifically prohibited therein forever.[27]

That was a busy day for the emerging Republican party in Illinois, for at Ottawa the county convention was in session, and yet another at Union Grove in Putnam County. At the latter place Owen Lovejoy was called up for a speech and responded with a few characteristic remarks. Here too the Rockford resolutions were adopted. A summer of intensive activity by the Liberty party vanguard led by Lovejoy, Eastman, and Codding, who was the most active organizer of the new party, prepared the ground for a move from the county level to the formation of a state party. A promising event in this connection came two weeks later when a German anti-Nebraska convention met at Bloomington. The *Free West* observed: "Illinois, the most servile of the free states, is fast moving toward a state organization of this kind." [28] In the belief that they had judged the pace of the movement correctly, the new party managers published their historic call:

STATE MASS CONVENTION

A convention of all the citizens of the State of Illinois who are opposed to the repeal of the Missouri Compromise and to further extension and consolidation of the slave power, and in favor of the overthrow of the existing State and National Administration, which are pledged to the support of slavery, will be held on the 5th day of October A.D. 1854 at 2 o'clock, at Springfield, for the organization of a party which shall put the Government upon a Republican track, and to secure to non-slaveholders throughout the Union their just and constitutional weight and influence in the councils of the nation. Papers throughout the State, please copy.[29]

The time and place chosen by the Illinois radicals showed the breadth of their hopes for the organization. The state agricultural fair would be in progress at Springfield in the first week of October, with thousands of farmers, merchants, and their families streaming into town for the occasion. Stephen A. Douglas was expected to speak to the assembled people. Abraham Lincoln had announced that he too would speak out, in rebuttal of his Democratic foe. Thus the state capital would be a busy, packed, and exciting town for three days. What better opportunity of time and place to array a new party before the people.

108

6

Anti-Nebraska Breakthrough: 1854

"He will 'make the fur fly.' "

—Chicago Tribune

Thousands of Illinois people eagerly crowded into Springfield on October 3, 4, and 5, 1854, to look upon a rich array of prize hogs and cows, wheat and corn, flowers, pumpkins, and vegetables. They also came to listen to the well-advertised oratory of Senator Douglas, Abraham Lincoln, and the state's antislavery leaders. The Nebraska Act, the most explosive issue of the day, had aroused the Whig politician from Springfield and he had announced that he would speak at the second annual state fair of the Illinois State Agricultural Society. The promised debate between Douglas and Lincoln doubtless drew most of the crowds to the fair.[1]

On the afternoon of October 3, Senator Douglas presented his doctrinal defense of the repeal of the Missouri Compromise—stating that just as the states had rights to govern their own "domestic institutions," the territories should enjoy the same rights. In effect, Douglas was defending the rights of slaveowners to move their "domestic institutions" into the territories of the United States. Here in central Illinois, with large numbers of Southern-born people, Douglas might expect to meet with a trifle more warmth than he had been accorded recently in Chicago or across the expanses of the northern counties. Loud cheers greeted the senator, according to the next day's issue of the Democratic *Illinois State Register*. Although he was defensive of the Nebraska Act, Douglas scored a point when he attacked the bigotry of the anti-foreigner and anti-Catholic Know-Nothings in the Whig party ranks. This was a clear effort to expose the Whigs and damage the already dying party, and it was an effort to solidify his own position in the dividing Democratic party. Douglas's remarks could at least slow the loss of his German-born followers. But he could not stop influential leaders of his party from openly opposing him. Outstanding among them was Connecticut-born Judge Lyman Trumbull, who had come up to the fair from the southern Eighth Congressional District and had dissected Douglas's arguments on the evening of October 3.[2]

The next day Abraham Lincoln strode up to the platform at the Statehouse to rebut his old political foe. Most people had shed their coats in the balmy October afternoon. As he launched into his speech Lincoln also removed his coat and rolled up his shirtsleeves. He had had a brief term in Congress during the war against Mexico, which he opposed in principle, and had returned to a fairly comfortable Illinois country law practice. That he had voted in the House forty times for Wilmot's "Jeffersonian proviso" might be a clue to Lovejoy's faith in him when other abolitionists looked with suspicion on a man who had favored Henry Clay's Compromise of 1850. In the following years he had been cautiously silent in public on the slavery question. His private, far-ranging discussions with his partner William Herndon, his own independent thinking, but above all the mass outburst against the Kansas-Nebraska Act broke Lincoln's silence.[3]

Now at the Statehouse he came forward to confute Douglas and his doctrines. He had spent hours on end that summer studying the question, consulting the law books, reviewing the Constitution, gathering the facts, and depositing notes in the stovepipe hat he used as a file. He had then assembled a speech that was devastating to Douglas's "popular sovereignty." Lincoln sketched the history of the Missouri Compromise and its repeal, then struck out boldly against the wrong of slavery: "I think . . . that it is wrong; wrong in its direct effect, letting slavery into Kansas and Nebraska. . . .

"This *declared* indifference, but, as I must think, covert *real zeal* for the spread of slavery, I can not but hate. I hate it because of the monstrous injustice of slavery itself. I hate it because it deprives our republican example of its just influence in the world. . . .

". . . What I do say is, that no man is good enough to govern another man, *without that other's consent*. I say this is the leading principle—the sheet anchor of American republicanism." [4]

The speech was qualitatively different and on a higher political and emotional plane than any he had made before, notwithstanding the quality of his funeral oration on Henry Clay in 1852. Unlike the rhetoric of most country politicians, this speech was filled with careful logic, eloquence, and honest emotion. It was a speech that sprang from an incisive perception of the danger inherent in the situation.

Lincoln's refutation was not an abolitionist's, and it brought the assemblage to its feet cheering. The women waved their handkerchiefs in approval. Paul Selby, editor of the Morgan *Journal* of Jacksonville, Illinois, thought this speech was "one of the noblest efforts of Mr. Lincoln's life, and advocated the truest and boldest anti-slavery doctrine." Herndon was rapturous. Horace White, a twenty-year-old reporter for the Chicago *Tribune* at the fair, wrote fifty-four years later that Lincoln's speech made such a profound impression on him that he felt under its spell to that day. Only the *Illinois State Register* sneered and turned a cold shoulder.[5]

While the applause and cheering echoed through the State-house, Lovejoy and Codding made their way down to the front of the hall and announced a meeting of the Republicans to take place that evening in the Statehouse itself. The Republicans had hoped to hold a mass meeting there on the afternoon of the fourth, but Lincoln had been granted the use of the hall and had spoken at that time. They therefore hastily changed their plans and recessed to hear Lincoln. Lovejoy had tried during the day to persuade Lincoln to meet with the Republicans in the evening. They were willing to unite with him, on Lovejoy's urging, but the Springfield attorney had not then clarified his position. When he learned that the Republicans wished him to speak to their convention, he declined. This rejection he signified by hitching up his buggy and riding off to Tazewell County to attend court there.[6]

The Republicans who finally assembled in convention were twenty-six former Free Democrats and Free Soilers. Among them was an old-time antislavery stalwart, the Reverend Thaddeus B. Hurlbut, who had stood at the side of Elijah Lovejoy in 1837 and who had been an organizer of the state antislavery society. He was named a member of the Republicans' committee on resolutions. After a temporary organization was effected, adjournment was approved until the next day. But that night the committee on resolutions huddled around a table in the dingy office of Erastus Wright. Under the light of a couple of tallow candles the committee drew up a set of resolutions that would later prove a source of embarrassment to Stephen A. Douglas.[7]

Rebuffed by the state's foremost Whig—and their goal of broad unity far from realization—the Republicans nevertheless proceeded to business. On a motion by Lovejoy, seconded by

112

Codding, the convention nominated the first candidate of the party for public office. He was John E. McClun of McLean County, nominated for state treasurer; and this was the only nomination. Later McClun declined, and James Miller was named to run. The next piece of business was the appointment of a state central committee. Among those named were the Reverend Ichabod Codding, secretary of the committee; Zebina Eastman; David J. Baker of Madison County; Major N. D. Coy of Knox County; N. C. Geer of Lake County; Abraham Lincoln of Sangamon County; A. G. Throop of Cook County; and J. B. Fairbanks of Morgan County. When Lincoln's name was proposed, questions were raised regarding the harmony of his views with those of the convention. Only Owen Lovejoy rose to endorse Lincoln's position on the slavery question and urge his appointment. However, the meeting failed to establish a firm Republican organization like those in Wisconsin, Michigan, and other states.[8]

Two or three weeks after the unsuccessful meeting of the Republicans, Codding notified Lincoln of his appointment to the central committee. Lincoln declined the nomination and expressed his consternation over the action of the radicals. Yet he attempted to maintain a friendly but not enthusiastic attitude toward them. Indeed it was one participant's opinion that Lincoln had run away, and had replied so stiffly to Codding's notice of nomination only because he did not know the true contents of the resolutions adopted at the convention. Paul Selby believed that Lincoln could easily have agreed with these resolutions. Since all Lincoln saw was a "fraudulent platform" printed in a Springfield paper, Selby wrote, "it follows very naturally that he did 'misunderstand' the real position of the convention." Nor did Douglas let Lincoln off easily from the charge of guilt by association with the radicals. He confronted Lincoln with the resolutions four years later at their famous debate in Ottawa.[9]

What was the nature of the resolutions? Paul Selby insisted that they represented a conservative platform aimed solely at halting the expansion of slavery into the territories. The *State Register* had tried to make it appear that the new party adopted resolutions of a more radical nature at a meeting held in another place earlier that year. The heart of the platform drawn up in Wright's little office is embodied in this resolution:

"That slavery can exist in a Territory only by usurpation and in violation of law, and we believe that Congress has the right and should prohibit its extension into such Territory, so long as it remains under the guardianship of the general government." This was less than the usual radical demands for defiance of and repeal of the Fugitive Slave Law. It was intended to win over broader groups than radical abolitionists.[10]

These were the times when, as Horace White observed, "the men in the northern counties . . . were obliged to consider the situation of their friends in the central and southern counties, and were thus restrained from taking immediate steps to form a new party." "Abolitionist" was still an epithet in Illinois, and prevented men like Lincoln from uniting with them. Even though he abhorred slavery in principle and the Kansas–Nebraska Act in deed, he could not bring himself to enter the ranks of the Republicans at this time. Yet one of their number later asserted that a large proportion of them were as conservative "as was Mr. Lincoln himself" on the slavery-extension question. Nevertheless, Lincoln must have been extremely sensitive to the epithet, for his retreat to Tazewell tacitly acknowledged it. How could he ignore the current propaganda stigmatizing Lovejoy and Codding, even if they had been recognized as "two Congregational clergymen, whose lips had been touched by a live coal from off the altar of eternal justice." [11]

During that summer and fall Lincoln had been campaigning for the election of Richard Yates to Congress from the Seventh

District. Lincoln himself was a candidate for the lower house of the state legislature, but hoped to be elected by that body as United States Senator. When the reaction to his Springfield speech was fully assessed, his Whig colleagues urged him to go in hot pursuit of the Little Giant. Consequently when, on October 16, Peoria welcomed Douglas for a speech, Lincoln also appeared to present his rebuttal. This was in large measure the same one delivered at the state capital. This time Douglas made a pretense of surrender. He proposed and won Lincoln's agreement to a mutual retirement from further debate during the fall campaign. Lincoln did go home, but Douglas's "withdrawal" lasted two days, at the end of which he turned up in Princeton, where local Democrats escorted him with fanfare to a face-to-face encounter with the local lion of abolition, Owen Lovejoy. He was the Bureau County anti-Nebraska candidate for the state House of Representatives and also party campaign manager. Douglas was the first to speak, for a half-hour. Lovejoy replied, for another half-hour. The senator then held forth for the rest of the afternoon until dark, giving Lovejoy no chance to reply. But Lovejoy had struck blows for the antislavery position. Douglas ran off to other speaking engagements and protested that he had broken the "Peoria truce" with Lincoln only because he was persistently "bantered and badgered" by Lovejoy. The Democratic senator thus revealed that his opponents, though divided, may have had sufficient grounds for uniting.[12]

Their failure to join forces with Lincoln and other anti-Nebraska Whigs and Democrats did not, however, deter the Illinois antislavery Republicans from conducting an exemplary congressional and state campaign. Anti-Nebraska men became prominent in the Whig and Democratic parties, and Owen Lovejoy led former Liberty party men and Free Soilers in contests for state legislative posts. So compelling was the need for unity that the *Free West* came out vigorously for congressional candidates Richard Yates, W. B. Archer, and Archibald Williams, all Whigs, and Lyman Trumbull, Democrat, on the sole issue of opposition to the Kansas–Nebraska Act. The Whigs' Chicago *Journal*, on the other hand, supported Republican nominees Elihu B. Washburne of Galena and Jesse O. Norton of Joliet in the Third District, as well as Democrat Trumbull and its own James Knox, anti-Nebraska Whig.[13]

The rewards of broad unity could be discerned in the 1854 contests. Liberty men, if not too deeply immersed in old-line purism, must have rejoiced at the election results in November. They were victorious, although only a fraction of their program, nonextension, served to unite the voters and the leaders. A majority of the state's congressional seats went to anti-Nebraska men: in the First District, Washburne; in the Second, James H. Woodworth; in the Third, Norton. In the Fourth, the Whig Knox was victorious, and in the Eighth, Trumbull won. Four of the nine districts were won by Douglas Democratic party-liners. In the Seventh District Yates, the anti-Nebraska man, was defeated by only one vote.[14]

In the state Senate, anti-Nebraska men were in the majority; in the state House of Representatives, anti-Nebraska men made a telling sweep, claiming a majority of fifteen in that house. Among the Whig candidates for the state legislature Abraham Lincoln was elected as a Whig from Sangamon County. Owen Lovejoy was at last elected to his first public office. He found the election results gratifying, "inasmuch as I have been cursed & abused & vilified for a long series of years." He told Giddings that "a great deal of wrath" had been brought down on him. Some had said Lovejoy had lost his influence. Now it was pleasing to win "an endorsement from my fellow citizens that these things that have been said are lies." Giddings had come into the state from Ohio to speak in the campaign, and so had Cassius Clay from Kentucky. At least one vote, Lovejoy acknowledged,

116

had been won for him by Giddings's appearance during the campaign. Others in the election had also benefited by the Ohio congressman's visit. The state had gone anti-Nebraska, Lovejoy wrote, and Giddings had "contributed to this result." [15]

The exultant editors of the *Free West* drew two conclusions from the election returns: Unity was the guarantee of victory, and disunity led only to defeat. For example, it was demonstrated that where Whig, presumably anti-Nebraska, men ran alone, they were beaten by the better-organized Democratic machine. Such were the results in the Fifth, Sixth, and Seventh Congressional Districts. On the other hand, in the central Third District, its southern sector of counties overwhelmingly anti-abolitionist and pro-Douglas, anti-Nebraska men joined hands across party lines and elected Jesse O. Norton as a Republican. Moreover, Codding had played an important part in the campaign for Norton, and a fearless frontal attack had been made against Douglas's legislation. But where the candidates such as Williams in the Fifth and Yates in the Seventh Districts exhibited "a foolish timidity over the 'odium of abolitionism,'" defeat was a sure consequence. In any event, the one big conclusion enthusiastically drawn by the *Free West* was, "the Whig party is dead." It was not the first remark of the kind, for in August Whig Attorney General Usher F. Linder had expressed his bereavement by saying, "The Whig party is dead, and I am left a widower." [16]

Those elected as Republicans in 1854 in Illinois were actually the candidates of fused sections of parties and it would be more accurate to call them fusion, or anti-Nebraska, candidates. As such they won by majorities greater than those of the Free Soilers and antislavery Whigs in 1852.[17] Surely now was the time to finish the work and organize a firm state Republican party. The demand for it grew among antislavery men hopefully eyeing the presidential elections of 1856. It was only a year and ten months off, and Lovejoy, Codding, and Eastman were sure, now that they had had success at the polls, that their sole task lay in creating the new fusion party. For old Liberty men, for Lincoln, for Trumbull, and for their cohorts, 1855 would be a year of probing, of shuttling back and forth, of realignments.

Lovejoy conferred with Eastman at Chicago in January, 1855, before the opening of the Illinois legislature. What the two anti-slavery leaders discussed is not recorded, but not long after Lovejoy took his seat it became obvious that he would stir a fresh breeze in the lower house.[18]

At the same time, Lincoln had declined his credentials to the Statehouse in order to free himself to contend for Democratic James Shields's United States Senate seat. Lincoln's retirement from office-seeking was at an end. The furor over the Nebraska Act had made it clear that there was an issue on which an opposition party could win. Lincoln hoped the Whig party could be revived to fill the role, but the Lovejoy forces believed a fusion of the anti-Nebraska elements in all parties was the answer. The contest in the state legislature in February, 1855, afforded Lincoln the opportunity to win an important office and give the Whigs new life. If successful, he could avoid fusion with the Lovejoy radicals and, in challenging the powerful Douglas machine, elevate his struggle to national notice. The prospects seemed good, because Shields had little if any chance of election by the anti-Nebraska legislature. Only highly respected Judge Lyman Trumbull or Lincoln could win in this situation, although there were other hopefuls and dark horses.

The *Free West* early made clear its preferences. An editorial of November 30, 1854, proclaimed that the next senator "should be a radical." It suggested that the brilliant James H. Collins, if alive, would have been the ideal standardbearer, for he had been an unwavering antislavery man. But among the living . . . the state of Illinois could do itself credit in "the election of Owen Lovejoy"—or Codding; even a Whig like Yates and an anti-Nebraska Democrat like General William Bissell might be favorably considered by the abolitionists. But as for Lincoln—"We could not advise the republicans to support for this station Lincoln, or any of the moderate men of this stamp. He is only a Whig and the people's movement is no Whig triumph." Thus were the editors riding high on the victory at the polls earlier in the month.

Two weeks later the *Free West* elaborated bitterly on its anti-Lincoln position: "Mr. Lincoln is a Know-Nothing, and expects the full vote of the Republicans as well as the influence of the Know-Nothings . . . he has got sense enough to make a good Senator because he is not a Know-Nothing by nature . . . and he is reported to be a Good Fellow at heart. . . . Our opposition to [Lincoln] is based upon shortcomings on the Republican basis. . . . He is reported to be a Compromise Whig—attached to that mummy of a Whig party. . . .

"He dares not oppose the Fugitive Slave Law—and he would not pledge himself to go against the admission of any more Slave States. If these cannot be gotten from him, of what service would he be in the Senate when the slavery question comes up?" [19]

If this had been the unanimous outlook of the Republicans, fusion would indeed have been a mirage. But fortunately for all sides there was a moderating group centered around the recently converted Chicago *Tribune* that looked favorably on Lincoln. Prominent among the leaders was Dr. Charles H. Ray, who had owned and edited the Galena *Jeffersonian* and was a friend of Elihu B. Washburne's. Ray had hoped Lovejoy would succeed in bringing Lincoln into the new party at Springfield in October, 1854.[20]

Owen Lovejoy's support of Lincoln in this period waxed and waned rapidly, and grew again. He had defended Lincoln against the sectarianism of some of his comrades at the premature Republican convention. But in the contest for senator in the state legislature on February 8, 1855, the *Free West* reported, Lovejoy had voted—from first to last ballot—for Lyman Trumbull. Yet the *House Journal of the Nineteenth General Assembly of Illinois* showed Lovejoy voting for Lincoln on the first three ballots. James Shields intimated to Charles H. Lanphier, editor of the *Illinois State Register,* that the radicals had proposed a deal with Lincoln. He urged the editor to get "proof of the pledges required by 'Lovejoy & Co.' as the price of their votes for Senator . . . those Republican radicals would be 'politically doomed.' " Lincoln had pursued the post with all the political aids at his command. He also enlisted local lieutenants like Leonard Swett and Judge T. Lyle Dickey to line up votes. At one point, during December, 1854, Swett reported to Lincoln, "Dickey says he has hopes of Lovejoy!!" The double exclamation is significant. However there seems to be no evidence that Lincoln made a deal with Lovejoy and the radicals, despite Shields's dark hints. In the end, after a complex and exhausting battle that threatened to end in deadlock, Lincoln released his votes to Trumbull, thereby guaranteeing that Democrat's election—at least he was an *anti-Nebraska* Democrat.[21]

Lovejoy's record in that session of the legislature was marked with distinction, especially in carrying forward antislavery objectives. Certainly his prestige among his constituents was vastly enhanced by his participation in the state government. Among those who knew him only as a thundering radical, dangerous, intemperate—as Stephen A. Douglas delighted in having him pictured—Lovejoy began to make compelling good sense. His principled and adroit remarks on the floor of the Statehouse won him new friends and prepared the way for him in national government. Above all, he rallied around him some of the masses who would guarantee fusion of antislavery forces in his state.

Appointed to the House standing committees on Education and Licenses, as well as to the chairmanship of the House Committee for the State Library, Lovejoy lost little time in plunging into the parliamentary battle.[22] A new sound was heard in the House—the new spirit breathed into the language and precepts of Jefferson and Paine. Though Lovejoy seemed to meet conservatives halfway, as he had in 1848 in measured replies to queries, first things came first.

Thus, hardly had the session commenced than Lovejoy introduced a bill to repeal all laws disqualifying colored persons from testifying in courts of justice. If repealed, a small measure of civil rights would be restored to free Negroes, for they could then at least go into courts to protect and defend their lives, their rights and property. But so deeply had the virus of anti-Negro prejudice infected Illinois that Lovejoy and the radicals were forced to accept a tabling of his bill on January 11.[23]

Lovejoy's most moving and significant action was to introduce on February 6, 1855, three resolutions that would instruct the senators and representatives from Illinois in Congress to carry out antislavery Republican policies. The first would prohibit slavery in all the territories of the United States then under its jurisdiction and those to be acquired in the future. A second resolution would instruct Illinois lawmakers in Washington to vote against the admission of any more slave states; and a third resolution instructed the federal legislators to introduce bills repealing the infamous Fugitive Slave Law. Bold and courageous as an Underground Railroad operator and in defense of his principles, Lovejoy now was constrained by the temper of the times to go no further—at this moment no one with political sense would demand abolition of slavery in the states. Anti-extension was the limit of feasible political abolition.

The Chicago *Tribune*'s man in Springfield was evidently captured by Lovejoy that day, and some of his observations are

121

worth repeating. First of all, in an advance notice that Lovejoy would speak on February 6, the correspondent wrote: "This is the first opportunity that Mr. Lovejoy has had to give his views upon all the questions growing out of the Slavery Question, and there is a general feeling he will 'make the fur fly.' " [24]

The gallery and lobby filled up long before the meeting opened. When Lovejoy commenced, all the seats were occupied, and all standing room taken by intent listeners. Lovejoy read his resolutions, took one at a time and spoke on each. The *Tribune* writer was transported: "I have never heard the subject so ably handled and the facts brought up with such irresistible force . . . but the great feature of the speech was on the Fugitive Slave Law."

In the course of his speech Lovejoy was interrupted several times by messengers and messages from the Senate. After one such stoppage he quipped, "I administered a purgative dose to the State Library the other day, and it would seem that the Senate must have found access to some ipecac in quantities larger than homeopathic." [25]

In his opening he assaulted the repeal of the Missouri Compromise: Why did not the Democrats repeal the whole compromise, why had only half been recanted? In 1821, Lovejoy demonstrated, the slave states had been willing to prohibit slavery in the Louisiana Territory, then practically all the territory possessed by the United States, providing Missouri were admitted as a slave state. Therefore, now, Lovejoy argued, repeal the whole compromise, let Missouri become a free state—the Democrats having repealed the abolition of slavery in the territory.

Stephen A. Douglas, chief spokesman for the Kansas–Nebraska Act, was the subject of special attack in this speech. Lovejoy asserted that Douglas had been in support of the Missouri Compromise in 1848, 1850, 1852, and even up to 1854. Suddenly in January, 1854, the fiery little senator opposed it. Lovejoy attributed the change to Douglas's fear that abolitionist and Whig support of the Wilmot proviso would unite the two groups. This unity was what Lovejoy hoped he could achieve. If it could be consummated, such a political fusion would threaten the power of the Douglas Democrats.

Squatter sovereignty, Douglas's defensive doctrine, was torn apart by Lovejoy. His indignation over the moral wrong of slavery could not but grip men and women who listened. "I do not admit that these 'sovereigns' or any other sovereigns, have any right to convert man into a chattel, into goods, into four-footed beasts. . . .

"No power on earth has the right to make a man a slave," Lovejoy asserted. "If that is the case, someone may ask, why don't you go for abolishing slavery in the States? I do not go for it simply because I have not the power, if I had the power, you could rely upon my doing it. Had I the power I would abolish serfdom in Russia. If I had the power I would dot the European Continent all over with Republics. I have no more power to enter the State of South Carolina and abolish slavery there by an act of Congress, than I have to go into Brazil and abolish it there. But we have the power to do it in the Territories, as they are under the exclusive jurisdiction of the people of the United States."

On this basis in particular, Lovejoy called on all, regardless of party, to pass his resolution and make it United States policy. That was the plank of the Republican party, he proclaimed, the party that "had stepped forth like Minerva from the head of Jupiter, full grown, and fully equipped for the battle, and has already indeed gained no inconsiderable victories. And here is one old, fanatical abolitionist voting with the majority in the Illinois Legislature."

At this point someone in the gallery shouted out, "Your allies deny that you are an abolitionist."

Lovejoy replied forcefully: "If anybody denies that I am an abolitionist, he denies erroneously. I have no doubt, what is the truth.

"I am an abolitionist,
  I glory in the name."

The House rocked with applause. Lovejoy then spelled out for his audience what an abolitionist was, in his opinion. "My abolitionism is just what I state here. I do not acknowledge it to be all you may fancy it." For example, his abolitionism included asking as an act of justice for the Negro that he might have the means to an education.

Then he attacked the Fugitive Slave Law. For it he summoned up his heaviest blows. In his argument he cited the Constitution, Madison, and Jefferson—these Founding Fathers recognized no property in man. Madison deliberately used the terms "person and labor" rather than "servant or servitude." The Constitution, Lovejoy asserted, speaks only of "persons held to service or labor, under the law of the States."

Lovejoy held up to ridicule the execution of the Fugitive Slave Law. In Kentucky, he observed, the slave is made an article of property like an ox or a horse. The master sends his dogs after him, leads him back as he would a stray horse or ox. The master does not obtain a magistrate's warrant.

"It would be a fine operation," Lovejoy said, "for a Constable to take out a warrant from a Justice of the Peace, and seizing the brindle ox by the horn or the old grey mare by the mane, read his warrant, and arrest them in the name of the Christian people of the Palmetto State!"

How did the Fugitive Slave Law affect the masses of white Americans? Lovejoy declared it "degrading to us as American citizens."

124

"I avow myself a disciple of the Higher Law."

Now, with his soul afire, Lovejoy proclaimed: "If you ask me to seize that trembling fugitive woman, I tell you plainly, in the face of fines, in the face of imprisonment, and with God's grace, that stood by my brother—in the face of death itself—I tell you I will not do it!"

"My Nebraska friends, if you fancy this transformation [of Americans into informers and slave-catchers] you may make the experiment, but I apprise you if they [slaves] get on the underground railroad they are safe in spite of you."

Men and women in the gallery were electrified, even moved to tears. Members of the House were as deeply shaken by the speech. The Chicago *Tribune* correspondent was so transfixed that he could not "pretend to give you even an outline of the speech. . . . When it was closed Mr. Lovejoy was no longer pointed out as the 'notorious abolitionist,' but as an enlightened Christian and eloquent defender of free institutions." Circulating among the crowds, the correspondent talked to many who had never before heard an antislavery speech. They had believed the worst distortions of the antislavery platform. Now, the reporter wrote, "with scarcely an exception, they say they fully endorse all Lovejoy said."

Reporting the afternoon session, the same correspondent recorded: "This has been a great day for the state and the cause of Humanity. For the first time in the history of Illinois, a regular Abolitionist, in his place in the Hall of the House of Representatives, has made a speech in defense of his principles, and hundreds of persons heard for the first time, the enunciation of such principles from one whose history and character are a guaranty that he would nothing extenuate."

By the time the legislature adjourned, the *Free West* printed a glowing letter from Erastus Wright of Springfield: "Lovejoy, it is said, made the greatest speech ever made in the State House.

. . . His very opponents accord to him candor, honesty, talent, courage, justice, and true American principles. . . .

"It is encouraging," Wright continued, "to see those who belonged to the old rickety parties slacking the cords, untying the knots, examining the ground, and analyzing the dose they are called to swallow. Yes, even here in the borders of Egypt, the sagacious Lincoln, the penetrating [Stephen T.] Logan, the cautious [Benjamin S.] Edwards, and the persevering [Samuel C.] Parks are found occupying elevated ground, which betokens a better day coming." [26]

In a burst of missionary zeal Wright urged that Lovejoy's speech be printed as a pamphlet for, "we must have it circulated. . . . It must go into Egypt." This was approved by the editors, who acknowledged widespread requests for reprints. The problem was money. An estimated $150 would finance an issue of ten thousand to sell at three or five cents each.[27] These were prodigious plans for the men of Liberty, but the *Free West* itself expired in July. The ambitious project was never carried out.

Without a supporting newspaper, and lacking funds, the men who stood behind Lovejoy failed to spread his message. Furthermore, Illinois, still lagging behind other states in the fusion movement, was not ready to accept Lovejoy's antislavery position. This was reflected in the votes on his resolutions. The first passed on February 7, 1855, by a vote of 41 to 32. The second and third were defeated by votes of 33 to 40 and 35 to 47 respectively. Nevertheless, with his motions Lovejoy became big news, even as far east as New York, where Horace Greeley's *Tribune* thought an account of the debate on his proposals in the Illinois legislature fit to print on page one. The closeness of the votes indicated the gaps still to be closed in the ranks of antislavery and anti-Nebraska men. It was evidence too of how persistently old Liberty men would have to fight to enact into law their program of Negro emancipation.[28]

7

The Illinois Republican Party
Is Organized

> *"We are in company with abolitionists."*
> —*Abraham Lincoln*

Lovejoy tried to draw closer to Lincoln in the summer of 1855 during a relatively quiet political season in Illinois. His hopes were still high for a single party of anti-Nebraska forces in the state, and his efforts toward fusion received added impetus from the stormy events in the Kansas territory.

Kansas became the frontier of war between slavery and anti-slavery groups. Clashes broke out between bands of Missouri and Southern squatters, on the one hand, determined to bring in their slaves and, on the other, Free Soil emigrants from the Midwest and Northeast hoping to establish farms in the territory. Missouri raiders invaded the territory to make illegal land claims and to win elections with illegal votes. Acts of violence were committed against Free Soil settlers throughout the year. Proslavery mobs attacked newspapers and churches, drove settlers out of their homes, tarred and feathered some, and rode them on rails. Even territorial Governor Andrew H. Reeder, an early advocate of the Kansas–Nebraska Act, was threatened with hanging because he ordered new elections in six districts where Free Soil protests against fraud had been filed. Secret societies of proslavery men terrorized settlers from New England and the Midwest and took the law into their own hands.

Violence, lawlessness, and sectional strife had been forecast when Douglas fought for his bill. Little more than a year later, Lincoln expressed not only his own despair over the divisive law but the dismay of millions of Americans when he wrote to his friend Joshua F. Speed: "I look upon that enactment not as *law*, but as *violence* from the beginning." [1]

The unfavorable reaction to Douglas and his bill continued to be demonstrated during the year after its passage. Anti-Nebraska majorities were elected in fifteen states, one of them Illinois. There Trumbull's victory over Shields proved a high price for Douglas to pay. Furthermore, 117 representatives and 15 senators pledged to nonextension were elected to Congress. Finally, the Republican party was established in a number of Northern states and was riding high on a wave of success.

Reading these signs of the times as favorable for the fusion movement in Illinois, Lovejoy and his colleagues renewed their efforts to complete what they had begun in October, 1854. During the summer of 1855 Codding, Lovejoy, and Eastman, with the help of Giddings of Ohio, tried to revive the prematurely organized Republican party. Judging by the bitter reaction of the Democratic press, they probably enjoyed popular approval. For example, in September, 1855, the Joliet *Signal* protested violently against Joshua Giddings's "perambulating the northern sections of the state with the Reverend Ichabod Codding, organizing the Republican party . . . a nigger-stealing, stinking, putrid abolition party." On the other hand, this party proved not abolitionist enough in any state for Frederick Douglass. He wrote that it would be "retrograding, instead of advancing," to join the

Republican party, although he conceded it was "anti-slavery as far as it goes." In the main, however, the new party seemed to be a little more acceptable in Illinois than previous third-party attempts.[2]

Waiting for the acceptance must have seemed endless to some old Liberty party men. There would have to be more conferences, conventions, more letters and visits and consultations with the rank-and-file faithful, with the middle-roaders, and even with some of the johnny-come-latelys.

For their part, the last would be measuring the force of the new political winds, taking sights on the shifting landmarks. Lincoln's journalistic friends, if not Lincoln himself, had written with self-assurance on July 27, 1854, in the *Illinois State Journal:* "There will be, in our opinion, no large third party. There have always been but two large permanent parties in the country; and when the Nebraska matter is disposed of, the members of the Free-Soil party will fall into the ranks of one of the two parties."

Despite rebuffs of this kind and the insults of the Joliet newspaper, the abolitionists did have impact considerably beyond their own ranks. Their incessant work forced members of the old parties to take antislavery and anti-extensionist positions. As a result, conservatives were never able to enclose or foreclose the influence of the abolitionists. The national Democratic and Whig parties had shunned the slavery question for more than twenty years, but in 1854 and 1855 a verdict was forced by mass disaffection. The voters, aroused at last by the slaveowners' voracity for territory, wealth, and power, discarded what had long been taken for granted: a perpetual two-party system.

Horace White, reminiscing on these times, recalled: "At the beginning Lovejoy and Codding were the only ones who were entirely footloose and had a clear view of the course before them. The others [Lincoln, Trumbull, etc.] were constrained by the fogginess of their environment to feel their way and to move with caution." [3] Yet men like Trumbull, Judd, Cook, Palmer, and "Long John" Wentworth of the Democrats; and Lincoln, Yates, and even Orville H. Browning of the Whigs would have to move with the masses if they wished to move at all.

Eastman, Codding, and Lovejoy appreciated how well Lincoln stood with the masses, hence their concentration on him as the focal point of united political action. Years of existence against odds had sharpened the abolitionists' wits and had required besides dogged tenacity, a nourishing ideology, faith, conviction, above all, flexibility—to know how to wield the balance of power, as they had learned to do in the late 1840's, and to advance their principles at the same time. Lovejoy and Codding had learned how to meet the middle-roaders, travel with them, yet remain firm on principles. Such flexibility they had to practice daily now, and the test came in the approach to and winning over of Lincoln.

Lovejoy, who apparently had undisturbed confidence in Lincoln, must have hammered this point across to his comrades: Go for Lincoln, bring him in, he is the political lodestone we need. Having won over enough of his abolitionist friends to his conviction, Lovejoy must have gained their agreement to press their cause with Lincoln. He wrote to Lincoln on August 7, 1855, asking him to come into the ranks of the Republican, or fusion, movement. Unlike his stand-off letter to Codding of the previous November, Lincoln's reply to Lovejoy conceded much in attitude, tone, and thought. Acknowledging the powerful antislavery belief long latent in him, Lincoln told Lovejoy: "Not even *you* are more anxious to prevent the extension of slavery than I." Yet he admitted, "just now . . . I fear to do any thing, lest I do wrong." [4] One drawback was Lincoln's friendship with local Know-Nothings, or American party men.

The nativist and anti-Catholic movement had, through the American party, won startling victories in Massachusetts, Pennsylvania, New York, and elsewhere during the 1854 elections. This was partly due to the party's Free Soil and anti-Nebraska position. But the narrowly anti-Catholic and anti-foreign elements in the movement pressed their advantage and destroyed it in riots and murders of foreign-born citizens. As a result, the Know-Nothings rapidly lost support. However, in Illinois they stubbornly clung to their organization and managed to influence state politics. In 1855 the party continued to be influential around Springfield and in southern Illinois.

Surrounded as he was in Springfield by old courthouse cronies, Lincoln's outlook on fusion was dimmed by their opportunistic flirtations with Know-Nothingism. On this basis Lincoln justified his inability to move openly toward organizational unity with the Lovejoy Republicans. He feared to antagonize many in the capital city who were "mostly my old political and personal friends," men with whom he was at ease, who jawed with him in Speed's store, or who might share a room at a village inn as they rode the law circuit. Recognizing how weak was the excuse of personal ties, he told Lovejoy that he hoped the Know-Nothing organization would die of itself without his having to come out openly against it. "Of their principles," Lincoln wrote, "I think little better than I do of those of the slavery extensionists. Indeed I do not perceive how any one professing to be sensitive to the wrongs of the negroes, can join in a league to degrade a class of white men." Lincoln assured Lovejoy, however, that he was not against fusion if achieved "on ground which I think is right." He even believed it could be done at that moment, "if it were not for this K. N. ism." Moreover, Lincoln believed that without winning over elements of the organization, anti-Nebraska forces could not "successfully combat the Nebraska democracy." In closing, Lincoln indicated when he might be able to meet with Lovejoy, but there is no record of such a meeting.[5]

131

Eastman apparently was assigned by the Republicans to seek another approach to Lincoln. With Cassius Clay, Eastman visited Springfield some time in the fall of 1855 to determine Lincoln's antislavery beliefs, his position on fusion, his availability for office. The first stop of the two abolitionists was at the home of one of the Underground Railroad operators. This person had at times retained Lincoln's services. He assured Eastman that "Mr. Lincoln was all right on the Negro question; he gave money when necessary, to help the fugitive on the way to freedom." [6]

This was indeed a strong and reassuring recommendation for a man denounced a few months earlier in Eastman's *Free West* for adhering to that "mummy" of a Whig party. Perhaps it was a further confirmation of what Lovejoy privately knew or believed about Lincoln. It was unmistakable evidence for the radicals that Lincoln was at least traveling in the right direction. This minimum requirement would recur as a theme in Lovejoy's speeches as he fought for Republican unity during Civil War days.

After the preliminary visit with the Springfield Underground Railroad agent, Eastman climbed the dark stairway to Lincoln and Herndon's law office. He was making a call on William Herndon, junior partner of the firm, to ascertain whether Mr. Lincoln really was "all right" since "there was a prospect of his being a competitor of Judge Douglas." Herndon and Eastman rambled through a miscellany of subjects practical and intellectual, theoretical and prosaic, for two hours.[7]

Herndon had considered himself an abolitionist long before this interview—ever since his student days at Illinois College when that school was dominated by Edward Beecher and other comrades of Elijah Lovejoy. When Douglas's Nebraska Act exposed the country to the threat of slavery, Herndon pitched in to help the radical abolitionists. He contributed money, circulated pamphlets and papers, and spoke to as many groups as would listen to him. Lovejoy, Eastman, and Codding might count him in their number, even if for Lincoln he was sometimes "too rampant."

Years later the editor recorded what Herndon said about Lincoln: "He has been an attentive reader of your paper for several years; he believes in the Declaration of Independence; and he is a great reader of the abolition papers. He is well posted. That he might get all sides of the question, I take Garrison's *Liberator* and he takes the *National Era* and the *Western Citizen* [probably the *Free West*]. Although he does not say much, you may depend upon it, Mr. Lincoln is all right; when it becomes necessary he will speak so that he will be understood." [8]

Stroking his rich black beard, the editor walked down the wooden stairs from the law office, reviewing what he had just learned. He was satisfied of the lawyer's "all-rightness." But about Lincoln's immediate availability and willingness to fuse, Eastman learned nothing more than what he and Lovejoy already knew from correspondence. They were two matters of which Herndon could not speak and Lincoln would not—for the present. Yet at this time Lincoln did divulge something of his purposes and ideas in letters to his friend Speed and Judge George Robertson of Lexington, Kentucky. Speed had traveled with Lincoln on a steamboat from Louisville to St. Louis in 1841. The sight of shackled slaves on board was a "continual torment" to Lincoln and he reminded Speed of this. Speed admitted the abstract wrong of slavery but insisted on the legal right to own slaves. Perhaps in clarifying his stand on slavery for Speed, Lincoln was at the same time clarifying for himself. On August 24, 1855, he wrote: "It is hardly fair for you to assume, that I have no interest in a thing which has, and continually exercises, the power of making me miserable. You ought rather to appreciate how much the great body of the Northern people do crucify their feelings, in order to maintain their loyalty to the constitution and the Union.

133

"I do oppose the extension of slavery because my judgment and feelings so prompt me; and I am under no obligation to the contrary. If for this you and I must differ, differ we must." This was a reference to the situation arising out of the Nebraska Act. Speed believed in the act, although he strongly condemned the unfair and violent tactics used in the 1854 and 1855 Kansas elections. Lincoln, however, condemned the law itself that sanctioned such violence. He was convinced that as a result Kansas would seek admission to the Union with a proslavery constitution. Lincoln saw little hope for any other course there. At about the same time he told Judge Robertson that he considered "peaceful, voluntary emancipation" of the slaves hopeless. Lincoln also confessed to Speed his indecision on party affiliation: "You inquire where I now stand. That is a disputed point. I think I am a whig; but others say there are no whigs, and that I am an abolitionist . . . I now do no more than oppose the *extension* of slavery." [9]

Like Lincoln, the southern Illinois Democrat Lyman Trumbull stood so well with the masses that he too must be approached on the fusion question. At about the same date that Lovejoy had written Lincoln, he had sent off a proposal of unity to Senator Trumbull. Thus the anti-Nebraska leaders of the two major parties were asked to consider the calling of a "state convention of all those opposed to the repeal of the Missouri Compromise irrespective of party." Trumbull pointed out to Lovejoy that in his part of the state, bordering on Kentucky, the idea of fusion would be anathema to Democrats. He pointed to the obstacles of "side issues such as Know Nothingism and the Temperance question." At this time, a fusion convention of those opposed to the spread of slavery, Trumbull believed, would stand little chance of success.[10]

At least Illinois men of good will were making themselves clear to each other, although no startling, open political develop-

134

ments toward antislavery unity occurred. Understandings were growing. Reflection, assessment, inquiry—these were the actions of a quiet political year in Illinois. Yet civil strife in Kansas in 1855 disturbed the nation, sharpened sectional attitudes, and demonstrated that the extension of slavery must be halted.

Among the scores who believed this were at least a dozen Illinois newspaper editors who called themselves Anti-Nebraska Editors. Their determination to act on the political front was affirmed in the first weeks of 1856. What Lovejoy, Codding, and Eastman had hoped to achieve in October, 1854, now in 1856 eleven editors, some former Whigs, some former Democrats, proceeded to promote decisively: the union of Illinois antislavery and anti-extension men in a *new* party.

It was indeed an eventful week, February 22 to 26, 1856, when the editors gathered in convention at Decatur. During that week the xenophobic American party met in a boisterous convention at Philadelphia. Across the state, at Pittsburgh, political abolitionists and anti-extensionists were conducting the first major national conclave of the various people's movements, parties, loose associations, individuals, in short, a national Republican party organization. This was where Owen Lovejoy became one of the superintendents in the formal creation of the party.[11]

Back in Decatur eleven editors and the lawyer Abraham Lincoln hammered together a platform capable of holding and uniting all antislavery, anti-Nebraska forces. The principal resolution centered on the slavery question. The conferees disclaimed interference with slavery in the states where it then existed. They concurred in a general belief that the slave states were entitled to rights guaranteed by the United States Constitution. On the specific matter of slavery extension they resolved:

1) That we are in favor of the restoration of the Missouri Compromise, or in other words, that we will strive by all legal

means to restore to Kansas and Nebraska a legal guarantee against slavery, of which they were deprived at the cost of the violation of the plighted faith of the nation;

  2) That we hold the settlement of the true relations of the General and State Governments to slavery, and the restriction of slavery to its present authorized limits, as the paramount question for consideration.[12]

This declaration of purpose became the basis for organizing a new party in Illinois. As an immediate guarantee, the editors called for a state convention to meet at Bloomington on May 29 next. To supervise the birth of the anti-Nebraska, or Republican, party a state central executive committee was appointed. Of necessity its members came from among leaders of the old parties. The moderates at Decatur chose moderates to superintend. Although the biographer Beveridge claims that some of the 1854 Republican stalwarts were in the Decatur convention, the composition of the 1856 committee does not bear out the assertion.[13] Lovejoy, Codding, Eastman, and Farnsworth were not in the convention and were not named. Herndon, who was named to the central committee, had strong abolition sympathies but had never been known as a leader of the Liberty or Free Soil parties. Paul Selby was an exception, and even he had been known as the editor of a Whig newspaper. Although the irony of the situation was readily apparent to abolitionists, they were filled with satisfaction that their lead had been followed at Decatur.

While the Decatur convention was under way the militant radicals and other anti-extensionists were gathered at Pittsburgh in search of the larger prize—a new party on a national basis.

The chairmen of the Republican state committees of Ohio, Massachusetts, Pennsylvania, Wisconsin, and Vermont in January, 1856, had issued a call for a mass convention to organize their separate parties into a national one. More than four hundred delegates from sixteen Northern and eight Southern states

136

assembled in the iron city. Although no roster of delegates was preserved, newspaper accounts recorded some of those present. Joshua R. Giddings was sent from Ohio's Western Reserve. Charles Reemelin came from Cincinnati. Michigan sent Zachariah Chandler. Indiana delegated Giddings's son-in-law, George W. Julian, who was to be elected chairman of the committee on national organization.[14]

The Illinois contingent consisted of Owen Lovejoy, Ichabod Codding, John H. Bryant (a Princeton triumvirate); John C. Vaughan of the Chicago *Tribune* (a South Carolina antislavery man); John H. McMillan; William F. M. Arny; A. Danford; and Wait Talcot.[15]

Lovejoy was one of a small number of delegates who met on the evening of February 20 in the Monongahela Hotel to consult on the preliminaries of organizing the convention. The participants failed to arrive at a harmonious decision, and the meeting broke up "with ill feeling." At eight o'clock the next morning another meeting was held, this time as a committee with one man from each state. Lovejoy was the Illinois representative. Lewis Clephane of the District of Columbia; Lieutenant Governor Kinsley S. Bingham of Michigan; and the wealthy New Yorker Edwin D. Morgan were some of the other leaders. Apparently they resolved their differences, for the convention was able to commence the next day.[16]

At eleven o'clock on the morning of Washington's one hundred and twenty-fourth birthday the first session of the convention was called to order in Lafayette Hall. The Honorable Lawrence Brainerd of Vermont read the call and asked John A. King of New York to act as temporary chairman. The Reverend Owen Lovejoy then opened the proceedings by reading a prayer that roused a "suppressed murmur of applause" when he asked God to enlighten the mind of the President of the United States [Pierce], and "turn him from his evil ways, and if this was not possible, to take him away, so that an honest and God-fearing man might fill his place." [17]

Horace Greeley of the New York *Tribune* was warmly applauded after a brief speech. Then the convention tumultuously called for Giddings. The veteran congressman obliged, yielding to the roof-raising cheers of the delegates and observers. He then introduced the next speaker, Owen Lovejoy.

Every man and woman present knew and respected that name. Many had been alive when Elijah had been martyred, many had grown up in the intervening nineteen years to learn of him and how he had died for freedom of the press and liberty for all Americans. They had heard, too, of Owen Lovejoy and his dramatic fight in the abolitionist cause. When Lovejoy stood up to speak he was fired with indignation over the violent outbreaks in Kansas against Free Soil settlers.

In the sea of faces Lovejoy could see the strength of the anti-slavery movement, now combined with its allies and prepared to take the first big stride toward national political power. Characteristically, he "did nothing extenuate." He tore into the Pierce Administration, and denounced the incursions of Missouri border ruffians into the affairs of Kansas. He let it be understood that the events in Kansas ought to arouse such a storm of indignation that every man would rather be a martyr than submit to the pro-slavery laws of the Kansas legislature. As for Lovejoy himself, he hurled out the challenge: "Who would not lose his life in such a cause? In defense of Kansas I will offer myself as a captain, and if not wanted in that capacity, I will shoulder a gun and go as a private. If I use my Sharp's rifle, I will shoot in God's name. I am for war to the knife, and the knife to the hilt, if it must be so." Lovejoy's impassioned call to arms was received with hurrahs and amens.[18]

After order was restored, Francis Preston Blair of Maryland was elected president of the convention, with Julian, Vaughan, and McMillan among the vice-presidents. Blair proceeded to pour a balm over the excitement left by Lovejoy's thrust. This aristocrat of a powerful political family injected a sadly misplaced note of middle-groundism. Blair declared for the Compromise of 1850. Later Julian wrote that Blair "misconceived the spirit and purpose of the convention . . . the convention was not beating a retreat to the finality platforms of 1852, but marching in the opposite direction." [19]

When the afternoon session convened, the delegates were prepared to get down to business. A committee of one from each state was appointed to draw up an address and resolutions. Another such committee was created to plan a national organization. In the latter Julian was elected chairman, and Lovejoy sat as his state's spokesman. While these undramatic tasks were being accomplished a most significant message was read. From Philadelphia Thomas Spooner had wired: "The American party is no longer a unit. The national council has gone to pieces. Raise the Republican banner. The North Americans are with you." The party leadership had split over the slavery question. Almost a year earlier, in June, 1855, the national convention had been marked by the withdrawal of twelve Northern state delegations because they would not accept a platform endorsing the Nebraska Act. During the year, the sharp division over the repeal of the Missouri Compromise deepened. Finally, in the national nominating convention in February, 1856, the hostile factions could no longer be reconciled and the party split into Southern Americans, who favored the Nebraska Act and the Fugitive Slave Act, and Northern Americans, who wanted no further extension of slavery. Following the logic of this position, the Northern Americans sought to join with the Republicans. The result was a tightening of the lines for the coming election campaigns of 1856 and 1860.

As if to underscore this development and assert the strength of the Republicans, Charles Reemelin of Cincinnati, speaking in that afternoon session at Pittsburgh, lashed out at Know-Nothingism and bigotry. He had been a Democrat, together with thousands of other Germans, but his party's course on the Nebraska Act and on the slavery question in general had alienated him and his compatriots. They had turned to political independence and finally to the Republican party. Reemelin was plainly slamming the door on nativism for the new party.

Ichabod Codding from the old Liberty guard of Illinois reminded the convention of the pioneer efforts of men like Lovejoy and himself. The New York *Times* reported him as applauding "the firmness with which the Free Soil men of the Union have made their long stand against the encroachments of the slave power." [20]

After several ten-minute speeches by delegates from each of the states, Julian reported back with a plan of national organization: Edwin D. Morgan of New York to become chairman of the party's national committee; a national nominating convention to be held June 17 in Philadelphia. Julian further reported a recommendation that state, county, and district committees be formed and that these in turn organize Republican clubs in every town and township. State delegations to the June convention would be chosen on the basis of twice the representation in Congress. Lovejoy rose to amend the proposal in an effort to widen the base of the convention. His proposal to elect three delegates from each congressional district was adopted. The report was approved by the delegates, and thus on February 23, 1856, the national Republican party "became a fact." [21]

From the resolutions committee came a demand for freedom from slavery in Kansas and other national territories, and the unifying platform of restricting slavery to where it then existed. This was a big compromise on the old abolitionist programs. When Frederick Douglass read of the Pittsburgh convention's

140

work, he deplored this latest watering-down of abolitionist principle: "Nothing said of the Fugitive Slave Bill—nothing said of slavery in the District of Columbia—nothing said of the slave trade between states—nothing said of giving the dignity of the nation to Liberty—there is not a single warm and living position taken by the Republican party, except freedom for Kansas." [22] It was sharp criticism that could as well be directed at the Lincolnian conclusions of the Decatur conference of editors. But eventually Douglass altered his appraisal and became a staunch member of the new party.

Lovejoy and Codding and the radicals could nevertheless be proud and happy with their contributions. They had capped their long struggle over the years with two days of work that helped to produce this new party. Although their maximum program was not adopted at Pittsburgh, they had at least succeeded in winning broad support for the obvious minimum.

It was a considerable advance for the antislavery people, and was in part due to their willingness to "lose themselves in a larger movement committed to the essential articles of their political faith," as Julian later wrote.[23] For the two Illinois preachers "whose lips were touched with fire" it would nevertheless be difficult to achieve at home the same kind of unity they found at the Pittsburgh convention. Although the ground was being prepared for the new party in Illinois by the Decatur Anti-Nebraska Editors' convention, there were many old party loyalties to overcome. Yet there was hope of success. In other states large numbers of Democrats, Whigs, and American party people had broken with their parties to join the Republicans. Why not in Illinois?

In anticipation of the Bloomington convention on May 29, Herndon had gone out on a speaking tour, appearing at a number of local anti-Nebraska conventions. Lincoln, although a counselor of the editors, still held himself away from the Republicans.

He hoped that fusion might be made with some of the local Know-Nothings on "middle ground." Getting wind of this trend of thinking, John H. Bryant wrote Trumbull that he would have none of it, he would not go for such middle ground. Herndon also sharply disagreed with the middle position based on a Know-Nothing alliance and broke with the editors of the Illinois *Journal*. Dr. Charles H. Ray, now in command of the Chicago *Tribune* and pushing its circulation to new highs, also made his feelings clear to Trumbull. In a letter written early in May, Ray asserted that the coming Bloomington convention must write a clear-cut resolution opposing Know-Nothingism. Such a move was necessary to avoid alienating the large German population.[24]

The Germans were too strong a political force to be lost to the Republicans; rather, they were to be welcomed as allies, for they had been among the first to react against the Nebraska Act. Since they had settled by the thousands on the farms and in the towns of Illinois, they could not be ignored, insulted, or wished away. Their energy made political life in the state far more complex for hack politicians. If the sharp-minded New Englanders threw a kind of pepper into the political stew, the Germans with their democratic and socialist bent added the salt. In the last analysis their numbers alone must have been an overwhelming force against nativist tendencies.

The backstage squabble between Lincoln and his cronies on one hand and Ray, Bryant, Herndon, and the Liberty men on the other was not resolved until the whole cast of players assembled in Bloomington. Before the curtain could rise, though, one of the largest parts in the drama had to be assigned. All knew who should play that part, but he was cautious and deliberated long, as was his habit. Lincoln was, as Herndon put it, "sorter so & not so." The younger lawyer, actively fulfilling his assignment on the central committee of the anti-Nebraska convention, was determined to have Lincoln commit himself openly to the new organization. (Hadn't he once recently assured Eastman of the radicals that Mr. Lincoln was "all right"—and that he would be, at the right time? Wasn't this the time?) It rankled Herndon to think that "Whiggery & Know-Nothingism tried to hold" Lincoln.[25]

His chance to do something about it came with the call for a Sangamon County convention to elect delegates to Bloomington. Herndon signed Lincoln's name to the call while the senior partner was in Pekin. Whether or not it was a forgery, or otherwise unauthorized by Lincoln, is not so important as Lincoln's reply (about May 15) after Herndon informed him of the deed. Lincoln wired: "All right; go ahead. Will meet you—radicals and all." Exuberant after his own fashion, Herndon wrote Trumbull on May 19, "I have never seen him [Lincoln] so sanguine of success, *he is warm.*" [26]

At Bloomington, Lovejoy too was warm. When Judge J. O. Cunningham stepped off the train from Champaign, he found Bloomington alive with anti-Nebraska partisans. He particularly noted "the athletic personality of Owen Lovejoy, making love to the abolitionist haters of the center and south." [27]

Lincoln had arrived, and was using his talent for persuading and conciliating on some old friends, fellow Whigs, and anti-Nebraska Democrats. Lincoln had to strain a bit to hold conservatives Jesse K. Dubois, Orville H. Browning, and bring along David Davis (the last hating Lovejoy "with a burning intensity"). To Norman B. Judd and other Democratic foes of Senator Douglas who came into town to fuse, Lincoln, as political catalyst, had to say, "Our party is fresh from Kentucky and must not be forced to radical measures; the Abolitionists will go with us anyway, and your wing of the Democratic party the same, but the Whigs hold the balance of power and will be hard to manage. Why, I had a hard time to hold Dubois when he found Lovejoy and Codding here; he insisted on going home." [28]

In the end all the players stayed, and Bloomington on May 29

143

became the scene of triumph for unity. George Schneider, Adolph Meyer, and Francis Hoffman of the German leadership were there. Dubois, Browning, Lincoln, and Yates came from the Whig ranks. Even within this contingent one had to distinguish between old-line and anti-Nebraska. Joseph Gillespie and Ozias M. Hatch, two of Lincoln's friends and legal colleagues and lately of the seriously damaged American party, joined the proceedings. Norman Judd, John M. Palmer, and Trumbull came from the Democrats. Codding, Lovejoy, Herndon, Eastman—and their adherents—completed the roster of leading actors in the Republican or "People's party" pageant.[29]

At an open-air meeting the night before the convention Governor Reeder of Kansas detailed the terrors of life in that state. He was followed by other eyewitnesses of Kansas events, and as speaker after speaker stepped back from the veranda of the Pike House, even conservative Whigs were moved to demonstrate their feelings. The reaction to Kansas taken together with the news a week earlier that a South Carolina congressman brutally caned Massachusetts Senator Charles Sumner following a rousing speech on the crime against Kansas, encouraged the desire to halt the expansion of slavery. Every shade of nonslaveholding thought was impelled to react to the caning of Sumner and the sack of Lawrence, Kansas.[30]

On the morning of May 29 Isaac N. Arnold stood on the main stairway of the Pike House and "with almost tragic emphasis" read aloud to assembled citizens the accounts in that morning's Chicago newspapers of the burning of the Free State Hotel and press of Lawrence. Crowds in the Pike House lobby and in the street outside were shocked and ashamed. The excited demands for reprisal set the stage for the organization of the Illinois Republican party.[31]

Later, at Major's Hall, the convention opened with the election of Palmer as president. Lincoln became chairman of the

144

nominating committee. Lovejoy played hardly any role in organization, merely accepting appointment by Palmer to the resolutions committee. In general, the radicals had little to do. The die had been cast, and all the participants were resigned to fuse on the key issue of nonextension.

As Browning opened a round of speeches, he "sought to lay the ghost of Abolitionism." He reiterated his belief that slavery had been one of the compromises of the federal Constitutional Convention and "was sacredly protected by the supreme law." Nevertheless he was willing to fuse with others to halt the expansion of slavery.[32]

Lovejoy followed the conservative Browning. His reputation had preceded him, and many who knew him only by what enemies said of him fully expected to see the "Raw Head and Bloody-Bones of the Abolitionist Ogre, who surely must be of kin to Auld Clootie." Fully aware of the caricature, Lovejoy knew that he had an opportunity to correct impressions and win many friends. He devoted himself to the single unifying question before the convention.[33]

A writer for the Chicago *Democratic Press* thought: "Many who heard Mr. Lovejoy for the first time were agreeably disappointed by his declaration of sentiments on the political aspects of the slavery question." The ever-ebullient Herndon remembered Lovejoy "like Otis of colonial fame . . . a flame of fire." Judge Cunningham, in retracing the history of the day, recalled that Lovejoy "carried his miscellaneous audience with him. He did more. He broke down much of the unreasonable prejudice against himself and secured for himself a hearing before an audience in Illinois without danger of insult, a treatment he could not, before then, expect." [34] Cautious Whigs and Democrats now could happily consider Lovejoy "all right." Ward Hill Lamon, though, never ceased opposing Lovejoy, if one judges by his *Life of Abraham Lincoln,* published in 1872. Lamon insisted then that

Lincoln "never sided with the Lovejoys. . . ." In the same work he reflected that although the Republicans united at the Bloomington convention, "the most noted Abolitionists were in it, the spirit of the Lovejoys was present. . . ." [35]

Lincoln, following Lovejoy as a speaker and summing up and closing the convention, projected such brilliance as to capture all his auditors. For an hour and a half he delivered his heart's and his mind's best. The Alton *Courier* reported that Lincoln "came upon the platform amid deafening applause. . . . He was here ready to fuse with anyone who would unite with him to oppose the slave power." This was the famous "lost speech" of Lincoln, so named because no one wrote it down. Reporters for Chicago and Alton newspapers were too absorbed by the dramatic speech to take notes, and Lincoln was believed to have spoken neither from manuscript nor notes. But one participant, at the age of seventy-six, recalled that at one point Lincoln "stood as if on tip-toe, his tall form erect, his long arms extended, his face fairly radiant with the flush of excitement," as he said: "We do not intend to dissolve the Union, nor do we intend to let you dissolve it." The writer of this account may have been recalling another speech by Lincoln, his "house divided" speech of July 16, 1858, when similar words were uttered. On the other hand, Lincoln was believed to have wanted to say this in 1856 but was dissuaded from doing so. At any rate, either the content of the speech itself, or the memory of Lincoln delivering it, lasted in the mind of at least one witness for almost fifty years. [36]

Although it was not preserved, the speech remained vivid for Herndon: "His speech was full of fire and energy and force; it was logic; it was pathos; it was enthusiasm; it was justice, equity, truth, and right set ablaze by the divine fires of a soul maddened by the wrong; it was hard, heavy, knotty, gnarly, backed with wrath." When Lincoln concluded, the audience was on its feet cheering, telling "how deeply their hearts had been touched." [37]

Above all else, Lincoln's "lost speech" signified the unification of the anti-Nebraska forces in the state. Lincoln and his old Whig colleagues, and John M. Palmer, Norman Judd, and the anti-Douglas Democrats must receive much credit, as they have, for this important consummation of new party unity. On the other hand, Lovejoy, Bryant, Eastman, Codding, and the radicals deserve a large share of the honors for having persevered in antislavery political organization for a decade and a half before the others.

The convention unanimously approved resolutions for party unity; against extension of slavery into territories "heretofore free"; for restoring the Missouri Compromise; for the immediate admission of Kansas "under the constitution adopted by the people" of the territory; an anti-Know-Nothing resolution; and a final resolution approving Lyman Trumbull's performance in the United States Senate. A central committee with conservative hue was appointed for the new party. Also, candidates were nominated for state offices in the election that year. William H. Bissell led the ticket as candidate for governor. He had been an anti-Nebraska Democrat and a hero of the Mexican War, ironically one fought to enlarge the domain of slavery. Finally, the Bloomington convention named a state delegation to the Republican national nominating convention opening in Philadelphia on June 17, 1856.[38]

With his heart full of warm recollections and gratitude Zebina Eastman, speaking for his comrades Lovejoy and Codding and the old Liberty men, wrote, "there was no longer any opposition to Mr. Lincoln from the most radical of the abolitionists. They understood him; they knew that he was wholly with them; that the great inspiration of his life, was the restoration of the doctrines of the Declaration of Independence, to the administration of the government." [39]

At a large Republican campaign rally at Kalamazoo, Michigan, in August, Lincoln anticipated Eastman's estimate. He took the occasion of this appearance to reject unflinchingly efforts to discredit him. As Jefferson had been when his enemies called him a "Jacobin," as Franklin D. Roosevelt and other liberals were baited by political foes as "red," Lincoln was baited by his contemporaries as a "black Republican," an "abolitionist," a "radical." Lincoln's reaction to the epithets showed a marked change from his position in 1854. At Kalamazoo he said: "They tell us that we are in company with men who have long been known as abolitionists. What care we how many may feel disposed to labor for our cause?" [40]

8

Lovejoy Is Elected to Congress: 1856

"Illinois has repented."

—Western Citizen

While Lincoln now was disposed to act with the abolitionists in the Republican party, so too was Frederick Douglass willing to move in 1856 from the high ground of radical abolitionism. The Negro leader's decision to reverse his stand and endorse the candidates came after careful examination of the existing political relations. In Douglass's words, "Beyond all controversy, the commanding and vital issue with Slavery at the approaching Presidential election, is the extension or the limitation of Slavery." This was the unifying issue that had created the Republican party and in 1856 was the inspiration of the first national Republican nominating convention.[1]

Unlike the conventions of the Democrats and Whigs, the pervading spirit of this one was high indignation and moral zeal. The Democrats strained to hold back sectional resentments; and all sorts of deals attested to the cynicism and barrenness of principle among them. Northern elements backed Stephen A. Douglas for presidential candidate, but the convention instead chose James Buchanan of Pennsylvania, who was considered more sympathetic to Southern aims. John C. Breckenridge of Kentucky was named his vice-presidential running mate. The fragmented and dying Whig party, finally convening in Baltimore in September, 1856, endorsed the Southern Know-Nothings' nomination of Millard Fillmore for the Presidency. Fillmore was a Whig who supported the Compromise of 1850 and while President had enforced the fugitive slave laws. He had no chance of winning in 1856, but his candidacy was feared because it might weaken the Republicans by attracting Northern conservative Whig votes. Nevertheless, the enthusiastic new party marched on to its nominating convention.

Six hundred Republican delegates and twice as many observers surged into Philadelphia on June 17, battered away at each other's favorite sons, and indulged in some log-rolling. Throughout, they harked back to the eighty-year-old Declaration of Independence. In the end they emerged with a significant and challenging platform and the most colorful presidential candidate that year or in many a recent campaign: the pioneer pathmaker John C. Frémont of California.[2]

When delegates from Kansas entered Musical Fund Hall, they were hailed as heroes. Owen Lovejoy was loudly called for, to make an address. Henry Wilson of Massachusetts; Joshua Giddings of Ohio; and David Wilmot of Pennsylvania received tumultuous ovations. When Wilmot, as chairman of the platform committee, reported the planks, each was thunderously applauded. Foremost was the demand for an end to the expansion of slavery. Then came a plank calling for the immediate admission of Kansas as a free state. Southerners' schemes for a territorial grab in the Caribbean, documented in the Ostend Manifesto, received a howling condemnation. The New York *Tribune* had labeled it a "Manifesto of Brigands" in 1854. Now, at the convention, it was denounced as "the highwayman's plea that 'might makes right.' " A railroad to the Pacific, and river and harbor improvements were important economic demands in the platform.

Though antislavery radicals played their part, they did not dominate the convention. Lovejoy, Giddings, Thaddeus Stevens, and Zachariah Chandler of Michigan were matched by less thoroughgoing antislavery men such as Charles Francis Adams of Massachusetts; Alphonso Taft of Ohio; and John Bigelow and Edwin D. Morgan of New York. Even the Illinois contingent showed a "moderate" coloration. Besides Lovejoy, who was "ultra," the Prairie Staters were George Schneider of the *Staats-Zeitung*, Jesse O. Norton, Cyrus Aldrich, W. H. L. Wallace, John M. Palmer, Norman B. Judd, W. B. Archer, and others.

In the balloting for a vice-presidential candidate, Lincoln received 110 votes, which rather surprised him, a little-known Midwestern lawyer. The final decision was to run William L. Dayton of New Jersey for this position.

By no idle coincidence, the first day of the convention fell on the anniversary of the battle of Bunker Hill, a symbol of the Revolutionary War for freedom and nationhood. The day was an appropriate one for Lovejoy to raise the question: What was the destiny of the nation?

"To drive Negroes?" he asked the assembled hundreds.

"No! No! No!" they thundered.

"To win territory by all sorts of filibustering," he asked, "and then desecrate it by introducing slavery on its soil?"

"No! No! No!" was the roaring reply.

It was to maintain and illustrate the self-evident truths laid down in the Declaration of Independence, Lovejoy declared.[3]

He had expected to make only a few brief remarks, but the audience encouraged him to develop his ideas at length. Greeley's *Tribune* reported that "the feeling against the truculence and aggression of the South was most significantly manifested during Mr. Lovejoy's address."

In the afternoon session Lovejoy took part in the debate over admission to the convention of a group from the Northern wing of the American party. This group was then meeting in New York City and had sent a letter to the Republican convention seeking to become a part of it. Giddings had initially moved to table the communication and it had been done, but later he opened up the question to reconsideration. A number of delegates maintained that the convention had invited the North Americans and was obligated to receive them. Lovejoy took the floor to state emphatically that the convention had not invited them as a group. It had, he said with considerable approval from the Republican delegates, "asked them to come as individuals and unite for freedom." With a long glance backward toward Illinois, Lovejoy said that he wanted the convention to know that "if the North Americans were received as an organized body of Know-Nothings, that demagogue, Stephen A. Douglas, would tickle the senses of the foreign-born citizens of Illinois and Illinois would be lost." [4]

This was recognition of the key role to be played by the politically articulate masses of German-speaking voters. They had generally followed Douglas and the Democrats, but had turned away from him because of his role in promoting the Kansas-Nebraska Act. The opportunities to win them to the new Republican party were only beginning to mature, and might wither if the nativist Know-Nothings were absorbed in the party. In the end the Republican convention relegated the question of affiliation to a committee, and adjourned without accepting the American party as a group. The North American party later nominated Frémont as their national candidate and offered no little embarrassment to the main body of Republicans.

Sixteen years after the clamor for a Hard Cider "backwoods"

hero and his meaningless platform, Americans were treated to another emotional campaign, this time one with a lofty moral tone. The Free Soil platform adopted by the Republicans won them support from some of the finest intellects in the nation. Washington Irving proclaimed his intention to vote Republican. Ralph Waldo Emerson and William Cullen Bryant, long the editor of the New York *Evening Post,* lent their weight to the cause of the new party. Walt Whitman, who had been fired from the editorship of the Brooklyn *Eagle* in 1848 for expounding Free Soil sentiments, wrote a moving essay condemning slavery, "The Eighteenth Presidency." In it he bared the pusillanimities of Fillmore and Buchanan and the falsities of two hard-shell parties. Whitman called upon the "Workmen! Workwomen! of America" to listen and support the new party.

Mass meetings drew huge crowds. In Pittsburgh, one hundred thousand people attended a Republican rally. In New York, twenty thousand listened to Nathaniel P. Banks, formerly of the American party and now Republican Speaker of the United States House of Representatives, who spoke from the balcony of the Merchants' Exchange. On July 4, almost ten thousand people assembled in Princeton, Illinois, to hear Burton C. Cook of Ottawa, Joseph Knox of Rock Island, and Lincoln and Lovejoy. Later that summer, when Lincoln spoke to a Frémont rally in Kalamazoo, Michigan, thirty thousand were present. Other demonstrations in the Midwest drew vast crowds: fifty thousand each at Indianapolis, Indiana; and Beloit, Wisconsin; and thirty-five thousand at the state fair at Alton, Illinois. These were gratifying expressions of interest and support for the new party. At the same time, however, Democratic and Know-Nothing meetings were not small. In Illinois, Senator Douglas attracted tens of thousands to rallies for Buchanan and Breckenridge.[5]

Republican pamphlets and throwaway literature deluged the people. Sumner's "Crime Against Kansas" speech circulated widely, as did German-language pamphlets. Typical appeals to workers were headed: "Southern Slavery Reduces Northern Wages," "The Poor Whites of the South." Frémont and Freedom clubs and Pioneer Clubs conducted torchlight parades proclaiming "Free Labor, Free Speech, Free Men, Free Kansas, Frémont," *"Gegung Ausbreitung der Sklaverei," "Für Freies Kansas und Freie Arbeit."* [6]

Free Negroes of Boston pledged support for Frémont and Dayton but made it clear that the Republican party did not yet come up to the real needs of the colored man: "It is not an antislavery party . . . we do not pledge ourselves to go further with the Republicans than the Republicans will go with us." Frederick Douglass took a similar stand. Only six months earlier he had shunned this party. Now he wrote: "But let us not be unreasonable or impatient with the Republican party. In considering this defect in the Anti-Slavery character and creed of the Republican candidates, it should be borne in mind that they now stand in respect to this doctrine precisely where the Liberty party stood ten years ago." Despite these criticisms, Douglass led the Northern Negroes in voting for Frémont and Dayton. His action helped to cement the solid national front presented by the various elements in the organization.[7]

In Illinois, however, the front of Republican unity was breached not long after the homecoming from the spirited Philadelphia convention. Resentment against Lovejoy, because he was considered to be a radical abolitionist, threatened to split the young party in the struggle for the Third Congressional District nomination. On July 2, a Republican congressional district convention at Ottawa nominated Lovejoy. This was considered to be compensation to some radicals who were disappointed that abolitionists received no positions in the state party apparatus. As C. L. Kelsey of Princeton explained the Ottawa nomination, "We felt then the need also of asserting our own equal manhood.

We were not only good enough to vote, but good enough to be voted for, and we determined to test and vindicate it in the person of Owen Lovejoy." [8]

A first, informal ballot gave Lovejoy 25 votes; Leonard Swett, who was Lincoln's favorite, 18; and Jesse O. Norton only 9. On the regular ballot Lovejoy and Swett each gained one vote. Then the convention adjourned for twenty minutes. When it reassembled Swett and Norton withdrew and their votes went to a dark horse, Churchill Coffing, in an effort to concentrate the opposition to Lovejoy. The maneuver was unsuccessful, for Lovejoy was nominated by a vote of 30 to 24. The Urbana *Union* cheered the result and hoisted Lovejoy's name to its masthead a week later. The Democrats thought it was great fun that he had been chosen over Swett, this "Rev. Notorious Abolition-Banner-Trailing-Union-Sliding-Lovejoy." [9]

When Lincoln first heard of his friend Swett's defeat, he said, "it turned me blind." But he controlled his anger and "after much anxious reflection" decided not to oppose Lovejoy's nomination. Only two days after the Ottawa convention Lincoln was a featured speaker at the Independence Day rally at Princeton for Republican candidates. He came away from the meeting impressed with the popular respect and admiration for Lovejoy. He quickly got in touch with his old Whig law colleagues Henry C. Whitney and Judge David Davis, to inform them of his feelings about the Lovejoy nomination. On July 7 Lincoln wrote Davis: "I was, by invitation, on my way to Princeton; and I really thought of turning back—however, on reaching that region, and seeing the people there—their great enthusiasm for Lovejoy—considering the activity they will carry into the contest with him—and their great disappointment if he should now be torn from them, I really think it best to let the matter stand. . . ." He wrote a similar letter to Whitney.[10]

There was much dissatisfaction among Republicans in the

southern part of the district over Lovejoy's victory at Ottawa. They complained of being mistreated by the convention and seemed less disposed to accept the nomination than Lincoln. They hastened to call a convention of bolters from the July 2 convention, this one to take place in Bloomington on July 16. Among the signers of the call were Asahel Gridley, Isaac Funk, and Whitney. The first two were wealthy in banking, railroads, and farm properties; the last was a leading lawyer. Another disappointed man, Cyrus Aldrich, confided to David Davis that he could "see & almost feel . . . disastrous & deplorable effects everywhere" from Lovejoy's nomination. Aldrich feared that even in his own Second Congressional District John Farnsworth who, Aldrich said, "had heretofore been classed as an abolitionist," would be brought out for the nomination. The Bloomington *Pantagraph* which for two weeks before the July 2 convention had editorialized in favor of Swett, admitted that the result was unexpected and two weeks afterward decided to come out enthusiastically for Lovejoy. Indeed, the boldest type, equal in size to that used for Frémont's name, was used to set OWEN LOVEJOY in the masthead of the editorial page, and the line was kept there throughout the campaign.[11]

Dickey complained to his son John that "Rev. Owen Lovejoy, a rank old-fashioned *Abolitionist*," had got the nomination and that about half the delegates at Ottawa on July 2 had bolted. They had nominated the judge as a candidate "who would not only oppose the introduction of slavery in Kansas, but would at the same time be *true* to the acknowledged rights of the South under the Constitution, embracing their right to recapture runaway slaves. . . ."[12]

Dickey was to some extent aware of the error he and the other conservatives made in opposing Lovejoy at this time. He told his son, "I am stemming a terrible current without any reasonable certainty of success." This was grudging recognition that some

156

conservatives had taken a more exact measure of the political winds and had altered their courses accordingly. Lincoln was one of these. Jesse W. Fell, the Quaker businessman and publisher of the Bloomington *Pantagraph*, was another. His editor, Edward J. Lewis, expressed their thoughts about the matter in the newspaper, then one of the most influential in the state. They went so far as to defend Lovejoy's past efforts in the antislavery movement. An editorial of July 23 asked, "Does voting for him subject you to the imputation of 'ultra Garrisonian abolitionism'? We have shown you that he is himself the farthest removed from Garrisonism." Even so, the *Pantagraph*, speaking from a strict nonextensionist angle, conceded Lovejoy's right to advocate abolition of slavery in the District of Columbia. Although the Republican platform at Philadelphia did not go that far, the *Pantagraph* nevertheless was prepared to consider abolition in the District an open question "on which we are at liberty to differ, just as we may differ on the question of a protective tariff." The Fell-Lewis endorsement of Lovejoy was unequivocal: "We want in Congress men of ability and eloquence who may be relied on with perfect confidence to resist the extension of slavery. Nobody doubts that on this question OWEN LOVEJOY will be as true as steel." [13]

Davis lost little time in checking his own disappointment when he saw for himself on July 16 at Bloomington that Lovejoy was as popular in the McLean County seat as he was at Princeton. But the bolters persisted. In the evening of the 16th they held a meeting to ratify their nomination of Dickey that afternoon. Dickey's solemn presentation aroused little enthusiasm. Gridley, who followed him on the platform, woke up the meeting with his cutting sarcasm. He denounced Lovejoy as a "nigger thief," and the audience sensed something of life and conflict in the proceedings. A quick adjournment might have buried the occasion in obscurity. But Lovejoy was present, much to the surprise of the audience and the chagrin of Dickey and Gridley. He was called upon and obliged by speaking, but with considerable effort to overcome his "evident embarrassment." His voice shaking with emotion, he confessed that he had no heart for "this personal contest." He said he had come expecting to find scarcely a friend but had found many sympathetic listeners.[14]

Lovejoy conceded the federal government's impotence to abolish slavery in the states, but he reasserted its power to do so in the territories. He argued for an amendment to the Fugitive Slave Law to give slaves the right to have trials by jury and to testify in their own behalf. He spoke about his opposition to the doctrines of Garrisonian abolitionism in former years. He then riddled the "nigger thief" charges. He pleaded guilty to aiding fugitives and concluded by asking, "Who of you would not do the same?" The applause that met this question was a white flag of surrender and a signal of humiliating defeat for Dickey. Half a century later, Ezra M. Prince, the McLean County historian, recalled the spell cast by Lovejoy. Comparing his speech to those of other eminent orators—Wendell Phillips, Charles Sumner, Abraham Lincoln, Robert G. Ingersoll—all of whom he had heard speaking, Prince wrote that he had never heard "any oratorical display superior, if at all equal to the address of Mr. Lovejoy on that occasion." [15]

A further effort to air the discontent over Lovejoy's nomination was made in Bloomington on the evening of July 18 in a public meeting at the courthouse. Gridley and Fell were present, as were others of a variety of viewpoints. Gridley opposed a resolution ratifying Lovejoy's nomination. Then Fell and others spoke in his favor and offered enthusiastic support. A "Mr. Abbott of Stout's Grove" said he had come ten miles to attend the meeting and found that the people of Bloomington were behind the times. In the country, he said, "there is but one voice. The people [are] not only for the nomination of Mr. Lovejoy but heartily and cordially so." This opinion had been under-scored a few days earlier by meetings of the Republican clubs of Urbana and West Urbana, which had repudiated the bolters. It was evident that Dickey had little chance of success and that someone would have to explain the facts to him lest he destroy the only political haven for the former Whigs.[16]

Davis took on this task and made immediate efforts to dissuade Dickey from further contesting Lovejoy's nomination and thus splitting the party and weakening its opportunities for local, state, and national victories. "I did not dream that you would have taken the nomination for Congress . . ." Davis wrote to Dickey. Significantly, he emphasized that the feeling in the southern counties of the district made any moves against Lovejoy harmful to the party. "The readiness with which many persons support Lovejoy is surprising," he reported. Davis attributed this support to the feelings over the outrages in Kansas, the gen-eral conduct of the Pierce Administration, and the attack on Senator Sumner, which, he wrote, "have made Abolitionists of those who never dreamed they were drifting into it."

"These principles," Davis continued, "and the feelings which underlie them were more active and vigilant than the principles which you and I entertain, and hence, in a very great measure the nomination of Lovejoy. Many men again express great re-grets that he is nominated, but think that he will vote right on the question of the extension of slavery, and are willing that he should vote his Abolition sentiments in other respects rather than send a Democrat to Congress who will vote to uphold slavery further.

"A third class think he was fairly nominated and should be sustained. . . . Again there are another class of people who think that this fusion was of all elements and whoever adopts the fusion platform should be voted for, no matter how wrong the other sentiments are." Davis hastened to add that he was try-

159

ing to justify "simply as reasons (unsatisfactory to us as they may be) why the people are predisposed to vote for Lovejoy." Here, then, was the heart of the matter, according to Davis: "I think the grand reason of it all is that his [Lovejoy's] views and opinions are becoming the views and opinions of a majority of the people." [17]

Davis, like Lincoln and others in their former Whig circle, was understandably saddened by Lovejoy's success. Yet, what could he do? "This nomination of Lovejoy deadens enthusiasm, dispirits and causes all people who really love the Union of States to pause. . . . I am told that the sentiment of this town is in favor of Lovejoy. . . . But it may be asked what you and I and those who think with us are to do. Simply to vote for, and eschew the others. . . . We, the old Whig party, will be stricken down during this campaign. Had we not better bide our time, brush up our armor for future operations? . . ." [18]

Davis refused to yield entirely to the Lovejoy forces. He looked for ways to head off Lovejoy but could see none at the time. If it were only a question of time and money, no matter how great, the effort would be worth while, and the expense would be no obstacle. But even if Davis and his friends could persuade the Democratic candidate Uri Osgood to withdraw, "success is, to say the best, problematical." [19]

In his consternation over Dickey's insistence on running, Davis applied pressure through Dickey's son-in-law, W. H. L. Wallace. On July 19, he implored Wallace: "I know that he will be beaten. . . . Pray, prevent him from running." Davis was convinced that "about all the old Whig lawyers [in Bloomington] gave in their adhesion to Lovejoy." Despite such warnings Dickey remained in the race, and his stubbornness disturbed friends of Lincoln.[20]

"Do you not think a few of our men are acting very foolish over this Lovejoy nomination?" asked J. E. McClun of Bloomington in a letter to Lincoln on July 21. McClun wanted Lincoln to prevent Dickey from running, since his advice would be strong with Dickey. However, there is no evidence that Lincoln personally acted on McClun's suggestion. McClun had good reason to make such a plea, for he was convinced that Lovejoy's popularity was growing so rapidly that if the election were held that week he would win by a majority of 300 over Dickey and Osgood.[21]

Lovejoy, said McClun, had done himself much credit while in the legislature in Springfield. Besides, he added, "he is with us on the Republican platform and is an able vindicator of it." Even if Lovejoy had been "somewhat ultra" in the past, he is "glad of the opportunity that this Republican movement has given him to take a more conservative shoot in politics." Lovejoy would be "useful & successful. . . ."[22]

When Dickey stopped in Rock Island at the end of July, [Joseph] Knox tried to dissuade him from running as an independent against Lovejoy and urged him to write to Lovejoy "on any real or imaginary differences" between them. Knox hoped Lovejoy's replies would satisfy Dickey and his friends. There was just such an exchange of views. Dickey put several direct questions to Lovejoy, dealing mainly with the intent of the Constitution's framers with respect to fugitive slaves, and with the laws and Supreme Court decisions on the same subject. Dickey feared that Lovejoy's position might be unjust to Southerners.[23]

Lovejoy answered that he believed the framers of the Constitution studiously avoided using the words "slave" and "slavery" because they anticipated that the institution would be eliminated in the states by the actions of those states themselves "and then there would be no permanent record that it ever had an existence." If a case in the Supreme Court went against him, as a citizen, he would submit to its mandate but as a member of Congress, he would vote in accordance with his convictions. As

Andrew Jackson had done, he would " 'Swear to support the Constitution as I understand it.' " Although Dickey's queries were on matters "not now in issue before the people," Lovejoy said, "it is but right that I should say that if elected I shall take my seat in Congress with a heart loyal to the Constitution of my country against which I never entertained a thought or uttered a word." Lovejoy said that he stood on the Philadelphia platform of the Republican party, which had been adopted by the convention that nominated him at Ottawa. He reminded Dickey that "there is a South distinct from the slave holding nullifiers and disunionists who now control the government and who seek to rule or ruin." Whether this reply affected Dickey in any way is unknown but the many pleas and urgings that he withdraw from the election must have registered on the judge.[24] Forced to plow a field full of boulders, Dickey quit the race on September 13. But while the threat from that quarter to Lovejoy was in process of dissolution, a brief but disconcerting effort to make Lovejoy appear more extreme in his antislavery views than he was, came from another source. The *Flag*, an Illinois conservative Democratic paper, reported that the Illinois state convention of the Radical Abolitionist Party at Joliet on July 31 had endorsed the "Black Republican State ticket, Frémont and all, and was particularly emphatic in holding up Owen Lovejoy, Abolition candidate for Congress from this District, as a model Abolitionist." This small and uncompromising abolitionist party had rejected the course many antislavery people had followed after 1848 and particularly in 1856 when they settled for the Republican anti-extensionist platform. The party's standardbearer in 1856 was Gerrit Smith, but the party, even in its stronghold in New York State, polled an insignificant number of votes. The party was regarded as extreme and dangerous by many not in its ranks and the *Flag* in Illinois attempted to smear Lovejoy by linking him with it. Even if he might have been sympathetic toward the

162

party, Lovejoy's own utterances gave the lie to the *Flag*'s charges. Moreover, the *Pantagraph*, attempting to repair any damage done by the Democratic paper, denied that the Radical Abolitionists endorsed the Republican ticket, or any part of it. Except for the eloquent support of the Republican party in their convention by the Negro orator H. F. Douglass of Canada West, the *Pantagraph* maintained, the party "unanimously rejected" his views and strongly supported Gerrit Smith. That was the end of the matter, and the threat to Lovejoy was dissolved.[25]

Lovejoy seemed to be in an impregnable position by midsummer, for he retained the nomination and campaigned up and down the district and the state for Bissell for governor and for Frémont and Dayton on the national ticket. Except for the disgruntled in Dickey's camp, all elements of the new party exerted themselves to make a lasting impression on the voters in this their first national campaign. Here is a sample of the campaign schedule that brought Lovejoy and Lincoln and the others together a number of times: Herndon, Lovejoy, and Norton were the principal speakers at an all-day rally in Urbana on September 17. Lincoln spent the day as an auditor, for in the evening he was to be a main speaker. On September 24 at Decatur three members of the Chicago newspaper fraternity were the main speakers in a morning session—William Bross of the Chicago *Democratic Press;* John Wentworth of the *Daily Democrat;* and Vaughn of the *Tribune*. In the afternoon Senator Trumbull and Lincoln were the main attractions. In the evening Lawrence Weldon, later the United States district attorney for the southern district of Illinois, and Owen Lovejoy wound up the day's activities. During Lovejoy's speech, rowdies threw eggs through a window into the room where he was speaking and spattered some members of the audience.[26]

The next day, September 25, an all-day rally was addressed by Lovejoy, Trumbull, and Lincoln. The *Pantagraph* reported that

Lovejoy's irresistible logic and overwhelming eloquence made his speech the main topic of conversation after the meeting. He was besieged by people from all parts of the state to speak in their localities. Trumbull was applauded rapturously, and in the evening Lincoln was received with equal enthusiasm. The editor of the *Pantagraph*, when asked by readers and friends why Lovejoy had not appeared in McLean County, replied that he went wherever duty called and could not restrict his appearances to his own large district of some two hundred thousand inhabitants. For example, he added, Lovejoy had one day addressed a monster meeting in Chicago, the next day another in Galesburg, the next one in Beloit, and on the fourth day one in the extreme southern part of the district—"wherever he can do the most good." [27]

A week after the Springfield meeting Lincoln joined Lovejoy on the stand at a rally in Marshall County, before a crowd of two thousand at Lacon. On October 7 twenty thousand persons filled the town of Ottawa as they descended from railway cars and from wagons to rally and listen to speeches by Lincoln, Trumbull, Lovejoy, Bross, Yates, and several German orators. On October 8, Lincoln, Trumbull, and Lovejoy spoke in Joliet, and on the 9th in Peoria. Finally on the 10th Yates and Lovejoy favored Bloomington with their presence before an audience of ten thousand. Fell called the colorful meeting to order and McClun presided over it. When Lovejoy spoke he repeated essentially what he had said there on the evening of July 16 when he had surprised Dickey and Gridley. And, to cover the vast crowd while Lovejoy was speaking, Yates and Swett stood in a wagon which had been drawn up at the outer edge of the assemblage and addressed the people there.[28]

As for Lovejoy's chances of winning, hopes were high for a smashing victory. The Lockport *Telegraph* believed that his opponent Osgood had "injured himself with the humane and thinking class wherever he has spoken." Osgood's "demagoguery and bull-neck coarseness," the editor wrote, only aroused loathing and "scorn in our inmost soul," and since the North had tolerated demagogues in Congress long enough, and "Illinois has been almost damned with them," it would be refreshing to elect a man like Lovejoy. Here was a man, the editor went on, "whose teeth won't chatter, whose knees won't smite together every time some lordly slave breeder threatens to dissolve the Union." These were fair reflections of the attitude of Fell's *Pantagraph.* Lewis urged that Lovejoy be elected by such a majority that would shame the "political scavengers" who had been slinging mud at him since his nomination. Not even Frémont, he asserted, was so maliciously abused as Lovejoy was from one end of the state to the other. "Almost all the crimes of the Decalogue, and a legion of others [of] which the Decalogue makes no mention, have been laid to his charge," the editor stated.[29]

Such loyal support was, of course, good for Lovejoy, especially in the southern part of the district. Although party unity seemed to be assured, an accusation almost on the eve of the election disclosed an active undercurrent aimed at defeating Lovejoy. On October 31 the Republican central committee of Vermilion County sent off a long, detailed letter to the De Witt County committee alerting it to what it suspected was a scheme "set in motion by some Old Line Locofocos, some, to a certain extent disappointed Republicans, and some pro-slavery Fillmoreites, for the purpose of defeating Mr. O. Lovejoy at the coming election." The evil genius, they charged, was the Honorable David Davis who, as leader of "the clique," had on a visit to Danville summoned one of the staunch old Whigs of the county, "for the avowed purpose of being talked to and having his mind embittered against Mr. Lovejoy." The Vermilion County committee members were "mortified to know that Judge Davis will resort to such means, but it is so!" [30]

Even though the gentlemen of the Vermilion committee had not originally favored Lovejoy as a candidate, they did accept his nomination. They saw a large vote for him in their county "unless there is some unfair and dishonorable means resorted to." If the leading and influential Republicans succeeded in their plot to beat Lovejoy, the committee warned, they would be *persona non grata* in Vermilion: "It *must* and *will* forever damn them in this county should they hereafter be proposed as candidates for any office."[31]

Davis, despite his advice to Dickey, was indulging in desperation politics. On November 3 his friend Clifton H. Moore in Clinton finally said to Davis what was necessary: "I know what you think of Lovejoy's nomination but it is suicide to attempt to defeat him." The chilling thought was that this had to be said only hours before the election.[32]

While this bitter struggle was going on in the Third Congressional District, a less fratricidal aspect was displayed during the campaign for Frémont and Dayton in Illinois. Such leading lights as John P. Hale, Nathaniel P. Banks, and Governor Charles Robinson of Kansas came in to aid the national Republican ticket. It was a foregone conclusion, however, that the Democrats would win the state for Buchanan and Breckenridge; but they were upset in the state and congressional contests. Republicans were elected in the first four congressional districts, and Bissell and Francis A. Hoffman won the top state posts. In the Third Congressional District the "rank old fashioned Abolitionist" ran 6,069 votes ahead of his Democratic opponent.[33]

Lovejoy could justly be proud. He had fought this campaign as he had fought them all since his first nomination a decade earlier. He told Gerrit Smith that he had had "an arduous campaign, though on the whole a pleasant one." To liberty-loving souls like Lovejoy, Codding, and Eastman this triumph of 1856 was the sure sign of their correctness and the fall of those who would ostracize abolitionists. It was the answer firm to the gang of drunks who had murdered Elijah Lovejoy at Alton, and to the respectable people who had whitewashed the murderers but who had inspired the murder. It was with Elijah's death in mind that the *Western Citizen* in 1846 had written: "When Owen Lovejoy shall fill a seat in Congress by the votes of the people of Illinois, then let it be said that Illinois has repented. . . ." He had faced up to the abuse over his Underground Railroad activity during the campaign and was gratified to write when it was all over, "I . . . justified it and the people sustained me." [34]

When he departed from Princeton to take his seat in Washington, the Hampshire Colony Congregational Church resolved: "That we highly appreciate Mr. Lovejoy's long and able ministry among us, a period of seventeen years," and they approved of his efforts in the pulpit as well as in "the philanthropic and reformatory movements of the day."

If he went to Washington to serve under a Democratic President and in a predominantly Democratic Congress, it was nevertheless a sign of better things to come for the Republicans that Lovejoy and many other men like him were sent to occupy the opposition seats. The Democrats would hold the reins of government but they could not overlook the ninety-two Republicans in the House who were elected to the 35th Congress. They would be a formidable group of rivals facing their own one hundred and eighteen Representatives. Nor could the Democrats be certain of the votes of the twenty-six Know-Nothings who also were elected in 1856. Apart from the Republican strength facing them in the House and Senate, the Democrats were elated, for they also considered the Supreme Court to be safely theirs. The real cause for uneasiness came in knowing that Republicans were moving toward future majorities in the heavily populated Northern states. Illinois was prominent among them and its Third Congressional District, with the largest constituency of any district in the Union, had taken a lead with Owen Lovejoy toward a victory in 1860.

9

In the Thirty-Fifth Congress

"Those that go their own gait, erect, stepping with freedom and command, leading not following."

—*Walt Whitman*

Lovejoy did not take his seat in the 35th Congress until it convened in December, 1857. This was due to the old practice under the Constitution that left a "lame duck" Congress sitting from election day in even-numbered years until March 4 in the following odd-numbered year when the Congress adjourned; nine months later the newly elected Congress commenced. In the thirteen months after his election Lovejoy turned his concern to personal affairs. Like other prairie farmers that year, he was hard hit in the inflationary flight of the economy aggravated by frenzied speculation in railroads and land and various commodities. Loose and uninspected banking also contributed to the appearance of prosperity in the mid-fifties.

The rocketing economy was reflected in high prices farmers paid on their purchases from the cities as money became more and more difficult to lay one's hands on. A British subject of long residence in America observed that "by 1857 more than $800,-

000,000 had been invested in idle western land and lots, held for speculative rise, and but one quarter paid for." The New York *Tribune* noted dourly: "Our city merchants and bankers owe those of Great Britain, the country owes the cities, the farmers owe the merchants, in short, two-thirds of us are in debt." By midsummer of 1857 the false prosperity dissolved into economic depression.[1]

Whatever his immediate needs, Lovejoy, now forty-six years old, must have felt uneasy about his large family's future. His quest for financial aid took him to Gerrit Smith, from whom he sought a loan of three to five thousand dollars. This wealthy abolitionist was considered one of the best businessmen in the state of New York and "one of the most benevolent in the nation." At the close of 1856 Lovejoy went straight from his election victory celebration to Smith's upstate New York home. Smith recommended that Lovejoy try to arrange a loan in New York City, then as now the financial center of the nation. If he failed, he was to write to Smith. After wearying and fruitless applications to some of the prominent men in the city, Lovejoy complained to Smith that New Yorkers "seem to think there is nothing secure and stable outside of New York . . . they think the world outside of New York is a floating island." Even the philanthropic merchant and antislavery leader Lewis Tappan knew no one in December, 1856, who would lend to Lovejoy. He was prepared to offer the greatest security, presumably his farm—"as secure as anything earthly can be." Lovejoy visited in Massachusetts, then in Utica, and returned to Princeton in January. Since the mails were slowed by winter's hold on the Midwest, he had received no reply from Smith—"everything is locked up in Ills. till the Lord opens the Lakes," Lovejoy noted. He need not have worried. A draft forwarded by Smith on Christmas Eve reached Princeton on January 20. Smith wanted no interest and advised Lovejoy to apply for a license to practice law in the local courts. Lovejoy promptly followed this advice and prepared to form a law partnership with a Mr. Farwell. There is no evidence of this venture into law except for the license granted to Lovejoy in April, 1857; one of the signers was John D. Caton, Chief Justice of the Illinois Supreme Court and the man who had presided over the Agnes-Nancy case in 1843.[2]

That winter Lovejoy despaired about the health of his good friend Joshua Giddings, the dean of antislavery men in Congress. His illness was serious enough for Lovejoy to say, "I shall mourn his death as a personal loss, and I had hoped to have his counsel should I live to reach Congress." Giddings did recover, and the two went on to fight side by side against slavery. Lovejoy enjoyed good company in the House of Representatives, for among his colleagues were veterans of antislavery struggle on one level or another. Among the Illinois Republicans were John Farnsworth of Chicago and Elihu B. Washburne of Galena. Schuyler Colfax of Indiana went back to his House seat as a Republican, while Galusha Grow of Pennsylvania's north central counties joined him under the banner of the new party. Anson Burlingame and Nathaniel P. Banks of Massachusetts, the latter recently connected with the American party and Speaker of the 34th Congress, were also returned on the nonextensionist platform.[3]

On the way to Washington late in November, 1857, Lovejoy stopped in New York City, where Senator Seward of New York treated him and some other friends to an evening at Niblo's. Lovejoy wrote his stepdaughter Lucy, now a young woman of twenty: "Niblo's is not a theatre but a pantomime exhibition." His sensibilities were upset by what he saw there—"Well, they had dancing & I concluded that if you went and saw what I did once would do you." One of the ladies in Seward's party remarked that, after the girls had danced once or twice "they could not have shown anything more than they had exhibited." Lovejoy confessed that he was not "particularly fascinated with any of it."[4]

In Washington at last, he stayed at the National Hotel along with fellow boarders Hale, Clark, and Mason W. Tappan, all of New Hampshire, and Burlingame, "with several others of like stripe." As he got around the city and met some of its noted persons he was moved to report that "the great men dwindle very much as you approach them." [5]

On the Democratic side of the House Lovejoy came up against hard-hitting and wily parliamentarians. Alerted to the threat against it inherent in the 1856 election returns, the Administration party prepared to fight tooth and claw to retain its supremacy. The Democrats controlled the House, and although they seemed to have a clear majority, it was a shaky one because of the split in the ranks between Northern and Southern wings. On the other hand, the cohesive group of Republicans presented a serious challenge to Southern Democratic power, particularly to those aggressive members fretful over the possible contraction of the domain of slavery and the slave economy. To the slave-owners the name of Lovejoy was already anathema, and they considered all Republicans usurpers and subversive. Their contempt for Negroes as well as for their white allies, they summed up in the epithet "Black Republican," which Northern Democrats like Douglas in the Senate used in an extravagance of Republican-baiting. One of the leading "Black Republicans" selected for attack was Lovejoy.

Standing on the threshold of political prominence in Washington, he need not have been concerned about his abilities, which he deprecated in a letter to Gerrit Smith, for he had a vigorous state party back of him and he had learned much from the fight in the state legislature in 1855 over antislavery policies. But now he would have to carry out his aims on the national level, where he would also be expected to fight for a broad platform. He now had to be the representative not only of antislavery men but farmers, merchants, educators, even speculators —the whole population of the rich central prairie of his district.[6]

As a new member of Congress, he was bound at first to suffer the humiliation of being ignored by the Speaker, even when he rose in his place and sought the floor. In the meantime he watched the tumult of the chamber as other members simultaneously shouted for the Speaker's attention and noisily summoned page boys amid the riffling and rustling of papers, the scratch of pens, the loud conversation in a group of seemingly inattentive legislators. The hubbub in the House of Representatives, it was said, was worthy of hackmen hawking fares at the New York or Chicago railroad depots. But the power of the Speaker of the House was as great as Captain Ahab's aboard the *Pequod*. Mr. Speaker appointed the committees and ruled the House with the rap of his gavel. That great prize of debate, "the floor," was his to give almost at will. Would Lovejoy, too, learn the tricks of parliamentary procedure and use them to gain lofty ends? [7]

The Democratic Administration of President Buchanan was soon thrust into awkward and straitened positions by the effects of the depression on the federal budget. The squeeze on money had an embarrassing effect on Administration policies, for, however posed, they revealed the struggle over slavery as the decisive one involved in almost all other questions. The Southern enemy increasingly narrowed the path and blocked the way to progress, and in response antislavery radicals became more and more the leaders, scouts, and guides of the emancipation movement. Lovejoy, taking his part in the congressional opposition to Buchanan's policies, never let it be forgotten that whether it was the Kansas constitutional question, the currency question, the Utah "war" of 1857, or appropriations to be voted for the army, all of them were inseparable from the struggle to limit the power of the slaveowners.

Unlike most newcomers, Lovejoy headed into debate within two weeks of the session's opening. His initial effort came not directly on the slavery question but on a fiscal matter, the treasury note bill designed by the Buchanan Administration. Lovejoy opposed the measure. J. Glancy Jones of Pennsylvania, a confidant of the President and a friend of Southern members, pointed out that revenue from dutiable goods had fallen because those goods had not been withdrawn from the warehouses and sold. Jones explained further that the Secretary of the Treasury had asked for authority to issue twenty million dollars of treasury notes "in the contingency of this state of things." Besides, Jones warned, "does he [Lovejoy] not know that there is danger of a deficiency in less than a month from this time?" [8]

Lovejoy took the floor on December 21, 1857, and spoke at length, enumerating his objections to the bill. He objected to the "hot and indecent haste" with which the chairman of the Ways and Means Committee, Jones, tried three or four times "to screw us up to a vote upon it under the previous question, without scrutiny and without analyzing and sifting this measure." Lovejoy called it the most important measure before the legislature that session.

"Except Kansas," a member reminded.

"Yes, of course," Lovejoy replied. "I always except the 'peculiar institution' and its expansion. That is the one paramount thing."

Lovejoy declared the treasury note bill deceptive. "It will be called a loan, but in reality it is converting the Government into a great shinplaster machine, to flood the country with irredeemable currency." This was the true view of a son of the soil—give him hard money every time. It had been the Democrats' own credo to oppose paper money and Lovejoy needled them about it: "The Gentleman from Virginia seemed surprised that there were any members on this side of the House in favor of a hard currency and against the banks."

The freshman congressman stated what he considered paper money should be. In doing so he forecast his position in a monetary controversy a few years later that would disclose cracks in the unity of Civil War Republicans. This was how Lovejoy put the matter:

". . . when you undertake to build up national prosperity, by means of a paper currency which does not represent dollar for dollar, and is not convertible into specie, it will not stand. But, Sir, when you build it upon hard money, upon a metallic currency you have built your house upon a rock, and it will stand the test of all the storms that may beat upon it."

Lovejoy's suspicion about the Administration's use of the money to be raised was probably his most compelling reason for objection. "I cannot vote for this bill because I do not know what is to be done with the money," he said. Glancy Jones hastened to assure him that the government would pay debts, according to law. Lovejoy insisted: "Sir, I want to know what the money is voted for." Lest this bumbling tenderfoot of the prairies pry into the heart of the bill and spring its secret, Glancy Jones explained as if to a schoolboy: "I thought I had sufficiently explained it. . . ." Lovejoy fired point blank: How much of the money "is going to be used . . . in sustaining usurpation in Kansas?

"How much is to be used to force, at the point of the bayonet, upon the people of Kansas a government for which every person in the United States knows they never voted and never will?" he demanded in alluding to the proslavery state constitution adopted at a convention in Lecompton, Kansas, in November. Less than a quorum of the sixty delegates decided to make Kansas a slave state, and antislavery people in and out of Kansas felt betrayed and angered. In addition they had ample reason to believe proslavery men in Washington, up to the President, supported the rigged elections in Kansas. Finally, they suspected, as Lovejoy did, that the Buchanan Administration might send troops to Kansas to impose the proslavery constitution.[9]

John Letcher of Virginia interrupted to ask if the gentleman were aware that a vote was being taken in Kansas upon the Lecompton constitution that very day, "so the President cannot want money for that purpose." Lovejoy snapped back: "I knew that the party in power can play such 'fantastic tricks' as make Heaven blush, and that other place smile with joy." The members laughed audibly. Finally Lovejoy challenged the constitutionality of the treasury note bill, asserting that there was no power to issue treasury notes. He scorned any precedents that might be cited and warned "mechanics and laborers, and the industrial classes" that the bill was only an overture to despotism and "one grand banking system." After lengthy debate the House overrode Lovejoy's energetic forensic by a vote of 118 to 86.[10]

Whatever the outcome of the bill, old politicians had been treated to a spirited display of one radical Republican. The country was now to be exposed to a voice different from the solemn tones of "practical" men. Wherever the *Congressional Globe* went, the bristling ideas of a faithful abolitionist penetrated.

As the session progressed, Lovejoy developed a sure grasp of legislative intricacies and displayed sharp wit in swift sallies upon opponents. When the filibustering manipulator of Central American republics, William Walker, ran into obstacles to his stuffing Nicaragua into his pockets in 1857–1858, Democrats sprang to his defense. Walker enjoyed Southern Democratic support even though he had trespassed on United States neutrality laws in organizing on United States soil his invasion of Nicaragua. What endeared him to the Southern power bloc was his repeal of Nicaraguan laws against slavery and his promise to revive the slave trade. When he was first arrested in December, 1857, Southern state legislatures called for his release; and a public meeting at Mobile demanded repeal of the neutrality laws. In all, Walker was hailed as a hero. Nevertheless he was put on trial but wiggled through a divided jury to freedom under a *nolle prosequi.*

Lovejoy in the House on January 5, 1858, intruded on a series of moves by Southern representatives to repeal the neutrality laws ensnaring Walker. He protested against what he called a farce: "And when the [repeal] act is passed, we shall hear gentlemen, with a pathos that thumps the heart like a triphammer, portraying the scene.

"We shall hear how gracefully Bill Walker, the pirate, moved towards the gallows; how heroically he met his fate; with what majestic tread he took his stand upon the dead fall! And ah! when the knot shall have been adjusted—our admiration all gone —with an overwhelming emotive power of veneration, we shall have to prostrate ourselves on the very earth, and look up admiringly to the dangling buccaneer! Sir, my admiration will go forth to the sheriff, and not to the criminal.

". . . I am not willing that even this preliminary debate should go out to the people with no voice of protest against this idea of cloaking a man with heroism, and making him a martyr when he is simply a rascal." [11]

In another debate on slavery, in an exchange with Lucius Gartrell of Georgia, Lovejoy recommended to that gentleman's reading Deuteronomy 23: 15–16, as well as the Eighth and Tenth Commandments. Deuteronomy admonished: "Thou shalt not deliver unto his master the servant which is escaped from his master unto thee. . . ." Gartrell asked, "Does the gentleman consider the African equal to the white man?"

"That depends altogether upon his character, Sir," was Lovejoy's rejoinder as the House burst into laughter.[12]

About ten days later Lovejoy sat listening to the dreary discussion of items in the army appropriation bill. It irked him to hear the brand of buncombe being issued about pensions for soldiers' widows and orphans. The House Committee on Invalid Pensions reported a bill to the floor to pay the claims of soldiers of the War of 1812, or their widows and orphans. Lovejoy pointed out that the claims were not a matter of legal right, but requests for gratuities from the government. Furthermore, he said, nine out of ten of the claimants were not widows and orphans of soldiers. Rather, Lovejoy declared, the object of the bill was to satisfy the demands of speculators and land-sharks "into whose hands the claims have gone." Getting the floor again after other members had spoken, Lovejoy proposed referring the bill to the Committee of the Whole on the State of the Union where the bill could be more carefully considered. "If we do anything in this matter," he said, "let us do it for the benefit of surviving soldiers and their widows and orphans, and not for the everlasting cormorants who come here and urge the kind of claims which it is here proposed to originate." [13]

It was often said of Lovejoy that on the subject of slavery his soul took fire. He demonstrated this passion when he made his first major, lengthy address in the House of Representatives on February 17, 1858, opposing the admission of Kansas as a slave state. He stood at the clerk's desk before the House and the crowded galleries, which listened attentively to his "clear and emphatic utterances." The memory of his brother's martyrdom, the pledge a decade earlier that he would not flinch in the face-to-face encounter with slaveowning congressmen stirred Lovejoy as he opened his attack:

"What Achilles' wrath was to Greece, slavery is to our country—the prolific spring of woes unnumbered. Not the discussion, not the agitation of the subject of slavery, but the existence of slavery itself."

He deplored the identification of the South with slavery, and called upon its "true heroic men" to take an oath of fealty to freedom and "forswear allegiance to slavery." Lovejoy hoped Mason and Dixon's line could disappear and "let the country be one united whole; the rights of all equally respected, equally sacred."

Aiming his main attack at the Dred Scott decision and President Buchanan's defense of the doctrine that slaves are property, Lovejoy declared: "I confront it at the very threshold, and deny it." He reminded the House that in all classes, in every section, there had always been Americans who regarded slavery as a wrong and looked for its extermination with "earnest and often patient hope." Slavery was "the relic of a barbarous age."

The heart of his argument probably was contained in these excerpts:

"[Slavery] claims the right to annihilate free schools—for this its very presence achieves—to hamper a free press, to defile the pulpit; to corrupt religion, and to stifle free thought and free speech! . . . It claims the right to transform the free laborer, by a process of imperceptible degradation, to a condition only not worse than that of the slave. Yes, sir, while the border ruffians are striving, by alternate violence and fraud, to force slavery into Kansas, the President and Chief Justice, by new, unheard of, and most unwarrantable interpretations of the Constitution [in the Dred Scott decision], are endeavoring to enthrone and nationalize slavery, and make it the dominant power in the land. . . . And all this upon the false, atrocious, and impious averment, that human beings are property! Again I meet this doctrine, and spurn it. The Supreme Being never intended that human beings should be property."

Since the Constitution had been cited by the President and by Chief Justice Roger B. Taney to uphold their pronouncements, Lovejoy examined this aspect and presented a strong case for the opposite. In the Dred Scott decision Taney led the Court in declaring the Missouri Compromise unconstitutional and denying that Congress had the right to legislate for the territories. The effect of the decision was to open every territory to slavery. Negro slaves, by the decision, could not be freed by being taken to free soil. The Court overstepped propriety, accuracy, and its own prerogatives when it also rendered an opinion that Negroes were an inferior race and had "no rights which a white man was bound to respect." As for President Buchanan, his message to Congress at the beginning of the session had called upon the Constitution for authority in assuming "that human beings are property in the absolute and unqualified sense." But Lovejoy insisted that he could find nothing in the document that expressed or implied that idea. Were the President and the Chief Justice not uttering untruths? Lovejoy asked, "Do they not contradict the entire history of the country?" He revived Madison's account of the Constitution's making; that the delegates in 1789 had kept out of the document any mention of slavery.

Now, Lovejoy asserted, men were proposing constitutional sanction for carrying "human chattelism" into Kansas. By such logic, he believed, neither Kansas nor any other state could ever prohibit slavery; and no more free states could ever be added to the Union.

Lovejoy posed some stinging questions: "If human beings are property . . . why has Federal legislation declared the slave trade piracy? Is it piracy to go to the coast of Africa and trade in elephants' teeth, or in palm oil, or in any other articles of commerce that may be produced there? . . .

"How often is it that when slave owners lie down upon the death couch and look the future in the face, they emancipate their slaves? Did you ever hear of men emancipating their cattle in their last will and testament?"

In a soaring flight of oratory, Lovejoy proclaimed: "What now is our country's duty, destiny, and true glory? To go marauding over the territories of weaker nations like buccaneers and poltroons, to extend the area of slavery; to hunt down fugitive slaves and take them back, manacled, to bondage; to break down the dykes of freedom. . . . No! . . . The true mission of this nation, the work assigned, the trust committed, is to reduce to organic form as we have already done, and now to illustrate before the world, the great and ever-enduring truths that I have recited, and thus to exemplify before the nations of the earth the principles of civil and religious freedom and equality, and so teach them that their monarchies and despotisms are usurpations." [14]

The speech in the House was called "the as yet master effort of Mr. Lovejoy . . . no new member fills a higher place on the Republican side of the House." Another was convinced that "Lovejoy has proved himself a national man of the first water . . . among the bright stars in the National Capital." The Galena *Advertiser* of March 11 was particularly impressed, because Lovejoy was "more moderate on the slavery question than many shrewd Southern men would wish him to be." Lovejoy knew that some of his highly charged remarks were considered "ultra" by some. The principles invoked in his speech were not new to antislavery veterans, "but they are to thousands who will read them in my district." He apparently also felt that the speech would do some good in the British antislavery papers, possibly to help raise funds overseas for the antislavery cause, for he asked a friend in New York to forward some copies to London. The New York *Tribune*'s Washington correspondent made Lovejoy's "rousing speech" his lead item. The writer said that Lovejoy had combatted very effectually "not only the political but social, moral and theological fallacies by which the ultra slaveholders strive to bolster up the institution." At home, the country weekly of Champaign County, the *Central Illinois Gazette*, spread the text of the address across its columns. By April 1 the reaction was so favorable that the Urbana *Union* and the Danville *Independent* placed Lovejoy's name at the head of their columns, signifying grass-roots sentiment for him as their candidate for reelection to Congress. In effect this launched his 1858 campaign.[15]

In the meantime Lovejoy, encouraged by the response to his

speech, became involved in an almost impish examination of civil and military finances. Lovejoy seemed to delight in upsetting that dream of war contractors: the unquestioned and speedily approved appropriation. Lovejoy was always asking embarrassing questions. To his friends, this affair, beginning in March, 1858, was known as his "Exposure of the Utah War Contracts."

The Utah War began when President Buchanan dispatched an expedition of United States Army regiments to quell an alleged Mormon rebellion in the Utah territory in the summer of 1857. Although troubles between Mormons and non-Mormons over religious and legal matters was chronic, there was little foundation for highly colored and very dubious reports of violence that reached Washington. Nevertheless, no investigation was made of accusations against the Mormons, or of Mormon charges against corrupt Gentile officials and judges in the territory. Bitterly resenting armed federal intervention, the Mormons prepared to defend themselves, by force if necessary. But before any real clash took place, the bloodless "war" ended in a negotiated settlement in May, 1858.

Under the aggressive leadership of Brigham Young, governor of the territory, Superintendent of Indian Affairs there, and leader of the Church of Jesus Christ of Latter-Day Saints, the Mormons had prospered in Utah. The gold rush to California brought gold-seekers and other immigrants into Utah on their way West and Mormons did a brisk business with them. One member of the church succeeded in 1856 in winning a lucrative monopoly contract for delivering the mail and the freight and supply business from Independence, Missouri, to Salt Lake City, by underbidding the firm of Hockaday and Magraw, which had conducted this business. The monopoly control by the Mormon merchant irritated the losing bidder as well as other merchants. These contractors looked to the federal government to pull their chestnuts out of the fire for them. W. M. F. Magraw had con-

181

nections in the White House and presumably made good use of them; in 1857 he was named superintendent of construction of military wagon roads in the territory, and John M. Hockaday was appointed district attorney of the Utah territory.

Contractors generally were hurt by the economic depression, and by the termination of army supply contracts made to serve expeditions in Florida against the Indians. In their desperate need for new contracts and for money they sought to use the Utah troubles to recoup their fortunes. They let their friend in the Cabinet, Secretary of War John B. Floyd, know that they wanted to profit from the impending "Utah War." And it was against them that Owen Lovejoy in the House of Representatives directed his penetrating questions.

Although representatives of the Mormons had urged President Buchanan to send a commission of investigation to Utah, and although efforts were under way to settle the dispute between the Saints and federal officials "without the army" early in 1857, Buchanan finally ordered the troops out of Fort Leavenworth. The persistent efforts of the Utah congressional delegate, Dr. John M. Bernhisel, to seek a bloodless and inexpensive settlement "scarcely helped Floyd's appropriations," according to a recent historian. The Virginia-born Secretary of War, who had argued in Congress in 1824 that it would be wise to take over the Far West by Southern action, now in 1857 seemed so sure he could put over the Utah expedition that he began to endorse bills of favored contractors. One in particular, Russell, Majors and Waddell, received negotiable paper signed by Floyd, and banks were told that they could lend money on his signature. The contractors would be paid for services out of deficiency appropriations by a willing Congress.[16]

A contemporary writer charged that more than $6 million in contracts were distributed to relatives and friends of congressmen who were wavering in their votes for admission of Kansas as a slave state under the Lecompton bill. He said that a $4.5 million contract for transportation of army supplies in 1858 went—without prior advertisement—to one firm in western Missouri "whose members distinguished themselves in an effort to make Kansas a Slave State, and now contributed liberally to defray the election expenses of the Democratic party." [17]

But the Democratic party was treading soft ground in 1858. A depleted Treasury could hardly replenish the pork barrels being opened by members of the Buchanan Administration. Further embarrassment came when the Democrats, who, having insisted that the way out of the depression was not through government spending, were now proposing through Secretary Floyd that contractors be paid millions of dollars out of the funds of the United States government. To make matters worse, the payment was proposed to come from a deficiency appropriation by Congress. And to make matters even more complicated, federal forces were being sent into a territory in outright contradiction of the Democratic principle of nonintervention. The departure could only alienate the scores of Democrats who honestly believed in Stephen Douglas's popular sovereignty doctrine as well as play into the hands of the Republicans eager to make the most of the embarrassment of the Administration. The consequences of Floyd's and Buchanan's actions could be grave, for if federal intervention were permissible in Utah, why not in Kansas, where antislavery men had been asking for it to prevent a proslavery state government and constitution. And why not extend the doctrine to intervention against slavery in territories and states at some future time? worried slaveowner representatives might easily have asked.[18]

Against such a political and economic backdrop, Lovejoy and a handful of other Republican congressmen stepped on the stage. James L. Orr of South Carolina, Speaker of the House, recognized Owen Lovejoy during the session of March 24, 1858, when Lovejoy offered a resolution requesting the Secretary of War to "furnish this House . . . with a full statement of all contracts made in connection with the Utah expedition." The move was defeated instantly by a single objection. However, Lovejoy soon resumed the attack from another angle.[19]

Throughout the discussion in the House from March 24 to April 19 and afterward, Lovejoy hammered away at the idea that the military branch must be subordinate to the civilian in the government. He was willing to support the army's needs in protecting persons and property, but he kept up a running attack on what he believed to be the army's extravagance. "I am not willing to vote money blindly for the Army," he said. In a debate on another money bill, the general deficiency bill, he sustained his attack against military extravagance. He wanted to know, for example, why $89,000 should go to pay Indian agents when only $69,650 was proposed "for agriculture."

"Now, how many of these agents are honorable men," Lovejoy stated, "I do not know. How many of them cheat the Indians out of their annuities, and teach them to get drunk I do not know. . . . But I know this: that we pay more for these agents and subagents to take care of the Indians than we do for the immense interests of agriculture throughout this agricultural country." [20]

Bearing in mind the effect on the farmers in his district, Lovejoy on April 2 divulged that he had it "from one of the contractors" that he got ninety-eight cents per bushel of corn delivered at St. Louis and that he contracted to sell fifty thousand bushels. Yet, Lovejoy said, the St. Louis *Republican* reported that farmers were paid only thirty to thirty-three cents per bushel.

"I want the farmers of Illinois to know that while it is difficult for them to sell their corn at from 20 to 25 cents per bushel, the Government is paying its pet contractors 98 cents per bushel in St. Louis who buy it for 30 to 40 cents; and I want them to understand that it is shrewdly suspected that all these contracts have an intimate relation with party politics." He was probably hinting here that bargains were being made between the Administration and some representatives for votes to pass the act admitting Kansas as a slave state.[21]

As Lovejoy took his last poke at the nest, the Democratic hornets broke into an angry buzzing. Protests long and bitter were heard: Who is the contractor? they wanted to know. Where do you get your information? What impudence to make such allegations! Come, now, there is no truth in the accusations. But Lovejoy, like the cat playfully pawing the mouse, replied that he had asked for the true facts through his resolution. Since the House defeated it he had only this recourse: to rely on newspaper accounts and the statements of individuals.

Lovejoy explained his understanding of the contracts in question: The contractor received so much for transporting beef and other provisions to Utah; if Mormons or Indians attack, the government insures the loss. Lovejoy asserted he did not know "how much it would take to get up a band of Indians to do that. . . . This is an imputation of the contractors." Lovejoy did not suppose "they are without some human nature." Teasingly he said, "I know that if they get a contract under this Administration, it is presumptive evidence against them."

He deplored the expedition into Utah, labeling it "the war of plunderers and contractors." Lovejoy maintained that he had yet to learn the point of collision between the Mormons and the United States. "It is not fair to butcher the masses of people there because they are polygamists, when you have been winking at it so long." He would rather see a law passed, which if disobeyed would then permit the legal use of men and money to enforce it. He would vote for such a law.

William Smith of Virginia insisted on knowing whether Lovejoy's charges were rumor or fact. Lovejoy parried: "It may be that I have obtained it [the information] in conversation, and that I do not feel at liberty to make it public." The House laughed at him as much as with him.[22]

Phelps, again on the defensive, replied that the deficiency appropriation was necessary because the last session of Congress had not anticipated a war in Utah in the army's budget.

Three days later, on April 5, the House approved Lovejoy's resolution of inquiry. Apparently House Administration leaders thought it wiser to do so than to permit Lovejoy to prod too deeply. When Secretary Floyd supplied figures and other data to justify army expenditures in Utah, Letcher of Virginia spoke in his defense, and again asked Lovejoy "in all kindness, to let us know who this libeler of the Secretary of War is."

Lovejoy stated simply that he alone was responsible for what he said in the House. Later he did reveal that his informant was "a gentleman who represented himself to me as a contractor" in a casual conversation on the steps of a hotel. Since he considered the facts more important than the man's name, he said he went immediately to the House to introduce his resolution. Lovejoy sidestepped any further questions of identification. He was more intent on questioning Secretary Floyd's statements. He noted disdainfully that "we ask for the contracts and they send in a statement here which answers the demand of the resolution about as well as the return of a skeleton would answer the demand for the man. It may be very good as a study of comparative anatomy, but it does not answer the demand, and is not the contract. An old dead contract is sent in, one stated to be annulled, and I presume it is." The Secretary had been evasive, Lovejoy believed. "Who cares anything about those annulled contracts? We want the living contracts," he demanded.[23]

Letcher baited Lovejoy by suggesting the Illinoisan desired the contracts for horses himself. (One of the products of Lovejoy's farm was horses.) Lovejoy bit for the bait and claimed he could fulfill a government contract for three months "at one tithe of what it costs." The Virginian played with Lovejoy: "I did not know the Gentleman from Illinois was a fighting man, or probably the Secretary might have spoken to him on the subject."

"I presume I am as able to fight as the gentleman," Lovejoy flashed back.

He extricated himself from the personal exchange and resumed the offensive against the contracts. "I understand . . . that this item covers a period of twenty months. How is it that, when this is for the year ending June, 1858? . . ."[24]

But his time on the floor was up and he was forced to yield to Letcher. This Administration spokesman's stinging yet supercilious reply was wide of the mark on the true nature of the contracts. Lovejoy's effort was defeated for the time being, but the Administration withdrew with open wounds.

There were indeed many such embarrassing questions to be asked of the Buchanan Administration. Perhaps if Lovejoy; Benjamin Stanton of Ohio; George W. Jones of Tennessee; and Israel Washburn of Maine had been able to pursue the matter further than they did in the House, they might have uncovered evidence to substantiate later charges against Secretary Floyd. He was forced out of the Buchanan government in 1860 because his improper actions in other instances made him a costly appurtenance for Buchanan. Floyd joined the Confederacy after the bombardment of Fort Sumter and was remarkable only for his incompetence as an officer in the Civil War.

One of the later charges against Floyd cast him as a plotter against the United States, as one who prepared for the secession of 1861 by dispersing the army and supplies in order to make the North impotent when the time came. Judge Joseph Kinney, the Utah territory's congressional delegate in 1864, while pleading for the admission of Utah as a state, accused Floyd of sending an army of ten to fifteen thousand men to the Mormon territory, at a cost of about $40 to $50 million "for the purpose of preparing the way by crippling the North, with a view to the rebellion which is now upon us." This former chief justice of Utah further charged that Floyd did this to impoverish the Treasury of the United States. Although no documentary evidence was presented against the former Secretary of War, he was seriously suspected by Lovejoy and fellow Republicans in 1858.[25]

Lovejoy's final move against the Administration's spending came in a debate in June on the naval appropriation bill. His particular objection was to an amendment authorizing $1.2 million for five "steam screw sloops of war." This project was pushed in the climate of Manifest Destiny imperialism, when some Americans were openly declaring the Gulf of Mexico *mare nostrum.* Another facet of his thought was revealed in these remarks made while moving an amendment to strike out the appropriation:

"Mr. Speaker, to my apprehension the most preposterous of all preposterous things is, that in order to keep the peace you must go armed to the teeth. It is an absurdity, applied either to an individual or to a nation. . . . It is preposterous, unchristian, and tends toward barbarism. Besides that it is utterly useless. These few gunboats—what will they do? Absolutely nothing. . . . They are no means of defense, but merely a means of depleting the Treasury. . . . In Mr. Jefferson's day they had to hitch up mules and haul these boats up, and put sheds over them to preserve them; and when they wanted them they were utterly useless: and so these will be." [26]

Having made his point, he withdrew his amendment, which was after all a device to gain the floor.

At summer's approach, the Congress adjourned. Lovejoy had broken ground and cultivated the political soil for his future labors. He would perhaps have taken a rest if Illinois had faced no political contests that year. But it was 1858.

10

Campaign for Reelection in 1858

*"Don't say a single word abusive of Love-
joy."*

—*David Davis*

Bureau County's Republicans early in 1858 had already begun
the campaign to reelect Lovejoy while the new congressman was
still in Washington, active in the first session of the 35th Congress. They commenced publication of the weekly *Bureau
County Republican* in Princeton on January 14, and readers
thereafter were treated to accounts of Lovejoy's parliamentary
exploits. On February 18, for example, the newspaper carried
the story of a hot exchange of words over fugitive slaves between
Lovejoy, the Washburn brothers, and Galusha Grow on one side
and Lawrence M. Keitt and John McQueen of South Carolina;
William Barksdale; Reuben Davis; and Lucius Q. C. Lamar of
Mississippi on the other side of the House of Representatives.

The reason for the *Republican*'s existence became apparent on
March 11, when in effect it started to play up news about Lovejoy. Readers were cautioned that there was "a plot on foot
among certain Old Fogy politicians in the district" to defeat the
election of Lovejoy. The uncomplimentary reference was to

Judge David Davis and Judge Dickey, the latter still smarting from his failure to overthrow Lovejoy's nomination in 1856. The two judges were being accused of plotting to pack the June 30 Third Congressional District convention with their cohorts. A skeptical observer might dismiss the *Republican*'s alarm signal, but when Lincoln, who was gathering force for his campaign for a seat in the United States Senate, could not suppress his apprehensions about the scheme against Lovejoy, it was plain that the party as a whole had something to fear. Three days before the newspaper appeared, Lincoln had written to Lovejoy in Washington, alerting him to the dangerous plans being hatched at home. Lincoln was on the law circuit at the time and passed through Lovejoy's district swapping yarns and picking up the latest political gossip. But when Lincoln wrote to Lovejoy he was not relaying mere political gossip. He had reliable information that some of the judges and lawyers of the Eighth Circuit bar, notably Davis, Lamon, and Swett, opposed Lovejoy's nomination.

Lincoln pointed out to Lovejoy: "Your danger *has been* that democracy would wheedle some republicans to run against you without a nomination, relying mainly on democratic votes." Lincoln had "seen the strong men" of the party, who, while "tempted by the enemy," had in the end seen the affair "in the proper light." In his letter to Lovejoy he carefully remarked: "I think it is not expected that you can be beaten for a nomination; but do not let what I say, as to that, lull you." He asked that the letter be confidential because some "highly valued friends" might not like him "any the better for writing it." Lincoln ended with a cordial postscript, "Be glad to hear from you." [1]

Lovejoy's response to these political warnings was immediate. He rushed out letters to his constituents, enclosing a lithograph portrait of himself. He urged his close political friends back home to look to the election campaign and protect his interest,

190

and their own of course. He had already had favorable signs in March when the Urbana *Union* and Danville *Independent* urged his nomination. This support from the southern part of his district was valuable. Nevertheless the Bloomington *Pantagraph* had not yet committed itself to Lovejoy, and this was a prize worth winning.[2]

The congressman's correspondence proved effective, according to the *Republican*, which reported on April 8 it had seen a letter from an "influential Republican" in the southern part of the district who felt Lovejoy was winning friends where in 1856 there was bitter opposition to him. Lovejoy continued to campaign by mail particularly for the control of delegations to the forthcoming nominating convention. He instructed his supporters to hold primary meetings in the towns to elect delegates to the June 30 convention in Joliet, but he complained that some Republicans were calling meetings too early to suit his convenience, that they were inconvenient for his friends to attend, and that they were designed to defeat him. Despite his efforts to postpone the primary meetings until he could get home, "certain moldy politicians" succeeded in calling county conventions by capturing certain central committee members, as the *Republican* charged. These county meetings were scheduled to take place in the first week of June.[3]

In the meantime Jesse O. Norton, David Davis, and Ward Hill Lamon proceeded with backstage moves to snatch the nomination away from Lovejoy. But the strength of Lovejoy among his constituents forced the schemers to confine themselves mainly to covert actions. A public fight would ruin them and eventually defeat Lincoln's chances for the United States Senate.

Davis had made inquiries about his chances to be the Republican congressional candidate, and Wallace had his heart set on getting it. Davis's "smothered ambition to go to Congress" was evident in a confidential letter he sent to Lamon instructing him to go "prudently" up to Urbana and "find out how the land lies." With Judge J. O. Cunningham leaning to Lovejoy in Champaign County, and the Urbana *Union* already boosting Lovejoy, the situation in that county had to be handled carefully. Davis urged Lamon to "stick a pin wherever it needs sticking." Lamon was to report back to Davis so that he might "see where it is necessary to operate to the best advantage." Above all, Lamon was to be "prudent and cautious—Don't say a single word abusive of Lovejoy," Davis wrote.[4]

This respectful fear of Lovejoy's strength was underscored by Davis's final advice to Lamon. He reminded him that Lovejoy would be home about June 10, a few days after Congress adjourned. Davis suggested that Lovejoy would have three weeks to "go around this whole district & pray & preach & talk to people—He will accomplish something—You may rely—It is well to anticipate all that we can." [5]

The opponents of Lovejoy chose to concentrate on a McLean County convention at Bloomington on June 5. Delegates from several counties had toyed with a number of names they hoped to propose—Wallace and Davis foremost among them. Finally Davis was selected to lead the contest in his home city and county against Lovejoy. Here he could be strong, since even the *Bureau County Republican* conceded Bloomington to be "the very hot bed of [Lovejoy's] enemies." [6]

Some sharp-eyed person in Urbana must have seen Lamon's maneuverings in Champaign County, and eventually word came to the ears of the Urbana *Union* editors. They labeled Judge Davis the leader of the bolters opposed to Lovejoy in 1856. Another Lovejoy partisan took up the fight in a letter to the editor of the Chicago *Tribune*. Signing himself "Fair Play," this writer complained that Davis had attempted to sabotage Lovejoy's election two years earlier and that even now Davis had "no more sympathy with the vitalizing principle of the Republican party than an Egyptian mummy." Davis was charged with refusing to vote for Lovejoy and with having persuaded others not to vote for him in 1856. Lincoln, under the pen name "A Republican," adroitly came to Davis's defense in a letter to the *Tribune* deploring the attack and asserting that the judge participated in "no plot or movement against Lovejoy's re-nomination." In the coming election, Lincoln asserted, "Judge Davis expects Lovejoy to be nominated, and intends to vote for him, and has so stated without hesitation or reserve." Davis was grateful for Lincoln's letter to the *Tribune*, but he still berated the abolitionists.[7]

In the prelude to the Bloomington convention Davis forces had scoured the district for delegates, and Lovejoy had dispatched a stereotyped letter to "Sympathizers and Abolitionists," according to an opponent, for the same purpose. The fight for county delegations became bitter. Davis forces, plainly outnumbered and out of tune with the growing antislavery sentiment in the district, were forced to fight hard to gain control of McLean's ten delegates to the district convention. Aside from Will, Bureau, and La Salle, heavily populated and heavily pro-Lovejoy, McLean was the only other county entitled to ten or more votes. Vermilion held seven, Champaign and De Witt four each, and Livingston two. Even if Davis were successful in these central and southern counties, he could not beat the thirty-six or more votes Lovejoy would control from Will, Bureau, La Salle, and some smaller northern counties. A hint of the general strategy was dropped by Clifton H. Moore, a delegate from Clinton: "If it is impossible to nominate [Davis] we will do the next best thing to defeat Lovejoy." Come what might, the portly judge went into the Bloomington meeting adamant and, "like one of the bulls of Bashan," pressed on for the nomination.[8]

One version of Davis's role in the convention was published by Robert H. Browne in 1901, forty-three years after the event. With a precautionary word as to the lapse of time and its possible effects on memory, here is the essence of Browne's story. As the son of Nimrod Browne, a construction engineer engaged in building Illinois state buildings and schools, he was acquainted with Stephen A. Douglas, Abraham Lincoln, David Davis, Owen Lovejoy, and Asahel Gridley. For a while young Browne worked in the offices of Davis and Gridley. He became engrossed in the antislavery cause while at the Rush Medical College and in a short time came to know, admire, and work with Owen Lovejoy, who was twenty-five years his senior. Browne became secretary of the Champaign County Committee of the Republican party in 1857.

On June 5, 1858, he and Judge Cunningham attended the Bloomington meeting as delegates, apparently representing Republicans of McLean County as well as Champaign County. The judge was a respected citizen of Urbana; he had been publisher of the *Union* in that city and at this date was co-publisher of the *Central Illinois Gazette*. He was chairman of the Champaign County committee of the party.

Browne said that on the morning they arrived in Bloomington a sharp struggle was in progress between Lovejoy forces and their opponents. The votes Browne and Cunningham carried with them were immediately vied for, the contest for votes being so close, according to Browne, that Champaign's could nominate or defeat Lovejoy. By noon they ascertained that four of their votes would be sufficient to "renominate Mr. Lovejoy, and that we could vote for him and compliment some other gentlemen with the other four votes as we liked." After full deliberation, the Champaign men concluded that Lovejoy "deserved the approval and indorsement for faithful and generous service in Congress, where he had made a manly defense of the cause and our people, then the most populous district in the United States."

Leaders of the Lovejoy people as well as those of the Davis

group besieged Browne and Cunningham. They were called on and argued with during the luncheon recess. But they did not disclose their intentions. They maintained a discreet silence. Before the recess was over, Lovejoy's opponents had measured the sentiment of the delegates and applied their most persuasive efforts to win over votes. Judge Davis approached young Browne in an austere and authoritative manner. He demanded to know why Browne was not conferring with "those who desired the nomination of some Republican who could be elected rather than training with the Abolitionist, Lovejoy." Davis's patronizing manner irked the younger man, who was laboring under the disadvantage of having been an employee of Gridley and Davis when he was a college student a few years earlier. Maintaining his composure as best he could under the circumstances, with "the almost furious leaders prevailing and raging all about," Browne replied that he and Cunningham represented their county and would not recognize Davis's or any authority except that of their own people. Only they could have the right "to catechize or arrogate the right to dictate" what to do. He told Davis they understood Lovejoy was "no more an Abolitionist than I was, and had been such for years as he [Davis] well knew, and that was the belief of thousands of like-minded voters in our district."

Davis's heavy body and big head shook with anger. He roared out his condemnation of "Lovejoy and agitating Abolition supporters." He had apparently surmised that the two Urbana men would cast their votes for Lovejoy. Pointing his finger menacingly at Browne, the judge lectured: "You had better training than this. Mr. Lincoln's prudent interest should have left a deeper impression on you." Davis then stormed away.

While this scene was unfolding, the two men had been walking along toward the courthouse, followed by several zealous men of both factions. They overheard Davis's and Browne's hot words and concluded that the Champaign delegation would vote for Lovejoy and therefore his nomination was certain, so far as Champaign and McLean Counties were concerned. They ran into the meeting room and broke the news as they interpreted it. The hundred or more Lovejoy friends and delegates cheered and shouted their enthusiasm so loudly they drowned out "all remonstrance of Davis and his little crowd, who had gathered about him." The Davis forces left at once, "chagrined, outwitted, and beaten . . . for the time at least." The convention reassembled and renominated Lovejoy. And this is how Browne's story of the convention ends.[9]

"We are thrashed out completely," said one of the Davis men. "You never saw Abolitionists flock out so in your life . . . every one of them turned out to the rescue. I am not only mad, but tired of this Nigger Worshipping. If Lovejoy is to be the nominee, I am ready to vote for a Douglas Democrat." Davis's own post mortem is revealing: "The Abolition element is successful here and very proscriptive. They are entirely in the ascendancy . . . the truth is that the county is for Lovejoy. The Whig part of the Republican party is proscribed. . . ." Realistic politician and businessman that he was, the Bloomington judge made the situation quite plain for Wallace when he told him: "If it was not for saving Lincoln for the United States Senate a pretty good outbreak would follow. I don't believe Lovejoy can be beaten if nominated and there is no use of bolting." Ward Hill Lamon was flabbergasted by the results at the McLean meeting. But when the La Salle meeting at Ottawa a few days later came out strongly for Lovejoy, poor Lamon cried out: "I believe the whole country is fast going to the devil!" Nevertheless he reported to Lincoln: "So we all can, but acknowledge—*beaten*. Judge Davis is, of course, out of the field." Lamon was depressed and feared that "Lovejoy's election [to] a second term, will put the Congressional District irredeemably in the hands of the Abolitionists." [10]

196

Judge Davis also reported to Lincoln: "The result in the different counties in favor of Lovejoy has not disappointed me." What a comedy the rotund judge was playing—one day pressing for the defeat of Lovejoy, another day blithely not disappointed by his own defeat! Carrying on the pose of imperturbability, the judge told Lincoln that although his colleagues Jesse O. Norton, Dickey, Wallace, and Joseph O. Glover (Ottawa's mayor) had been hopeful of capturing the northern part of the district away from Lovejoy, he, Davis, saw ten days before the McLean convention that the result that transpired was inevitable. Yet, he told Lincoln, he felt it was necessary to "run through, otherwise the Northern friends would conclude that we had deserted them." [11]

The judge was not completely reconciled to Lovejoy, however. He complained that a paper in Bureau County was "very abusive" of him, and that the Chicago *Tribune* was still running bitter letters against him. Nevertheless, he reported to Lincoln, he had made every effort to quash the wrath and indignation of the anti-Lovejoy forces. "I have been busy in season and out of season to keep things quiet—and to prevent any hostile demonstrations." He was convinced that if the opposition to Lovejoy had not sought and gone through with the primary meetings, it would have broken out in some other form, possibly to the detriment of Lincoln.

Lincoln continued to receive reports on the Lovejoy nominations in the county meetings. When the Urbana meeting on June 19 concluded, James W. Somers was able to report another resounding victory for the antislavery congressman. "We did all we could for our worthy friend Judge Davis, but the friends of Mr. Lovejoy were too numerous and we had to withdraw the Judge's name and permit our delegation to be instructed for Mr. Lovejoy." Somers was wry about the result: "We may congratulate ourselves that we will not have to labor much for *his* election because *that* is a *sure thing*—" [12]

Lincoln read and heard a variety of impressions of fact and fiction about the nominations in the Third Congressional District. Among the foolish ones was the idea that Lovejoy could still be defeated, possibly by a so-called independent Republican running against the antislavery man. Lamon had so hinted in his letter of June 9 when he suggested that Will and Kankakee counties "can yet be controlled against Lovejoy." How desperate were the abolition-haters. Only four or five days before the state Republican convention that would name a senatorial candidate, these disappointed conservatives were prepared to split the party wide open with a dangerous affront to Lovejoy and the antislavery element. For Lincoln this might have been disastrous.[13]

Lincoln would have no part of the splitting maneuver. Bluntly, the senatorial aspirant had to tell Lamon and through him the conservatives that he depended, in fact, on Lovejoy's victory in the Third Congressional District. The antislavery leader plainly controlled Republican politics in his district, which was distinguished by its consciously antislavery population. Radical or not, and more likely because he was radical and forthright and electric, Lovejoy daily won the support of growing numbers of people who were rapidly coming to his conclusions. In the face of such popularity Dickey, Davis, Lamon, Wallace, and others had to fall back, while the realist in the Springfield law office who aspired to be in the Senate collaborated with Lovejoy. The others for one opportunistic reason or other followed Lincoln's lead. Even hot-tempered Davis had assured Lincoln he had been aware that "your election to the Senate might be hazarded by a miss-move—" [14]

This then was the heart of the matter: Lincoln needed Lovejoy; and Davis, Lamon, and the others needed Lincoln. If Lincoln was to be elected over Stephen A. Douglas by the Illinois legislature, he had to win friendly representatives from the central counties. Here was the doubtful area. Northern Illinois had become solidly Republican, while the Democrats seemed to be unbeatable in the opposite end of the state. Since Lovejoy's district extended across the central portion of the state and he would have something to say about local legislative candidates, Lincoln and his followers had to recognize Lovejoy's strategic importance.

To run an "independent" against Lovejoy was to ask for embarrassing repudiation by the antislavery voters. Lincoln put the matter thus to Lamon: "it will result in nothing but disaster all round. In the first place whoever so runs will be beaten, and will be spotted for life; in the second place, while the race is in progress, he will be under the strongest temptation to trade with the democrats, and to favor the election of certain of their friends to the Legislature; thirdly, I shall be held responsible for it, and Republican members of the Legislature, who are partial to Lovejoy, will, for that, oppose me; and lastly it will in the end lose us the District altogether." [15]

Before the Republican state convention assembled at Springfield on June 16, about ninety-five county meetings had resisted the blandishments of Horace Greeley to make Douglas the Republican senatorial candidate and had scorned the wavering of some Illinois Republicans on this proposal. Greeley, hoping to widen the split over the Kansas question in the Democratic party, supported Douglas. He believed that Douglas acted like a Republican in the debate over the admission of Kansas. Some Illinois Republicans concurred in this belief and were willing to back the Democratic senator. However, Lincoln and his friends acted quickly to suppress such a development on a state scale. Instead, the county meetings emphatically endorsed Lincoln. Among them, the Bureau County Republican convention at Princeton on June 12 resolved that, "Abram [sic] Lincoln is our choice for the seat in the United States Senate, now occupied by Stephen A. Douglas, and . . . the Republican party in this state will be wanting in fidelity to itself if it does not sustain him." When the state convention began on June 16, fifteen hundred delegates full of "electric fire" came into Springfield to demonstrate that Lincoln was their "first and only choice" for the position. The favored candidate was prepared with an acceptance speech, so certain was his nomination.[16]

In the address, Lincoln analyzed the main problem facing the nation as a result of the Nebraska Act. He said that slavery agitation had not only not been stopped by the Act but had "constantly *augmented*." Lincoln did not think it would cease "until a crisis shall have been reached, and passed." He then quoted the biblical prophecy, from Mark, "A house divided against itself cannot stand." He demonstrated that the Dred Scott decision and the Nebraska Act worked together not only to perpetuate slavery in the South but to give it legal sanction anywhere in the country —in all states and all territories. He called for the overthrow of "the power of the present political dynasty," for which purpose, Lincoln declared, it was necessary to maintain the complete unity of the Republicans—"of strange, discordant, and even hostile elements." Lincoln had not been so firm in his anti-extensionist assertions and so bold in his faith in the unity of the Republican party since the lost speech of the Bloomington convention of 1856. The force that had brought him to speak out against the Nebraska Act in 1854, that is, the aggressiveness of the slave power, was still at work. It moved Lincoln as it moved the growing number of Americans fearful of the consequences of slavery imposed upon the whole nation.[17]

When Lincoln tried out the speech on a group of friends the night before its public delivery, he elicited dismay and regret. Someone called it a "d————d fool utterance." A more circumspect listener declared it "ahead of its time." Another felt it would drive away voters fresh from Democratic ranks. Gridley thought it showed "high independent character" but he doubted that it could help Lincoln that year. This "d——d fool utterance" turned out to be the famous "house divided" speech, charged with antislavery thought and sentiment.[18]

Perhaps most objectionable to conservatives and cautious Republicans were Lincoln's direct attacks on President Buchanan, Supreme Court Justice Taney, President Pierce, and Senator Douglas. Lincoln made it quite plain that he suspected those four had worked in concert to bring about the Dred Scott decision. "We find it impossible," Lincoln said, "to not *believe* that Stephen [A. Douglas] and Franklin [Pierce] and Roger [B. Taney] and James [Buchanan] all understood one another from the beginning, and all worked upon a common plan or draft drawn up before the first lick was struck." A conspiracy charge, or one bordering closely on it, was not to be taken lightly. Moreover, Lincoln was taken to mean he favored a division of the country over the slavery issue when he was merely commenting and warning of its dire possibility: "I believe this government cannot endure, permanently half *slave* and half *free*. I do not expect the Union to be *dissolved*—I do not expect the house to *fall*—but I *do* expect it will cease to be divided. It will become *all* one thing, or *all* the other." [19]

Lovejoy embraced Lincoln for the speech. "It sounds like God's truth from the mouth of the prophet," he exclaimed. "Do good? Yes," Lovejoy said expansively, "and shatter the doubtings of thousands of weak and timorous souls who are under the ban of pro-slavery sympathizing and small despots all about us. They can now defy these in the strength of Lincoln's leadership. To the faithful it is a new hope. . . ." [20]

Lovejoy could endorse Lincoln's position, for he and his abolitionist friends had held it for years. It strengthened the growing collaboration between the two men, and could only bode well for the cause of human liberty. One of its immediate practical effects was to fortify the antislavery wing of the Republican

201

party in the state, which, personified by Lovejoy, proved invincible two weeks later in the district.

When the Third Congressional District convention met on June 30 in Joliet, Lovejoy was nominated by acclamation. The courthouse where the delegates met was close to railroad tracks and the deliberations were not made easier by freight trains running and backing directly under the windows. Ringing bells, puffing steam, and rattling wheels led one observer to comment: "Joliet ought to remove either her court house or her railroad." Inside the courthouse, however, the convention was marked by a spirit of party harmony. This meant simply that the Davis forces had been routed and acknowledged their defeat. Apparently they had accepted Lincoln's word and, showing better grace, also accepted Lovejoy as the candidate for reelection. The Lovejoy forces naturally were gratified by the result and predicted his vote would go over twenty-five thousand in November.[21]

Lovejoy rose to quiet the acclaim that greeted his name and made an acceptance speech of rare candor. In it he reviewed his record in the House of Representatives and clarified Republican and abolitionist strategy. Besides its cheering message of party unity, the speech demonstrated Lovejoy's skill and sincerity. Because of its importance in clarifying the relations between radical Republicans and Lincoln, a major portion of it is reproduced here.

Mr. Chairman and Delegates:
I do not rise for the purpose of general discussion. But I should do injustice to my own feelings if I did not express my obligations to you and to those you represent, in having placed my name, in the flattering manner in which you have done it, before the Third Congressional District for re-election. To say that I was not highly gratified at the result would be mere affectation. Gentlemen, I am gratified and thankful

in view of this endorsement of my course in the councils of the Nation, and this highest testimony of the continued confidence of my constituents—thankful beyond the power of expression. I never was much in the habit of parading my feelings before the public. When moved deeply, whether by emotions of joy or sorrow, I am prone to silence. But I cannot help saying my heart, as well as my lips, thanks you for this token of approval and confidence. . . .

As to the words in which the formulas of our faith shall be expressed, it is to me a matter of little consequence. —I believe that the love of freedom and the hatred of oppression undergirds and vitalizes the whole republican movement. The principles of our fathers in regard to human liberty and equality still live in the hearts of their descendants, and will find appropriate expression and suitable exponents. I am content with the Philadelphia platform. I took my place there in '56, and there am content to stand till some future convocation of the Sons of Freedom, clothed with rightful power shall construct a new one. . . .

For myself, I hate slavery with a deathless and earnest hatred, and would like to see it exterminated, as some time by some means it must be. But because I thus feel towards slavery, it does not follow that I shall seek its extermination in unjustifiable modes. It does not follow that because I am opposed to monarchy that therefore I should be in favor of fitting out a naval armament to dethrone Queen Victoria. I am content to fight slavery in modes pointed out in the Constitution, and in those modes only. I do not think, however, that we need to be very apologetic when we tread on the corns of slavery. The defenders of slavery do not act thus. . . .

As to antecedents the less we say the better. The sooner we forget what we have been, and only remember that we are Republicans now, the better. The original and varient elements of our party had to be melted in the crucible of our common cause. I am not in the habit of alluding to my antecedents, not because I am ashamed of them, but because I am proud of them. When I am accosted therefore as I have often been, "Why, you have changed, you are not as radical and rabid as you used to be," my uniform reply has been, "it is no matter who has changed, so that we are all right and all together *now*." But if any are determined to push this heraldic investigation to see whose political escutcheon has a bar sinister upon it, I shall not only not decline, but welcome the search. But still, I repeat it as my earnest and deep conviction, that the sooner we forget that we were old liners in any direction and remember only that we are Republicans now, the better. I am told that fears are expressed about the southern part of the district and the southern part of the state—fears that Lovejoy will frighten away Kentuckians. Now I submit that was tried on in '56 till it was worn out. The southern part of my district has given me a more cordial and unanimous support than the northern, for the reason, probably, that I am better known here than there. —But I can tell you that Lovejoy has no trouble with the Kentuckians, it is the renegade Yankees that support slavery that bother him. I have had many a cordial pressure of the hand and kindly gleam of the eye from those same Kentuckians. After hearing me advocate my principles, and God knows I never concealed them, they have often said to me: "I am just as much of an abolitionist as you are." I do not care to make any allusion to the campaign of 1856 which might have the appearance of boasting, but I must be permitted to say that any one who talks about Lovejoy's loading down the ticket must himself be ignorant of the history of that period, or, presume on the ignorance of others.

It is asked if I am for Lincoln? My reply is that the Republican party was not organized for the benefit of any man—it was not made for Lincoln or Lovejoy, or any one else, but it was organized for the purpose of giving political efficiency to those principles of freedom with which, in theory, our government is instinct, but which have of late in its administration been crucified. I am no hero worshipper. And now I am prepared to say that I am for Lincoln, not because he is an old line Whig—to me this is no objection and it is no commendation—but I am for him because he is a true hearted man, and that, come what will, unterrified by power, unseduced by ambition, he will remain true to the great principles upon which the Republican party is organized. I am for him for the same reasons that you and those you represent, are for me. —Why have the people of this District risen in their majesty, and poured out to the primary meetings in multitudes through streams and mud, and honored me with this unanimous nomination by acclamation? Was this because they wanted to honor me as an individual?

Not that, but because they thought I had been true to those principles which they cherish and love as above all price and above all individuality. For this reason I am for Lincoln, and whoever is in Abraham's bosom cannot I think, be far from the Senate.

And here I wish to express my satisfaction with the resolution approving the course of my colleagues. I can cordially and very sincerely bear my testimony to the constancy, fidelity and ability with which they discharged the duties of their positions. I trust it may not be amiss for me to express the hope that they will be returned.

Friends, brethren, yes, I will say brethren, let us be true to our principles and God will crown our efforts with success.[22]

Lovejoy quickly set off to tour the district. The long campaign had never really been without a break for him. All the striving of the 1840's and even the triumph of 1856 were merely phases in the process of political growth. Now in July, 1858, the flaming orator of the prairies went out on Independence Day to make a speech to his friends and neighbors in Princeton; then on to Bloomington, where he drew large crowds, with two thousand reported at one rally; then to De Witt County in the bottom of the district, where he attracted an overflow crowd at the courthouse. Lovejoy multiplied friends for the Republican party as the antislavery party, even here in the hotbed of his foes.[23] Foremost among the friends, the *Pantagraph* on July 2 declared, "Once more we throw our flag to the breeze with the name of Owen Lovejoy for Congress inscribed thereon."

205

Robert H. Browne had been accurate in his observation about the anti-Lovejoy men after the Bloomington struggle—"chagrined, outwitted, and beaten . . . for the time at least." Their acquiescence at Joliet was short-lived. All through July they met and planned some retaliatory blow against Lovejoy and Lincoln. In their desperation they had allowed abolitionist-hating prejudice to blind them to political reality. They had constructed for themselves and others the implausible doctrine that Lovejoy and Lincoln had captured the Republican party for Negro equality, amalgamation of the races, and the bloodiest abolition their ire could devise. In all this their leader was Judge T. Lyle Dickey of Ottawa, aided by the Joliet *Signal*'s charges that there was a "deal" between Lincoln and Lovejoy. For Dickey apparently there could be no reconciliation with Lovejoy or the modified abolitionism he professed at Joliet and a hundred other places, nor with Lincoln's belief plainly uttered at Springfield. Dickey made a choice—to step out of the Republican party and nominate an "independent" candidate against Lovejoy. In this political adventurism some Republicans joined Democrats in plans to vote for Churchill Coffing, again the standardbearer of the Republican bolters. In the face of Lovejoy's demonstrated popularity in the district, the Democratic candidate, George W. Armstrong, was not a significant threat as such. But Coffing's candidacy could be used by Dickey, who had a following among former Whigs, to split the Republican vote. Thus the decisive contest in the Third District was not to be between Republican and Democrat, but between men of the same party. As Davis observed about the nature of the Republican party, it was "a confederated—not a consolidated party." [24]

When Henry C. Whitney heard of the plot to run Coffing, he wrote Lincoln on July 31 detailing the danger to Lincoln's election. According to Whitney, this was how Dickey's plan would work against Lincoln and Lovejoy: Dickey would wait to see the results of the Bureau and La Salle County conventions to nominate candidates for the state legislature "being such as are prominently talked of and are Abolitionists *sui generis*." Dickey and his friends would then announce the nomination of Coffing. Whitney learned from Dickey what the line of the bolters would be: "The story which Dickey &c will undoubtedly raise (as he had already broached it to me) that if Lovejoy &c get a balance of power of Abolitionists in the [state] Legislature they will demand Lovejoy for the Senate &c will intimidate many republicans & cause them to vote wrong that feel a great preference for you" [Lincoln]. But there is no evidence that Lovejoy ever desired to contest Lincoln for the Senate seat. Whitney implored Lincoln to use his great influence with all the principals: with Lovejoy to urge him to drop David L. Hough of La Salle as a state legislature candidate "and the rest of those well known ultra abolitionists & take up men less obnoxious"; and with Judge Davis to urge him to go into La Salle to speak with Dickey and Coffing.[25]

Whitney's own hatred for abolitionists was plainly expressed. Like Davis, he was considerably upset by Lovejoy's invincibility and professed to work for Lincoln's best interests by opposing the abolitionists. The main trouble with "those stinking abolitionists," according to Whitney, was their "greediness," which might cost Lincoln his election. He thought the avowed abolitionists would vote for pro-Lincoln candidates "who ever they are." He too missed the point of Lovejoy's increasing popularity when he wrote that the abolitionists' "salvation & all their worldly political prospects depend upon their hanging on to the skirts of the Republican Party." It was not so clear, Whitney told Lincoln, that on the other hand Republicans like Coffing and others who hated abolitionism, would support avowed abolitionists.[26]

The complications now setting in as a result of Dickey's and Coffing's maneuvers were too much for Whitney and other old-line Whigs. He strongly urged Lincoln to take a serious hand in this dangerous game: "You may rely upon it that matters in Lovejoy's district must be managed with more shrewdness & less recklessness." [27]

Davis received a copy of Whitney's letter to Lincoln, and the judge sent a confidential letter to Springfield supporting the suggestion that conservative Republicans be nominated for the state legislature in Bureau and La Salle Counties. "The best checkmate to Dickey & Coffing is to nominate unexceptionable men," the judge said. "It may be the class of men like Hough could succeed—But *now* is not the right time to try experiments. The Abolitionists proper have the greater prize in Lovejoy and they ought to be willing to forego the lesser prize until the State is won." Davis also gave Lincoln the impression that he could do nothing with the Lovejoy forces or with the Dickey bolters. He urged Lincoln: "You may know how to operate the thing, or rather to engineer it in Bureau & La Salle—but I don't know how to do it." The judge's consternation was succinctly put in the instruction to Lincoln: "Burn this letter." [28]

The Lincoln and Herndon law office in Springfield became an unusually busy one on August 2 as the senior partner penned several letters. Writing to Whitney, he promised to write immediately to Lovejoy, and to Ottawa's Republican leaders Burton C. Cook and Mayor Joseph Glover. To Cook, Lincoln repeated essentially all that Whitney reported about the scheme afoot in Bureau and La Salle. He asked Cook to keep his eye on the situation, and sent off a similar letter to Lovejoy.[29]

Immediate replies came from Lovejoy and Mayor Glover, the latter speaking for himself and Cook. Both correspondents assured Lincoln that they would resist Dickey's maneuvers and would keep their counties "all right" for Lincoln. Lovejoy did not know of any "Douglas Republicans" in Bureau County "unless it means Douglas men who are becoming Republicans which

I think is the tendency at the present." At any rate Lovejoy had no doubts that his county would send "a clean Republican to the Legislature, whatever his antecedents . . . I mean to try & keep my district all right & the counties connected with it." [30]

A few days later Lovejoy's hand appeared in an editorial of August 12 on "The Conservative Element" published in the *Bureau County Republican*. The main argument was the implicit one that Dickey was threatening Lovejoy *and* Lincoln. The editorial expressed confidence that the conservatives could not defeat Lovejoy. The editorial scorned Dickey's accusation against the two men, that "the Republican party of Illinois unfortunately has passed into the control of the revolutionary element of the old Abolition party, and those who have adopted and paid court to that element."

The *Republican*'s editor asserted a week later in an article on "Conservatism" that the abolitionists did not create the issue of slavery. He asked, "Did Elihu Burritt's World Peace Congress [in 1851] bring on the Crimean War?"

For the third week in succession, the editor, still hammering away at Dickey, ran an editorial in the August 26 issue entitled "The Original Sorehead." It was hoped, said the editor, the judge would be nominated by the Democrats' Third Congressional District convention. "We know of no other man we would rather see beaten," he teased.

As the last of these acid baths was being administered, the big contest in the state for Senate office had already begun in the debate between Lincoln and Douglas. In this series of verbal tangles Douglas adopted the abolitionist-baiting line of the "soreheads" and tried to smear Lincoln with the poison of guilt by association with Owen Lovejoy.

On August 21, 1858, streams of Illinoisans converged on the pleasant green town of Ottawa, set at the junction of the Fox and Illinois rivers eighty-four miles southwest of Chicago. The occasion was the first of seven formal debates between the Democratic and Republican candidates in the forthcoming senatorial contest. The arrival of the two men was hailed with brass band music, cannonades, and resounding cheers. Douglas's four-horse carriage was escorted into town by a cavalcade. Lincoln, when he stepped off the Chicago train, was led to a carriage embellished with evergreens and escorted to the home of Mayor Glover. "Vanity Fair never boiled with madder enthusiasm," wrote the Chicago *Press and Tribune* man on the scene.[31]

As Lincoln and Douglas took their seats on the stand in the town square they were flanked by such notables as the district's congressman, Owen Lovejoy, the mayor, and the aged Indian Chief Shabonna. Before them were gathered between twelve and fifteen thousand enthusiasts and partisans.

Douglas seized the offensive as he opened the debate at 2:30 and struck out at Lincoln and Lovejoy. He threw up to Lincoln the charge that he and Trumbull had conspired in 1854 to "abolitionize" their parties and deliver them to Lovejoy and his radical abolitionist colleagues. He further accused Lincoln of surrendering to Lovejoy by accepting entirely the radicals' program of 1854. Finally the senator charged that Lovejoy had pressed Lincoln for an antislavery commitment in exchange for votes of anti-Nebraska men in the February, 1855, contest for United States Senator. The Little Giant interlarded these accusations with Republican-baiting, belaboring the phrase "Black Republican." His whole performance seemed intended to throw Lincoln off guard and to bowl over his supporters by pitching the campaign into the narrow confines of intraparty skullduggery. Suppose Lincoln admitted the charges? He would thus be eliminated as a force in politics, Douglas might have reasoned. Suppose Lincoln denied the charges? He would then have alienated the strong antislavery wing centered around Lovejoy and the old-time Liberty and Free Soil men. The new party would be split, and Douglas could once again safely rule the state's political life.

In the course of the debate Douglas read out the platform of Lovejoy and his radical coworkers who had gathered at Springfield in October, 1854. He attempted to show that this became the platform of the Republican party now facing him, that it was an ultraradical one and *ipso facto* evil. To the senator's dismay and chagrin, and some anger, the crowd cheered each of the points of the program as he read them. Douglas snapped back, "Now, gentlemen, your Black Republicans have cheered every one of those propositions [again the crowd yelled its approval] and yet I venture to say that you cannot get Mr. Lincoln to come out and say that he is now in favor of each one of them."

Lincoln rose to make his hour-and-a-half reply, as agreed. The tall lawyer, speaking in his high-pitched voice, denied outright that he and Trumbull schemed to divide the Senate positions. As for the resolutions, Lincoln could truthfully say he "never had anything to do with them." He had made his famous withdrawal to Tazewell. Lovejoy was there on the platform to corroborate his statement. Furthermore, Lincoln pointed out, when Lovejoy went into the legislature in 1855 he "complained of me that I had told all the old Whigs in his district that the old Whig party was good enough for them, and some of them voted against him because I told them so." Lovejoy was forced to hold his tongue although he too had been indicted by Douglas. In the audience, however, there were dozens of antislavery men not governed by the fine points of platform etiquette, and they heckled the senator.

At one point while Douglas was speaking Lincoln himself, now angered, interrupted caustically. Two Republican committeemen yanked Lincoln away from the front of the stand, one of them saying, "What are you making such a fuss for?" A little later when Lincoln interrupted he was again pulled back by someone on the platform. One eyewitness years later recalled that Douglas "was occasionally coarse in his expressions" and at one juncture accused Lincoln of deliberately misstating something. Douglas roared, "I will bring him to his milk." Lincoln jumped to his feet, a stern expression on his face. This time Lovejoy grabbed Lincoln's coat, pulled him back, and "whispered something that induced him to take his seat." Meanwhile Douglas spun out the theme of Lincoln at the "Black Republican party" convention. It could not be denied, notwithstanding the protests of the crowd, that the senator presented a powerful case that might disconnect moderate antislavery men from the Republicans.[32]

In the evening the Republicans capped the day with a noisy rally of their own. A band led them in a procession to Mayor Glover's house to carry off his guests, Lincoln and Lovejoy. The procession then banged and tooted on to the courthouse for "one of the most enthusiastic meetings that was ever gotten up." Lovejoy was loudly called for. He stepped forward in the balmy summer evening, took off his collar and cravat, opened his vest and shirt and went at it. The friendly Chicago *Press and Tribune* correspondent said he had never listened to a speech "so full of eloquence and magnetic power." The Chicago *Journal* correspondent called it "one of his characteristic sledge-hammer efforts." Both writers were so exultant that neither one wrote down what Lovejoy said. They were carried away by the excitement of the evening, just as the masses, solidly Republican, formed a torchlight procession after Lovejoy spoke and paraded the streets with loud "hurrahs for Lincoln" until late that night. The Republicans were satisfied with the day and predicted victory. "The general opinion," said the Chicago *Journal*, "is that in the Third Congressional District, at least, Douglas is 'a dead cock in the pit.' "[33]

Realistic politician that he was, Lincoln could not rest easy after the Ottawa encounter. He campaigned down into the central and western counties, then made his way back up to La Salle in the Lovejoy district. On August 27 he was scheduled to go up to Freeport in the northern tier of the state for his second debate with Douglas. Stopping in Mendota in the northwest corner of La Salle County on the night before the debate, Lincoln entertained about a dozen men who urgently requested that he drop the questions he proposed to ask Douglas the next day. David Davis brought Leonard Swett along. Although Swett was reported to have been silent during this Mendota meeting, he also was reported to have told Lincoln after the Freeport debate, "I think it complicates the situation, and will not add to your strength for the senatorship." Robert H. Browne wrote that "none of our abolition section were expected" at Mendota and seats were not provided. But Lovejoy sent a message to Lincoln that day saying, "The cause is prospering. I believe a Lincoln man will be elected from every legislative district in my Congressional district. Stand firm on the Springfield speech" [the "house divided" speech]. Browne, who may or may not have been present at Mendota, wrote that Lincoln's "auditors and comforters" were pained to hear from Lovejoy and "made grimaces at the mention of his name." [34]

Douglas undoubtedly knew the strength of Lovejoy, Farnsworth, and the antislavery elements in the northern counties and reserved his special maledictions for them in the heart of their territory. If the Democratic candidate could throw shadows of doubt on the Lovejoy-Lincoln connection, he could split the Republicans. His strength in the southern counties would aid him. Besides, an outdated apportionment of seats in the legislature would work in his favor. The Freeport debate thus presented Douglas a tantalizing opportunity.

Douglas, stung twice by Lincoln's opening speech, unleashed a barrage at Lovejoy in the course of his reply. He portrayed Lovejoy as the evil genius guiding Lincoln and Trumbull. Douglas read verbatim what he believed to be the Springfield resolutions of Lovejoy and his colleagues. But what he read turned out to be a set of resolutions passed at a convention held in Aurora, Illinois, in August, 1854. Truly a radical antislavery platform, most of it was never again adopted by the Lovejoy group of abolitionists, certainly not at Springfield two months later. Whatever their real desires, the radicals had cautiously committed themselves at Springfield to a moderate program of nonextension. Douglas had unknowingly overreached himself in attempting to tie Lincoln hand and foot to Lovejoy.[35]

Douglas pressed on: "Lovejoy [before the vote for senator in 1855] insisted on laying down certain principles by which to govern the party." Lovejoy's three antislavery resolutions of February 6, 1855, were then read aloud to the huge crowd. The mass approval of the resolutions was signified by shouts of "good, good," and by roaring cheers, causing the Little Giant considerable discomfort. But by his own words he canceled the charge against Lovejoy. He demonstrated that the 1855 legislature approved only one of the resolutions, and that by a close vote of 41 to 32. The other two, more far-reaching in their antislavery intent, were defeated 40 to 33, and 35 to 47. Douglas asserted that those who voted for Lovejoy also voted for Lincoln in that earlier Senate contest. Yet Douglas failed to see or explain the reluctance of men supposedly controlled by "Parson Lovejoy" to sanction all his recommendations.

Lincoln demolished the senator's criminations by showing that in 1854 and 1855 anti-Nebraska men in the northern part of the state were for strong antislavery measures. The resolutions that Douglas had read "were local [to Aurora] and did not spread over the whole state." Proceeding with his usual careful argument, Lincoln pointed out that when the Republican party was formed in 1856 the diverse elements did agree upon a common platform. But in doing so, Lincoln asserted, those (like Lovejoy) who held "more extreme notions" yielded for practical purposes

214

of organization. Douglas's "blackmail" charges could only fall flat after this rebuttal.

Still angered by the wild accusations made at Ottawa, Lovejoy longed to confront the senator on the platform at Freeport, but the set nature of the debates precluded such a scene. He sat through the second debate, again keeping a disciplined silence even when Douglas argued more against Lovejoy than against Lincoln. But after the debate, when Benjamin Shaw, a Republican editor, suggested that Lovejoy speak, the congressman was more than ready. Someone fetched a dry-goods box and set it up as an improvised platform in front of the town's hostelry, the Brewster House. Earlier Douglas had asked Lincoln if he would return fugitive slaves. Lincoln's stand was well known—he did not believe in the unconditional repeal of the Fugitive Slave Law —but he treated Douglas's question with silence. This was the question that Lovejoy pounced upon, and in "scathing philippics" from the perch on the dry-goods box he lashed Douglas and others who voted for the slave-catcher's law.[36]

Between debates with Lincoln, Douglas continued to hammer at Lovejoy. At Joliet in September, Douglas tried again to force a wedge between Lovejoy and Lincoln. He asked the "Black Republicans": "How can you expose yourselves to the ridicule and contempt of mankind by professing to be fighting for principle, and yet supporting Mr. Lincoln with one set of principles, and Lovejoy and Farnsworth with another?" [37]

Lovejoy's presence on the speaker's stand inspired the reporter for the Democratic Chicago *Times* to make an improbable charge that he acted in the rudest, most brazen manner.[38]

Back home the *Republican* in Princeton reported that Lovejoy had been on the platform by invitation and that he had maintained his dignity throughout the meeting. Douglas, the *Republican* writer said, had been insulting.[39]

Lovejoy's impassioned response this time came at an overflow meeting in Young's Hall at Joliet in the evening. Peter Stewart, a beloved Scotsman and a captain of the Underground Railroad, introduced the congressman. Lovejoy spoke for two and half hours, delighting his audience, but the speech went unrecorded.[40]

Pending the third debate between the senatorial candidates at Jonesboro on September 15, Lincoln and Lovejoy continued to campaign unceasingly against Douglas and the "soreheads" Dickey and Coffing. Both leading Republicans made a grand harvest on September 8 in Paris, Edgar County, just south of Lovejoy's district. State Treasurer James Miller and Lovejoy came into Paris on the morning train, somewhat unexpectedly. The curiosity with which some of the town's most respectable citizens regarded Lovejoy was mixed with some terror, according to the Chicago *Press and Tribune* correspondent. "Evidently many of them expected to find him wearing horns and a tail," he ventured. But after this reception Lovejoy, in the absence of Lincoln, took the stand and spoke for half an hour. At this point a noisy procession marched in with "Old Abe," who had just arrived on the three o'clock train. Lovejoy yielded the stand, and Lincoln held forth for about two hours. His concluding words brought three resounding cheers. Someone proposed an adjournment till evening, when Lovejoy and Richard Oglesby would speak. But the crowd loudly cried down that idea and insisted that Lovejoy go on speaking "and pitch in right smart."

Lovejoy did that for an hour, with frequent interruptions from the crowd. "If that's what they call Abolitionism, I'm an Abolitionist," was the unexpected reaction of Republicans as well as of old-line Whigs, the *Press and Tribune* reported. Lovejoy pleased the community so much he was asked to speak again in the evening. This time a half-hour on the platform at the courthouse permitted Lovejoy to sway even some hard-bitten American party men who admitted their agreement with Lovejoy. "One of the best speeches that ever came out of a man's mouth," was the reply of one of them to a reporter's question. "No more Abolition than I've believed in all my life." [41]

One Dickey supporter recorded his sour rejection of Lovejoy. In a letter to W. H. L. Wallace written on September 8, A. Wardlow informed him that the abolitionists had "backed down and come to the conclusion" that it was best not to monopolize all the offices. They had, Wardlow wrote, nominated an old-line Whig from Peoria for the state Senate. Wardlow was not sure of the man's position but insisted only that he would not support Lovejoy for the United States Senate in 1860. That Lovejoy might be Trumbull's successor in the Senate was an idea Wardlow attributed to the abolitionists. However, not even the *Bureau County Republican* had suggested the possibility. Yet so far had fear of Lovejoy gone that at least one of Dickey's supporters could believe and then repeat the political guess. Wardlow required only that the Peoria nominee "not . . . go for Lovejoy." [42]

The great debates between Lincoln and Douglas ran on into September and October, but Lovejoy played no part in them after the Freeport engagement. During that debate and afterward Douglas was forced to state that slavery could be rejected by the people of a territory before it became a state. This contradicted the Dred Scott decision and drove a wedge between Douglas and Southern Democrats. Lincoln succeeded not only in this master stroke but in disproving Douglas's accusations that Lincoln was a mere tool in the hands of Lovejoy and the radical abolitionists. Moreover, Douglas was forced to state his extremely unattractive notion that the Founding Fathers established the nation for whites only. Yet Lincoln's lack of knowledge about the races of mankind led him to concede the inferiority of the Negro. His saving grace, however, was a conscientious desire to eliminate, at least restrict, the spread of slavery. Douglas did not care whether slavery was voted up or down. Lincoln cared very much. In this

217

he was indeed acting like Lovejoy, or vice versa. The important point was not who followed whom but whether men of good will acted *together* to rid the nation of slavery, a distinct evil. Lovejoy carried the message across the prairie counties in his own fashion, as Lincoln did in his. Lincoln, for example, insisted in the final debate at Alton on October 15 that the real issue was the wrong of slavery. Lovejoy likewise put this matter foremost in his speeches on the campaign trail, as he had in his speeches on the floor of the House of Representatives: the paramount issue is slavery.

In spite of conservatives like Dickey, Lovejoy enjoyed prominence during Lincoln's campaign as much in his own right as in the reflected glory from the senatorial candidate. Dickey's machinations, Davis's earlier table-thumping, and Douglas's maledictions against Lovejoy and Negroes were to no avail. The slavery question persisted in being the most important before the nation and the state of Illinois.

Lovejoy's victory, which had been predicted early, was significant. While Elihu B. Washburne's winning vote fell in the First District by 2,000 and Farnsworth's declined in the Second Congressional District, Lovejoy increased his margin over his 1856 triumph. His majority then was 6,069; now, after Coffing had dropped out of the race in October, Lovejoy's margin over Armstrong was 7,375, with gains scored in every county in the district. The Bloomington *Pantagraph* was especially gratified that he had gained in the southern counties, notably in De Witt, where he had run behind Osgood by 105 votes in 1856. Lovejoy's total vote in 1858 was 22,373; his Democratic opponent Armstrong polled 14,998.[43] If Republican candidates in other districts could have matched Lovejoy's gain, Lincoln's election might have been assured, for among their other accomplishments the Republicans had won statewide majorities for their gubernatorial candidate. But because of the antiquated apportionment law which in effect negated the popular vote in the state as a whole, the Douglas Democrats commanded fifty-four votes in the state legislature to Lincoln's forty-six. The Democratic senator's victory was nevertheless gained at a considerable price. His answers to Lincoln's second question at the Freeport debate alienated the Southern wing of his party and deepened the Democratic split. On the other hand Lincoln received favorable national attention, which contributed to his nomination and election to the Presidency in 1860. Nevertheless in 1858 Lincoln and his friends were sad and frustrated by his failure to win the Senate seat.

One who refused to keep his anger and disappointment to himself was Henry C. Whitney, Lincoln's circuit-riding colleague. He had been in Springfield on January 5, 1859, the day the Illinois General Assembly elected Stephen A. Douglas to the United States Senate. For Whitney, as for many Republicans, the day was depressing, the more so as the Democrats went out "to paint the town very red." Whitney, Leonard Swett, and Augustus M. Herrington found themselves in a room at the St. Nicholas Hotel and, commiserating over Lincoln's defeat, each offered his analysis. Herrington was for uniting all Illinoisans regardless of party for Douglas for President in 1860. Swett was disgusted, and tired of backing a loser.

Whitney, incensed, left the others and went over to Lincoln and Herndon's office to grieve with the younger partner. On his arrival he found Lincoln instead. Whitney upbraided Lincoln for "adhering to Lovejoy, and the Abolitionists; and thus courting defeat." Lincoln, sad and spiritless, according to Whitney, showed him the election figures of Lovejoy's victories in 1856 and 1858. "It is the people, and not me, who want Lovejoy," Lincoln said, "The people have not consulted me on the subject. . . ."[44]

11

His Reputation Is National

"Nobody can intimidate me."
—*Owen Lovejoy*

Lovejoy went back to Washington in the winter of 1858 to complete his first two-year term in Congress more confident than ever of the political course he was steering. The voters of the Third Congressional District had sealed their faith in Lovejoy by electing him to a second term, which would start in December, 1859, the 36th Congress of the United States.

Eighteen seats in the House were lost by the Democrats in the 1858 elections. Northern voters, resentful of the Administration policy with respect to Kansas, swung over to the Republicans and the Anti-Nebraska Lecompton Democrats. In October, Indiana, Pennsylvania, and Ohio sent an overwhelmingly Republican group to the House. Administration favorite J. Glancy Jones was rejected in Pennsylvania, but Thaddeus Stevens was elected as a Republican. In November, New England voted a solid Republican ticket and New York, New Jersey, Michigan, and Wisconsin also voted Republican. However, Administration losses were caused not only by its Kansas policy but by its position on the tariff and homestead issues, and the Republicans returning in December, 1858, for the final term of the 35th Congress took heart from these signs and pressed their advantage. Lovejoy, for one, hastened to Washington to play his part in badgering the hurt Buchanan Administration.

Early in the session he playfully and sardonically opposed the Administration's consular and diplomatic bill, observing that it would be better if the wastrel emissaries of the nation in foreign cities were recalled and replaced by men who could at least understand the languages of the countries in which they were stationed.[1]

Lovejoy also objected to transferring the office of Indian affairs from the Interior department to the War department. He announced he would never by his vote "give control of the Indian tribes into the hands of the War department, whose tender mercies are cruelty, so far as the Indians are concerned." This proved to be one of many agile thrusts at the army, which Lovejoy considered to be inept, cruel, corrupt, and unnecessarily expensive to the country. Not least of his objections to the military was the charge he made that it was being used as an instrument of the slaveowners' imperialist objectives.[2]

His battle with the army was a continuation of the exposures made in the first session of the 35th Congress. Scathing remarks punctuated his speech against the army appropriation bill on February 18, 1859: "The genius of our country is that of peace; . . . we do not want an army, as the despotisms of the Old World do, to sustain our Government; and, consequently, that we ought to reduce our Army to the lowest possible amount, and depend upon it simply as a nucleus around which volunteers could gather in time of actual war. We do not want an Army to be used in unjust and aggressive wars; and, whenever there is really just occasion for war, hundreds of thousands of citizen soldiers will rush to the battle-field. . . . That is all the Army we need. Why, sir, every year we grind out a grist of officers, and they come out of the hopper with epaulets on their shoulders, and green and red stripes up and down each side of their pants." (Laughter greeted this remark.) ". . . the head of our Army [the officers] has swelled out of all proportion to the body, and become monstrous; and we keep up this establishment of privates on purpose to make places for the officers ground out to order annually." [3]

Earlier in the debate that day Lovejoy had offered an amendment to reduce the army and have it shorn of frontier duty. For him, this activity was one of its most mischievous, and he said so at some length, much to the discomfort of the Administration's defenders. Although his amendment was defeated, he struck at a sore spot.

"I am opposed to this whole idea of protecting our frontiers by the Army of the United States. . . . Often wars are got up on purpose to have the Army ordered to the out-posts, in order to raise the price of town-lots and of provisions. . . .

"I protest against this use of the Army. That was the main use of the army which was ordered to Utah. I made the remark here a year ago, when the deficiency bill was up for consideration, and when we heard an Alpine ululation all through the Hall, careering through the galleries, about the rascalities of the Mormons, and that they should be exterminated; that they were not fit to live because they preferred white concubines, while in other parts of the country the concubinage of the blacks was preferred. But as soon as the ten million [dollar] deficiency bill passed, all this outcry ceased; and there has not been a word uttered on the floor of the House since about the rascalities of the Mormons—not a word. I appeal to the members of the House if that is not the fact. Soldiers were ordered out to Utah. We paid $10,000,000 for this service; and one firm made $1,500,000, and now generously proposes to give up the contract, if we pay for all the old wagons and oxen. I want to hit the Army between the horns, to cut it down to the skeleton, and hang it up, so that it may afford a model for the study of comparative anatomy of an army. All we need of an army is the engineer department." [4]

Lovejoy was joined in the opposition by Benjamin Stanton of Ohio; Linus B. Comins of Massachusetts; and Philemon Bliss of Ohio. Comins peppered the discussion with a quotation from the Vicksburg, Mississippi, *Whig* about the almost comical disproportion of officers to men in the army: "We have no privates . . . ," the newspaper lamented. Reuben Davis of Mississippi was so enraged that he blurted out an irrelevancy that was also a revealing glimpse into the intentions of some Southerners: "we are ready to defend ourselves without arms against any force the northern states could send against us with arms." Bliss agreed with Lovejoy's opposition to the use of troops on the frontier and added his own objection to use of the army as a *posse comitatus*.

Three days later, on February 21, Owen Lovejoy delivered one of the "scathing philippics" against slavery that made him famous in his time. The speech went into the record under the title "Fanaticism of the Democratic Party," but its contents were aimed at the conscience of the whole nation.

Beginning with an appraisal of President Buchanan's message to Congress, Lovejoy ranged over a wide array of questions related to slavery. On efforts to create a *mare americanum* in the Caribbean, Lovejoy had this to say: "So also in regard to Cuba. The *real* object of its purchase is not the *avowed* one . . . but in spite of all, we are asked to purchase this island, and to place $30,000,000 in the hands of the Executive, to begin the negotiations—that is, to buy up the officials!

"No, it is not for the benefit of commerce, nor to guard against invasion, that we are asked to purchase Cuba; but it is for the benefit of slave-breeders and human-flesh mongers. . . ."

223

Lovejoy pointed to the President's message—"you will find its entire texture to be slavery. Every topic is discussed with reference to its bearings on the subject of slavery. And yet the Democrats, with an impudence that challenges our admiration for its sublimity, turn to us, and say, 'Do not agitate the subject.'"

The Illinois representative grappled with another phase of what he called the "fanaticism of the Democratic party"—"It identifies slavery with the nation, and especially with the South." He had always been "reckoned as ultra, and extreme as most on the subject," Lovejoy said, "and yet no one has ever heard me say anything against the South." He had been careful always to attack slavery and not the South. Again he defined his method: "I propose to assail [slavery] only in those modes justified by the Constitution."

Democrats had taunted Republicans with being merely a sectional party. Lovejoy replied by asking the right to speak freely in the South. "Allow us free access to the minds of the non-slaveholders of the South, and in one year we would have more Republicans votes, in proportion, in the slave states, than there were Democratic votes in the free states." It seemed a boast, but beneath Lovejoy's utterance was his awareness of the Republicans' speedy growth since 1856. His own startling successes among southern Illinois voters gave him additional confidence. The speech was packed with emotion and with lengthy arguments in refutation and contradiction of a whole catalogue of slaveowners' justifications for their system.

Dozens of newspapers reprinted Lovejoy's sensational address to the House. The Vermont *Caledonian* and the Concord, New Hampshire, *Democrat*, as well as the Rockford, Illinois, *Republican* reprinted the speech. As soon as the text was received in Greeley's office at the New York *Tribune*, compositors went to work picking the type out of the cases to set Lovejoy's words. When the papers came off the press, Lovejoy became a national name in homes and farms and offices across the North, a name to consider with fellow politicians Douglas and Lincoln.

Lovejoy further enhanced his national reputation by expressing his attitude toward German-born people in the nation. While at home in Princeton he had been queried by the editor of the Illinois *Staats-Zeitung* about the Massachusetts Republicans who were then supporting a law discriminating against the Germans. The proposed change in the immigration and naturalization laws would deny the ballot to foreign-born persons or the right to hold office until two years after their naturalization had been completed here. Lovejoy's letter of May 18 affirmed his belief that the naturalization laws should remain as they were. He clearly opposed any change that would prejudice the rights of adopted citizens. A similar view had been expressed by Lincoln in a letter to another leader of the German community. The implications for the next national election undoubtedly entered the thinking of Lincoln and Lovejoy in taking these positions for justice. They were, after all, practical politicians.[5]

Already by May, 1859, speculation over the 1860 presidential candidates had begun. The Lake County *Citizen* of Waukegan, Illinois, although not in Lovejoy's district, tipped its hat in Lovejoy's direction by calling for a Republican candidate solid on the only important issue, slavery. In Princeton, the *Bureau County Republican* took up the *Citizen*'s lead. Its editorial of May 6, reserving the Vice-Presidency for Lovejoy, compared Lincoln and their own favorite. The editors still hugged Liberty party doctrine and discounted Lincoln for being too deeply imbued with conservative Whiggery. Lovejoy, they proclaimed, was bold, enthusiastic, and without equivocation on the subject of slavery. His reputation was national, they boasted with some justification, for Lovejoy in Congress was reaching a national audience.

A sad exception to the shower of praise at this time was an

open letter from Owen's brother Joseph, who had collaborated with him in publishing the memoir of the martyred Elijah Lovejoy. Joseph had traveled far from the ideas he and his brothers held in 1837 and 1838. Once a temperance advocate and champion of the poor and the imprisoned, Joseph C. Lovejoy became for a short time a spokesman for the special interests of liquor merchants, according to the *Free West* in 1855. Four years later, in March, 1859, his open letter was printed as a pamphlet attacking Owen. Opponents of the congressman had published it, with introductory remarks by the editor of the Washington *Union*, a Democratic newspaper patently hostile to Owen Lovejoy.[6]

Joseph's letter was an undisguised effort to embarrass Owen and to defend the South's system of slavery. Joseph confessed, "It was one of the early dreams of my early life, that the conditions of mankind might be greatly improved by sudden political changes. . . . I am compelled to cancel many things that I have said on the subject of slavery. . . . I might have once said what, or nearly what, you have said in your late speech in Congress. . . . But my convictions at the present time are, not only that the slaveholders have a complete vindication of their present position, but they are entitled to be looked upon as benefactors to the country and to the human race."

To cap his defection from the antislavery cause, Joseph wrote, "American slavery is a redemption, a deliverance from African heathenism." He attempted to shore up this assertion with a repetition of the meanest racist attacks on the Negro.

How Owen reacted, or whether he even stooped to reply to this Democratic maneuver, is unrecorded. But any man would recoil from the kind of closing Joseph put to his letter: "You may possibly succeed (but heaven prevent you) in the attempt you are making . . . but the day of your success would be the hour of your [the Republican party's] dissolution." The document was signed, "affectionately, your brother, Joseph C. Lovejoy."

The long recess of the House gave Lovejoy an opportunity to spend the summer with his large family and occupy himself with the management of his farm. It was one of the largest and richest in the vicinity of Princeton, and Lovejoy had continued the stock breeding begun by the Denhams. A visitor in 1858 had found it "in a highly cultivated state . . . free from weeds as its owner's mind is from political errors." The thousand acres of level fields provided grains and corn for feed as well as for market, and also produce for the family larder. In October, 1859, Lovejoy took time out to compose a lengthy poem extolling the farmer and delivered it before the Bureau County Agricultural Society. The poetaster spoke through the mouth of the professional farmer, to "My fellow farmers, brothers of the plow."

> Serf, slave, and villain, are the terms applied
> To those who labor, sons of pride.
> But here the laborer is a man of wealth,
> The bone and sinew of the commonwealth;
> Invested with the franchise of election,
> He spurns control, and scoffs at all subjection.

There followed a paean to the soil, to plowing, to methods of farming. He injected his conception of money into the catalogue of thoughts:

> Good money by this must be silver or gold,
> Either white, or else yellow, hard, solid and cold.[7]

As fall was turning the fields and woods to browns and grays, Lovejoy went to New York to confer with Republican leaders and antislavery men. Charles Sumner had returned from a visit abroad, where he had gone partly to restore his health after Brooks's assault, partly to meet with friends in England. Lovejoy joined Schuyler Colfax, Horace Greeley, Charles A. Dana, Oliver Johnson, and others in inviting the senator to make a public address either at the New York Academy of Music or at Plymouth Church in Brooklyn. The signers of the letter of invitation congratulated Sumner on his return and told him that thousands of friends and admirers "watched your health for years," and "would like to meet you face to face." Sumner apparently was unable to fulfill the plans of his well-wishers.[8]

About a month later the 36th Congress convened amid national excitement over the execution of John Brown. His abortive attack on Harpers Ferry in October had failed to begin an anticipated slave insurrection. Nevertheless the bold stroke by Brown brought him to international fame as a liberator and roused fear, anger, and hatred in the hearts of the slaveowners. In great panic, the government of Virginia hastened to do away with Brown lest, living, he might inspire and lead a revolution of Negroes and whites against the slaveowners. He was rushed to trial on the day of his indictment and at first was denied the right to engage his own counsel. Only six days later he was found guilty of conspiracy with slaves to rebel; murder; and treason; the last an impossible crime since Brown was not a citizen or resident of Virginia. But the verdict of death was pronounced on Brown and the twenty-one Negro and white young men who shared his idealism and were his meager liberating army at Harpers Ferry.[9]

John Brown standing on the gallows at Charlestown, Virginia (now West Virginia), on December 2, 1859, made a dignified figure, serene in the moment of approaching death. He had been called mad, but he had seen with unusual clarity where slavery was leading the country. In the solitude of his jail cell he had written his prophecy, and on the morning of his execution he handed it to the jail guard: "I, John Brown am now quite *certain* that the crimes of this *guilty land:* will never be purged *away;* but with Blood. I had *as I now think:* vainly flattered myself that without *very much* bloodshed; it might be done." At the moment of his execution bells were rung in Chicago, Illinois, and in Concord, New Hampshire, and in dozens of other Northern cities and towns. Guns were shot off in salutes in many cities. Crowded public protest meetings assembled in others. Garrison spoke to a packed Tremont Temple in Boston. At Albany an all-day demonstration was held. Ministers like Dr. George B. Cheever in New York and Reverend William H. Furness in Philadelphia spoke to large audiences. Black bunting hung from buildings in Cleveland while five thousand people listened to a prominent churchman. America's best minds expressed their sympathy with Brown's ideas and praised his character. For Thoreau, Brown was an angel of light, and for Emerson, he was a new saint. William Cullen Bryant wrote, "History . . . will record his name among those of its martyrs and heroes." [10]

Momentarily appeased by the hanging of John Brown, Southern leaders enjoyed an uneasy success. Governor Henry A. Wise of Virginia had panicked, and so had most Southern leaders. They transformed their discomfiture over Brown into hatred of Northern men in general, and turned their most intense animosity on the Republican party and its leaders. Emotion was stirred to such a point that a number of Southern congressmen went armed with pistols and knives into the House of Representatives ready to threaten and issue open challenges to duel. They were haunted by the idea of John Brown, for he also reminded them of the slave revolts of Nat Turner and Denmark Vesey, symbols of what the slaves could do if organized and aroused to armed struggle for their freedom. Some of the Southern spokesmen became quarrelsome and exceedingly self-conscious guardians of "the peculiar institution." When antislavery or anti-extensionist Republicans spoke in the House, Southern representatives replied angrily and revealed the insecurity under which they lived. The institution of slavery was under siege on the economic front, inasmuch as the industrial and capitalist North was rapidly moving along, with the free farmer class, to domination of the national marketplace. On the other hand the plantation system of production grew at a much slower rate, which provided the base of the slaveowners' fears. And in the political arena the new Congress supplied obvious cause for further Southern worry, for the Republicans who would dominate it came on a platform pledged to restrict slavery and advance the interests of industry and Northern agriculture.

Sumner returned to his seat in the Senate fully prepared to legislate the end of slavery. Antislavery men among the one hundred and nine Republicans in the lower house were Owen Lovejoy; Thaddeus Stevens and Galusha A. Grow of Pennsylvania; Justin S. Morrill of Vermont; Elihu B. Washburne of Illinois; and Schuyler Colfax of Indiana.

On the first day of the session J. B. Clark of Missouri moved to disqualify candidates for the speakership who had signed a public endorsement of Hinton Rowan Helper's *Impending Crisis of the South* (1857). This book denounced Southern leadership and was considered the work of a renegade, inasmuch as its author was a Southerner. Helper was not truly antislavery, but his book's marshaling of facts on the slave economy struck at the exposed sensitivity of the South to its weakness vis-à-vis Northern capitalism. Republicans had endorsed the book as a confirmation of their charges against the South's leaders. Among the signers of the endorsement were sixty-eight members of the House of Representatives, with Owen Lovejoy and Schuyler Colfax leading the list. The intent of Clark's motion became comically obvious when it appeared that all the Republican aspirants for Speaker had signed the Helper endorsement. The House rejected Clark's motion, but a bitterly fought and long-drawn-out parliamentary battle was thus begun.[11]

230

The Democrats obstructed almost every motion concerning the speakership. They created confusion, delayed voting, and harangued endlessly. The leading Republican candidate for the important position was John Sherman of Ohio, who could get no more than 111 votes when 114 were necessary to elect him. Having no real chance to elevate a Democrat, the Southerners hoped to create such confusion that weak Republicans would finally swing away from Sherman in order to break the deadlock. Republican strategy was to allow conservatives to go out front and speak for the party. Radicals like Lovejoy remained in the background in order to rob the Southern fire-eaters of a chance to entrap the House in violent conflict.

Lovejoy was convinced that the Republicans would prevail in this great test of their strength as the challenging party. In a letter to Henry Asbury of Quincy, Illinois, he wrote: "Yours of the 20th containing prescriptions for the disunion democrats was duly received & shown to my colleagues. We hope to give them a Republican Speaker which may possibly *relieve them* & then a President & *that* I think will cure them. This cry of disunion has become a miserable farce. They have been croaking it for the last forty years as it began in 1820." [12]

On the day that Lovejoy was predicting success in capturing the speakership for the Republicans, Sherman withdrew from the contest. He yielded to William Pennington of New Jersey, a dark-horse candidate, who was elected on February 1 when the forty-fourth ballot was taken. A former Whig and a supporter of the Fugitive Slave Law, Pennington nevertheless satisfied the Republicans by his determined stand on blocking slavery in the territories. He threw the advantage to the Republicans in organizing the House committees. John Sherman became head of the Ways and Means Committee, Owen Lovejoy was made chairman of the Committee on Public Lands, and Galusha Grow headed the Committee on Territories. The latter two were prominent for their advocacy of homestead legislation. Justin S. Morrill's talents were to be displayed in writing tariff laws as a member of Sherman's powerful committee. Elihu B. Washburne was appointed chairman of the strategic Commerce Committee, and Colfax was named chairman of the Committee on Post Offices.

After two months of wasteful struggle the House at last was able to begin its work of lawmaking. Sherman proclaimed a sense of relief and security in the land. Even Democrats seemed to acquiesce and settle down to business. But in the South fresh threats of secession were already sufficiently loud to interrupt any progress on the economic issues that dominated the calendar in the House of Representatives: tariffs, internal improvements, Pacific railroad bills, homestead legislation. Such proposals were favorable to the emerging capitalists who would benefit from them, as would the nation in general, according to the spokesmen of industry. As measure after measure won approval in the House, Southern fears grew. Only their control of the Senate and the Presidency saved the Southerners from utter defeat.

Lovejoy's part in the Republican offensive was to introduce and fight for a homestead bill. On March 26, 1860, he reported the bill out of his committee. Six days later, in a division along party lines, the House passed the measure, 115 to 65.

On March 26, Lovejoy called the attention of the House to a speech he had prepared but would not deliver, and it was inserted into the record. The speech dwelt on the role of government in the United States—"What is beneficial to the people cannot be detrimental to the Government; for in this country the interests of both are identical," he stated. "With us the Government is simply an agency through which the people act for their own benefit." [13]

Lovejoy had helped in promoting the homestead bill. For thirty years there had been a growing demand to provide free public land for settlers, and the movement had been reflected in bills introduced in the national legislature. But in session after session Southern votes or a presidential veto had defeated the proposed law. Grow had introduced such bills ever since his first term in the House in 1853. In the reshuffling of Republican committee chairmen in 1860 Grow's leadership in the homestead fight was passed on to Lovejoy, who had already established himself as a leading farmer spokesman. Grow became the party Whip and guided Lovejoy and the House in passing a homestead bill without debate.

In the Senate, Democrats emasculated the bill and reframed its terms in a patchwork compromise. Grow refused to accept the Senate version and, with Lovejoy, persuaded the House to pass the original bill. At this point it became necessary to submit it to a conference committee of both houses. The Senate named Andrew Johnson of Tennessee, champion in the upper house of a beneficent bill; Robert W. Johnson of Arkansas; and James Harlan of Iowa. The House conferees were Lovejoy, Grow, and James H. Thomas. When this group submitted its work to the full bodies, the new compromise bill passed by a sizable majority. Then the Southerners played their trump: In June, President Buchanan vetoed even this watered-down homestead bill. In doing so he was indulging in partisan politics, and inadvertently supplying the Republicans with a winning issue. The campaign of 1860 was already under way when Buchanan rejected the measure, and he was hopefully attacking the Republicans as well as the Douglas Democrats, who also supported homestead legislation. What at first seemed a sure victory for Lovejoy's first major drive to pass a bill was thus bogged down in the mire of sectional vindictiveness.[14]

Earlier in that session, on April 5, Lovejoy had made a speech that became national news. With the House in Committee of the Whole on the State of the Union, Lovejoy was recognized and took the floor for an hour. He addressed himself to the slavery

233

question. As he began to speak, Williamson Cobb of Alabama rose for a point of order but decided not to press it. But so tense was the atmosphere that Lovejoy, seeing the bitter faces of Southern lawmakers and hearing their mumbled objections, adamantly insisted he would speak "with the gentleman's permission, or without it." The Southerners wanted him to confine his remarks to a particular bill before the House. But the Chair, occupied by Israel Washburn of Maine, finally ruled in Lovejoy's favor: Under the rules of the Committee of the Whole he need not be limited to the bill in question.

Lovejoy proceeded to make one of his impassioned indictments of slavery. A member called out, "You are joking." Lovejoy assured him he was in dead earnest. As he warmed to his topic he slowly moved across the area in front of the Democratic benches. Suddenly Roger A. Pryor of Virginia jumped up from his seat as if to meet Lovejoy head on, shouting "the Gentleman from Illinois shall not approach this side of the House, shaking his fists and talking in the way he has talked." The Southerner was so enraged that he blurted out, "It is bad enough to be compelled to sit here and hear him utter his treasonable and insulting language." Then Farnsworth of Illinois was on his feet insisting, "It is not for the Gentleman to say what is treason and what is not." John F. Potter of Wisconsin, a giant of a man, stood out in the aisle, reminding the Democrats that for eight weeks the Republicans had listened quietly while they were denounced in violent language. Firmly, like a stern father reproaching a wayward child, Potter stated, "And now, sir, this side *shall* be heard, let the consequences be what they may."

Already Southern members were feeling their belts and hips, knowing they might want to use their firearms or knives. Pryor could not be calmed; Lovejoy stood his ground. Tempers were rising throughout the House. Above the noisy exchanges of insults and threats the clicks of pistols could be heard. The astonished Chairman looked on the scene for a moment, stunned, and then ordered members to resume their seats. Samuel S. Cox of Ohio joined the Southerners to demand that Lovejoy speak from his seat. Pryor seized on the point, shouting, "He shall not come here gesticulating in a menacing and ruffianly manner."

Potter reminded Pryor he was doing the same thing at that moment.

The Chair again ordered all to take their seats. William Barksdale of Mississippi shouted at Lovejoy, "You shall not come upon this side of the House." Garnett B. Adrain of New Jersey suggested that Lovejoy continue from his seat, adding, "We all know him [Lovejoy] to be a man of courage, and that he cannot be intimidated." Simultaneously the two men in the center of the fracas called out:

Pryor: "No one wants to intimidate him."

Lovejoy: "Nobody can intimidate me."

The noise of scuffling shoes and men muttering rose, as thirty to forty congressmen ranged themselves behind Lovejoy and Pryor. Men were turning red with anger and exchanging challenges—about where Lovejoy should speak—while the Chair tried desperately to order men to their seats. Potter, Elihu B. Washburne, and William P. Kellogg assured their opposite numbers that Lovejoy would speak and should speak according to the rules of the House. Washburne made a grab for the hair of Barksdale and came away with his wig instead. In the meantime the Chairman had called the Speaker and relinquished the Chair to him. The Sergeant-at-Arms danced his mace about while the Speaker rapped and rapped the gavel and demanded "Order! Order!" Barksdale was livid with rage by now and almost shrieked as he yelled, "Order that black-hearted scoundrel and nigger-stealing thief to take his seat, and this side of the House will do it." The Mississippian itched to use his cane. Lovejoy stood still and "looked him calmly and steadfastly in the eye."

235

John McQueen of South Carolina added his anger to the mounting feelings on both sides. But already some clear-headed members were shouting from all sides of the House, "Sit down! Sit down!"

Once again the Speaker sent members to their seats, and this time they complied, as groups of two and three gradually moved away from Pryor and Lovejoy. They too resumed their seats. Having restored order, Speaker Pennington turned the chair back to Israel Washburn.

Lovejoy was again recognized. Rising to speak, he assured the Chairman that he did not wish to violate any rule of the House. William W. Boyce of South Carolina interjected, "Then behave yourself." Ignoring frequent sallies of this type, Lovejoy again asked if it was permissible to speak from a place in front of the Speaker's desk. A round of sharp and curt remarks by several members ended in the granting of permission for Lovejoy to speak from a place in front of the Clerk's desk.

Lovejoy began again to enumerate and to attack the grounds on which slavery was justified. Lucius J. Gartrell could be heard proclaiming loudly from his seat, "The man is crazy." Lovejoy did not go for the bait.

He was saying that "the practice of slaveholding has a tendency to drag communities back to barbarism . . . and were it not for the Christian women" who came from the North and intermarried with Southerners, and Southern women themselves, "in spite of the unhappy influences of slaveholding, the slave states would be as far back in barbarism as the State of Mexico." Otho R. Singleton of Mississippi wanted to know immediately if Lovejoy were making "an insinuation or slur on the women of the South." He insisted: "I want to know that distinctly and emphatically; because if he does, I will hold him personally accountable for it." Several members, perhaps suppressing their laughter, assured Singleton, "Oh, no. He gives all praise to the women of the South. . . . He compliments them."

236

Singleton still failed to understand and repeated his threat to Lovejoy. The Chair ruled him out of order, and the gentleman from Illinois went on to the constitutional question in regard to slavery. He demonstrated, as he had many times in a quarter-century, that the Constitution never did sanction slavery. Lovejoy upheld that basic document but he did not believe in "the construction put upon it by those who claim its recognition and sanction of the practice of slaveholding."

Barksdale could not contain himself as he said, "No, sir; you stand there today an infamous, perjured villain." John D. Ashmore of South Carolina ignored the demand for order from the front of the chamber, and concurred: "Yes, he is a perjured villain; and he perjures himself every hour he occupies a seat on this floor."

"And a Negro-thief into the bargain," Singleton added heatedly.

Lovejoy did not know at that moment how bloody were the thoughts of his opponents. In the near-riot earlier, Martin J. Crawford of Georgia had quietly taken his place in the mob at the center of the House floor and cocked his pistol in his pocket. "I had made up my mind," he wrote later, "to sell out my blood at the highest possible price." Such was the mood of the angry men scowling at the Illinois antislavery leader. For the moment they were leveling only their verbal fire at him. Lovejoy proceeded with the watchful boldness of one confident he was on the side of truth and correct principles; and the support of his Republican colleagues sustained him. Later he wrote: "The Republicans were on hand and behaved nobly. I think we should have whipped them [the fire-eaters] badly if they began it." [15]

He went ahead with his speech, pouring on "a rainstorm of fire and brimstone as hot as I could," he wrote his wife, "and you know something of what that is. . . ." [16] Standing at the Clerk's desk, Lovejoy claimed the right to endorse *Impending Crisis* or any book—"The Bible or the Koran, Young's *Night-Thoughts* or Tom Moore's *Anacreon*, Jonathan Edwards on the Decrees or Tom Paine's *Age of Reason*." The right to speak freely should be an American's even in Richmond or Charleston, Lovejoy asserted, but "I cannot go into a slave State and open my lips in regard to the question of slavery—"

"No," shouted Elbert S. Martin of Virginia, "we would hang you higher than Haman!"

Southerners' tempers were again boiling, and now Barksdale lashed out at the abolitionist, "The meanest slave in the South is your superior."

With great self-control Lovejoy concluded his remarks on slavery and the Constitution, on Helper's book, and on the right of free speech.

"Now what about John Brown?" he asked. Millions would be interested in Lovejoy's answer, for it would be the answer of a leading spokesman of radical antislavery thought in the government. "Let's have it!" several cried out as Lovejoy began. He described John Brown as "like a wounded lion with his head upon his paws," after the old man had been struck down in the fire engine house at Harpers Ferry. While the bearded Brown lay hurt this way, "a saber cut upon his brow, bayonet gashes in his side, the blood oozing out . . . certain little specimens of the canine species" prodded him with questions about his companions in the raid. Lovejoy's bitter reference to the "specimens" meant Governor Henry A. Wise of Virginia, Senator J. M. Mason of that state, Congressman C. L. Vallandigham of Ohio, and army officers Brevet-Colonel Robert E. Lee and Lieutenant J. E. B. Stuart. Lovejoy, reconstructing the scene, told the House that they wanted to know if Giddings, "the old war-horse of the Western Reserve had been on the 'expedition.'" Brown slowly raised his head, "cast a disdainful side glance upon the inquirer, growled out a contemptuous negative, and reposed his head as before." Later Lovejoy wrote to Giddings, who had lost his seat

238

in the House in 1858, to tell him that "the lion scene has been admired" and made a sensation across the land. Congressman Vallandigham hung his head, Lovejoy reported, when the scene was being described, especially when Lovejoy came to "the old 'war-horse.' " [17]

Continuing his speech, Lovejoy said: "In regard to John Brown, you want me to curse him. I will not curse John Brown. You want me to pour out execrations upon the head of old Ossawatomie. Though all the slaveholding Balaks in the country fill their houses with silver and proffer it, I will not curse John Brown. I do honestly condemn what he did, from my standpoint, and with my convictions I disapprove of his actions, that is true; but I believe that his purpose was a good one; and that so far as his own motives before God were concerned, they were honest and truthful; and no one can deny that he stands head and shoulders above any other character that appeared on the stage in that tragedy from beginning to end. . . .

"He was not guilty of murder or treason. He did unquestionably violate the statute against aiding slaves to escape; but no blood was shed, except by the panic stricken multitude, till [Aaron D.] Stevens was fired upon while waving a flag of truce. The only murder was that of [William] Thompson, who was snatched from the heroic protection of a woman, and riddled with balls at the railroad bridge. Despotism has seldom sacrificed three nobler victims than Brown, Stevens, and [Albert] Haz[lett]."

Lovejoy then asked, What right has this Caliban upon earth? Slaveholding laws have "the same moral power and force that rules among pirates have for the division of their spoils." After repeating essentially what he had said to the House a year earlier, Lovejoy asserted flatly, "Every slave has a right to his freedom . . . every slave has a right to run away, in spite of your slave laws." If he were a slave, Lovejoy argued, he would fight for his freedom, over "the carcasses of the slain." These would be his declarations of liberty: "Give me my freedom. Hands off. Unthrottle that man. Give him his liberty, he is entitled to it from his God." Supported by such views, he did not consider it harmful or wrong to help a slave run away from his enslavement.

A voice accused Lovejoy, "You steal them."

"Who steals," Lovejoy replied, "when a man comes and takes my child from my hearthstone? Who steals, when he comes and takes the babe, flesh of my flesh, and bone of my bone? Who steals?"

Seeing that his time was almost up, Lovejoy said so, but Adrain proposed extending his time. Singleton objected. Smarting under Lovejoy's scathing argument, he stated: "No, sir, any *gentleman* shall have time, but not such a mean, despicable wretch as that!"

Nevertheless Lovejoy continued for at least another fifteen minutes. After discussing the questions of free labor versus slave labor and the freedom of the territories, Lovejoy lifted the storm clouds for a moment. Smiling, he said, "Now, gentlemen, I know you are in no mood to take a little advice." He did not say what the advice was, but the House laughed with him. "I tell you I love you all," he added and again the laughter rolled through the chamber.

McQueen dourly repudiated "your love."

"Sinners did that to Christ," Lovejoy reminded, "but he loved them still." A ripple of laughter could be heard from some members.

"I do not think he loves you much," McQueen shot back.

"I am afraid that I am not much like him," Lovejoy said.

Then he made a solemn plea to slaveholders to emancipate their slaves. The Illinois congressman, in a reversion to moderate antislavery doctrine, urged gradual emancipation: "If you say that you want a quarter of a century, you can have it. But I insist that this system must ultimately be extinguished."

What was the alternative to voluntary emancipation?

"Refuse to proclaim liberty throughout all the land, to the inhabitants thereof, and the exodus of the slave will be through the Red Sea. . . . By and by some Marion will be found, calling his guerrilla troops from the swamps and everglades of South Carolina; and Patrick Henry will reappear in the Old Dominion, shouting, as of old, 'Give us liberty, or give us death!' "

A minute later an exhausted Lovejoy was uttering the last words of his oration. Martin of Virginia made an anticlimactic renewal of his threat to hang Lovejoy as they had John Brown—"as high as Haman."

The weary prairie preacher could only say, "I have no doubt of it." The gavel of the Chairman banged, and a hubbub of congressional private talk arose. Lovejoy moved quietly away from the Clerk's desk and returned to his seat amid congratulatory handshakes and thanks for his efforts.[18]

Lovejoy had not prepared a written draft of the speech ahead of time, nor had he any prior notion of the effect it would have. He confessed afterward, "I had *thought* the matter over. . . ."[19]

On the Democratic side of the House there were angry demands to expel Lovejoy. Someone proposed that such a resolution be introduced, but nothing came of the idea after an evening of feverish intramural discussion. Lovejoy was confident that "they will not be fool enough for that." He was too fatigued to write all the details of the fracas to his family, but he was exhilarated by the fight. He thought he had never "said anything more savage in the pulpit or on the stump." With some pleasure he told his wife, "It seems like old times to be in a storm." And to a friend, Lovejoy exulted that "I have made a ten strike without any expectation of it. The fire-eaters made a row and helped me to notoriety." Senator Henry Wilson of Massachusetts told Lovejoy the fire-eaters "acted like a turkey on a hot grate. . . ."[20]

That night and the next day all of Washington was aflame with gossip. The names of Lovejoy, Potter, and Pryor were buzzed about in the barrooms and boardinghouses along the Potomac. Telegraph keys clacked accounts of the speech over the wires to New York, Chicago, Boston, and Richmond. In thirty-three cities from Charleston, South Carolina, to Concord, New Hampshire, and as far west as San Francisco, newspapers carried the story. The Sacramento *Daily Union*, Mobile *Daily Advertiser*, New York *Herald*, Lancaster *Ledger*, Louisville *Courier*, Memphis *Avalanche*, and Newark *Evening Post* were only a few of the journals that helped spread the name Owen Lovejoy from coast to coast. The taciturn Washington *National Intelligencer* compressed the boiling session of the House into this terse description: "his remarks were quite denunciatory, and led to no small degree of excitement." The Peoria *Daily Transcript* commented: "the tendency of Lovejoy's speech we believe to be good." Greeley's *Tribune* ran news of the event for two days and on the third editorialized against the Southern fire-eaters who had at first obstructed the choice of a Speaker for eight weeks and then attempted to deny Lovejoy his right to speak. The *Tribune*'s Washington writer was James S. Pike, a native of Calais, Maine, and quite sympathetic to Lovejoy. He felt that the speech was fiery but excellent to circulate in an edition of two million copies. Pike wrote that Lovejoy had managed to produce "as many daguerreotypes and crayon drawings of slavery" as could be packed into an hour's speech, and that the pictures drawn by Lovejoy "blaze with a fervent heat." Lovejoy was pleased with the New York newspaper's attention.[21]

Besides enjoying the acclaim of the Republicans throughout the North, he became more than ever idolized in his home district. Local newspapers in Illinois spread the text of the address across column after column. The Bloomington *Pantagraph*, the *Bureau County Republican* in Princeton, and the *Central Illinois Gazette* of Champaign, deep in the farm region, all celebrated "The Speech of Owen Lovejoy." [22]

12

The Election of 1860

"I see a moral revolution effected. . . ."
—Owen Lovejoy

The fight on the floor of the House on April 5 was only one sign of many that the country was headed toward irreconcilable conflict. That process was made irreversible by the stubbornness of the slaveowning class against the growing power of the industrial and merchant capitalists, and by the sharpening division within the political parties. For example, the solid Democratic reign of eight years was fast weakening by the spring of 1860, and further rule by Southern-dominated administrations was threatened by the gains of the Republicans and by the considerable number of "popular sovereignty" Democrats. Senator Douglas as the principal advocate of that policy was the leading contender for the presidential nomination. Other Democrats, however, were extremely displeased with him for his position; and his nomination was blocked at the Democratic national convention in Charleston, South Carolina, in April, 1860, by the bolting delegations of seven Southern states.

The seceders reassembled in Richmond in June and adopted a platform bluntly denying Congress the power to do anything to abolish or halt the expansion of slavery in the territories. They based themselves on the Dred Scott decision, which they interpreted to mean that slavery was now not merely a sectional but a national institution. If it was formerly wrong to touch slavery in the states, it was now deemed wrong to touch it anywhere. The Southern Democrats nominated John C. Breckenridge of Kentucky as their presidential candidate and Joseph Lane of Oregon as his running mate.

Meanwhile the regular Democrats reconvened in Baltimore on June 18 and wrangled over delegates' credentials for three days. Virginia's delegation withdrew and was followed by those of North Carolina, Tennessee, California, and Oregon. Hopelessly disrupted, the Democrats nevertheless managed to nominate Douglas for President and Herschel V. Johnson of Georgia for Vice-President.

Although the divided Democrats were thus placed in an embarrassing position, there was some solace for them in the possibility of a split in the six-year-old Republican party. Ultra-conservatives, mostly former Northern Whigs and Southern Know-Nothings, met in Baltimore on May 16 under the label of the Constitutional Union party. The platform ignored the slavery question and set no higher sights than those defined by the disastrous nativist prejudices of the past six years. Even the knowledgeable merchants and manufacturers who were the main support of the new party conceded that it was of little use in the contest of 1860.

By far the most promising party in 1860 was the regular Republican party, especially because it faced up to the slavery question, however limited its approach. Moreover, the Republicans indulged the spirit of enthusiasm for national economic development, with the homestead question catching the popular fancy.

These two matters had now captured the attention of the increasingly populous Northern, Midwestern, and Pacific states, and were reflected in the platform written at the national convention in Chicago beginning on June 16. Meeting in the giant wooden Wigwam, the Republicans agreed that slavery must be prohibited in the territories. But they also continued to shy away from touching slavery in the states where it existed. The promise of free homesteads, for which Lovejoy had been working in the few weeks before the convention, was emphasized in the platform and was considered a sure vote-getter. Furthermore, the protective tariff was advanced in the platform as a pledge of better wages for workers, good prices for farmers' products, and adequate profits for manufacturers. The Pacific railroad and other internal-improvements planks written into the platform were effectively designed to win support across the country. The railroad proposal appealed not only to sectional economic interests but to the national imagination and desire for expansion over the continent. And not least of the appeals to the voters was the plank practically dictated by the German delegates—an antinativist one clearly repudiating Massachusetts' prejudicial naturalization law.

The process of compromise that worked in bringing out the platform also operated in the selection of candidates. Although William H. Seward of New York went to Chicago optimistic of his nomination for President, the party was well stocked with capable leading men ambitious for the prize. Eventually Lincoln was nominated, in no small measure because of the adroit and shrewd dealings of his managers, who could take advantage of his position midway between Seward's growing cautiousness on the slavery question and the reputed radicalism of another contender, Salmon P. Chase.

In Lovejoy's district, the Princeton Republican newspaper had written on April 12 that it favored Chase or Seward for President on the ground that they were stronger antislavery men than Lincoln, whom it recommended for Vice-President. The Champaign *Central Illinois Gazette* was confident in April, 1860, that Lovejoy's "too familiar voice" would be heard in the next session of the House, as clear and bold as it had been, but there was no indication yet of its preferences on the national ticket. The Germans in the district considered Seward their choice, but the Peoria German Republican Club was willing to support "Chase, Lincoln or any other representative Republican." But men like Edward Bates of Missouri or Simon Cameron of Pennsylvania would not do for the Germans. In February, 1860, they circulated resolutions to this effect among other German clubs in the nation and to Republican leaders. Their congressman, Owen Lovejoy, received a copy. He replied that he was in agreement with their prescription for a presidential candidate and said that the club's resolutions "breathe the true spirit and present the true principles and policy. . . . Let us have a standard bearer who can inspire confidence and awaken enthusiasm, and we will kindle a fire that will burn the sham Democracy to the lowest Hell." [1]

Together with fellow Illinois Republicans, Lovejoy rejoiced in Lincoln's nomination and in the choice of Hannibal Hamlin of Maine for Vice-President. Yet despite the effective behind-the-scenes maneuvering of David Davis and others in Chicago in Lincoln's behalf, there were many questions unresolved. Before a truly united Republican leadership could wage an effective, unified, and enthusiastic campaign, Seward forces in New York, among others, had to be mollified. Lovejoy appears to have been assigned as an emissary to promote party harmony with the New Yorkers, for he received a request to speak in the East. [2]

In his letter of congratulation to Lincoln, he said: "I suppose you are knee deep in letters of congratulations & that I am somewhat tardy in offering mine, although perhaps as sincere as those

247

that have been earlier." A note of ruefulness crept into the letter when Lovejoy wrote: "I have seen enough of political life to know that it is not altogether a bed of roses. You have the advantage of being without entanglements & will go into the White House as free I trust as you are now. It would be a treat such as the nation has not enjoyed for a long time to have the offices seek the men rather than the men the offices." [3]

Engaged as he was in shepherding the Homestead Bill through the House, Lovejoy had to rely on the home papers and the district party to fight for his own nomination. He shared the Champaign paper's confidence in his renomination and reelection, but as an experienced politician, he knew he could take nothing for granted. Late in May he asked Jesse Fell to get David Davis to consent to placing the name Owen Lovejoy at the head of the *Pantagraph*'s columns. If the *Pantagraph* did this for Lovejoy, he was sure that other papers in the district would follow suit. Lovejoy had no fears "as to the result, but it would be gratifying to have it done in some such way." If Davis, or Fell, or both did not agree with him, Lovejoy was willing "with entire cordiality" to let matters take their course. He had his wish, and his campaign for reelection was thus under way, with the influential and perceptive Jesse Fell acting for him in absentia. The *Central Illinois Gazette* proposed on June 13, as it printed a call for the Third District Republican convention at Bloomington on June 27, to give Lovejoy "the most rousing, overwhelming, tremendous majority." The Danville *Republican* copied the *Gazette*'s recommendations. The *Gazette* also observed that "there are many reasons why Mr. Lovejoy will at this time receive the active support of all shades of opinion in the party, even of men who are not disposed to like him in all respects. . . ." This was doubtless a reference to the Davis followers.[4]

Acknowledging his debt of gratitude to Fell for his support inside the party organization, Lovejoy wrote from the House of

Representatives on June 16: "We are now working under the lash as our time is limited and I can only thank you for your letter and express my obligations to you for your constant and efficient aid. If I can do something in the cause of human freedom you will feel compensated. I think it will be all right in the convention." The only threat seemed to be a rather weak one from Ward Hill Lamon. William W. Orme, who was a friend of Davis and Lamon, seems to have quashed that ambition, for in a discouraging letter to Lamon he wrote: "You wouldn't do for Congress for you wouldn't reflect the *high moral tone* of this District—Lovejoy does do that." It was an allusion to Lamon's weakness for alcohol.[5]

The House of Representatives adjourned on June 25, and Lovejoy left the Capital speedily to confer in New York with Seward's manager, Thurlow Weed, and with Governor Edwin D. Morgan in Albany. He paused at some of the New York cities, "speaking a word for 'Old Abe' and the good cause." The session at Washington had been an arduous one for Lovejoy, and he almost regretted his engagements, although he found the audiences "good and enthusiastic." On June 27 he was dining with Weed and Governor Morgan at Albany. At about three o'clock in the afternoon he was pleasantly surprised to receive a message from Bloomington. Fell had telegraphed the news of Lovejoy's nomination by a unanimous vote. Republicans who had bitterly opposed Lovejoy two years earlier had now come to be among his warmest political friends. Lovejoy hastened to assure Fell that he hoped to be "worthy of such friends and such constituency." Although the congressman did not elaborate on the results of his conversations with the New York leaders, he did write that "everything looks promising." [6]

At the Bloomington convention, Fell had fought for a resolution authorizing Lovejoy to be at liberty to cover the entire state during the campaign. The publisher was convinced that the

249

whole Republican ticket would be strengthened by Lovejoy's boldness in going into southern Illinois towns. Some hesitated because of that region's reputation for proslavery and Democratic solidity, but Fell finally won unanimous approval for Lovejoy's tour.[7]

With hardly any rest from his months of strenuous congressional duty, Lovejoy began his prodigious swing around the state. At one meeting in the Wigwam erected in Princeton, fifteen hundred people came to hear their congressman discuss the Republican platform. Lovejoy concentrated first on the homestead bill and on the threat posed to it by the system of slave labor. Then, turning to a consideration of Lincoln, he avowed that Lincoln would give the country honest administration. Expanding on Lincoln's mental and moral superiority over the Democratic candidate, Douglas, Lovejoy predicted a Republican victory even in crucial New York. The meeting was then taken over by the Princeton Brass Band and finally Ichabod Codding, in a witty and penetrating speech, argued for equal rights for Negroes.[8]

From Princeton the two old radical comrades set out separately to stump for Abraham Lincoln. Codding struck the trail in Wisconsin, and Lovejoy proceeded immediately to Illinois' Macoupin County. Here a crowd of twenty thousand, gathered in a woods, whipped things up for the Lincoln and Hamlin ticket, and listened to speeches by Lovejoy, Norman Judd, and John M. Palmer. "We had a meeting overwhelming in numbers and irrepressible in enthusiasm," Lovejoy wrote to Fell. "I had, as they say, a perfect success." He assured Fell that "No one will doubt the wisdom of your counsel hereafter in regard to my going into Egypt. I was as glad for you as for myself." [9]

July 31 found Lovejoy and Senator Trumbull speaking to about nine thousand people packed into the fairgrounds near Champaign-Urbana. Lovejoy followed the senator on the stand and spoke to the assemblage "as to his personal friends." On

August 6 he spoke again at Paxton in Ford County. He appeared at the Springfield Republican convention on August 8 and then resumed his ambitious tour of the Sixth, Seventh, and Eighth Congressional Districts in the bottom of Illinois, once a stronghold of proslavery people. At Springfield he succeeded in charming his audience and winning over Benjamin S. Edwards, a distinguished conservative old-line Whig lawyer of that city. Edwards, who was seated on the speakers' stand, had been a bitter opponent of Lovejoy and earlier had denounced him. But on this occasion he stood up to shake hands with Lovejoy and congratulate him on his speech. This fraternization in full view of thousands became a celebrated incident in the memories of Springfield's Republicans. Although Lovejoy had not converted the entire region, his magnetic eloquence was winning friends for the Republican cause. Yet the path was not always strewn with roses. Some southern Illinois crowds proved to be thorny, and so did some officials of the railroads that passed through that portion of the state. These gentlemen, Lovejoy complained, "refuse passes to all, at least to me and they say all." He appealed to Thurlow Weed for financial assistance, since the local committees were "not rich except in good works & beside that I prefer to work or fight on my own hook." He felt justified in making the appeal on the injunction, "Ye who are strong ought to bear the infirmities of the weak." Whether the plea brought help is not known.[10]

At the same time, Lovejoy pleaded with Seward to come out to Illinois and make a speech in Princeton. His neighbors in the county and the district at home apparently had preferred Seward over Lincoln, and their disappointment was "sore and deep." Lovejoy hoped the dean of the Republicans would come and speak for party unity to elect Lincoln. Lovejoy assured the New Yorker, "We could gather an assemblage of 20,000 people. They cannot all hear you but they can 'see the blessed wig!' " Seward had already agreed to appear in Chicago at the behest of the

Republican state committee. But Lovejoy preferred that the senator come to Princeton "at *our* request & not under the auspices of the State Com. If it is at all possible & consistent I hope you will do us, what we should esteem a *very great favor*." [11]

A weary Lovejoy returned briefly to Princeton to rest and answer his mail. Seward had written that he would visit Lovejoy, but would not speak at a meeting in Princeton. Lovejoy renewed his plea, asking only that the New York leader lend the magic of his name and presence. "I do not wish to tease you," Lovejoy wrote, "but it would be very gratifying & useful if it were consistent with your views of duty & propriety." [12]

As the summer waned, the campaign's tempo increased. Lovejoy was everywhere in the state but in his own district. He had conferred with Fell early in September, and the two men had worked out a schedule of speaking engagements. Lovejoy was irresistible and in demand by Republicans in most of the state. Although his own district was considered safe, he still made efforts to bring out Seward; one way was through a letter personally delivered by fellow Princetonian John H. Bryant, who went East to confer with Seward at Auburn, New York.[13]

Whatever it was that compelled Lovejoy to insist on Seward's appearance was the same force that made him write at this time to Charles Sumner, the Massachusetts antislavery senator. Hearing from the state committee that this eminent New Englander was expected in Illinois, Lovejoy asked him to set aside a day for an appearance at Ottawa, "a large town in my district." Since he had nothing to fear from Democratic opposition in his district, and he had the unanimous nomination of the Republicans, the reason for Lovejoy's concern is obscure. He did not offer Seward any explanations, except to speak of disappointments. To Sumner, he merely said, "For reasons which I cannot explain I feel very desirous that you should comply with my request." One plausible explanation may be that Lovejoy was apprehensive that in his almost continuous absence from the Third District, opponents might attempt to undermine his campaign as they had in 1856 and 1858 with an "independent" nomination. If he could bring such national stalwarts as Seward and Sumner into Princeton or Ottawa, he could overwhelm any "independents" who might dare to raise their heads. Or Lovejoy may have feared that disgruntled Republicans who had preferred Seward over Lincoln might bolt the party in a leftward direction toward Gerrit Smith, who had been nominated by the very small group of abolitionists organized as the Radical Abolitionist party. If the Eastern leaders assured the local people—who might still doubt Lincoln's strength on the slavery question—that Lincoln was all right with them, then perhaps Lovejoy could prevent disaffection.[14]

A shred of evidence in favor of the latter explanation is in this incident: Benjamin Shaw recalled that he had heard Lovejoy speaking in Amboy, Lee County, urging abolitionists to support Lincoln, "they generally having refused to do so," said Shaw, "for the reason that the Republicans did not propose any action leading to the abolition of slavery." Almost fifteen years after the turbulent one-idea struggle in Liberty party ranks had seemingly been settled, here was Lovejoy still exhorting radicals to drop their sectarianism. As long as the Republicans were anti-extensionist, Lovejoy advised, the abolitionists ought to get in and ride with them, inasmuch as they were going in the same direction.[15]

Despite his political fears, Lovejoy mounted the campaign with characteristic energy and indomitable enthusiasm. With Wide-Awakes sporting uniforms and thumping drums and adding noise and color to Republican rallies, Illinois partisans took on the flush of victory. One dazzling demonstration took place in Princeton, as eight to ten thousand people stirred up the town on Saturday, September 29. Brass bands and colorful floats led a parade of people on horseback, on foot, and packed in wagons. Some of the mounted riders carried rails as symbols of support for Lincoln.

253

Thirty-three women attired in white, with blue headdresses, represented the states of the Union, and one lady in green stood for Kansas territory. They received continuous cheers and applause as they passed through the streets. A sturdy contingent of two hundred and fifty Swedish people marched, followed by a wagon with thirty-five colorfully dressed women. Lincoln and Hamlin banners were flown everywhere, and the air was filled with songs of victory. Lovejoy spoke to and with the crowd for three hours, and his colleague Isaac N. Arnold rounded out the program with a half-hour platform speech.[16]

Four days later Chicago produced a spectacular exhibition on a larger scale, when Seward appeared before seventy-five thousand people in a gigantic open-air rally. So dense was the throng that many could not hear the voice of "Mr. Republican," although they could see his precise gestures on the platform. The New York senator, who had been deeply disappointed at the convention in this city only a few months earlier, made a direct statement to the crowd that they must vote for Lincoln. Much of his speech analyzed the nature of the slavery issue. He pointed out that slavery demoralized the white people, besides oppressing the Negro people. The effect, he exclaimed, was to rob white people of the moral courage to oppose the "institution." [17]

The senator singled out Lovejoy for special mention, as if in direct response to the fervent pleas from Princeton during the summer. He hoped that every district in the United States would choose men "as brave, as truthful, as fearless and as firm as Owen Lovejoy." A wave of applause endorsed the statement.

Lovejoy himself went into the Wigwam that afternoon to extoll Lincoln and the Republicans' forward-looking platform before an overflow crowd. Once again he hammered away on the homestead issue and received a wild ovation. Republicans, hewing close to the demands of the people, captivated Chicago that Tuesday, October 2.[18]

Lovejoy's oratory was so compelling that other states wanted to see and hear him. The Indiana Republican state committee called him in to exercise his talents at South Bend on October 5, and he was scheduled for an appearance at Racine, Wisconsin, on October 16 (which he was unable to make), and another at Burlington, Iowa, on October 27. His home state schedule during October called for him to make speeches almost every day in Livingston, Boone, Will, Lawrence, Marion, Christian, Woodford, La Salle, McLean, and Pike Counties. Lovejoy was due in Rock Island on October 12 and across the state in Chicago on October 15.[19]

By that date Pennsylvania, Indiana, and Ohio had already been delivered to Lincoln and his party in early elections. These three states for Lincoln were in addition to all of New England and the old Northwest, which were generally conceded in his column by mid-September. It was thus made clear that the country would most likely go Republican in November and, to celebrate the October victories in the three states, Chicago mounted another huge rally. The streets were thronged as a Wide-Awake escort accompanied Congressman Lovejoy and his family by torchlight from the Briggs House, where they were guests, to the Wigwam. Again the structure was unable to accommodate the mass turnout. Overflow crowds encircled the building on the outside. Inside, with Lovejoy on the platform were Galusha A. Grow and Schuyler Colfax, representing two of the states already recorded for Lincoln.[20]

Lovejoy, the main speaker, had a rollicking good time with the audience, beginning with the homestead issue and then going on to the slavery question. He spelled out the harassment of Republicans by their opposition in the Congress, especially on the homestead bill, and generally by tactics of delay and obstruction. Douglas and other Democrats, he explained, complained that Republicans would not let Congress deal with other questions because of the "interminable Negro question." On the other hand, the Democrats obstructed such bills as the homestead, Pacific railroad, telegraph, and tariff. As soon as the homestead bill was passed in the House of Representatives, Barksdale of Mississippi moved for adjournment in these words: "Mr. Speaker, I move to adjourn, we have done iniquity enough for one day." Lovejoy related this incident to the packed Wigwam and asked, "What iniquity? We had passed a broad, liberal, munificent, just Homestead Bill." But, he asserted, the Democrats had stripped the bill down to a skeleton.

Comparing the two parties' approaches, Lovejoy said that the Republicans would give the settler a homestead upon any of the unoccupied public lands; the Democrats would say, 'You may have any lands that are left after they have been offered for sale.' The Democrats would say to the poor man, 'After the capitalists have entered what they wish—after the speculators have taken the lion's share, then you may have the refuse—the swamp lands and the sand hills, to take possession of them.'

"We told them," Lovejoy said, "to choose from all the public lands—they might have the cream; the Democrats told them they might have the blue skimmed milk after the cream was taken off." Cheers and laughter rang through the hall, then a great ripple of laughter greeted Lovejoy when he said, "As I say to the people frequently, if they prefer bonny-clabber to cream, they ought to vote the Democratic ticket."

Lovejoy was making the strongest possible appeal to the masses of Irish and German workers of the Chicago area. They were the pro-homestead vote and the anticapitalist vote. It must be admitted that Lovejoy was less than frank in failing to acknowledge the heavy capitalist support of the Republicans; nevertheless, his appeals won the wild approval of the throng in the Wigwam.

Turning to the slavery question, he reminded his listeners of his brother's death, then hastened to make a distinction between opposition to slavery and opposition to the South. For himself, he had no quarrel with the South. He opposed only slavery and its effects on the rights of white as well as black men, North or South—the corrosion of their religious and civil rights. Lovejoy was not about to let racist talk about Negro equality wipe out the Declaration of Independence; "I will not give up the Declaration of Independence which comes to us baptized in the blood of the purest patriots that ever lived, because there is a miserable prejudice against the colored man." The election of Lincoln was a certainty that Lovejoy foresaw as a rebuke to disunionists and slavery proponents. "We will elect our man, and when we elect him, I tell you we will inaugurate him, and he shall administer the government. He will replace the Judges as they die; and we will add to their number if they won't die." This breathtaking challenge of the Taney-dominated Supreme Court drew cheers and loud laughter from the crowd.

When he said, "I must close," they roared, "Go on! Go on!" But he did close with another acknowledgment of the Republican sweep in Pennsylvania, Indiana, and Ohio. "In this news," Lovejoy said, "I see an earnest of our coming triumph. I do not see in it offices and patronage, and honor and promotion to men; but I see a moral revolution effected; I see the spirit of freedom revived here and everywhere." "I behold it going into the slave States," he continued, "and the slave States commencing a system of emancipation, and finally emancipating their slaves and ridding the country of this evil; and in that bright future, now close at hand, I behold a free American Republic reposing proudly among the nations of the earth." Great applause shook the big wooden hall, and Lovejoy called for three cheers for the Declaration of Independence, three cheers for the Constitution and Union, three for Pennsylvania, Indiana, and Ohio—and as if this did not produce pandemonium enough, Lovejoy called for three cheers for Old Abe and the whole ticket. The audience responded with wild enthusiasm.

Here was one old fanatical abolitionist, as Lovejoy might have put it, winning the masses for Abraham Lincoln and the most far-reaching platform in American electoral history.

As election day approached, Lovejoy was covering the big cities in Illinois. On November 1 he reappeared in Springfield. The next day he spoke in Alton, the city so full of unhappy memories for him. Twenty-three years had passed since those days of danger; and only six years since Lovejoy and a handful of zealots had tried to deliver the antislavery Republican party in Springfield. Here he was now, in the city that had cast him out, respected as a national champion of freedom for all men.[21]

The *Bureau County Republican* signaled Lovejoy's coming victory. The editor observed that Lovejoy had been heard in almost every county in the state, and had devoted the entire last four months to the presidential campaign. Lovejoy had "by the power of his logic and unequalled eloquence revolutionized Egypt. . . . No other man has done as much as he has for the success of Republican principles." The people owe him a debt of gratitude, the editor wrote, urging them to repay Lovejoy at the ballot box on Tuesday, November 6.[22]

A final engagement at Ottawa on November 3 concluded Lovejoy's circuit. Then he rested to await the outcome of the contest. The people poured out on election day to shower him with a majority of eleven thousand votes. The *Republican* had been justified in its prediction in July that Lovejoy would win by ten or twelve thousand votes.[23]

Amid the party rejoicing over Lincoln's triumph, the people of Princeton went wild over the local returns. Wide-Awakes lit their torches and provided a "Grand Illumination" as a stand was hastily knocked together in front of the American House facing the lawn of the county building. A cheering procession called on

Lovejoy, then on Codding, and escorted them to the speakers' stand. Lovejoy spoke briefly, saying that he felt "we have great cause to rejoice; we achieved a victory second only to that our fathers achieved in the Revolution." Then he introduced his old comrade, Codding, as "the best stump speaker in Illinois." Fittingly, Codding capped the celebration by reminding the people of the night of November 7, 1837. This modest veteran abolitionist had not forgotten the principles underlying the people's victory in 1860—the irrepressible demand to abolish slavery and uphold the rights of Americans, Negro and white. While abolitionists like Douglass, Garrison, and Phillips had been reluctant at first to join or support the anti-extensionist Republicans, they had overcome their doubts and backed Lincoln. He at least represented the antislavery sentiment of the country and would serve as the wedge to dislodge the power of the slaveowners. Lincoln and the Republican victory forced the practical unity of abolitionists and the anti-extensionists, however weak Lincoln was on the fugitive slave question or on the equality of the Negro with the white man. Seeing this as the outstanding feature of the election, Codding's joy was more than personal. With Lovejoy he acclaimed the revolution achieved at the ballot box. The "era of freedom" had arrived.[24]

Lincoln and the Republicans were chosen by the voters to usher in that era. Although his popular vote was only thirty-nine per cent of the total, his majorities were in the populous states of the North. The party's platform helped to win increased Republican majorities among the workers and the foreign-born people in states with electoral college votes large enough to guarantee Lincoln's legitimate victory. But constitutional or not, Southerners had long before the election made clear threats to withdraw from the Union, in the event of a Republican victory.[25]

13

The Secession Crisis

*"Entertain no proposition for a compromise
in regard to the extension of slavery."*
—*Abraham Lincoln*

The senator from South Carolina, James H. Hammond, reacting to Lovejoy's stormy antislavery speech of April 5, 1860, a few days after the event, predicted that for the season there would be no crisis—"But as everybody has a revolver and the South does not intend again to be surprised into hearing another Lovejoy speech, a general fight in one or the other House with great slaughter is always on the *tapis* and may occur any day. . . ." Hammond, who had once advocated the death penalty for abolitionists, described the rapidly deteriorating relations between the sections: "No two nations on earth are or ever were more distinctly separate and hostile than we are." Seven months later, and only a day before the national elections, another Palmetto state leader, Congressman John D. Ashmore, wrote passionately that a Republican victory would be intolerable and that he would rather see the Republic go down "two thousand fathoms deep into the ocean" than to see his section submit to "Black Republican rule for one day or one hour." He wrote: "The booming of 100,000 cannon and the slaughter of an hundred Waterloos would be music to my ears and gladness to my sight rather than see S. C. the victim of Lincoln, Seward, Sumner, Wilson, Lovejoy, Helper *et id omne genus.*" [1]

Threats of proslavery Southerners to dissolve the Union culminated in decisive action within a few weeks after Lincoln's election to the Presidency. By February 1, 1861, seven states, led by South Carolina, had severed their connections with the United States and formed the Confederacy. In response to South Carolina's demand for all federal property in the state, Major Robert Anderson's contingent hustled out of Fort Moultrie the day after Christmas, 1860, to occupy Charleston harbor's strong defensive site, Fort Sumter. It was plain that every American who had not committed himself to one side or the other would have to do so in the rapidly approaching civil war.

Although Owen Lovejoy had declaimed often on the moral evil of slavery and had pleaded with Southern slaveholders voluntarily to free their slaves, he differed little from other political, or constitutional, abolitionists on the proposition that the federal government should prohibit slavery in the territories but not interfere with it in the states where it existed. However, when the Southern war party broke the Union, and he heard extremists using moderate men to extract concessions for slavery through compromise schemes, he refused to recognize the word "compromise" and fought to prevent the dissipation of federal power and the dissolution of the Union. He displayed extraordinary implacability on this issue of secession in the last session of the 36th Congress that convened on December 3, 1860.

The country's predicament, now that it was threatened by the departure of some Southern states, was made no more comfortable in the days following Lincoln's election by the accident of a repudiated Administration still in office, at least until March 4,

1861, and an Administration regarded as at least ambivalent toward the secessionists. Nor did the movement of Northern businessmen toward compromise make matters easier for the Union. Bound as Eastern merchants were to the slave states' cotton economy, many of them in New York, Boston, and Philadelphia, seeing financial ruin ahead, strongly favored concessions to the seceding states. This approach was followed by conservative Republicans and by supporters of Douglas, Breckenridge, and Bell. On the other hand so antislavery a man as Horace Greeley was at first ready to let the South go, although his sincerity in this position has been regarded as questionable. Other Republicans concurred with pro-Union Democrats in expressing a readiness to consider peaceful secession, or compromises to hold the slave states with guarantees of a constitutional amendment forbidding any action against slavery in the territories or in the states. Moreover, radical abolitionists like Garrison and Phillips expressed their satisfaction that the union with slaveowners was dissolved. However, in a few months they became supporters of the war against the rebels, a war ostensibly to restore the Union.[2]

Opposed to conciliatory approaches to the slave power were Lovejoy and other political abolitionists, Lincoln and a number of leading anti-extensionists, members of President Buchanan's crisis Cabinet like Edwin M. Stanton, and segments of the labor movement in Louisville, Baltimore, Philadelphia, Cincinnati, Chicago, Alton, Illinois, and other Northern and border cities.[3]

Lovejoy maintained that the federal government should not deal with the rebels except to quash their insurgency and require them to surrender to the United States the federal property that they had seized unlawfully. A considerable number of moderate and radical Republicans shared this position. Accordingly, Lovejoy, Thaddeus Stevens of Pennsylvania, John A. Gurley of Ohio, and Charles B. Sedgwick of New York joined in distinguishing themselves in the House by their consistent hostility toward compromise. The Vermont and Wisconsin delegations to Congress found it impossible to consider compromise. Senators Charles Sumner, Benjamin F. Wade of Ohio, Preston King of New York; and Lyman Trumbull of Illinois were equally adamant against concessions to the slave states. These men really did not have to be told, as Lincoln was moved to tell his friend Representative William P. Kellogg of Illinois: "Entertain no proposition for a compromise in regard to the *extension* of slavery." Lincoln wrote to Trumbull and Elihu Washburne: "On that point [of no compromise] hold firm as with a chain of steel." The group around Lovejoy and Stevens needed no urging; they rejected compromise at least as vigorously as the President-elect and often more so.[4]

Although Lincoln, judicious as ever, fought compromise through his correspondence with leading Republican congressmen, he held his tongue until after his inauguration. On the other hand, Lovejoy was free to mount the attack instantly, as the compromise resolutions rained on the Clerk's desk in the House. When the Committee of Thirty-Three, representing every state then in the Union, was appointed to sift the compromise proposals in the House, Lovejoy told a New York friend, "The bluster about Union is mere sham. We have been fooled into appointing a com. but not by my vote."[5]

On December 17 Lovejoy struck sharply at disunion. A resolution introduced by him was aimed at the secessionists and their impending attack on Major Anderson in Charleston harbor. It read in part, "we deprecate the spirit of disobedience to [the] Constitution, wherever manifested, and . . . we earnestly recommend the repeal of all . . . nullification laws, so called, enacted by the state legislatures, conflicting with, and in violation of, that sacred instrument . . . and it is the duty of the President to protect and defend the property of the United States." The resolution was approved that day 136 to 0, with the Southern group of representatives refusing to participate in the vote.[6]

On that same day Representative Thomas B. Florence of Pennsylvania brought in a resolution amending the Constitution to recognize property in slaves, but Lovejoy jumped to his feet with an objection that disposed of the proposal. Throughout that day and almost every day in the following months Lovejoy found himself denounced, the target of unmerciful insults and charges, yet he seemed to thrive on the attacks.

On January 7, 1861, when the House debated a resolution approving of Major Anderson's move, Representative Thomas S. Bocock of Virginia said he wanted to show the country that "I, for one, am anxious to quench this firebrand introduced into this House today." Lovejoy met him head on in cross-discussion: "And I am anxious," he declared, "to let the country see that we are ready and willing to sustain the Government." Republicans waged a steady fight to bring the resolution to a vote; Democrats objected, prolonged debate. Lovejoy was on his feet time after time to raise points of order to overcome the filibuster. Finally he declared, "I object to everything that is not in order." However, debate continued and the resolution was adopted, 124 to 56. On the same day, the Committee of Thirty-Three reported a number of compromise resolutions. Lovejoy minced no words in telling the House: "I hope we shall not consider any more of these resolutions proposing compromise. I hate them." A week later Lovejoy's persistence temporarily blocked adoption of a master compromise of the committee.[7]

That was the set of proposals by Senator John J. Crittenden of Kentucky intended to perpetuate slavery in states and territories south of the old Missouri Compromise line, 36° 30', but now extended to the Pacific. Slavery would be prohibited north of the line. New states could have slavery or could prohibit it as their constitutions decreed. The Fugitive Slave Law would be strengthened, the slave trade between slave states could not be prohibited by Congress, nor could it abolish slavery in the District of Columbia nor in the states. Lincoln and the Republicans overwhelmingly rejected the proposals. In retrospect it seems that if seriously proposed, such a solution to the problem revealed either ignorance or willful disregard of rapidly changing sentiment in the North against compromise and concession. Crittenden's compromise also ran into the aspirations of Northern capitalists for expansion of the United States across the continent.

On January 16, Lovejoy was attacked for fostering a military dictatorship over the South with his resolution of December 17 supporting Major Anderson. Representative Martin J. Crawford of Georgia, continuing the harassment of Lovejoy, wanted to know how the Illinois legislator could force a government on the South. Suppose slavery were forced upon you of the North? the Georgian asked. Lovejoy picked up Crawford's opening with this rejoinder: "We have done it for years," he said amid laughter, "pro-slavery Presidents and Congresses have always ruled us heretofore." Crawford denied this and replied, "We have never elected a President of the United States by the people of the slave states alone." Lovejoy snapped back, "No, sir; but we have elected pro-slavery men." [8]

Lovejoy expressed a more fully developed view of the state of the Union on January 23. In a major speech that burned the ears not only of the secessionists but also of Northern compromisers, he hammered away at those who in his opinion were willing to foreclose on freedom. He made no effort to restrain his attacks on members of his own party who were inclined to appease the slaveowners, no matter how close he might once have been to those fellow Republicans.

"Who made the government?" Lovejoy asked. Not "we the states" but "we the people." Therefore no state could dissolve the Union, not even the people of one state. Only "we the people of the United States," Lovejoy contended, could do so.

Speaking on South Carolina's demands that Major Anderson surrender Fort Sumter in Charleston harbor, Lovejoy charged that the Southern cry of coercion was a mere pretext for "stealing United States property by Georgia and South Carolina."

Lovejoy was adamant in his refusal to have the government do anything "for the redress of any wrong, real or imaginary, until the threat of disunion and rebellion is removed." In his estimation there were no wrongs to be redressed. Even if there were, he would do nothing for their removal until "this game of secession has been played out."

He next turned to analyze the Committee of Thirty-Three with piercing logic and righteous bitterness. Lovejoy argued that the compromise proposals reported by Chairman Tom Corwin of Ohio would sow the seeds of a future harvest of trammeled liberties. The most offensive to Lovejoy of Corwin's five proposals was a constitutional amendment that would forever prevent abolition of or interference with slavery in any state. Another unacceptable one called for repeal of personal liberty laws and faithful execution of the Fugitive Slave Law. In less than thirty years, Lovejoy asserted, "we will be asked to yield to the clamor of the slaveholding interests and pass an amendment to the Constitution prohibiting the publication of anything from the press, or the utterance of anything from the lips 'intended' to excite servile insurrection." Lovejoy continued: "this innuendo is aimed . . . at the antislavery literature of the free states, to the suppression of free speech and the putting down of fanatical men like Lovejoy." Representative William M. Dunn interposed to assure Lovejoy that nothing in the report of the committee could be construed to interfere with freedom of speech or the press. Lovejoy replied that he was referring to remarks of Chairman Corwin, that he predicted "future aggressions of the slave power if we yield to its demands now." Besides, Lovejoy said, the disguised assaults of Corwin on antislavery, or even the abolition press, seemed to suggest and invite such aggressions.

Later in this major address Lovejoy insisted that the history of compromise taught that the slave power was insatiable in its demands. Lovejoy went on to discuss the Republican party's opportunities, its responsibilities and duties, its weakness and its potential for progressive action toward freedom and democracy. Above all, Lovejoy fought against the danger of party dissolution, which he felt was an inevitable consequence of a compromise policy.

"Mr. Speaker, I want to say a word to my Republican brethren. Gentlemen, Republicans, you are asked to desert the party and the principles which you were proud to uphold before the people, and when you entered the House at the opening of the session; and the question is, shall we abandon the cardinal article of our faith—the prohibition of slavery in the Territories of the United States . . . ? Perhaps this drift towards a compromise foreshadows a purpose to organize a new party, 'sloughing off,' as the phrase is, the extremes, both North and South. In this new arrangement all the radicals like myself are to be left out! I wish you a very merry time of it, my masters. A very interesting play, *Hamlet* with Hamlet left out. There never was a party that had such a golden opportunity since the organization of the Government, as we had at the beginning of the session. What we needed was unity, firmness, decision.

"If we had been cool, calm, self-possessed, doing nothing to conciliate on the one hand, and nothing to irritate on the other, we should have had, ere now, a strap around the leg of this disunion courser. But no; like the old Whigs, having achieved a victory, we were affrighted at our own success. . . . We appointed a committee of compromise—a grave mistake for us, a carnival for the Democracy. . . ."

In turn, Lovejoy dealt with Seward and Lincoln, delivering a stern rebuke to the former and a precautionary defense of the latter.

"But the premier, as he is called, is for a compromise, I am told," Lovejoy said. "I do not know and will not believe that, until I am obliged to; although I confess, instead of philosophical and polished essays, sailing like a beautiful barge around Point-no-point, I wish the Cicero of the American Senate had turned his eye on the Catiline of Georgia, and said in the abrupt and vehement invective of the Roman consul, *'Quosque tandem abutere, Catilina, patientia nostra.'* "

As for Lincoln, Lovejoy went to great pains to protect what in modern terms would be called the President's "image." "It is said that our President-elect is for a compromise. This I do not, cannot, and never will believe until I have it from his own lips or from his own acts. I know he has too much regard for the common appellation by which he is familiarly known, of 'Honest Old Abe,' ever to believe that he will betray the principles of the Republican party, which were made distinctly and squarely in the last campaign, of inflexible, unalterable opposition to the extension of human slavery. But, sir, even if it were true that the President-elect and future Cabinet advise compromise, I will not follow their lead one step."

He hastened to inform all that "one 12-month of the administration of Abraham Lincoln will do more to disabuse the public mind than all the compromises and peace measures that can be patched up in Congress." He asked only a fair trial for the President-elect.

In the end, Lovejoy cautioned that if the Union and the Constitution were tampered with, if compromise and concession to states were pursued, every state would find a reason to secede and dissolve the Union. "By and by, Pennsylvania, if she cannot have protection for her coal and iron, which is her Negro, will dissolve the union." Illinois could do so over beef, New York over free trade, California over the issue of a Pacific railroad, Michigan over the clearing of the St. Clair flatlands, and so on, to the end of the Union.

The amendment proposed by Corwin to perpetuate slavery in the states Lovejoy exposed as a halter on the free choice of some of the states. Although the amendment would never allow slavery to be touched in the states where it existed, suppose Maryland, Virginia, or Kentucky "wants to touch it"—suppose "they want us to pay them something, and they will emancipate their slaves." The amendment would destroy the possibility of nationwide freedom—you bind the hands of the federal government and the slave states that might choose to abolish slavery. His final plea was: "Let the American people who made this government preserve it consecrated to freedom." [9]

"A jewel compared with the compromising effusions of Seward and other Senators and Representatives who think Union worth more than Liberty and that slavery should be preserved and principle smothered," exclaimed the *Bureau County Republican*. "Give us the man of courage like the fearless Lovejoy in the hour of peril!" [10]

On January 29, Thaddeus Stevens, the Lancaster ironmaster and rigorous democrat, broke a long silence on the secession question. When he spoke in the House, the old man displayed the vigor of his ideas, his piercing contempt for humbug and halfway men and the "homilies upon the Union and the jeremiads over its destruction. . . . The Southern States will not be turned from their deliberate and stern purpose by soft words and touching lamentations." [11]

If in December Lovejoy and Stevens had seemed to be far ahead of the party, now in January they expressed ideas on compromise that more conservative Republicans were forced to adopt, as being in their own interest. A modern scholar of the secession crisis has concluded that the "stiff-backed" Republicans like Washburne, Roscoe Conkling, and Lovejoy expressed "the real sentiments of the party." Owen Lovejoy is singled out: "Even though identified with the extreme antislavery radicals,

[he] was not out of step with his more moderate colleagues on this issue." The same scholar, in assessing the importance of the antislavery radicals, wrote: "In a very real sense it was this group which gave the Republicans their *raison d'être*, their driving force, and their only common principle, namely, opposition to slavery expansion. Without these men it is doubtful that the party could have survived." [12]

Another modern scholar has demonstrated that Lincoln and the radicals rather than the conservatives, in holding fast against compromise, really spoke for the Republican party, if not also for the people of the North. He points out that although the radicals may have been apprehensive over "the drift back to Whiggery" that they feared in December, 1860, "their apprehension was tempered by a basic regard for Lincoln." Lovejoy probably best exemplified this attitude.[13]

On the other hand, leading New York capitalists meeting in a conference on December 15, 1860, at 33 Pine Street in the heart of New York's financial district, appealed to the South to avoid hasty acts, adopted compromise resolutions, and threw their great weight against Lincoln's careful intervention against compromise. They may not have been aware of his efforts; nevertheless, the application of a business-as-usual rationale by them and by business groups in Boston and Philadelphia strengthened the secessionists in this crisis period. Soon, however, even these bankers, merchants, and manufacturers in the North changed their minds—by the end of January the obvious trend in the North was toward neither concessions of the 1860 Republican platform nor secession but toward enforcing the laws and upholding federal power. Objectively this was a trend toward the radical and Lincoln position so militantly expressed by Lovejoy, Stevens, and others in the radical wing of the Republican party.[14]

Businessmen who in December were prepared to make concessions, began to realize in January that the destruction of the

Union would injure their interests. They were also taking note of the growing resentment among Democrats and Republicans each time federal property was seized by the rebels. As these events took place, the separation between the sections deepened; and in the North, particularly in the Republican party, new forces developed against conciliatory measures. Added to Lincoln's influence, the radicals' intransigence was probably the decisive force in the party. In the end they spoke for the nation, because the people of the North were less and less inclined to support compromise, and it was quite clear, too, that most of the Southern people did not desire secession, rebellion, and defiance of the federal government.

An incident of Lovejoy's adamant stand against compromise was described by Miss Emily V. Mason, who lived near Alexandria, Virginia. Knowing that Miss Mason desired an appointment for her nephew Mason Rowland to the United States Naval Academy, a friend of hers, and Lovejoy's, Bronson Murray, formerly of Ottawa, Illinois, used his influence to arrange a meeting between the two sometime early in February, 1861. To her astonishment Lovejoy said he would make the nomination of young Rowland immediately, and urged Miss Mason to telegraph the young man "directly" to come in and get his appointment.

Although Lovejoy's directness and speedy action pleased her, Miss Mason was put under considerable strain by the congressman's "latest disquisition on abolitionism." He told her that he and his party went for "*war to the knife* till not a slave holder rested on American soil." He was not at all happy with Cassius Clay, a former co-worker in Kentucky's antislavery movement. Clay had come to Washington, Lovejoy said, "talking *Union* & making some men falter, but our boys will stand firm & not concede an inch to slave power." Miss Mason said some "fierce things . . . in reply." When she left, she felt that no "blessing" could come of an appointment of her nephew "from such *bloody*

271

hands." Yet she thought it a strange inconsistency and wondrous indeed that Lovejoy had consented to make the nomination, knowing how secessionist Rowland was. Lovejoy said he required no pledge from the youth as to his politics or his future actions. Even though Lovejoy flared up at the end of the interview, Miss Mason thought him "honest & generous" although " 'crazy' as are all abolitionists, and as Lincoln himself shows *he is* by his latest speeches." [15]

As slave state after slave state left the Union in January, removing its representatives from Congress, the futile effort to appease continued. From the Committee of Thirty-Three Corwin continued to report plans to change the Constitution in favor of the slave states. Border state representatives became the main protagonists of conciliation policy, while men like Lovejoy and Stevens led an unyielding struggle to break up the rebellion and punish the offenders. But what once might have been bloody altercations now were softened into contests of wits to block and overthrow motions and countermotions.

Lovejoy's name occurs frequently enough in the pages of the *Congressional Globe* during the secession crisis to warrant the conclusion that he had been assigned a role of leadership among House Republicans. His persistent demands on points of order, his brisk objections, indicate a commanding position. For example, on February 26, 1861, Corwin introduced in the House an amendment to his committee's report. Lovejoy leaped to his feet with a point of order in an effort to block Corwin's move to legitimize slavery forever in the states. Lovejoy demonstrated to the satisfaction of the Speaker and of the House that Corwin's modifications were out of order because they were not the creation of the committee then reporting. Corwin, stung, remarked sardonically, "I understand the gentleman from Illinois very well. His motives are very pure but they are objectionable to me." Lovejoy replied, "I have no doubt of it. Purity is always objectionable to the opposite. I speak politically of course." Appreciative members laughed loud enough for the clerk to hear. Lovejoy's point of order was sustained.[16]

Nevertheless, test votes showed a majority for Corwin's amendment. On February 27 it failed to receive the necessary two-thirds support required for a proposed amendment to the Constitution; the Crittenden proposal also was defeated. But on February 28 four Republicans changed their votes and three abstained, providing the two-thirds approval. In the Senate in the following last few days of the stormy and complicated session, Corwin's proposed Thirteenth Amendment was adopted by a vote of 24 to 12 and recommended to the states; Crittenden's compromise resolutions were defeated on March 2, only two days before the Lincoln Administration was due to take over the government, and by a close vote of 20 to 19.

An insistent gadfly in the House, Lovejoy expressed himself pungently in other surroundings as well. In January, when Crittenden had proposed dividing the territories between slave and nonslave states on a line to the Pacific, Lovejoy was reported to have made this statement in a Republican caucus: "There never was a more causeless revolt since Lucifer led his cohorts of apostate angels against the throne of God; but I never heard that the Almighty proposed to compromise the matter by allowing the rebels to kindle the fires of hell south of the celestial meridian of 36° 30'!" [17]

When asked by the New York *Times* Washington correspondent about one of his colleagues' conciliatory speeches at the outbreak of secession, Lovejoy answered, "We want no Melanchthons now; we want Martin Luthers. We want no one to write essays upon the Union and the sin and disaster of secession, but some one to throw the inkstand right at the head of the devil." [18]

Lovejoy spoke militantly of bringing the lawbreakers to

court, of punishing brigands who destroyed and stole United States property. Rebellion and secession in the name of slavery—indeed any rebellion that attempted to overthrow the new order about to be inaugurated with Lincoln—had to be repulsed, crushed.

Four more states seceded after Lincoln took his oath of office on March 4. Not even the Corwin amendment perpetuating slavery in the states where it existed, which had just passed both houses of Congress, could mollify leaders of the rebellion. Peace conventions, compromise resolutions, appeasing amendments to the Constitution, soft words for Southern extremists—none availed to conciliate the rebels. Sad as the prospect of disunion was to some wise and temperate Southern leaders, their control of events was dislodged. Not all of them were aggressive to the point of armed rebellion; nor were they as imperialist as the powerful men in the slaveholding class who envisioned slave states on the Caribbean islands in a *mare americanum*. Such a voracious appetite for slave territory could not be appeased, as Lincoln observed when he said, "A year will not pass till we shall have to take Cuba as a condition upon which they will stay in the Union." [19] But since the moderate Southern men did not control events, the battle was joined in little more than a month after the inauguration of the new President with the siege of Fort Sumter.

Confident of the new administration's ability to cope with the rebellion, Lovejoy had even expressed a hope for a speedy adjustment of the crisis. But on March 27 he wrote Lincoln from Bureau County: "If you do not mean to recognize the 'Confederacy' the Fort [Sumter] ought to be retained. I think we ought to fight not only for their sakes but for the sake of the govt." In less than a month the fort fell to Confederate guns and Lincoln had issued a call to arms. By April 25 Lovejoy had seen at least one infantry company raised in Illinois in response to the

President's and Governor Richard Yates's calls. At the departure of fellow farmers and townsmen Lovejoy made a brief speech congratulating them, and he proclaimed that he was ready to serve the people on the field of battle. If he could be of more use there than in the legislative halls, he was willing to go immediately. Lovejoy aided in organizing five companies of men from the county in fourteen days.[20]

Some were for making Lovejoy a colonel in command of a regiment—the 20th Illinois Infantry—just then forming in the southeast part of the county. To this proposal a correspondent of the *Bureau County Republican* replied, urging that Lovejoy remain in Congress, although the writer did not doubt the excellence of the representative's service on the battlefield. Down in Champaign, Judge Cunningham's newspaper looked askance upon such a view, protesting that Lovejoy was being denied the honor of serving his country in a military capacity. The *Central Illinois Gazette* denounced the opposition press, proposed Lovejoy as a natural leader who "has fought many a battle for the right, God and humanity." In the end a cooler view prevailed— Lovejoy retained his seat in Congress, where none could deny that his vigorous actions compared favorably to the victories of a regiment. As the new session got under way Lovejoy demonstrated his growing leadership of antislavery and Republican forces in saving the Union.[21]

14

For a Vigorous Prosecution
of the War

"Our object is to subdue the rebels."
—Thaddeus Stevens

In the post-election maneuvering for position, the antislavery wing of the Republican party submitted a bill to Lincoln for its share of the victory. This was perhaps a belated claim, since the principal deals had been made by Davis, Swett, and others behind the scenes at Chicago. Nevertheless Lovejoy apparently had hoped to win a Cabinet post for Joshua Giddings, who was now the grand old man of the political-abolitionist cause. It was hoped that he might get the Postmaster-Generalship, but Lovejoy told the elder congressman that there was "nothing so good in store for us," that Lincoln had not yet called on him for advice, and he did not feel like "obtruding it." Lovejoy may have been hasty, since his letter to Giddings was dated November 23, 1860, only a few weeks after the election results were tallied. Whether Lovejoy had anything directly to do with it is not clear, but Giddings was appointed consul general in Canada in 1861. Also, his old colleague Zebina Eastman was named United States consul in Bristol, England.[1]

At about the time Lincoln was making appointments to the Cabinet, Lovejoy is said to have joined Senator Benjamin F. Wade of Ohio in condemning the President-elect's choices as a disgraceful surrender to the South. This charge might be credible if it were not that Lovejoy exercised the utmost care in his relations with Lincoln. Whatever his discontent with the President-elect, he had since 1854 made prodigious efforts to work harmoniously with him. Of course, in the excitement of the winter days before the inauguration, and before the appointments were known, antislavery men released an acidulous barrage against Lincoln's selections. But if Lovejoy agreed with these men, he tactfully held his tongue in public.

He did join Farnsworth and Washburne at this time in privately reminding Lincoln that he "had not as stated proffered the Treasuryship to Chase." The three Illinois Republicans, who were of varying shades of antislavery origin, told Lincoln on January 18 that they "would be gratified" with the appointment of the Ohio leader. As far as Lovejoy and his colleagues were concerned, Chase's long years of leadership in the antislavery movement were among his strongest recommendations. They did not mention this qualification to the President-elect. They did say that they were fully convinced that appointing Chase "would be highly satisfactory to an overwhelming majority of the Republican party." Thus the matter stood in mid-January when every species of office-seeker was on Lincoln's doorstep. When the new President announced his Cabinet on March 5, Chase was named Secretary of the Treasury. Although we do not know whether Lincoln disagreed with the three Illinoisans' measure of "an overwhelming majority," his appointment of Chase was a politic redemption of their claim, and a response to the urging of such influential Republicans as the editors of the Chicago *Tribune*.[2]

Lincoln appointed Chase as much to balance the influence of his Secretary of State, Seward, in the Cabinet as to meet the widespread demand in the country for the appointment. Few in the antislavery ranks were overjoyed with the "defeated candidates club" that Lincoln was forced to knock together. Middle-grounders in the Cabinet like Montgomery Blair of Maryland sickened stalwarts like Thaddeus Stevens. Yet even Stevens downed his anger and contempt and proved to be the able commander of Congress alongside Lincoln against the common enemy.

Lovejoy had by this time also made his peace with Illinois conservative Republicans. Probably through the good offices of Jesse Fell, the congressman arrived at a modus vivendi with David Davis and his supporters in and around Bloomington. Certainly the prospect of victory with Lincoln had proved a unifying force for Republicans. The threat to the country posed by the slaveholders' rebellion was the final and decisive one. Yet what a bizarre twist of politics it was that threw Davis and Lovejoy together in April, 1861, when the abolitionist was urging the appointment of Davis to the United States Supreme Court.[3]

Whatever lesser issues divided Northern men, most rallied to the defense of the Union. Stephen A. Douglas stepped forward from his bitterest defeat to stand by the Constitution and Lincoln in the crisis. Lovejoy appeared in June, 1861, as a speaker at a meeting in memory of the Little Giant after he had succumbed to typhoid fever. Douglas's successor, taciturn and conservative Orville H. Browning, also rose above the party squabbles to stand by Lincoln and the Constitution and by inference with Lovejoy, as the campaign of 1862 showed.[4]

Lincoln's call for volunteers three days after the Confederate bombardment of Fort Sumter was quickly answered. Massachusetts, Pennsylvania, Illinois, Wisconsin, Ohio, and New York were in the forefront as their men came out to defend the nation and preserve the Union.

Abolitionists early declared their ideas of the most effective

278

way to win the war, of what steps must be taken to break up the slave power, the seat of the rebellion. Garrison and Phillips had spent the winter of 1860–61 arguing for peace between the sections, on one hand and, on the other, they had welcomed the departure of the slave states. Although the latter attitude was consistent with the New Englanders' disdain for the Constitution as a proslavery document that ought to be rejected as well as a Union with slaveowners, it proved to be no help in meeting the responsibilities of a war thrust on the nation. But the fall of Sumter, the popular response to Lincoln's call for volunteers, and perhaps their own honest recognition of the gross tactical error in welcoming dismemberment of the Union led the Bostonians to change their minds. Phillips expressed it pungently for his followers when he said, "Rather than surrender the Capital, cover every square foot of it with a living body; crowd it with a million men, and empty every bank vault at the North to pay the cost." Frederick Douglass wrote in the May, 1861, issue of his paper: "The simple way, then, to put an end to the savage and desolating war now waged by the slaveholders is to strike down slavery itself, the primal cause of the war." The Negro leader urged that it be done at once by " 'carrying the war into Africa.' Let the slaves and free colored people be called into service, and formed into a liberating army. . . ." [5]

Meanwhile Lincoln had called for a special session of Congress to begin July 4 for the purpose of raising an army and the money needed to conduct a full-scale war. To save and mend the Union he asked for at least four hundred thousand men and $400 million.

Even as the members of Congress were arriving in Washington for this session, abolitionists were proposing a course of action for the Republican party and the Administration. Gerrit Smith wrote to the editor of the New York *Tribune* that the war had only one object: to put down "the gigantic conspiracy against the Government." The most effective way to do this, according to Smith, was for the Administration to declare a policy permitting the enrollment of Negroes in the army; Negro troops would speed the Union's victory. Moreover, Smith asserted that the army should be neither for nor against slavery but the army should treat the Negroes who flocked into Northern camps as they would white people. Smith said the object of the war was not the abolition of slavery but he later added his endorsement of the growing demands for a proclamation abolishing slavery.[6]

Lovejoy gave no hint of his intended course in the coming session, but on June 27 the *Bureau County Republican* stated that he would vote for "a vigorous prosecution of the war." When Congress convened, Lovejoy was thrust into a position of leadership by the logic of his political history. Whereas Thaddeus Stevens, as chairman of the House Ways and Means Committee, took undisputed command of the wartime Congress, Lovejoy emerged as the voice of the antislavery sentiment in the land. Technically, his leadership was confined to the chairmanship of the House Committee on Agriculture, but on the floor of the House his most effective and dramatic actions were on the slavery question, especially—in this brief session—on the question of the "contrabands" of war.

General Benjamin F. Butler, in command of the army's Department of Virginia, had used this word to classify three runaway slaves who had walked into Fortress Monroe. They were supposed to work on construction of a Confederate battery but had run away from their master to Union lines on the night of May 23, 1861. General Butler refused to give up the three men to John B. Cary, a Confederate major, who had come under a flag of truce to claim them under the Fugitive Slave Law. Butler maintained that the seceded state in which their master resided had forfeited its rights under United States laws by the act of secession. "I shall detain the Negroes as contrabands of war," the general told Major Cary. The word of Butler's action, and the term he used, spread fast among the slaves in the area. Six days later sixty thousand dollars' worth of "contraband" came into Fortress Monroe. And this was not a localized matter. Free Negroes had been among the first eager volunteers for the Union army; slaves, whenever they could, flocked to army camps or hid themselves on naval vessels in the hope of finding freedom and a chance to fight for the liberation of their families. The status of the rising number of slaves insisting on their freedom in this fashion perplexed many generals. The commander of the Northern army, General Winfield Scott, was at first angered by Butler's decision but soon changed his mind. And as rapidly as Negro slave families flocked into army camps to seek freedom, their legal status and their physical welfare became problems for the Lincoln Administration. Secretary of War Cameron approved of Butler's policy and urged him to continue to give asylum to the fugitive slaves of rebels. Postmaster General Blair also backed Butler and, in writing to the general, informed him that the "contraband" question was to come up at a Cabinet meeting.[7]

The problem was difficult, because there was no prohibition in the Constitution against Butler's "fugitive slave law," as his policy was popularly named, nor any sanction for it. However, there was wide popular support in the North, especially among abolitionists and antislavery men like Lovejoy. In "liberating" the "property" claimed by the Confederate officer, General Butler was dealing only with the slaves of rebels aiding in the construction of Confederate forts. It was a necessary wartime measure, but the problem it attempted to solve became more perplexing with the influx of men, women, and children not necessarily slaves of rebels actively aiding the rebellion.

Since neither Lincoln nor Cameron laid down a broad policy,

281

the vacuum was filled by field commanders, who chose their own course of action. Many Northern officers, assuming the constitutional protection of slavery in the states, ordered the fugitives to be returned to their masters. More far-reaching toward appeasing slaveowners were Generals George B. McClellan and Robert Patterson, who ordered their troops to suppress Negro slave insurrection.[8]

Abolitionists, of course, argued for emancipation. Frederick Douglass, characteristically ahead of most men of his time, declared in June, 1861, that "Sound policy, not less than humanity, demands the instant liberation of every slave in the rebel States." [9]

Owen Lovejoy hastened to put such a policy into effect when he introduced a resolution on July 8 in the special session of Congress. Although Lincoln's presidential message to the legislature on July 4 promised not to interfere with slavery in the states, Lovejoy tried to extend General Butler's limited "contraband" action into an over-all policy for the United States Army. That there was merit to Lovejoy's resolution was made evident when the first of its four parts was adopted by the House, 93 to 55. It stated that "in the judgment of the House it is no part of the duty of soldiers of the United States to capture and return fugitive slaves." A second part, aimed at the material base of the slaveowners' rebellion, would have specified that the Judiciary Committee be instructed to "enquire into the expediency of the repeal" of the Fugitive Slave Law. But the House was too timid. Its failure to face up to the "contraband" question disappointed abolitionists in and out of the legislature. Lovejoy was nevertheless pleased that the House had approved even the first part of the resolution. Senator Sumner of Massachusetts sent over a note of approval and congratulation. Lovejoy thanked him and observed that "Our conservative people were timid and vexed but they had to vote right at last." [10]

Frederick Douglass commented in August, 1861, that with the

282

passage of Lovejoy's resolution "we seemed on the verge of the right path," but he deplored the government's continuing practice of forbidding slaves to come within Union lines. This persistence by the government, Douglass wrote, "evades, ignores the real issue." Nevertheless Lovejoy's resolution was "excellent." [11]

Gerrit Smith commended Lovejoy and deplored the indisposition of the House of Representatives to strike the Fugitive Slave Law. Lovejoy's resolution was accepted by Smith, Douglass, and other abolitionists as a sign of the change in public sentiment (the "growing public radicalism," as Allan Nevins phrases it).[12] Smith pushed the argument further. He called for the liberation of the slave as "one of the necessities and therefore one of the rights of the country. Let the President in his capacity as commander of the Army proclaim such liberation, and the war would end in thirty days. The slave question is the war question," Smith stated. In the main Lovejoy agreed with Smith but hesitated to lecture the President so sharply in public. Nevertheless, the position of Smith, Lovejoy, and others was fast becoming the position of broad sections of the American people. They were ready for it and would accordingly approve legislative actions by Stevens, Lovejoy, Trumbull, Sumner, and others in both houses of Congress. The old radicals were enjoying acceptance where once they had been scorned.[13]

Yet the abolitionists lost the first round in this first wartime session. Their efforts to convince the country that an antislavery, especially an emancipation, policy was a necessary one for the Union armies, went down to defeat. The object of the war for the Union side was, as Lovejoy and other Radical Republicans had said, to suppress the rebellion. To do so, they said, it would be necessary for the army to cease upholding slavery and to enlist Negro troops. But Congress preferred to accept a different guideline, one proposed by Kentucky's Representative John J. Crittenden. A day after the Union debacle at Bull Run the House passed without debate, 117 to 2, the Crittenden resolution, which proclaimed that the war was not being fought to oppress, subjugate, overthrow, or interfere with slavery in the Southern states. The resolution also said that the war was being fought to uphold the supremacy of the Constitution and to preserve the Union, with states' rights unimpaired.

Albert G. Riddle, from Ohio's Western Reserve, and Charles J. Biddle, a Democrat from Philadelphia, voted against it. If its words were not an outright surrender to the secessionist rebels, its spirit was, according to Stevens and Lovejoy. They scorned the resolution so thoroughly that they refused even to vote against it. Lovejoy remained in his seat, silent and somber. Stevens said a few days after passage of the resolution: "I did not like the resolution of the distinguished Gentleman from Kentucky because it looked like an apology from us in saying what were the objects of the war. Ask those who made the war what its object is. Do not ask us. Our object is to subdue the rebels." In the Senate, Sumner refused to vote on the resolution, and five colleagues voted against, while thirty approved it. Ten men, therefore, had the fortitude to resist panic over the disaster on the battlefield the day before. They would not be stampeded into courting the border states by surrendering the lives of millions of slaves.[14]

The special session met that summer for twenty-nine days and, in James G. Blaine's opinion, "In no other session of Congress was so much accomplished in so brief a time." [15] Besides providing for the enlistment of four hundred thousand men and raising the money to clothe, feed, and arm them, the Congress began to face up to the necessities of the war when it began the process of confiscating rebel property—in this case their slaves. Four million human beings in bondage represented billions of dollars in productive value enriching the Confederacy. This advantage had to be neutralized if the United States were to be united again. On August 6 the first Confiscation Act was passed, providing for the seizure of all slaves and other property used by the rebels to prosecute the war. The bitter lesson of the Union humiliation at Bull Run was embodied in the bill. For it was at that disaster that Union men saw Negro slaves being used by the Confederate army to back up white troops.

In the same session Lovejoy's differences with Eastern Republicans came out, especially in debate over the Additional Revenue bill. This centered around the raising of money through taxes to win the war. Lovejoy spoke as the farmer's congressman against the interests of capitalists. Other Midwestern congressmen also denounced a tax policy favorable to banks and corporations. Stevens, Pennsylvania ironmaster, asserted that a direct tax, under the Constitution, was a tax upon real estate, that is, upon land. Lovejoy believed that taxing the nominal holder of land (principally farmers) was unfair, for the holder of notes (mortgage and credit grantors) on the same land was free from taxation on those notes. Despite fundamental agreement on the broad aspects of strategy and antislavery action, Lovejoy and Stevens continued to find themselves on opposite sides of this and other tax proposals.

On August 3, three days before adjournment, when the discussion again centered on the Additional Revenue bill, Lovejoy bluntly stated his war policy: "We propose to confiscate all their [rebel] property, not merely to tax it." Bingham of Ohio teased Lovejoy about a confiscation measure: "The Gentleman's bill, unfortunately, has not yet seen the light. It is a thing he tells us is going to be. I will consider it when it comes." But on the final day of the session the first Confiscation Act, although not Lovejoy's, was passed—the commencement of a serious policy against the disloyal states and their slaveowning leaders. The act embodied a policy Lovejoy supported as a patriot and as an abolitionist.[16]

Keeping the Republicans on the right track toward suppression of the rebellion and emancipation of the Negro slaves as a war policy was no simple job, Lovejoy discovered in this session and those that followed. Republican votes for the Crittenden resolution, passage of only part of his own resolution protecting fleeing slaves, and generals permitted by the Administration to return fugitive slaves to their owners left Lovejoy with much to wonder about fellow Republicans. In turn some of them teased him and stood opposed to his proposals, and some went so far as to lecture him publicly. For example, Thurlow Weed's Albany *Evening Journal* and the Chicago *Journal* took Lovejoy to task for his July resolution. On the other hand the Waukegan, Illinois, *Gazette*, a Republican newspaper not in Lovejoy's congressional district, came to his defense: "We tell the Republicans and journalists that Mr. Lovejoy represents the true sentiments of the people—the true issue now before the nation." [17]

15

On the Battlefields: Summer, 1861

"The side of war that you get in newspapers is very different."

—Owen Lovejoy

Indignation over the rebellion, combined with a buoyant confidence, had produced among the people of the North a heady certainty that they could wage a short and decisive war. A knockout victory over the Confederacy was prematurely demanded of the Union army, with the war cry of "On to Richmond!"

During the special session of Congress that began in July, 1861, the clamor for a major engagement forced Lincoln to call upon the aged veteran, General Winfield Scott. He turned to Brigadier General Irvin McDowell, who, against his better judgment, prepared a plan of battle calculated to throw Confederate troops out of the approaches to Washington, send them reeling back beyond the Confederate capital, and crush the rebellion before the harvest moon. In the action that took place on July 21 along Bull Run, a small stream a few miles southwest of Washington, federal forces were badly defeated.

McDowell's plans were well drawn but were based on false

estimates of the rebel strength and of Major General Robert Patterson's ability to cut off Confederate reinforcements. The triumphant advance of Union forces up to about three that afternoon was reversed, and the Union retreat turned into a stampede as raw troops panicked, overtaking congressmen and other spectators.

Lovejoy, one of the effervescent congressmen who had demanded a victory in the field against the rebels, spoke to his neighbors in Princeton later that summer of having had "an irrepressible desire to see a battle." [1] On the morning of the battle he had climbed into a wagon with some of his colleagues and rolled out of the Capital to the battlefield. The procession of buggies, gigs, wagons, and horseback riders had the air of a picnic.

Lovejoy had been in the field, riding a horse behind a column of Colonel Samuel P. Heintzelman's troops, and remained after nearly all had retreated to Centerville. Then, giving up his horse to an officer, he set out to walk the six miles to Centerville. At one point he was cut off from escape, but managed to reach Centerville weary and exhausted. The bulk of McDowell's tired army was here, drawn up in line of battle at nine o'clock in the evening, expecting an enemy pursuit. But the enemy also miscalculated and failed to use his advantage. Lovejoy took over an abandoned ambulance wagon and delivered two wounded soldiers to the Fairfax hospital. It was four in the morning by the time he reached Washington.[2]

William Howard Russell, London *Times* correspondent, was one of the eyewitnesses to the disaster at Bull Run. His haughty and polished description of the bloody fray in the Virginia hills told his readers a story of hysteria and outright stupidity on the part of Union army men and United States senators and representatives. An experienced war reporter who had seen engagements of the Crimean War, among others, Russell nevertheless stirred up an angry fusillade of criticism against himself. The Chicago *Tribune*'s antislavery editor Dr. Charles H. Ray, who was on the battlefield in a "four-wheeler" with Lovejoy and Elihu Washburne, denounced Russell's account in the *Times*. Washburne thoroughly disagreed with it, and Lovejoy, no friend of English aristocracy and upper-class complacency, showed no sympathy for Russell's tale of troops running helter-skelter from the field at Bull Run. Lovejoy flatly contradicted Russell and said that the newspaperman had "made a fancy sketch, to our injury, instead of giving a true historical record of the event." [3]

Lovejoy said he saw no one run. He was merciless in denouncing General Patterson, and placed the blame for retreat on that officer. Of course, the abolitionist congressman could hardly have had any use for a general who insisted on turning fugitive slaves back to their masters after they had sought asylum in Union camps. Lovejoy considered Patterson's failure to halt Confederate reinforcements from Winchester as an act of a "half traitor and half imbecile." It was those fresh Southern troops who turned the battle from Union victory to Union defeat. Lovejoy also maintained that "had there been officers who had properly addressed the troops, they would, hungry and tired as they were, have been again rallied to the contest." On the retreat to Washington, Lovejoy said, the men were in disorder, they were weary, exhausted—they were like lost sheep, but not like frightened ones. There was no panic, Lovejoy insisted. [4]

There was panic, however, next day in the House of Representatives as the Crittenden resolution was overwhelmingly approved. Lovejoy's abstention from the vote on the proslavery manifesto was his way of scorning it.

A more formal step toward seeing a battle had been taken sometime in the spring or early summer. Lovejoy offered the regiment of infantry that he had succeeded in raising in Illinois to the War Department, which it accepted for "three years, or during the war." The Chief Clerk of the department had added the proviso that the regiment be ready for marching orders in thirty-one days. West Point officiousness must have amused the abolitionist as he read the Department's letter of acceptance. The Chief Clerk's letter of July 31, 1861, declared: "This acceptance is with the distinct understanding that this department will revoke the commission of all officers who may be found incompetent for the proper discharge of their duties." Subsequently some inner office consultations must have occurred, for when Lovejoy reached home on August 17, after a visit with friends in New England, he found a telegram from Simon Cameron, Secretary of War: "Fremont will be pleased to receive you as one of his aids. Report to him." [5]

Friends in Princeton had deliberately refrained from making Lovejoy's homecoming a special occasion, to test whether he had really lost ground with the people over his resolution on fugitive slaves earlier that summer. The brash local opposition newspaper, the *Patriot*, maintained that Lovejoy had suffered a loss of popularity. But when more than three thousand people turned out to a reception for Lovejoy on the evening of Saturday, August 24, the Bryant brothers and others in Princeton knew that their congressman had deep and powerful roots among his constituents.

Even so, the local Democratic paper, thinly clothing its Southern sympathies, subjected Lovejoy to acid attacks. One day he was denounced as a coward in the battle at Bull Run, but generally he was attacked as a fanatical radical, as he had been for over twenty years. Embittered Democrats claimed fealty to the Union while they denounced antislavery patriots like Lovejoy. Yet he turned the tables on them by proposing on September 3 to unite with Democrats in a single, Union, party for the purpose of suppressing the rebellion against "our common country." There seemed to be no takers.[6]

Three weeks after the unity letter appeared in the *Republican*,

Lovejoy left Princeton for duty under General Frémont in the Western Department of the army. Governor Richard Yates forwarded Lovejoy's commission as a colonel on September 25. Lovejoy had already taken a train to Quincy, Illinois, and boarded a Mississippi steamboat bound for St. Louis. He reached that sprawling metropolis on September 27 at a moment when its inhabitants were in a state of turmoil over General Frémont's bold proclamation of August 30, 1861, freeing the slaves of rebels in Missouri. Within a few hours after his arrival, Lovejoy joined the general's staff and was on his way to Jefferson City. He wrote from that place on September 28 that he had met at least one officer who was from his home district. Lovejoy observed that the officers he met were confident of success in their expedition into Missouri. As for himself, he wrote, "I think we shall not be disappointed but the issue of a battle depends on very trivial things sometimes." [7]

And sometimes, he might have added, a general's command depends on very large political considerations, as General Frémont discovered when his order ran into opposition in the White House. Frémont's order was conceived by him as a sharp *military* countermeasure to the guerrilla warfare in Missouri. He had come into command of an area from the Mississippi to the Rockies, and Illinois and Kentucky, in July, 1861. Missouri was the critical border state, and control of it could be of the greatest strategic value to the United States. If Missouri were to fall to the rebels, it was believed at the time that Kansas and the Southwest might give them maneuvering ground. Pro-Confederate people in Kentucky and southern Illinois might then also pull those states away from the Union. With them they might take control of the Cairo junction of the Ohio and Mississippi Rivers, the western banks of the Mississippi, the Missouri River, and three railways running from half to three-quarters across Missouri.

Since the fall of Sumter the state had been the political and military battleground of secessionist forces, on one side, under Governor Claiborne Jackson, who had replied insultingly to Lincoln's call for troops, and Unionist forces on the other side, gathered mainly in and around the city of St. Louis. Germans, Irish, Hungarians, and other settlers of European birth, many with experience in the democratic revolutions of 1848, were antislavery and pro-Union, and from their ranks came some of Frémont's top officers and many of his troops. He could expect from them diligent execution of his emancipation order and thus strike a blow at secessionist strength.

When Frémont arrived in Missouri on July 25, Unionists and secessionists were already at war. The situation was complicated by Washington's neglect of the Western front and by the tactics of the Blair family, who ran Missouri politics and who pushed Missouri prematurely into full-scale war, according to Allan Nevins. The Western Department of the army was "boiling with confusion, shortages, dissensions, and perils." Secessionist bands of guerrillas roamed the hills and plains harassing the state and threatening the Union position. Frémont had not received adequate troops, equipment, and arms; and when contingents finally did arrive they were green.[8]

"War is a terrible necessity at best," Colonel Owen Lovejoy wrote from the Missouri battlefield in October, 1861. "Its tendencies are all to demoralization. But I cannot see any way that we can avoid it. All there is sacred in our government depends on our maintaining its supremacy." For Lovejoy the war in Missouri consisted mainly in pursuing an enemy who would not stand still long enough to fight a decisive battle. After his train ride to Jefferson City, Frémont and his staff made their way to a camp that Lovejoy described as "west of the city on a hill or large knoll sloping on all sides except on the west." For a man of fifty years such as Lovejoy, used to a warm bed in his pleasant house in Princeton or in his rooms in Washington, the camp's accommodations, principally tents, left something to be desired. On the stopover in St. Louis he had ordered a cot, but this "luxury" was lost in the army's organized confusion. On his first night in camp Lovejoy made his bed under the open sky on a couple of boards. The next night he was fortunate in finding an empty tent and placed the boards on two trunks, just in time to be protected against "one of the most terrific thunderstorms I ever knew . . . the rain poured down all night, literally in torrents." The water flowed all night across the ground and through the tent.[9]

Camp life was full of alarms and excursions. One chilly October midnight came a call to arms. It was over a false alarm. The pickets had fired at someone "said to be a spy who had attempted to pass them." Officers and men were called up again in the morning before light. It was another false alarm.[10]

On the first day out of Jefferson City, Lovejoy marched ten miles, camping in a meadow near a stream on what was believed to be a secessionist's farm. The general christened the camp in honor of Lovejoy. "I presume," the colonel wrote, lightheartedly, "he [the secessionist] will value that part of his farm very highly hereafter." On the second day's march the Frémont men trudged through desolate country, passing only a few log houses. They stopped at the small town of California on the Pacific Railroad route, and the third day marched on across the broken prairies to Tipton and set up Camp Asboth as Headquarters, Western Department, United States Army. After a gloomy day of October rain the weather cleared.[11]

One serene Saturday evening Lovejoy sat down to write his impressions of army life. One of his pleasantest was of "the encampment of clean white tents in a bright day or a moonlight night when the fires are burning at the mouth of the tents." He went on to comment on the perplexity of commanding an army. Some portions of the army were scheduled to move southward toward the Arkansas border. Teams of horses and wagons had to

293

be requisitioned or confiscated to provide transportation. General David Hunter told Lovejoy one day that he needed a hundred teams and had no more than thirty or forty. When the troops finally arrived, they plunged "into the darkness of secessionism." [12]

By October 7 Frémont had organized a marching force of thirty thousand men, including five thousand cavalry, with eighty-six guns. The army moved across the state in order to control the rail lines at Sedalia, Rolla, and Ironton, and to take Springfield, thereby linking forces with loyalists in the southwest portion of the state. His objective was to put Union forces in a position to encircle and hold the western banks of the Mississippi all the way to New Orleans. The latter objective Frémont hoped, with his usual exuberance, to achieve in conjunction with Commodore Andrew H. Foote's gunboats on the Mississippi.

The western army headquarters had moved to Springfield by the end of October. Lovejoy had marched with the troops thirty miles on the day of their arrival in that city. On another march of twenty-seven miles, after the Frémont forces came to the small town of Warsaw, Lovejoy was so exhausted that, he said, "like Jacob I threw myself on the ground and my head on the saddle and went to sleep." [13]

When he entered Warsaw, his first stop was at the hospital to give comfort to the wounded. In a small room he found thirteen dead bodies ranged side by side in square boxes for coffins, with their feet toward each other. They had been killed a few days earlier. "They seemed to have been placed in their coffins just as they had been found," Lovejoy said. Then "another young man was brought in . . . his feet stripped and his skull . . . broken in." He had been found eight miles from the scene of conflict, and it seemed to Lovejoy he had been taken prisoner and murdered. They were all buried next day in one grave. The gruesome spectacle was more horrible than any Lovejoy had ever witnessed. He wrote that "tears were seen in many an eye unused to weeping. . . . The more one sees of war the more one loathes its horrors and execrates the causes that produce it. . . . The side of war that you get in newspapers is very different from what it is inside of the curtain." [14]

One of Lovejoy's duties under Frémont's command was to act as a member of a claims commission. The general had appointed the Illinois congressman to serve on a three-member body to hear the claims of Missourians who had been denounced as being disloyal. Their horses and provisions had been taken from them; or their fences were used as fuel for campfires; or their timber had been cut down by army personnel. Another member of the commission was Gustave Koerner, former lieutenant governor of Illinois, who wrote in his memoirs that Lovejoy "was more prepared to allow claims than I." He speculated that had the Princeton abolitionist lived to see the Union restored he would have treated the Southern states kindly.[15]

Less a matter of speculation was Lovejoy's attitude toward slaves who slipped into camp, as they did into Union army camps all across the United States. Sarcastically referred to as contrabands, these fugitives became valuable sources of information about enemy movements and jubilantly went to work to aid the army of liberation. When they came into General Hunter's and General Frémont's lines, it was considered a good joke in camp to make application to Lovejoy to have the Negro fugitives returned. Lovejoy squelched the "applications" so that they were definitely discouraged from reappearance.[16]

Throughout October, troops streamed into the camps at Springfield in a build-up of Frémont's forces for a fight near the Arkansas line. Lovejoy had written his sons "Chinky" and "Charlie" on October 6, "we expect to leave in the morning but I do not know where we shall go. I fear the enemy has run away and will not stay to fight." Two weeks later, from Warsaw, he wrote that "Fremont says he will give us a victory before we return but I am still doubtful about it." [17]

Mixed with the excitement of the military actions was the agitation over General Frémont's explosive emancipation order, confiscating property and freeing slaves of rebel Missourians, and even imposing the death penalty on saboteurs and civilians guilty of aiding the enemy. Lincoln's displeasure with Frémont was sharp, and in the first days of September the President lost little time in modifying the order. Disgust with and denunciation of the President's attitude spread among antislavery men, even affecting conservative Orville H. Browning.

In the end the Blair family prevailed even over the metallic and powerful will of Jessie Benton Frémont, who descended on the White House to argue for her husband's action. The general was relieved of his command of the Western Department on November 2, much to the dismay of antislavery men, and especially those politically advanced Germans and Hungarians in Frémont's entourage. So incensed were the foreign-born officers and rank and filers in the camp that Frémont had to forbid demonstrations.

On Monday, November 4, according to Lovejoy, Frémont departed for St. Louis with most of the staff accompanying him. Lovejoy remained in camp "as a battle was confidently expected by Generals [Franz] Sigel and Frémont." Throughout the tense period preceding Frémont's removal Lovejoy expressed no opinion in public. Nor in the extant private correspondence is there a comment from him on this issue. Yet by all his past actions and statements he should have acclaimed the general and denounced the pressure against him for his emancipation measure. It seems inconsistent, too, that this man of strong feeling should have remained in camp while the general made his sad but grand departure. It seems especially strange since Lovejoy was considered to be "one of the political advisers in the picturesque Frémont entourage." [18] Apparently he played no significant role in the general's emancipation order and its subsequent troubles.

When Lovejoy returned to Princeton after his tour of duty in Missouri, he did finally say that he did not think the removal of the general at the time was right, but at the same time he was not prepared to say how far the President was justifiable, "as doubtless he had much more evidence in the premises." Lovejoy believed the wrong was in appointing Frémont to his position in the first place, but he insisted that the Administration should be sustained in its acts in carrying on the war and the government.[19]

The anticipated battle with the Confederate forces did not materialize, for they were in retreat and Hunter decided against pursuit. Lovejoy had written, "Reasoning from what I considered the true policy of the rebels, I made up my mind that they would not fight us." [20] President Lincoln had himself suggested the course of action to Hunter, basing his suggestions on advice from the aged Winfield Scott. This was a disappointing ending to the grand march begun by Frémont. The colorful general, although surrounded by opulence and apparent wastefulness and even careless officers, nevertheless did initiate a battle plan of pursuit. He had at least decided to fight the enemy, rather than sit it out, as General George B. McClellan seemed so dangerously to be doing in the East.

McClellan had been put in command of the Army of the Potomac to secure Baltimore and Washington. But he refused to act on his theory of one big campaign to end the war quickly. The more men, matériel, and arms he received, the more he complained of the enemy's superiority. McClellan's obsession with thoroughness of organization, his tactlessness with his superior General Scott, and his vanity made the Army of the Potomac a standing one, not a fighting one. When his forces finally went into battle after long inaction, they suffered defeat at Ball's Bluff on October 21. Despite assurances from Generals James M.

Wadsworth and Daniel Sickles during the fall and winter of 1861 that their forces were in a winning position in the Potomac theater, McClellan still preferred to wait.

On the other hand, Frémont's emancipation order, although often denounced by historians as precipitate and insubordinate, was at least an effort to check the rebellion by a measure short of battle. Had it not been countermanded, it might have proved a master political move.

Lincoln's modification of the order was distressing not only to radicals but to conservatives. And when General Henry W. Halleck, Frémont's and Hunter's successor in command of the Western Department, on taking over on November 20, ordered that no fugitive slaves should be admitted within Union lines, they were even more upset. Halleck justified his order on the grounds that the slaves were being used as spies by the rebels. Antislavery men were enraged, and Lovejoy returned to Congress determined to press for a repeal of Halleck's order.

16

The Revolutionary
Thirty-Seventh Congress

> *"Emancipation is the demand of civilization. That is a principle; everything else is an intrigue."*
>
> —*Ralph Waldo Emerson*

Late in November, 1861, Lovejoy made a farewell speech to his constituents in the courthouse in Princeton's city park. He was about to depart for the crucial second session of the 37th Congress. There, Lovejoy and other antislavery men hoped to enact their program for freedom. He communicated his ideas to his Princeton listeners in a "powerful, sonorous, variable and supple voice, well at his command." In his alert blue eyes friends and enemies alike could perceive his intense sincerity.[1]

"This is a causeless rebellion," he asserted, with a clenched fist held high above him and quivering with indignation, "—it must be crushed out." In time of peace he had abided by the Constitution: "We have no power to abolish slavery—even though I hate and abhor it." But now that war and rebellion were thrust on the American people—"we must do anything to suppress the rebellion." In time of war the highest law for governments is self-preservation.[2]

He was to return many times to this theme to justify federal action in abolishing slavery. He cited John Quincy Adams, who had written that at a time of insurrection Congress should have the power of abolishing slavery. Theophilus Parsons, eminent Harvard law professor, had concurred, and so had James Monroe. "What right do we have to destroy slavery?" Lovejoy asked. "I answer briefly, that if we do not destroy it, it will destroy us." But how best to accomplish this task was the question that had yet to be answered. Partisans of right and justice and freedom differed on the means. As ever, in a revolution, radical measures were deemed best to secure not only the victory of arms but also the triumph of a new, liberating institution over the old, decayed, and repressive one.

Lovejoy's radical measure enunciated at Princeton was not novel, but it was startling and bold for its time. "After what I have seen [I do not think] we shall ever subjugate these [rebellious] States without liberating their slaves and putting muskets into the hands of all who will fight for us." Arm the Negroes; arm the slaves to fight for the restoration of the United States—he had proclaimed this message for almost a year.

Lovejoy did not expect everyone to think as he did, but he did wish to make clear what were his true opinions. "You will endorse them after a while," he prophesied and added whimsically, "but as I am bound to keep a little ahead, I want to declare them now." The Negroes are "our natural allies, our natural friends," Lovejoy said. He cited the example of General Andrew Jackson's employment of Negro troops to seal the victory at New Orleans in 1815. These men had served with honor, bravery, and distinction for their country, however oppressed they were. Anticipating and meeting head-on the objections of those who shrank from employing Negroes in the army and navy, yet who desired restoration of the United States, Lovejoy asserted, "If we can subjugate the rebels without Negroes, we can do it quicker with them." If the Herculean task facing the nation were to be accomplished six months sooner and save a thousand lives, ten thousand, twenty thousand, and two to three hundred million dollars, "we had better do it."

He wondered aloud that "Abraham Lincoln don't lift himself up till his heart reaches up to the great heart of God, receive inspiration from him, and then do his whole duty"—emancipate the slaves. The old radical was willing even to compensate slave-owners if necessary. "I am not particular about the means but I am earnest about the measure." What would Lovejoy do with the freed men and women? "I would let them stay where they are and work under the stimulus of cash instead of the stimulus of the lash," he exclaimed.

Slavery had been abolished by gradual emancipation in most Northern states after the Revolution. In 1787 the Northwest Ordinance abolished slavery in the Northwest territory, out of which came the free states of Ohio, Indiana, Illinois, Michigan, Wisconsin, and part of Minnesota. In 1794 revolutionary France proclaimed universal freedom for everyone under its flag, and Hayti in fact abolished slavery in 1804. Although in the United States the free Negro suffered all the pain of discrimination and denial of the right to vote, he was nevertheless released from the lifelong bondage his brothers faced in the Southern states, where slavery persisted. When Britain abolished slavery in 1833 her English-speaking former colony took serious note of the act. Many attempts had been made to discredit emancipation in the British West Indies, as an argument against emancipation in the United States.

Lovejoy admitted that at first there was "some trouble and inconvenience," but he denied that the action had failed or was not working well. "It is now working better for master and slave" after a generation. "I do not expect to get rid of a system like that without trouble: but inasmuch as the cancer must be cut out, inasmuch as we are on the table and the knife is ready, and our life depends upon our submitting to the operation, I say carry the knife to the bone even though it creates a soreness which it will take a generation to recover from." There was no use evading what must be done. "The people are getting ready for it and President Lincoln is advancing step by step just as the cautious swimmer wades into the stream before making a dive. . . . President Lincoln will make a dive before long." Tremendous applause greeted this seemingly unfounded prophecy.

Lovejoy concluded the courthouse meeting with a thunderous proclamation of his intentions: "I will be loyal not only to the Union but to my convictions—there is nothing that can induce me to ignore principles for which I have contended during the last twenty years. I tell you that Lovejoy is an abolitionist. You may write it all over him that under the present circumstances for the sake of the Union he is an abolitionist." Lest this seem like overbearing sectarianism, it should be said that Lovejoy also praised the Administration. He was careful to guard the hard-achieved unity with Lincoln.

In Washington on Monday, December 2, for the opening of Congress, Lovejoy had another opportunity to speak out for the severest war measures to crush the rebellion. This time the occasion was a "serenade and public ovation" given in the evening to General James H. Lane, now a senator from Kansas. Lovejoy had seen the gallant Lane "on the march, in the camp and on the field" in Missouri, and he had the honor that evening of introducing General Lane to the immense crowd. The *Bureau County Republican*'s correspondent reminded his readers that "Hon. Owen Lovejoy, the member from Illinois, who, everybody knows means fight," played an important part in the meeting.[3]

Lovejoy, rising to speak, acknowledged that this was the first time he had addressed a "popular audience in the federal city." He reiterated his belief that there should be no delay in abolishing slavery, for the good of the whole country. "Our national life is worth more than the life of slavery," he was quoted by the New York *Tribune*. If this was radical, Lovejoy maintained, slavery left itself no choice but to be cut out at the roots. "I am called a radicalist," he said, "I am a radical like Him who laid the ax at the root of the tree."

Passing from observations about himself, Lovejoy turned to Lincoln's obligation as President. He compared the President to "a certain individual, in olden times, who . . . head and shoulders above his contemporaries, was made king." This man, by refusing to destroy his enemies, by Divine command, lost his crown. Lovejoy won cheers and laughter as he completed the comparison: "I hope that no gentleman of later days, resembling him in height and station, will, by following his example, share his fate."

Lovejoy's remarks about the President were by no means subtle, and they disclosed some irritation. The background for them was readily recognizable in the day's events and in the hubbub over a dispute between Lincoln and War Secretary Simon Cameron. Lovejoy was merely giving voice to the current displeasure with the Chief Executive among the antislavery leaders in the Capital.

Cameron had included in his report to the President a paragraph in favor of the arming of slaves. The report had been distributed on December 1 to the postmasters for delivery to newspapers as soon as the President had delivered his message to Congress. Lincoln read the report sometime on Sunday, December 1, and in consternation immediately called Cameron to his office insisting the paragraph was offensive and should be suppressed. After this meeting and another one that had been hurriedly called, with Cabinet members present, the War Secretary yielded to the President.[4]

When the House met at noon on Monday, the members were

expecting the President's message. When it was not presented, the House in a mood of pique voted endorsement of Frémont's action of the previous August 30 and of Cameron's recommendation of Negro troops. The House did this by passing a resolution calling for the emancipation of the slaves of rebels in all military jurisdictions. As a fervent advocate of just such policies as Frémont and Cameron had proclaimed, Lovejoy was naturally irked by the President's action. Not only did Lovejoy speak out at the Lane reception, but he later joined Bingham of Ohio, Vice-President Hamlin, and several other legislators in a laudatory visit to Cameron's home. Several days later the Republican representatives in caucus unanimously supported the policies of confiscation and emancipation of all rebel-held slaves. Nevertheless, Lovejoy spoke up in the party gathering for earnest support of the Administration.[5]

The outstanding factor in the situation was the movement of opinion in Washington toward a radical use of the Union's vast potential. Lovejoy's prominent role at the Lane meeting gave "striking evidence of the mighty change in public opinion" in the Capital in the last three months. Lovejoy had been greeted with great enthusiasm. But if he had attempted six months earlier to speak "on the streets against slavery, he would have been dragged from the stand, and perhaps murdered," in the opinion of one Midwest correspondent. In that writer's words, that was "the character of the revolution in public opinion . . . here, where slavery still exists." [6]

The revolution in public opinion was only a reflection of the real revolution in social and economic relations then beginning to unfold. The overthrow of the slave labor system was in sight, and in this session the 37th Congress was to become a revolutionary Congress, the instrument for the first acts of manumission. Not even the moderate position of the President could now stand in the way. In his message of December 3 Lincoln had posted a monitory word against "radical and extreme" measures. He was aware of the widespread reaction against his suppression of Frémont's emancipation order in St. Louis, and he could feel the resentment against General Halleck's Order No. 3 of November. Yet he was anxious to pursue his own program of gradual, compensated emancipation, and his message to Congress made unmistakably clear what he wanted: "In considering the policy to be adopted for suppressing the insurrection, I have been anxious and careful that the inevitable conflict for this purpose shall not degenerate into a violent and remorseless revolutionary struggle. I have, therefore, in every case, thought it proper to keep the integrity of the Union prominent as the primary object of the contest on our part, leaving all questions which are not of vital military importance to the more deliberate action of the legislature . . . obeying the dictates of prudence, as well as the obligations of the law, instead of transcending, I have adhered to the act of Congress to confiscate property used for insurrectionary purposes. If a new law upon the same subject shall be proposed, its propriety will be duly considered. The Union must be preserved; and hence, all indispensable means must be employed. We shall not be in haste to determine that radical and extreme measures, which may reach the loyal as well as the disloyal, are indispensable." [7] Just those radical and extreme measures the President hoped to forestall were the instruments Lovejoy and his colleagues were prepared to introduce in the next few months.

Radical Republicans were vigorous leaders of Congress in this session. Thaddeus Stevens became the recognized political general in command of the House of Representatives, and lesser roles were assumed by Owen Lovejoy, George W. Julian, James Ashley, John A. Gurley, Bingham, Elihu B. Washburne, Roscoe Conkling, and Justin S. Morrill. Each had a special field of operation, but on the principal issue, slavery, Lovejoy stood shoulder to shoulder with Stevens in leadership of the House.

Whereas Stevens was brilliantly cool, Lovejoy stirred the emotions. The Great Commoner from Lancaster led from the heights of American revolutionary principle. Lovejoy, the martyr's brother, fought from equally high principles. Each was strong and aggressive on the slavery question. Although they agreed substantially on the main question, they differed sharply with each other on the money question, on taxation, even ultimately on a reconstruction policy. They complemented and supported each other on the floor of the House when advancing the principal antislavery measures. They had early differences of opinion about Lincoln—the Pennsylvanian could not share Lovejoy's optimistic confidence in the President. Yet by the spring of 1864, when the end of the war was in sight, reconstruction on the agenda, and the next Presidency was a matter of heated discussion, both congressmen favored Lincoln as the best possible man for the position. Lovejoy's support of Lincoln's reelection flowed directly from his support of the President during the fight for vigorous measures in the 37th Congress. No matter what his differences with the Chief Executive over the best policy for suppressing the rebellion, Lovejoy insistently spoke throughout the turbulent session for unity with Lincoln, whether on the floor of the House or on the public platform in various parts of the North.

Antislavery measures came by the dozens to the desks of Senate and House Clerks in the opening days of the session. Despite the President's message, many of the proposed bills were radical and extreme—aimed at confiscating rebel property and punishing rebel leaders by moving toward emancipation of their slaves. Trumbull in the upper house and Stevens and Lovejoy in the lower were among the first to introduce such legislation. On December 3 Lovejoy also took a leading part when he requested that the President's message be read.[8]

On the day before this he had introduced a resolution praising

Captain Charles Wilkes for his action in seizing the Confederate emissaries to London and Paris, James M. Mason and John Slidell, from the British mail steamer *Trent* in Bahamian waters on November 8, 1861. Wilkes, who had commanded the United States exploring expedition to the Pacific and Antarctica of 1838 to 1842, was known as an able scientist but as an impetuous and domineering naval officer. In 1861, as the commander of a cruiser commissioned to search for privateers, he was justified in searching the *Trent* for contraband, but not in deciding the question of a violation of neutrality. He had violated international law by not taking the *Trent* into a United States port and submitting the case to a prize court. The affair proved most embarrassing for the United States, particularly since public sentiment was with Wilkes; however, he had acted without authority and after a few tense weeks in which Great Britain visibly prepared to enter the war on the side of the Confederacy, the matter was settled amicably, and the envoys were released. By that time, however, Wilkes's action had been applauded by Secretary of War Cameron and Governor John A. Andrew of Massachusetts, and Lovejoy's resolution had been adopted as a joint resolution of both houses. The captain was lionized in New York and Boston, with a march down Broadway to a reception at City Hall. Secretary Gideon Welles, speaking for the Navy Department, approved Wilkes's deed, and General McClellan endorsed it as well.

The jubilation over the capture of Mason and Slidell was great among antislavery men, for these two were former senators who had been responsible for passage of the Fugitive Slave Law. Slidell had worked in the background of the Pierce and Buchanan Administrations and was their "evil genius." Mason had grilled John Brown after his capture at Harpers Ferry and had also made himself heartily disliked in March, 1861, by declaring that he owed no allegiance to the Union government, but meanwhile holding his Senate seat and collecting his paychecks from the United States Treasury. He was an outspoken secessionist.

The affair turned some Americans into jingoists, and Lovejoy became an excessive one. The very superpatriotism that he had deplored when he denounced the Mexican War he now spouted himself. On January 14, 1862, he arose in the House to object to an appropriation of thirty-five thousand dollars for United States participation in a world trade fair in London. Some members objected and expressed their hostility toward England, especially with the memory of the *Trent* affair fresh in their minds. Thaddeus Stevens suggested that they lay aside their hard feelings and refrain from boycotting the London exhibition. Roscoe Conkling took a firm stand and rather shortsighted view of things, but Lovejoy lost his composure and good sense. He would rather acknowledge that the country had submitted to disgrace by Britain and he urged that "we . . . stay at home till the time comes that we can whip that nation." [9]

He said that he had "literally wept tears of vexation" when Mason and Slidell were released from their Boston jail and were allowed to sail for Europe. He doubted the necessity for it and thought that arbitration might have turned up a more acceptable result. He hated the "surrender," and he hated the British government—even though, "I have never shared in the traditionary hostility of many of my countrymen against England." He meant to bequeath his hatred for the British government as a legacy to his children when he died and would charge his sons with the duty to enlist in a war with England, as "sooner or later it must, for we shall never forget this humiliation." [10]

The press on both sides of the Atlantic became involved in a minor controversy over Lovejoy's remarks. For his display of jingoism the Washington *Star* in February, 1862, took a shot at him by quoting the London *Examiner* in styling "Hon. Owen Lovejoy a 'ranting blockhead.'" On the other hand, the *National Republican* in Washington preferred to see Lovejoy as possible

White House material. In time a calmer view of the affair prevailed, and Lovejoy and others returned to the necessary tasks of fighting one war at a time.[11]

Among the bills already under consideration by Congress was a homestead bill introduced before the House by Lovejoy on December 4, 1861. He gave notice on that date that he would introduce a bill designed to prevent the army and navy from returning fugitive slaves. In the Senate, Henry Wilson of Massachusetts introduced a bill to abolish slavery in the District of Columbia. On December 5, 1861, Lovejoy introduced a bill to abolish the law requiring Negroes to carry passes while traveling to the North; it was referred to the Committee on the District of Columbia. In the Senate on the same day Trumbull introduced the second confiscation bill, which would free the slaves of "persons who shall take up arms against the United States, or in any manner aid or abet the rebellion." His lead was followed in the House when Gurley of Ohio on December 9 introduced a confiscation bill. Republican caucuses on the evenings of December 9 and 11 unanimously decided to support a policy of confiscating the property of rebels and freeing their slaves. These were embodied in Gurley's bill and in one introduced by John A. Bingham of Ohio. On December 20 Lovejoy tried, in a resolution that failed by two votes, to bring out of the Committee on the Judiciary a bill to confiscate the property of rebels, unconditionally liberate their slaves, and protect slaves from recapture by rebel masters.[12]

Also on December 9 Lovejoy launched a major attack on Order No. 3 of General Henry W. Halleck, on the ground that it was of aid and comfort only to rebellious slaveowners. Halleck had also issued a number of directives he considered necessary to tighten discipline and to make for effective corps action. The sin of Order No. 3 was its cold legalism barring fugitive slaves from entering the army lines. Many antislavery people in the country denounced Halleck as a proslavery general, and his order as cruel and inhuman, thrusting the fugitive back into the chains of slavery. Lovejoy's resolution at first would have required the Secretary of War to revoke Halleck's order. On the suggestion of William E. Lansing of New York, Lovejoy accepted a substitution of "request" for "require." The next day Lovejoy modified the language to make the intended action more acceptable to the President. In its final form the resolution respectfully requested the Commander in Chief to "direct" General Halleck to withdraw the order "or cause it to conform with the practice of other departments of the Army." [13]

Whereas Lovejoy was willing to postpone action on his resolution, a more uncompromising attitude was expressed by Stevens. He grimly suspected that Halleck desired "more to hunt down General Fremont than for any general principles." Stevens cited several cases of the cruel return or capture of runaway slaves even though they had supplied information and help to the army. Objecting to the return of escaped slaves "on the mere notion of the commanding generals," Stevens said "they deserve to have the epaulets stripped from their shoulders." The inference was that a higher authority approved Halleck's actions. Lest it be concluded that the President had a hand in the general's order, Lovejoy hastened to assure Stevens and the House that Halleck and other offending officers had no authorization from the President. "These orders are given by the generals themselves," said Lovejoy. Kellogg of Illinois, another congressman in Lincoln's confidence, supported Lovejoy's statement. Representative Francis Preston Blair, Jr. of Missouri, however, attempted to defend Halleck, claiming that officer did not intend to go beyond the laws of the United States and the policy of the government. Lovejoy demanded to know why Halleck did not merely detain fugitives. He said he had been assured by Generals Benjamin M. Prentiss and James H. Lane, and perhaps by General John Pope, that former slaves were friendly and helpful to the army.[14]

Representative Philip B. Fouke of downstate Illinois charged that Negro slaves could not be trusted, and claimed that one of them had led Fouke's own regiment into an ambush the previous November. Fouke angrily scolded Lovejoy: ". . . if my colleague would pay less attention to the Negro and more to the interest of the country we would get along much better with this war." To Lovejoy's chagrin there was applause for Fouke in the galleries and among some members of the House. The Speaker threatened to clear the galleries. In the end Clement L. Vallandigham of Ohio moved to table Lovejoy's resolution and the House agreed, 78 to 64.[15]

That was not yet the end of the matter, for on December 12 Frank Blair, Jr., revived it by raising a point of personal privilege. He wished to read into the record portions of an explanatory letter from Halleck. Lovejoy seized the opportunity to rebut what was evidently turning into an attack on himself and other antislavery legislators. He spoke now to confute the attempt being made to "show that I, and others, support this war not against the rebellion but against slavery." Again he stated that he was for "one grand and overshadowing purpose"—to put down the rebellion. The most efficient way to do this, he repeated, was to take away from the rebels their property and liberate their slaves. In saying so he was mindful of the country's impatience with the slow-moving war effort. He was opposed to carrying on the war to protect slavery. "I am opposed," he said, "to the Army of the United States being turned into slave catchers. I am opposed to any general being allowed to give orders to throw back upon their masters those who desire to escape, whether they are Union or secession, white or black." Replying hotly to Fouke's hostile admonition, Lovejoy stated if some soldiers won't fight unless they are allowed to return fugitive slaves, "then the Army is better off without them." The main point was plain:

Coddling the rebellious enemy must cease, and giving him aid and comfort by such measures as Halleck's Order No. 3 must also cease. The corollary must be a vigorous prosecution of the war.[16]

Lovejoy warmed to the fight and availed himself of opportunities to spur on the war effort. One of these occasions came during the debate on Roscoe Conkling's resolution to investigate the Union disasters at Bull Run in July and Ball's Bluff in October. Out of this move came the formation of the Joint Committee on the Conduct of the War, one of the most powerful congressional groups in the country's history. In the debate leading up to its formation Lovejoy's remarks came into frequent head-on collision with the views of Charles A. Wickliffe, a representative of border state policy. Another Kentuckian, and the best known of the border state men, Crittenden, opposed Conkling's resolution and warned against congressional trespass on military prerogatives. Yet his Democratic colleague Vallandigham of Ohio oddly enough upheld the principle of civilian control of the military authorities. This was also Lovejoy's view of the role of the military in a democracy—he had demonstrated it quite vigorously in his forays against the army in 1858 and 1859. Lovejoy asserted rigidly: "We have the right to arraign not only our generals, but even the President. We here represent the sovereignty of the people." He demanded that "our battles should be fought so as to hurt slavery," and enable the President to decree destruction of the mischievous institution.[17]

Lovejoy took the floor on January 6, 1862, to speak at length and very bluntly on the Conkling resolution. "The truth is, if I understand it, our want of success in this war is owing to the theory adopted by this Government in regard to its prosecution. The Government is holding the Army in a state of inactivity, for what reason? Not because the officers are not skillful and brave, not because the soldiers are not brave and efficient; but they are holding this whole Army in this stand-still position, and literally making it a *standing* Army. . . . We are waiting in the hope—in my opinion a vain and fruitless hope—that this rebellion will put itself down; that if we do not hurt them these rebels will return to their allegiance, and that, too, before a great while.

"If I understand it, it is that that is paralyzing the whole Army of the United States, and bleeding the people of the United States to the extent of $2 million a day. It is no wonder that the people are growing impatient; it is no wonder that that impatience is becoming earnest in many portions of the country, and is almost reaching a point beyond that of passive emotion. The whole nation is waiting for the Army to move forward. They have furnished the men and the money; and why does not the Army move?"

The fear of hurting slavery, Lovejoy stated, "is benumbing and demoralizing the whole Army." Although he did not know how to conduct the details of military affairs, he knew what military results should be brought about. Even Crittenden, he maintained, would not claim that the people and the army must stand and do nothing. He compared the people standing trustful, hopeful yet impatient, to John Brown on the scaffold waiting for his execution—"John Brown, whose soul, thank God, is marching on." He hoped that spirit would get through the whole army, "and then we will not be quarreling about Ball's Bluff and other defeats."

Lovejoy said he was not concerned with investigating incidental facts. He was more concerned that the nation had failed to live up to its basic principles, had failed to proclaim liberty to all the enslaved. "We have stood looking coldly and jeeringly on the suffering slave." "We are verily guilty concerning our brother, in that we have seen the anguish of his soul and we have not had compassion on him. We have denied his woes; we have seen him stripped and lacerated and wronged and outraged—four

313

million human beings made in the image of God." The time had come "to repent and proclaim liberty to the enslaved of the land," as Jefferson had foreseen this necessity years ago.

It was not in Lovejoy's opinion want of brains that prevented military success. It was want of heart among the generals. "We want a soul in this matter. The generals who conduct our armies have no soul or earnestness in the cause," he charged. "They go with kid gloves on their hands, and say, 'Generous, hospitable South Carolinians (the very vipers who hatched out the accursed rebellion), we will not hurt you if we can help it.'" He earnestly believed before God that "the reasons why we have had Ball's Bluff, Bull Run, and other defeats and disasters, is that God in his providence means to arraign us before this great question of human freedom and make us take the right position."

"Men jeer about the 'everlasting nigger.' You cannot get rid of him, sir. He will not down at your bidding. You might just as well try to wipe out Jehovah's government, and crumble the pillars of God's throne. In the Negro just now are embodied and represented here before us the rights of man. We have disregarded his right as long as God will allow us." This was where the real trouble lay. "It is not Stone, nor McClellan, nor in Halleck altogether. God uses these poor instruments to punish us." He naturally won some laughter and broke the tension.

In summing up and concluding this powerful offensive, Lovejoy said: "Now, Mr. Speaker, the people are determined to put down this rebellion, and I tell the Government, without the least ripple or shadow of unkind feeling toward a single gentleman . . . intrusted with the administration of affairs, and without believing for a moment that they are not true and loyal and earnest, although, as I think, acting on mistaken theories; I tell them that the people mean to put down this rebellion, and do not mean to stand with a rope around their neck always. This rebellion must be put down by the Government or without it. I know how the people feel, and I know that the slaveholding interest of one or two border slave states will not be allowed to control the destinies of this Republic." [18]

The clear offensive aimed at the border states and Lincoln's toleration of slavery in those areas touched off a bitter response from Wickliffe. A running battle between Lovejoy and the Kentucky congressman had been going on since December and whenever a bout between the two was in the offing, members knew that they were about to enjoy a first-class contest. As the combatants closed in for their verbal confrontation, members set down their pens, put aside papers, and postponed chats. In the December sortie Lovejoy had scornfully attacked the Kentucky volunteers bill as an attempt by the slaveholders in that border state to set up at United States expense a rear guard gendarmerie against slave insurrection in that state. "Whether it is to keep the slaves from rising or what not, I do not know," he declared. He was nevertheless opposed to establishing any force not part of the regular army of the United States. Stevens had joined in opposing the Kentucky scheme.

Wickliffe, with a fierce look, sprang to the defense of the Kentucky volunteers bill. He said that the Secretary of War considered it important and that it had been blessed with the unanimous vote of the House Committee on Military Affairs. Wickliffe was no less adamant in his proslavery interest than Lovejoy was in his antislavery. In a shrill voice the Kentuckian struck back as violently as he could. He hoped the bill would receive the unanimous vote of the House, "except that of the Gentleman from Illinois." He did not expect Lovejoy to support the bill, because, he said, Lovejoy "seems to have an idea that this is intended to do something to the Negroes in Kentucky." Later he declared heatedly, "I will pledge my honor to my friend from Illinois that he need not be afraid of a Negro insurrection in the State of Kentucky. We will take care of our servants there if he will just let us alone." [19]

Accepting this, not as the personal attack intended, but as an

315

aggressive affront and insult to the Negroes, Lovejoy with dark-ened brow retorted rather tartly, "When these gentlemen on the other side are hard pushed for an argument, they have a sneer for the Negro." Though this seemed to amuse some members, he assured them "it has no terror for me." It had been tried against him once or twice in this session, and ever since he had become a congressman, and he would only say to the gentlemen: "*Con-tempsi Catilinae gladios; non pertimescam tuos.*" He was thank-ful to God that, having met the question before the people, he was not particularly intimidated by any representative. "I come here," he declared, "with a larger majority than nine tenths of the gentlemen representing slaveholding districts have votes." He would not carry on the war in the interest of thirty thousand slaveholders. "I will carry on the war to put down the rebellion, and slavery must take care of itself," was his flat offer to the border state men.

Wickliffe pursued the attack by asking again if Lovejoy would vote to leave slavery alone in the states. Lovejoy asserted that the people meant to put down the rebellion by the speediest, most efficient means. Significantly he added: "I have no doubt that the Government will gracefully yield to the popular sentiment."

When Lovejoy asked Wickliffe if he preferred to see slavery rather than the Union preserved and perpetuated, the Kentuckian said he was for the Constitution and believed the Union *and* slavery would be preserved under it. Lovejoy deemed this evasive and asked anew, suppose it were impossible to preserve both, which shall go overboard? Wickliffe sidestepped the thrust and replied: "I would prefer throwing the Abolitionists overboard." Above the laughter of some of his colleagues, Lovejoy angrily answered: "That is tantamount to saying that the gentleman pre-fers seeing the Union go by the board rather than slavery; for in the sense in which he uses the term he makes them identical." He was for preserving the Constitution too, and the Union *and* free-

316

dom. After all, he pointed out, "To preserve, to embalm freedom was the great object of forming the Union and of adopting the Constitution. Slavery was local, casual, transient. There is the very point at issue," he claimed. At this point he challenged the man in the White House: "I would be willing to die a thousand deaths to have the grand opportunity vouchsafed at the present moment to the President of the United States . . . to be President, to be king, to be victor, has happened to many; to float down through future generations, to be embalmed in the hearts of mankind as a liberator, emancipator, to few."

The friendly Peoria *Daily Transcript* reported on January 16 that "the galleries applauded 'en masse' " for Lovejoy. The correspondent reported Lovejoy's opponents "one after the other, received upon the point of his bayonet and dismounted." The equally friendly Chicago *Tribune* observed on January 22 that Lovejoy was driving Wickliffe upon the ropes. Wickliffe's refusal to say if he was for the Union or slavery "leaves no doubt his true place is in the rebel conclave at Richmond."

Lovejoy's interpretation of the people's impatience received some confirmation in an incident in Washington on January 6. A gala reception was held for Horace Greeley in the Smithsonian Institution, where he also spoke under the auspices of the Washington Lecture Association. Government dignitaries were on the platform. Among them were President Lincoln; Senators Preston King, Henry Wilson, and Samuel C. Pomeroy; Secretary of the Treasury Chase; Speaker of the House Galusha Grow; Representatives Lovejoy, Stevens, Cyrus Aldrich, Wells A. Hutchins, and John A. Bingham. Colonel D'Utassy and other prominent civilian and military men were also present on the platform. When Greeley spoke of Frémont's proclamation of freedom for the slaves of rebels, the large audience rose to its feet and shouted like mad. According to one reporter President Lincoln and Secretary Chase were the recipients of this demonstration.[20]

This meeting was one of the accomplishments of the Washington Lecture Association, organized in November, 1861, by a group of young antislavery intellectuals in the Capital. One of them, William A. Crofutt, was Potomac correspondent of the New York *Tribune*. As secretary of the association he was charged with engaging such speakers as Wendell Phillips, William Lloyd Garrison, Greeley, Orestes Brownson, Bayard Taylor, Moncure Conway, James Russell Lowell, William Goodell, and others, at that time the eminent writers and antislavery personalities in the North. Crofutt had no difficulty in enlisting them but he met considerable obstacles in obtaining a hall large enough to seat an audience of two to three thousand. The only suitable places were either the House of Representatives or the amphitheater of the Smithsonian. The former was denied him by Grow and the latter by Dr. Joseph Henry, the respected scientist who was its director. Crofutt took his troubles to Lovejoy, with whom he had an acquaintance, "as a zealous young recruit might enjoy with a kind-hearted veteran." Lovejoy, incensed, exclaimed: "Henry's an old traitor. We'll bring him to terms." He led Crofutt to Schuyler Colfax, who turned out to be a friendly listener. Although Lovejoy exaggerated Dr. Henry's suspected sympathies with the Confederates, his good offices played a part in obtaining the Smithsonian's amphitheater. Later he was found among the notable persons on the platform for at least two lectures in the series.[21]

Two days later, on January 8, Lovejoy made another sweeping attack on the kid-glove approach of the Union toward the rebels. His sequestration bill of this date would have empowered generals in the rebel states to appoint commissioners of sequestration. They would be authorized to take real and personal property found without owners, for the use of the United States, and to convert property into money to go into the United States Treasury. Sequestered homesteads of not more than one hundred

318

and fifty acres would be auctioned to settlers who occupied them for three years. The remainder of such seized lands were to be surveyed and disposed of as any other such property of the United States. This bold and specific proposal was only in the form of a resolution instructing the Committee on Public Lands to report such a bill for the consideration of the House. However, the bill seems never to have emerged in that form, although the House approved the resolution 52 to 0.[22]

A token of the esteem in which Lovejoy was held among the people for his attacks on slavery was displayed in a letter he received from a Baltimore resident. He blessed the Illinois congressman for his reply to Wickliffe in the winter and spring debates. The anonymous author told Lovejoy: "Your speech mounts up to the higher regions of mind, soul, and spirit and brings the negro slave at one bound right up out of the sloughs of degradation and ruin." He urged Lovejoy to keep on driving— "The negro will understand you, and the white man will shrink from him, when he shall stand up clothed with the panoply of your little speech." [23]

17

The Fight for Emancipation Policies

"God be praised, the Nation's Capital is FREE!*"*

—Bureau County Republican

The issue of immediate emancipation of the slaves—by a presidential proclamation if necessary—dominated the struggle in the North for an effective political policy in the spring of 1862. Powerful forces for and against such a radical step were exerted. The President, anxious to hold the border states loyal to the Union, believed that Negro colonization in Africa or Central America was desirable. However, in order to retain the support of the border states he attempted time after time early in 1862 to press for gradual, compensated emancipation. Lovejoy and some radical Republicans were willing to make some slight concessions by giving support to the proposal to pay slaveowners. In the main Lovejoy believed that a militantly offensive policy against slavery and against the rebellious states was best. He was fortified in this belief by the growing sentiment for emancipation measures. But the ineptitude of General McClellan in fumbling the war in Virginia depressed hopes for a speedy victory and in turn for a defeat of slavery. Moreover, these failures fed the public's impatience and drew the people closer to the radical demands for a vigorous policy against slavery. In Congress and in the Northern states demands swelled for emancipation proposals and plans to confiscate rebel property and arm Negroes.

Lovejoy had echoed the sentiments of the people when he had demanded that the army take off its kid gloves and fight the rebels. That he was correct was made evident by public dismay over the faltering moves of the Army of the Potomac under McClellan, and by the public acclaim for Ulysses S. Grant's bold victories on the western front in capturing Fort Henry on the Tennessee River on February 5 and Fort Donelson on the Cumberland on February 15. Grant's assault on the forts and his demand for unconditional surrender delivered into the hands of the Union the key to the Mississippi valley by clearing western Kentucky of Confederate forces and by threatening the security of Nashville. Millions demonstrated their elation, when they heard the news, in Boston, Buffalo, Utica, Cleveland, Detroit, Pittsburgh, Indianapolis, Springfield, and Cincinnati.[1]

The rising demand for emancipation had been demonstrated in petitions signed by thousands of people and presented to the Senate on January 6. The pressure continued through January and February. On the day that Grant's army took Fort Henry, Sydney Gay, the managing editor of the New York *Tribune*, demanded that emancipation of slaves immediately be put into effect. A month later, prominent Republicans and abolitionists organized a mass rally for emancipation, at Cooper Institute in New York. The emancipation movement received unprecedented recognition when one of its foremost leaders, Wendell Phillips, visited Washington in March. He received a respectful welcome by Vice-President Hannibal Hamlin and Speaker of the House Galusha Grow; was introduced on the floor of the Senate by Senator Charles Sumner; spoke three times to large and exuberant

321

audiences in the Smithsonian Institution; and finally was received by President Lincoln for an interview.[2]

In the House of Representatives Lovejoy and Thaddeus Stevens marched in the van of the emancipation movement. With other radical Republicans, they were acknowledged the leaders of the struggle for an emancipation proclamation. Representative Abram B. Olin of New York on one occasion referred to Lovejoy as one of those who thought this "paper" measure the best way of fighting the war. Lovejoy interjected, "I want to fight with bayonets and bullets, and not with proclamations." Lovejoy in truth meant to fight with both.[3]

Lovejoy's "extreme and revolutionary" measure of December 20 was defeated, 62 to 60. Only seven months later, on July 11, 1862, a similar bill emerged from the Congress, and Lincoln hastened his efforts to provide a moderate substitute in the form of a gradual, compensated emancipation policy.[4]

Another of Lovejoy's antislavery and pro-Negro measures was one that he and Lincoln could unite on, publicly as well as privately. This was the bill to establish diplomatic relations with the Negro republics of Hayti and Liberia. Lovejoy's resolution of December 11, 1861, so instructing the House Committee on Foreign Affairs implemented Lincoln's recommendation to this effect in his message to Congress. On February 4, 1862, in the Senate, Sumner reported the bill from the Senate Foreign Relations Committee that authorized diplomatic relations with the two countries. Lincoln signed the bill on June 5, 1862.[5]

This was not the only sign of a close relationship between the President and the congressman from his home state.

Lovejoy's heart went out to the President that winter when the bright and much idolized Willie Lincoln died in February, 1862. The boy had been riding his pony in a chilly rain and had come down with a cold and a fever. He lay ill in his bed in the White House guest room for several days, unable to fight off the illness or to be helped by medicine. When the end came, his father murmured sadly, "It is hard, hard to have him die." Mrs. Lincoln wept for long hours.

Lovejoy tried to convey the meaning of the sad event to his younger children back in Princeton. The older girls and Mrs. Lovejoy had accompanied him to Washington and settled there for the winter. To the children Lovejoy wrote on February 23 that he had just been to the White House to see the President, who, he said, "feels very much the loss of his little boy Willie who is about the age of Parish" (Owen's twelve-year-old son, named after Elijah Parish Lovejoy). He said a few words about the boy lying in his coffin and told his children, "His father says he was a very gentle and amiable boy." To reassure them, he added, "Father feels very thankful that one of his little boys is not taken away and hopes they may not be." [6]

In the face of the President's pleas for gradual, compensated emancipation in March, 1862, Congress in the next month passed the bill which abolished slavery immediately in the District of Columbia. Lincoln signed the bill reluctantly. Yet if he yielded on this measure, so did radical congressional Republicans, notably Owen Lovejoy, when the House passed Roscoe Conkling's compensation resolution of March 10. The President had sent a message to Congress on March 6 requesting the adoption of a joint resolution, the heart of which was an offer of compensation to any state "which may adopt a gradual abolishment of slavery." Conkling had introduced the resolution in the words offered by the President, and the House passed it, 86 to 35, with Kentucky's delegation opposed even to this gesture in its interest. Abolitionists had rigorously resented and rejected the principle of compensation—the payment to slaveowners for an action that should, in their opinion, have been performed as a moral obligation—the abolitionists having consistently denied that the government of the United States could recognize property in man. Yet Lovejoy was found among the majority voting for the Lincoln-Conkling resolution, "warmly supporting the proposition to pay for slaves out of the Treasury of the United States." [7] He later defended the resolution, and his thoughts immediately after its passage probably were the basis for the *Bureau County Republican*'s remarks on March 20. Although "we" had faith in Lincoln, declared the editor, others, presumably radical antislavery men, were "sorely tried with Mr. Lincoln's reticence on the subject of slavery." The editor referred to the March 6 message of the President as an "Emancipation Proclamation"—though admittedly "short—somewhat obscure—barren of fruits." Nevertheless he supported it: "Let no one belittle this great act of the President. . . . It is great in underlying principle." He concluded: "Henceforth Mr. Lincoln is a historical personage."

Other such compromises as the one over Lincoln's message would follow by the abolitionist warrior. Nevertheless Lovejoy fought resolutely for more vigorous and more far-reaching confiscation and emancipation laws. Whereas other radicals were severe with the President, Lovejoy—"this old and ultra abolitionist," as he liked to refer to himself—was far more sympathetic and generous toward the Chief Executive. He "perfectly understood and appreciated" Lincoln's motives. [8]

While the House was considering the President's message, more victories were being scored by Union forces on March 8 and 9. Confederate General Sterling Price had at last been driven out of Missouri and defeated at Pea Ridge, Arkansas, on March 8. The next day the ironclad fighting ships, the *Monitor* for the Union and the *Merrimac* for the Confederacy, clashed off Hampton Roads, Virginia. The news reached Lincoln on March 9 that the *Monitor* had outfought the *Merrimac* and driven the Confederate ship toward Norfolk. Two such victories in two days gave the President cause for celebration. In the meantime, on March 8, Lincoln had reached the end of his patience with

McClellan and had demoted him from general in chief of all armies to general of the Army of the Potomac.

This move was received with joy by radicals, who had begun to suspect that McClellan might have had traitorous motives in failing to fight on the eastern front. How Lovejoy reacted is not known from the available records. It is safe to say, however, that he took heart from the action to press on his offensive against border state representatives. Sympathize though he did with the President's underlying principles, Lovejoy could not bring himself to coddle the men in Congress from Kentucky and Maryland who opposed immediate emancipation, or gradual, compensated emancipation for that matter. While Lincoln appealed to them, Lovejoy attacked them. While Lincoln pleaded in vain with them to agree to his plan, Lovejoy hit at their proslavery inclinations with such outbursts as this one of March 25: "Kentucky boasts of her loyalty, and then sends her sons to fight for slavery in the rebel army with bullet and bayonet, and her fathers here to fight for the same thing with voice and vote." Robert Mallory, a Union Democrat, was so deeply stung that he struck down Lovejoy's words as "a farrago of nonsensical fanaticism." John W. Crisfield of Maryland denounced Lovejoy as "disloyal as the man who draws the sword to strike down the Constitution." Lovejoy reminded his adversaries: "If it were not for the antislavery men of the country, the soldiers who are risking and laying down their lives . . . the gentlemen could not go home and live in peace if it had not been for these very antislavery men, these fanatics, my neighbors, of whom we the other day buried forty in one grave, every one of whom, fanatic as they were, fought and lost their lives in defending Kentucky, in defending the gentleman's home while he was here calling me a fanatic." Lovejoy was referring here to the men of the twenty-five Illinois regiments that had fought to capture Fort Henry.[9]

A few weeks later Lovejoy enjoyed a supreme moment of

exhilaration in voting for the immediate abolition of slavery in the District of Columbia. This was a goal antislavery men and women had sighted a generation earlier. It had inspired mass petition campaigns in spite of the gag rule. Before the District abolition bill became law, however, Lovejoy asserted his militant beliefs in more than one clash of oratory. When on April 10 Representative Charles R. Train of Massachusetts offered an amendment allowing aggrieved slaveowners to seek and get a trial by jury in the United States Circuit Court in the District of Columbia, immediate and sharp opposition came from Stevens and Lovejoy. The Illinoisan was blunt: "I am tired of this miserable twaddle about due process of law for the master when everybody knows that every slave in the District of Columbia and in the United States has been robbed of his freedom without process of law." [10]

On the same day, too, a congressman objected to the District abolition bill's figure of three hundred dollars as the compensation to be paid by the United States on each slave. His objection that this sum was not a fair market value—it was only half the average value of a slave, he said—earned him a sharp rebuke from Lovejoy. The latter cited the case of a Georgetown slaveowner who had one day pledged his consent to let a free Negro purchase his own wife and child for eleven hundred dollars. The owner reneged, and the woman and child and a six-month-old baby born since the pledge were sent into a Baltimore slave pen. Lovejoy scolded the "brazen men [who] stand up and talk about robbing, because we give only three hundred dollars a piece. . . . It is the sublimity of impudence." [11]

The bill abolishing slavery in the District had been introduced by Senator Henry Wilson of Massachusetts in December and reported from committee by Senator Lot M. Morrill of Maine on February 13. On February 27 Morrill had moved that the District abolition bill be made the special order of business on

March 5. Some delay occurred while Lincoln's gradualist message was delivered on March 6. On March 10 Lincoln held a frustrating meeting with border state representatives, who refused to accept his plan. On March 12 the Senate took up Wilson's bill and passed it on April 3. Sumner, Hale, and Wilson from New England led the fight in the Senate, where the bill passed 29 to 14.[12]

Meantime both houses had approved the Conkling compensation resolution, and on April 10 Lincoln gave his final assent. Stevens in the House moved that the Senate bill for District emancipation (with compensation) be taken up before all other bills. In the wide-ranging debate that day Lovejoy delivered a bitter denunciation of the District's slave traders. The bill passed in the House of Representatives after a debate in which Stevens, Lovejoy, and Bingham led the fight. Thus two paths to emancipation were opened, the gradualist one by the Conkling-Lincoln resolution, the immediate one by the District of Columbia abolition bill. At six o'clock that evening the members began to cast their votes on the District bill by voice vote. The ayes and nays echoed through the hall and stirred partisans in the galleries. When it came time for Lovejoy to vote, he pronounced the heartiest "Aye!" The proud satisfaction he felt when he voted aroused the galleries and brought from them a round of loud applause. Other votes were equally enthusiastic. Stevens, Ashley, Julian, Bingham, and others each enjoyed a moment of glory in casting a vote for freedom. The final tally was 92 to 38. The President signed the bill and made it law on April 16.[13]

"God be praised, the Nation's Capital is FREE." So wrote the Washington correspondent of the *Bureau County Republican*.[14]

In their jubilation the Negro people of Washington filled seventeen churches in the city to thank the Lord for emancipation. Negroes in the District looked upon Lovejoy as the "deliverer of the race." Frederick Douglass, thanking Charles Sumner for his speech on the bill in the Senate, prayed that God would sustain Sumner and "all the good men who surround" him. The congregation of Union Bethel Church in Washington was so transported that the pastor could not make himself heard. He tried to reach them with a powerful "Glory to God!" But a loud voice in the congregation cried out, "Glory to Lovejoy!" The pastor returned with a resounding "No! I tell you glory to God!" [15]

The fight continued for an effective abolition policy, and for its enactment. Specifically the fight was for an immediate emancipation policy and to win Lincoln to it. Crittenden of Kentucky knew this as well as Lincoln himself, and Lovejoy knew it. The old border state leader, who was a saintly and Christian gentleman to scores of Americans and a bulldog to others, aimed to capture Lincoln in the swirling struggle of March and April, 1862. The President's pleas had been thrust aside by Crittenden. The slender old man, his white hair falling carelessly over his bony forehead, stood on April 23 to speak on the confiscation bill before the House. His fear was that Congress might adopt one or more of the strict measures under consideration. His fear was, too, that Lincoln might become the executor of emancipation policies. The signs were plentiful—in the House more than a dozen confiscation bills were about to be recommitted (and were on April 24); the District of Columbia had been emancipated for a little more than a week; Lovejoy was advancing a bill for the abolition of slavery in the territories; and the President was urging a form of antislavery action, however gradual and partial.

It was no wonder therefore that Crittenden took the floor to appeal for a hands-off policy in regard to slavery, and regaled the House with what Lovejoy brusquely called "a solemn homily" on slavery. In it Crittenden made an enticing bid for Lincoln: "There is a niche in the temple of fame, a niche near to

Washington, which should be occupied by the statue of him who shall save his country. Mr. Lincoln has a mighty destiny. . . . But if he choose to be, in these times, a mere sectarian and a party man, that niche will be reserved for some future and better patriot." [16]

Promptly the next morning Lovejoy took the floor to reply to Crittenden. His speech was perhaps too long, sustained on too shrill a note, but it contained a generous sprinkling of pungent remarks. "It is the old story of garnishing the sepulcher of dead prophets and slaying the living ones," Lovejoy said. Referring to Crittenden's repetitious eulogy of the Constitution to uphold his defense of slavery, Lovejoy thanked him sarcastically and answered that the great document "knows no black, no white; knows no slave; but recognizes all men as entitled to the rights of men." As for the niche that Crittenden was reserving for the patriot in the White House, Lovejoy sketched one of a different design. With these words he opened the gates of glory to Lincoln:

"I, too, have a niche for Abraham Lincoln; but it is in Freedom's holy fane, and not in the blood-besmeared temple of human bondage; not surrounded by slaves, fetters, and chains, but with the symbols of freedom; not dark with bondage, but radiant with the light of liberty. . . . Let Abraham Lincoln make himself, as I trust he will, the emancipator, the liberator, as he has the opportunity of doing, and his name shall not only be enrolled in this earthly temple, but it will be traced on the living stones of that temple which rears itself amid the thrones and hierarchies of heaven, whose top stone is to be brought in with shouting of 'Grace, grace unto it.' " [17]

A rare compliment was paid Lovejoy when, before adjournment, twenty-five thousand copies of the "niche for Lincoln" speech were ordered. Salient quotations from the address were reproduced in the Chicago *Tribune* of Friday, April 25. At the least, Lovejoy's speech would help to increase the pressure on Lincoln to adopt the radical emancipation policy.

Meantime, General David Hunter, in command of the army's Department of the South since March, was issuing orders (on April 12 and May 9) that simply and directly freed *all* slaves in his military jurisdiction. The move was bolder even than Frémont's in Missouri, because Hunter did not restrict his emancipation orders to the slaves of those who took up arms against the United States. Furthermore his domain was a larger one, embracing the states of South Carolina, Georgia, and Florida. Hunter took a step in the direction that Lovejoy very much favored when he also approved the enlistment of Negroes in a regiment of their own.

Lincoln annulled the general's orders on the ground that he had usurped a function reserved exclusively to the President, and Lovejoy again, as in the case of Frémont, backed Lincoln's right to save for himself the task of emancipation. The Chief Executive's countermanding order cited his message to Congress of March 6 calling for gradual compensated emancipation, and again he exhorted the border state representatives to give support to his proposals. Again these men turned a deaf ear.

The Act to Abolish Slavery in the District of Columbia represented the first meaningful victory for the policy of immediate abolition. A second and more far-reaching victory was already being fashioned by Lovejoy and his Illinois colleague Isaac N. Arnold. This was a law that would abolish slavery in the territories of the United States, and wherever the United States had jurisdiction, whether on the highways or high seas, in federal dockyards or other federal establishments. This was to be the reply positive to the Dred Scott decision, which had restrained Congress from legislating on slavery. After Arnold introduced the bill on March 24, 1862, it was referred to the Committee on Territories, of which Lovejoy was a prominent member.[18]

Lovejoy reported out the territorial abolition bill on May 1 "to render freedom national and slavery sectional." After two readings it was recommitted and reported out again on May 8. Democratic Representative Samuel S. Cox of Ohio tried unsuccessfully to table the bill, and Kentucky's Charles Wickliffe, as expected, attempted to embarrass Lovejoy. Finally the House refused to take up the bill that day. But on May 9 Lovejoy's bill was made the special order of the day.[19] In the morning Lovejoy made an adroit move to use the news of the Union's military successes of the early May days to support his bill. On May 8 the capture of New Orleans by Admiral David G. Farragut and General Benjamin Butler had been announced, and the Union rejoiced in the knowledge that the Mississippi would be open from the Gulf of Mexico to Baton Rouge. It was a promise of ultimate Union control of the western fronts. On the same day good news also flowed in from the Army of the Potomac. McClellan had finally begun to move into Virginia and was sending Confederate forces back toward Richmond. After a month of maneuvering, McClellan's army took Yorktown on May 3 and Williamsburg on May 5.

Lovejoy introduced a resolution on the morning of May 9 giving thanks to General McClellan for the victories of the Army of the Potomac. The congressman thus helped to soften the image of harsh intransigence he held in the eyes of conservatives, and appeared to be more reasonable than they supposed. Next morning's New York *Times* thought Lovejoy's motion "was doubtless penitential and certainly eminently becoming." Springing to the defense of McClellan, the *Times* could not let its readers forget that "For months the radicals, of whom Lovejoy is the typical man, have delighted in denouncing the generalship . . . of the Commander. . . . The events of a week have shown the utter falsity of these criminations. What better could Lovejoy do—presupposing grace granted him to do it—than to make prompt

331

and ample amend to the insulted patriot. . . ." But the general was pleased by Lovejoy's resolution. He looked upon it as evidence the abolitionists seemed to be coming round to his view of fighting the war. "Are you satisfied with my bloodless victories?" he asked. "Even the Abolitionists seem to be coming round; judging, at least, from the very handsome resolutions offered by Mr. Lovejoy in the House. I look upon that resolution as one of the most complimentary I know of, and that, too, offered by my bitterest persecutors." [20] Even with such revised opinions of him Lovejoy proceeded cautiously.

In the afternoon Lovejoy proposed a substitute for his bill. In the newer version he eliminated a reference to freeing slaves on "all national highways." He did so in order that the House would accept a bill on which to base a debate. Immediately Cox, speaking for the conservative elements, asserted that the bill only helped the secessionists. He bitterly denounced this or any bill like it and even attacked Lovejoy's resolution in praise of McClellan as a "piece of Pharisaism on his part." Cox wanted to see the Union restored as it was, not the Union the gentleman from Illinois "wants to see." The Ohio conservative, who later wrote that Lovejoy had little understanding of the legislative process, complained peevishly, "I believe the people of the country are sick and weary of this legislation about the negro." William P. Kellogg of Illinois wondered whether the effect of the bill would not be to repeal the Fugitive Slave Law. He saw the bill providing places under United States jurisdiction wherein fugitive slaves could come and therefore be forever free. He felt it would be more manly to introduce a bill for the universal emancipation of slaves within the limits of the United States, "and boldly and fearlessly take the responsibility and the consequences." Arnold reminded his colleague that the bill on liberation in the District of Columbia was framed substantially like the one under debate, yet enemies of this bill had made no objection to that. Perhaps Kellogg was being hypercritical, he asserted.[21]

Throughout the afternoon, as the questioning and debating criss-crossed the House, Stevens, Lovejoy, and Arnold bore the brunt of the attack. Stevens backed up Arnold's reply to Kellogg. Lovejoy cited his victory in the Illinois Circuit Court when it reaffirmed the freedom of a slave who escaped from a slave state into a free state. By late evening, May 9, the debate was not yet near conclusion, and it was apparent to Lovejoy that the conservative opposition was still considerable.

When the House reconvened on Monday, May 12, Lovejoy offered a modification in the substitute bill of May 9. That earlier bill had been designed to "secure freedom to all persons within the exclusive jurisdiction of the Federal government to the end that freedom may remain forever the fundamental law of the land, and in all places whatsoever, so far as it lies within the power or depends upon the action of the Government of the United States to make it so. . . ." The enacting phrase then stated that slavery should cease and be prohibited in all the territories then existing or to be acquired or organized in the future; in all federal establishments; on vessels on the high seas; and in all places under federal jurisdiction where the national government is supreme. Taking note of the conservative trend against the bill, Lovejoy on May 12 offered a compromise in a motion to strike out the preamble and to change the title of the bill to read, "An Act to Secure Freedom to all Persons within the Territories of the United States." The omission of other places of federal jurisdiction was agreeable in the House, but Cox registered his acidulous opposition by suggesting the addition of these words to the title: "to carry out the Chicago platform and to dissolve the Union." The final vote on Lovejoy's bill was 85 to 50 in favor. Thus the wider frontiers of freedom were about to be embodied in law, if the Senate would concur and if the President would sign the measure.[22]

In the Senate, Orville H. Browning of Illinois reported Lovejoy's bill on May 15, and on June 9 Benjamin F. Wade of Ohio moved to take it up on the floor, with an amendment. The Senate agreed, 28 to 10, to strike out all after the enacting clause of Lovejoy's bill and insert instead, "That, from and after the passage of this act, there shall be neither slavery nor involuntary servitude in any of the Territories of the United States, otherwise than in punishment of crimes, whereof the party shall have been duly convicted." On June 17 Lovejoy moved that the House concur in the Senate amendment, and passage was assured. The vote was 72 to 38. Two days later the President signed the act.[23]

The importance of the territorial abolition law steered through the House by Lovejoy should not be underestimated. Reduced though it was by the Senate, it nevertheless legalized a principle adopted at first by only a handful of early abolitionists. Wilmot's proviso of the 1840's and 1850's had adopted the principle of nonextension of slavery from Jefferson. This had been a cardinal point in the platforms of the poor little antislavery parties, beginning with the Liberty party, and of the varieties of Conscience Whigs, Barnburners, and other dissident Democrats. Then, when the Republican party came fresh on the scene with mass support for its nonextension plank, men like Lovejoy, Lincoln, and Browning were enabled to unite their forces on common ground. Even so profound a leader as Frederick Douglass, speaking for the millions of slaves whose fate, after all, was the fate of liberty and Union, consented to unite on the nonextension principle as a minimum objective.

From the narrowly partisan point of view, Lovejoy's bill did its share to uphold the 1860 Republican platform. Republicans differed on the other questions—on tariffs, on money, on river and harbor improvements, on railroads, on postal rates—but on one question they were united: The slavery system must be kept out of the territories and confined to the states where it existed, for the time being.

Lovejoy's bill has further significance as one of the several

334

enactments of the revolutionary 37th Congress, which began to shift power from the slaveowners to Northern agriculture, industry, and finance interests. Among the other measures were the abolition bill for the District of Columbia, the Second Confiscation Act, the Homestead Act, the Pacific Railroad Act, and the Morrill Tariff. All were linked as the political offensive of the Northern interests in their basic economic struggle with the slavery system. Hereafter, slaves who entered free territory would become free. Slaveowners were thus forced to face the prospect that they could hope for no relief in the free territories when Southern soil was exhausted by cotton agriculture and the plantation system. The territorial abolition bill constituted, moreover, an assertion of federal responsibility to abolish slavery. It precluded the enactment of a Missouri Compromise or a Kansas-Nebraska Act or the rendering of a new Dred Scott decision. In that it did not provide compensation to slaveowners, it was an improvement over the District of Columbia abolition bill. Had the original bill been successful, slavery would have been banned not only in the territories but in federal shipyards, on vessels at sea under the United States flag, or in any other place where the federal government held jurisdiction.

Even though it was a weak measure from the point of view of the radical Republicans, the militantly pro-Union Chicago *Tribune* shouted its joy over the "Arnold-Lovejoy Bill." The editors had been somewhat disappointed in Lovejoy's compromise of May 12, noting that while the bill "rendered freedom national and slavery sectional," it did not "secure freedom to all persons within the exclusive jurisdiction of the United States." This was undoubtedly as much a pitch for the original bill as for some early measure of national emancipation of the slaves. But when the bill became law with Lincoln's signature on June 19, the *Tribune* editorially noted that the bill was cast in almost the exact words of Jefferson in 1784 during the discussion of the antislavery provisions of the Northwest Ordinance. The editors were elated indeed in that first week of summer; not only had slavery been abolished in the territories, but the Chicago platform had also been redeemed by passage of the Pacific railroad bill.[24]

The District and territorial abolition bills were cause for celebration by Negroes in New York and surrounding towns. On May 13 the passage of the first and the progress of the second brought thirty-five hundred colored people into a jubilee in honor of the legislation at Cooper Institute. Negroes came from Newark, Jersey City, Paterson, Williamsburg, Jamaica, Harlem, Flushing, and Tarrytown. Reverend Henry Highland Garnet as the main speaker brought forth tremendous cheering when he cited "the passage of Mr. Lovejoy's bill" in the House of Representatives.[25]

The people in the North and Congress continued the pressure for immediate emancipation throughout the land. Thousands of signatures on petitions for such a policy had been presented to the legislature. The confiscation bill before the Congress contained an emancipation clause that would free the slaves of anyone committing treason and of all persons who supported the rebellion. Moreover, direct action was taken by Congress on March 13 when it enacted a new article of war forbidding army and navy officers to return fugitive slaves. Congress and the people, in the days before and after the District and territorial abolition acts, were in a mood to extend the emancipation policy even to the rebel states.

In those spring and summer days Lincoln's hopes were slimming for gradual, compensated emancipation. Border state men continued to refuse his offers; and the inconclusive military advances on the eastern front almost within sight of Washington further depressed Lincoln's hopes. The Seven Days Battle from June 26 through July 1 on the Virginia peninsula had ended with Lee retreating toward Richmond, and with McClellan preferring

336

to find a safe base rather than to advance after a fleeing enemy. This frustrating Union victory was followed by a chorus of demands for vigorous attacks against slavery. General Lew Wallace proclaimed his willingness to use Negro troops, and in the Congress, where the Militia Act was coming up for consideration, legislators were receptive to the enlistment of Negroes. This was recognition of the earlier demands for Negro troops by Frederick Douglass and other Negro leaders; and of the offers by black men in New England and in major Northern cities to serve their country. Radical Republicans, who had supported the enrollment of Negro troops, were now in a position to increase their demands.[26]

By July 4, 1862, it was clear that the President would have to yield to his radical friends on the emancipation question. Even so careful a financial man as Jay Cooke confided at this time to Secretary Chase that his own feeling was growing stronger that slavery must be purged "either by some wholesale declaration as that of Hunter or through the operations of such a bill as that passed for the District of Columbia." With such sentiment hardening in the country, the crisis was rapidly approaching. The influential New York *Tribune* and Chicago *Tribune* as well as the New York *Evening Post* were not alone in pressing for strong emancipation measures. The Washington *National Republican*, the Harrisburg *Telegraph*, and the Portsmouth, New Hampshire, *Journal*, among others, also called for outright abolition of slavery. Lincoln's old friend, Governor Richard Yates of Illinois, urged him to wipe out the institution if it would help win the war. Governor John A. Andrew of Massachusetts and other leading governors in the North, reading the sentiments of the people, joined in the chorus for decisive emancipation. One week after Independence Day a conference committee of the Congress reported a bill combining revolutionary confiscation and emancipation measures. So far-reaching was the bill that it proposed to confiscate not only property in slaves but other property, including real estate, of rebels. Lincoln's particular objection to this latter section was that he believed it to be unconstitutional. Accordingly the legislature modified it to avoid a presidential veto. The President had decided to veto the entire bill and had prepared a veto message. On July 11, the House passed the conference committee's version of the confiscation bill and on the same day Lincoln named Halleck commander of the United States Army to overcome the growing uneasiness of the people with McClellan's procrastination. It seemed that Congress was now dominated by radical Republicans sure of their mass support in the country. On July 12 Lincoln was host at the White House to a gathering of border state members of Congress. Again he implored them to accept the proposals of March 6. Again he was met by unyielding refusal. He told them that he had aroused the country against himself when he annulled Hunter's orders. "The pressure is still upon me and is increasing," he said in explanation of why the border states must accept his offer in order to "secure substantial compensation for that which is sure to be wholly lost in any other event." But again he was met with a stern negative.[27]

The next day, Sunday, July 13, the President was resting at the Soldiers Home, which was his summer residence in the capital city. Among his visitors that day were Congressmen Arnold and Lovejoy from his home state. Arnold referred to "Lovejoy, the ultra-abolitionist" as "one of Lincoln's confidential advisers." Lincoln's agitation over the rebuff from the border state congressmen could not be contained and he said to the two legislators: "Oh, how I wish the border States would accept my proposition. Then you, Lovejoy, and you, Arnold, and all of us, would not have lived in vain! The labor of your life, Lovejoy, would be crowned with success. You would live to see the end of slavery." Even though he was pleading almost in desperation for his gradualist policy, he had apparently made up his mind to travel with the main antislavery sentiment of the country. On the same day he told Seward and Welles and Mrs. Frederick Seward, daughter-in-law of the Secretary of State, that he "had about come to the conclusion that it was a military necessity absolutely essential for the salvation of the Union, that we must free the slaves or be ourselves subdued." Two years later he explained his predicament: "I was in my best judgment, driven to the alternative of either surrendering the Union or issuing the emancipation proclamation." [28]

Lovejoy, who said in a letter to Garrison in February, 1864, "I have known something of the facts inside during [Lincoln's] Administration," also asserted that the Emancipation Proclamation was "*not* extorted from [the President] by the outward pressure." Lovejoy maintained in February, 1864, that he had learned from Lincoln's own lips that "he had written the proclamation in the summer, as early as June, I think—but will not be certain as to the precise time. . . ." The correctness of Lovejoy's recollection was to some extent supported by Thomas T. Eckert, Superintendent of the Military Telegraph in the War Department. Eckert said that the President began the writing in June. Lincoln went daily to the telegraph office of the War Department to escape the distractions of the White House. One morning he asked Eckert for some paper on which to write. Eckert supplied the President with foolscap and the President began to write. He continued to do so on his daily visits for several weeks. Finally he told Eckert that he "had been writing an order giving freedom to the slaves in the South, for the purpose of hastening the end of the war." [29]

It is difficult to understand then why the President continued to maneuver with the border state representatives. One interpretation of Lincoln's action was recorded by James C. Welling, editor of the Washington *Intelligencer*. He believed that the preliminary proclamation of September 22, 1862, "was issued primarily and chiefly as a *political necessity*, and took on the character of a military necessity only because the President had been brought to believe that if he did not keep the Radical portion of his party at his back he could not be long sure of keeping an army at the front. . . . Thus placed between two stools . . . he determined at last to plant himself firmly on the stool which promised the surest and safest support." Lovejoy was later publicly to assert a similar claim.[30]

That stool on which Lincoln firmly planted himself was the one supported by Stevens, Lovejoy, Julian, and other radicals in the House; Sumner, Trumbull, Wilson, and others in the Senate; and Douglass and the Negro people; as well as the growing sentiment in the country for emancipation. Their policy was firmly documented in the confiscation bill that passed in the House on July 11 and in the Senate on July 12. On July 17 Lincoln signed it into law. The Second Confiscation Act provided for the punishment of persons convicted of treason against the United States, by death or fine and imprisonment; the slaves of rebel masters were declared free as soon as they entered Union lines (a blow at the Fugitive Slave Law); the President was empowered to enlist Negroes to suppress the rebellion; and he was authorized to seize without warning the property of officers of the Confederate government, and after sixty days' warning the property of all others supporting the rebellion.

Lovejoy's leadership in the House during the spring of 1862 seemed to be guided by a lesson learned in Illinois politics six years earlier. That was, simply, to maintain a united front with Lincoln while using every tactic that would advance the main issue of abolishing slavery. He had by then become the deft tactician the times required of a radical. In every major utterance in the House he fought for his principles, yet upheld the Lincoln

Administration and avoided contending with the Chief Executive's gradualism.

The quality of Lovejoy's relationship with Lincoln is revealed in an address Lovejoy made before the Emancipation League in New York's Cooper Institute on June 12, 1862. In the audience were some of the city's most prominent men, including the millionaire Peter Cooper and Edgar Ketchum, Secretary of the Emancipation League. William Cullen Bryant came over from the *Evening Post* offices in printers' row to make an introductory speech in which he recalled the martyrdom of Elijah Lovejoy and pointed out that Illinois had given to the Union "a Republican President—a Chief Magistrate who urged upon the slave states the policy of emancipation." The poet then presented "fearless and resolute Owen Lovejoy" to the crowd assembled in the great hall on Astor Place. The lecturer of the evening looked out upon a half-filled auditorium, but such a circumstance by no means dismayed him. He had spent long hours preparing his speech, and he spoke for two and a half hours. The report in next morning's New York *Times* was lavish in praise of the address. A reading of the text in the New York *Tribune* reveals careful preparation, good organization and a more dispassionate tone than displayed in Lovejoy's earlier speeches on slavery. The headline writer, however, gave it biblical import by titling it "Freedom the Shekina of America." The praise by the *Times* writer must have caused Lovejoy to smile, for this was the very paper that had so icily greeted his resolution in praise of McClellan only a month earlier, on May 9.[31]

Lovejoy departed from the written text to approve the President's March 6 message as "another distinct landmark in our progress freedomward." He admitted "some think the butter spread rather thin" in the resolution of Congress for gradual, compensated emancipation. Nevertheless, Lovejoy maintained, "the Executive rail splitter . . . knows the thin end of the

341

wedge must first enter the wood. . . . So the Executive has taken the Abolition wedge, and struck it into the log of slavery." But, Lovejoy asked his audience to remember that "in very ugly and cross grained or frozen wood the blows have to be a little easy at first, or the wedge flies out. . . ." Even city dwellers could understand the woodsman's homely metaphors.[32]

Lovejoy kept the audience alternately laughing and applauding while he limned in more details of how Lincoln stood with antislavery people:

"The President is like a man driving a horse in the thills of a buggy, and leading another behind him by the halter-strap. . . .

"Now the President knows that the horse Radical that he is driving can go ahead, for he has by him been taken in handsome style into the Executive Chair. . . .

"Now I do not propose to dash ahead so as to throw the President out or break the carriage but to go steadily that the Executive can be assured that he is safe with the Radical steed . . . and then he will drop the strap and let the old conservative Rosinante go to grass.

"If the President does not believe all I do, I believe all he does." In other words, Lovejoy said, "If he does not drive as fast as I would, he is on the right road, and it is only a question of time."

In defense of Lincoln's slowness the congressman said no President, not even Washington, had been so beset with trials and difficulties. "The wonder is not that he should make mistakes but that he should make so few," Lovejoy said. He no more doubted the President's "antislavery integrity, his ultimate antislavery action" than he doubted his own. He urged then that the President be given a "cordial, loyal, and sympathizing support."

Lovejoy had spent at least two weeks preparing the lecture and "felt some anxiety about it," but in the end he was satisfied that it had gone off very well indeed. After the lecture, friends surrounded Lovejoy, exchanged greetings, continued discussion of

342

his remarks, and wished him well. Peter Cooper wished to thank Lovejoy especially for his defense of "the wise and politic course pursued by the President," but the speaker of the evening seemed so thoroughly occupied that Cooper could not bring himself to intrude. The New York *Independent*, an abolitionist newspaper more radical than Lovejoy, was also pleased and noted that "This was the first address which Mr. Lovejoy ever delivered in New York, and it won for him many new friends." [33]

Back home in Princeton, when John H. Bryant read the speech he lost little time in extolling it—"Its literary execution," he told Lovejoy, "is much more perfect, it is more compact, argumentative and epigrammatic, and at the same time less pretentious, if you will allow me to say so." The poet and brother of a poet nevertheless took occasion to remind his friend that Lincoln was dragging his feet on antislavery action. The President, Bryant believed, "seems to act with more decision on the wrong side, than on the right." Bryant feared that Lincoln's reputation among antislavery men "is not sustained by his acts, I hope it will not be but I fear." [34]

Despite such doubts and fears in the minds of some antislavery men, Lincoln moved ahead to strengthen Union forces by issuing a call for three hundred thousand men on July 1. Moreover, he had given some thought to the drafting of an emancipation proclamation, as Lovejoy and Eckert indicated. Also, Charles Sumner called on Lincoln on July 4 and pleaded with the President to issue the proclamation on that day. Lincoln, however, preferred to wait for a better military situation, as he implied in his reply to Sumner. He was still waiting for a decisive victory on the Virginia peninsula and for a favorable response from border state men. Neither materialized by July 13 when Lincoln divulged his plan to the Sewards and Secretary Welles, nor by July 22 when he called his Cabinet together and told them of his intention to issue the proclamation.[35]

Two events that added to the pressure on Lincoln were the passage of the Second Confiscation Act and the publication on July 19 of an "Address of the Republican Members of Congress." Eight senators and twenty-five representatives had written this message to the American people. In it the congressmen reasserted the necessity to free the slave and permit him to fight to defend "his native land." Lovejoy, of course, was among the signers. A New York *Tribune* editorial on the same date warned against the dangers of "a faithless, insincere, higgling, grudging execution" of the emancipatory provisions of the new Confiscation Act.[36]

Lovejoy was one of many Republicans who during the summer emphasized the call for the arming of Negroes. In doing so he was attempting not to harass the President but to strengthen his hand in carrying out the emancipation policy he was beginning to adopt. Lovejoy stopped in Milwaukee on July 31 to speak to a mass open air meeting in Washington Park. He urged full support of the President's call for troops. Two days later Lovejoy appeared as a featured speaker at a giant war rally in Chicago. By eight-thirty in the evening, it was reported, about ten thousand people gathered in the enclosure between the Courthouse and Washington and Clark Streets. The densely packed throng heard Governor Yates, John Sherman, and three of the state's most ardent antislavery congressmen—Owen Lovejoy, Isaac N. Arnold, and John F. Farnsworth. One theme united all the speakers. The government must enlist Negroes in the army to suppress the rebellion. Waves of cheers and shouts greeted the speakers, but probably none was so warmly welcomed as Owen Lovejoy from the Third Congressional District. He had long ago made an indelible mark in the memories of Chicagoans.[37]

Great applause shook the darkening streets when Lovejoy made his plea: "We want to take away [from the rebels] everything that will weaken [them] and strengthen our side." He explained why the country needed the Negro people: "These

Negroes know all the roads, all the swamps, all the country, and they are about all the loyal people in the South that have helped us, and I would proclaim freedom to them all, not for the sake of the Negro, but for the sake of the government."

He let the throng know he had "great confidence in the honesty and patriotism of Abraham Lincoln." Lovejoy regretted that the President was "merely unfortunate in some of his surroundings." He called for a proclamation of freedom for the slave for the sake of preserving the nation. The government, he said, should do as Tacitus said the Romans did—when they made a peace they also made the enemy's country a solitude. If the Republic could be saved in no other way than to make a solitude of the rebellious states, then Lovejoy urged the utmost warfare against them. This required troops—fighting men who loved their country. Enlistments were required to uphold the government—every able-bodied man was called for—black and white.

Lovejoy had also played on this theme in his Cooper Institute address and he continued to do so through the summer and into early fall as he campaigned for his reelection.

During that first winter and spring of the Civil War other questions besides the antislavery one confronted the people and the government. Economic measures, promised in the 1860 Republican platform and requiring implementation by the 37th Congress, were a homestead act, construction of a Pacific Railroad, and other internal improvements. One that was not foreseen in the platform, however, was the matter of financing the war. The money question arose in the winter of 1861–1862 as part of the financial crisis brought about by the government's difficulty in paying for the war by old and respected methods: taxation, or the income derived from internal revenue duties on goods, protective tariffs, and personal income taxes; borrowing, from banks and other private investors. Only eight months after civil war began the poor condition of the country's finances was made evident in December, 1861, when Secretary Chase reported that revenues were falling below his estimates while expenditures were rising far above the estimates. Moreover, as a result of the reaction in New York and other financial centers to the possibility of British reprisals in the *Trent* affair, United States securities declined by two to two and a half per cent on the New York stock exchange on December 16, 1861. Banks were subjected to runs on their gold supplies in the next several days, and on December 30 twenty-five New York banks out of forty voted to suspend redemption of paper money in coin. Philadelphia and Boston banks immediately followed suit; and they were followed by almost all the banks in the North. While the drain on their specie was great, the bankers are believed to have taken this step more to protect their reserves than to meet an immediate absolute necessity. Nevertheless the country was faced with a first-class crisis. If no uniform and dependable currency were available, speculators in the banking field could flood the country with worthless paper money. The government was therefore forced to act to assure that it would have money to purchase materials and supplies and to pay the soldiers. The magnitude of the government's needs dictated that it step into the situation and, to avoid chaos and collapse, create a new medium of circulation and give it respectability by declaring it legal tender for debts and obligations.[38]

In adjusting to the new demands put upon them, leaders of government and banking were forced to swallow old prejudices. Hard-money men like Lovejoy were compelled by the flow of events to give up ideas they had learned as young men—ideas that had aided Andrew Jackson in blunting the power of the Bank of the United States. Hard-money ideas had been the cherished ones in financial thinking since the founding of the republic, but the nature of the economy had changed in seventy-five years.

It was clear to a few men in those grim winter days that the gargantuan wartime enterprise would require an equally gargantuan purchasing power to sustain it. Thaddeus Stevens was one of a handful who ventured boldly to create the kind of purchasing power required. But Lovejoy opposed his party colleagues on this issue. The question arose, who should create the new purchasing power, the private banks or the government? If the banks were to do so at a time when they were relieved of the responsibility to redeem notes in specie, might they not indulge in issuing unlimited quantities of worthless notes? Should the government do so, as proposed in the first legal tender bills before Congress, the people would receive irredeemable government paper money. But the hope was expressed at the time that after the war emergency a grateful government would redeem the money, somehow.

On December 30, 1861, when the banks suspended specie payments, Congress heard a proposal by Representative Elbridge Gerry Spaulding of Buffalo, New York, for the issue of treasury notes which, though irredeemable in specie, would constitute legal tender. Spaulding was chairman of a subcommittee on loans under the powerful Ways and Means Committee, which was headed by Stevens. The Pennsylvania ironmaster at first objected strenuously to the legal tender clause in Spaulding's bill as unconstitutional, but under the pressure of arguments for the necessity of the provision he succumbed and voted for it. He reported the legal tender bill to the House, and joined Spaulding, himself a banker, in fighting for the bill.[39]

Many were the voices raised in objection to the bill. Lovejoy went so far as to offer a substitute bill to the Spaulding measure. The Illinois hard-money man scoffed at the arguments offered in favor of the legal tender bill. In the meager five minutes he was allowed when he took the floor on January 29, 1862, Lovejoy called the general idea of the bill a fallacy—"Believe that this piece of paper is a five dollar gold piece, and it is a five dollar gold piece; believe it is worth five dollars, and it is worth five dollars." To do so, he said, would be to make something out of nothing. "The piece of paper you stamp as five dollars is not five dollars, and it never will be unless it is convertible into a five dollar gold piece; and to profess that it is, is simply a delusion and a fallacy." He disputed the constitutionality of the bill: "I would admit the plea of necessity if I believed it; and think it is more manly to confess, as Jefferson did, that it is to attempt to torture the constitution into the support of a measure which everybody must see to be unconstitutional." He predicted that the bill would lead to ruin: "At every step your paper will depreciate more and more, until the expenses of the war will swell to such an appalling sum that redemption will be impossible, and repudiation inevitable." [40] But Lovejoy's five-minute speech was not entirely a jeremiad. He offered a set of positive proposals:

"First, adequate taxation, if need be, to the extent of $200,-000,000.[41]

"Second, adopt legislation that shall compel all banking institutions to do business on a specie basis. Every piece of paper that claimed to be money, but was not, I would chase back to the man or corporation that forged it, and visit upon them the penalties of the law. I would not allow a bank note to circulate that was not constantly, conveniently and certainly convertible into specie.

"Third, I would issue interest-paying bonds of the United States, and go into the market and borrow money and pay the obligations of the Government. This would be honest, business-like, and in the end economical. This could be done. Other channels of investment are blocked up, and capital would seek the bonds of investment."

Some of the ablest Republicans in the House joined Lovejoy in support of his substitute. Conspicuous were Roscoe Conkling,

Frederick A. Conkling, and Theodore Pomeroy of New York; Justin S. Morrill of Vermont; Benjamin F. Thomas of Massachusetts; Edward H. Rollins of New Hampshire; William H. Wadsworth and Albert G. Porter of Indiana; and Valentine B. Horton of Ohio. But even such a stellar array of opposition could not stop passage of the Spaulding bill, which seemed to Lovejoy a foregone conclusion. The final vote was 93 to 59, with these few Republicans breaking ranks to join the Democrats who made up most of the opposition.[42]

The bill became law on February 25, 1862, and authorized an issue of $150 million in Treasury notes, not bearing interest, declared legal tender for all obligations, public and private, except duties on imports and interest on the public debt. The notes were made convertible into six per cent bonds redeemable at the pleasure of the United States government after five years, to mature in twenty years.

This infusion of paper money failed to supply the demands of the wartime economy, even when combined with the revenue from customs duties, internal taxes, and sales of public lands. However, the problems of the banks and the Treasury were relieved by the issuance of the new notes. Nevertheless, the government resorted to the second legal tender act in July to pump more money into the economy. This time some of the opponents of the first bill voted in favor. Lovejoy continued to oppose the new money policy, denouncing it as pernicious, but promised he would not persist "in any factious opposition to what is a foregone conclusion." In the debate Representative Samuel Hooper of Massachusetts, a wealthy retired Boston merchant, said it was a question between bank notes and government notes and he preferred the latter. Lovejoy indicated that he was coming round to the positions of Hooper and Stevens when he said: "If anybody is to have the advantage of a depreciated currency—the advantage, in other words, of not paying interest on what they owe—

I say let the government have that advantage; and let the bankers share with the rest of us." Once again the argument of necessity won the vote in Congress.[43]

That was only the beginning of a process Lovejoy and other opponents of the first legal tender bill had predicted. Ask for this dose of paper money, they said, and you will start an endless series of demands for more and more paper money. They proved to be right, for the third legal tender bill became law rather speedily in January, 1863. Even the most unrelenting foes of the greenbacks, as the paper money was called, voted for this bill. By the end of the war a total of $432 million in greenbacks had been issued. More than this, Lovejoy supported a measure to tax bank notes out of existence and have them replaced by treasury notes. Speaking for the Northwest, Lovejoy proclaimed: "I express the united and earnest sentiment of the grain-growing states. If we must have a paper currency—that seems to be inevitable now—let us have a Government currency, and not a currency of a thousand irresponsible corporate bodies or associations. I ask it at the hands of this House on behalf of the Northwest." [44]

He disagreed with Charles J. Biddle of Pennsylvania "in regard to the right of annihilating this sort of irredeemable currency." Lovejoy considered it now to be the exclusive right of the federal government to issue notes and to make them legal tender as it had done, and he was opposed to conceding the right to the states. This was indeed a far cry from his argument against the constitutionality of the first legal tender bill. He now based his argument on the legal precedent announced by Associate Justice Joseph Story of the United States Supreme Court in Prigg vs. Pennsylvania, a case in which federal law on a subject was held to be preeminent over any state law on the same subject. But that case, Biddle answered somewhat incredulously, was the case of a fugitive slave. Lovejoy acknowledged this but asserted that

350

the principle laid down in the case was not limited in application to that particular case. He insisted that the states had no business to legislate in a field in which the federal government's legislation was "absolute and exhaustive." In addition Lovejoy chose this moment to unburden himself of opinions obviously long simmering in him against the banks that issued their own notes: "My conviction is, and has been, that these bank issues have been always unconstitutional, have always been a curse to the country, and never have been an advantage at all.

"I hold that this whole theory of banking is vicious, fallacious, and deceptive; and I believe that these banks have had more to do with our ever-recurring commercial disasters and collapses than any other cause whatever." [45]

Representative Frederick A. Pike of Maine, who had earlier raised the slogan of "tax, Fight and Emancipate," took Lovejoy to task for casting aspersions on the bankers, of his part of the country at least. Lovejoy, who voted with Pike on most questions of wartime policy, defended his statements by saying, "I have denounced neither banks nor bankers. I suppose bankers have the same human nature that other people have. If I were a rich man I might be a banker, but as I am a poor man I have my sympathy enlisted in behalf of the laboring men more than on behalf of the capitalists. I have simply denounced irredeemable bank paper." [46]

A little while later in the debate Lovejoy flatly asserted, "The people are satisfied with the Government currency." Pike pounced on the remark to ask if that were not irredeemable currency. Lovejoy did not deny it, but insisted that the government should have the exclusive privilege of issuing it—the people would have the benefit. He maintained that the people believed government currency to be good, whether it was or not. "They believe that it is good," he said, "that it is a mortgage upon the entire property of the United States, personal and real. . . .

351

They believe that these notes will sometime be paid. That is their faith, and it is mine." [47]

Speaking still as the spokesman of the Northwest, Lovejoy told the Congress to "give us a currency." If the House could not give the grain-growing states gold, as Lovejoy believed the legislature might have done, he was willing to have greenbacks, "and we will continue to pour out our products as we have our soldiers," in support of the Union. He then read into the record a lengthy communication from the Illinois State Agricultural Society that had apparently moved him to alter his position on the money question.[48] It is tempting to believe that the society's message foreshadowed the later positions of the Greenback and Populist parties, and to wonder how far Lovejoy would have gone with these grass-roots movements had he lived another thirty years.

Also, as a defender of his section's interests, Lovejoy joined Elihu B. Washburne in the Galena man's fight to legislate construction of a ship canal from the Mississippi to Lake Michigan. The wheat and corn states would then have a clear route to the Atlantic Ocean and then to the markets of Britain and the Continent. When Lovejoy spoke on January 15, 1863, in a debate on the ways and means bill, he devoted most of his time to the currency question but also injected a proud claim for the commercial interests of the Northwest. He bristled at the talk then current in the corridors of the capital that " 'the first gleams of peace will be from the Northwest.' " Such divisive talk was defeatist, and could only originate with the Copperhead appeasers. "I stand up here today to speak the voice of the Northwest," he announced. "The Northwest will never go to the South, and never will let the South go." Nor would his section separate itself from New England, New York, or Pennsylvania. "No, sir," Lovejoy told the whisperers, "we are going to the Gulf by the Mississippi, and to the ocean by New York. We propose to feed the world, and we will never surrender the privilege of going to market either way." In every parliamentary test Lovejoy voted with Washburne, but other sectional interests, notably Pennsylvania's, led by Thaddeus Stevens, proved too potent in their opposition. The Illinois Ship Canal bill went down to defeat on February 9, 1863, but not without a fight from the Prairie State men.[49]

Lovejoy also fought for two bills in 1862 that were to benefit the farmer. One was the bill establishing a bureau of agriculture, the other was the homestead bill. Lovejoy had been intimately connected with both, and had served in a leading position in the campaign for the latter in the 36th and 37th Congresses.

Washington in his last annual message to the federal legislature had suggested that a board of agriculture be established to collect and disseminate information of use to farmers. Although no such body was authorized by Congress, the farmer was not entirely forgotten. Henry L. Ellsworth, the first Commissioner of Patents, in 1836 began to distribute seeds through his office, although he had no official sanction. This proved a popular step among the farmers, and in 1847 Congress responded to the growing importance of the farmers by appropriating money for seed distribution. This was repeated in every subsequent Congress, but as the Northwest grew in population and productivity, and especially as its grain crops became a factor in international relations, the farmers felt that the time had come to establish a bureau or cabinet level department in the federal government to represent their interests.[50]

Lincoln responded to this growing demand by declaring in his State of the Union Message of December 3, 1861, "that an agricultural and statistical bureau might profitably be organized." Lovejoy as chairman of the House Committee on Agriculture was directly concerned and made responsible for carrying through the legislation required. On February 11, 1862, he reported a bill to establish "an Agricultural Bureau or Depart-

353

ment." Its special object would be "the development of the agricultural and productive interests of the country." On May 8 the bill finally passed in the Senate and a week later President Lincoln signed it into law. The bill set up a non-cabinet department at first, but eventually it was raised to cabinet rank. Lovejoy's bill had been a compromise between those who preferred a subordinate bureau in the Department of the Interior and those who pushed for a separate cabinet department.[51]

The *Bureau County Republican* was quick to give unqualified praise to the act: "The bill originated with Mr. Lovejoy, and was matured by him, and he secured its passage through the House. It is emphatically his measure, and to him are the farmers indebted for the first important movement by Congress looking directly to the interests of the man who cultivates the soil." [52]

The Homestead Act became law that same week. Lovejoy again played a leading part, at least in the introductory stages of the bill. He had introduced House Bill No. 7 on December 4, 1861, but was reminded by Clement L. Vallandigham that a similar bill was already in the Public Lands Committee, of which Wisconsin's John Potter was the influential member. The big man from the Badger State had stomped down the aisle of the House in April, 1860, to defend Lovejoy against the threats of Southern fire-eaters. But now he was opposed to Lovejoy on the technicality involved.[53]

Although the bill was sent to Potter's committee, it was virtually the same one that Galusha Grow had introduced in the previous Congress and for which he and Lovejoy labored diligently. Now, with the support of Republicans, who generally favored the measure as a matter of party policy, and a few Union Democrats, whose party before the war had long fought for the bill's principle, the House passed it on February 28. The Senate approved the bill on May 6 and Lincoln signed it on May 20. The act provided an opportunity for anyone twenty-one years of age or over to acquire one hundred and sixty acres of land; a citizen under twenty-one who was the head of a family enjoyed the same opportunity. The settler must pay fees of $34 on the Pacific Coast and $26 in other states for the land. Title was to be acquired after the settler spent five years in residence and improvement on his homestead; however, after six months of residence and improvement the claimant could take full title by paying $1.25 per acre.

Overlooking the rivalry between Potter and Lovejoy, the Princeton newspaper was happy to reprint the sentiment of the Aurora, Illinois, *Beacon*'s special correspondent in the Capital. He was sure the country would be indebted to Lovejoy and Potter for the bill's final success. "I don't know how it may seem to the people on the prairies," wrote "S.W.," "but to me, here, it looks as if Lovejoy was a name of growing strength, of influence, of power." [54]

At the moment of the bill's passage Lovejoy was beginning to foresee that rapacious land capitalists and "operators" like those described in Mark Twain's *Gilded Age* would very soon turn the Homestead Act into an instrument to gather up large holdings of timber, grazing, mineral, and fuel lands. Lovejoy had an inkling of how crassly acquisitive were the early industrial capitalists. He showed in the debate on the Pacific Railroad bill that he foresaw the grasp these men would take on lands supposedly set aside for the worker and the farmer. Nevertheless in May, 1862, Lovejoy's farmer constituents rejoiced that the long fight for the liberal land policy had come to a successful end. The story of the alienation of the public domain would come later, and indeed has not yet been widely told.

There was really no debate over whether the country needed a railroad linking the two ocean coasts. The Democratic and Republican platforms of 1856 each had included a plank favoring construction of a continental railroad. This had become a national aim, spurred on by visions of wealth in the West. The discovery of gold in California in 1848 gave substance to the vision. Others saw wealth in the West from exploitation of various natural resources, of real estate development, of continental trade, and ultimately of international trade with China and Japan via the transcontinental railway and the Pacific Ocean.

Railroads were concentrated in the eastern part of the country where only about nine thousand miles of rail routes had been built in the twenty years from 1830 to 1850. For the most part they remained local. Realizing that railroads meant trade, industry, and profit, towns and states vied for railroad construction with generous concessions, including wide belts of land, to railroad companies. In the next ten years, from 1850 to 1860, twenty thousand miles of track were added, five trunk lines crossing the Appalachians to points on the Ohio and Mississippi Rivers. The country witnessed a railroad construction and real estate mania broken only by the panic of 1857. Illinois by 1860 had more railroad track than any other state, and Chicago-based companies were eager to push through Iowa toward the West Coast. The lake city had already been linked to New York in 1853 and to Philadelphia in 1858. Why not to the far West as well? Combinations of American and foreign capital were mobilized to exploit the railroad fever of the ambitious promoters; and political leaders on local, state, and federal levels were acquired as friends of these railroad and real estate investors. Their most notable achievement was a grant to the railroad companies of two and a half million acres of the richest soil in America from Chicago to Mobile on the Gulf of Mexico. This plum was gained through the effort of Senator Stephen A. Douglas, an expansive friend of railroad interests and a heavy investor in them himself, and for more than ten years a promoter of the railroad to the Pacific.

The battle in the 37th Congress developed over means to organize, finance, and control the ownership of the railroad. In spite of the chaotic financial situation, the United States Congress was willing to appropriate hundreds of millions of dollars and make vast land grants to capitalists if only they would build this railroad. The Republican platform of 1860 had promised the continental road as a boon to the economy.

Lovejoy spoke on House Roll No. 364, the Pacific railroad bill, on April 17, 1862. He was, as he said, desirous of having this railroad built and he wanted only to get the best possible bill. As far as he could gather, the bill before the House that day "has been got up on the plan of what is familiarly called log-rolling, to suit some six, or eight or ten railroad companies; to get the votes which represent this railroad interest, that railroad interest, and the other railroad interest. It is supposed that unless the interests of these different railroad companies are conciliated, no bill can secure votes enough to become a law." [55]

Although Lovejoy was decidedly opposed to "converting Congress into a railroad company"—"We are not here as a railroad corporation," he said—he was just as decidedly opposed to the great give-away he detected in the bill of the House Select Committee. He was satisfied after reading the bill, section by section, that "under it this Pacific railroad can never be built." He did not doubt or question the integrity or honesty of purpose of the committee bringing in the bill, but he doubted "whether those who have engineered this matter outside of this House ever intended to build this road, unless by association of three or four sections of broken down roads, which they might do with the donation that we give them." The private enterprise involved was under no obligation to complete the road and the government would have no remedy, in Lovejoy's estimation.

Lovejoy insisted that the Pacific railroad be constructed by a "single indivisible company . . . held responsible for all the

357

obligations of the entire road." The proper principle for such an undertaking, he maintained, would be to provide for beginning at some given point, incorporate a company, and say to them, you shall have so much money after you reach a certain point, so much for so many hundred miles, and so much more for so many more hundred miles. This was the essence of Lovejoy's substitute bill, which was strongly supported by Senator William P. Fessenden of Maine, inasmuch as he considered it "the simplest, plainest, and most practical bill yet presented for the consideration of Congress." Frederick A. Pike of Maine and James F. Wilson of Iowa also threw their support to Lovejoy's bill.

Fessenden candidly stated that the Illinois representative's bill was based upon a company chartered by the state of Maine, and claimed that the company, the People's Pacific Rail Road Company of Maine, was made up of men among the most respectable in his state. Opposed to him was James H. Campbell of Pennsylvania, chairman of the Select Committee, who charged that the company was well known as the scheme of a "celebrated lottery-ticket projector." Why Lovejoy espoused the cause of this company is difficult to understand. Yet Fessenden, in speaking for Lovejoy's bill, stoutly maintained that "there are no speculative features about it, no mystery, no confusion, no difficulty." He said that under its terms "the company will subscribe to [United States] stock, will pay their subscriptions, and those subscriptions, the government bonds, and the lands will be used to build the road," and he promised it would be built as speedily as possible. If the amount of money appropriated by the Congress were insufficient, Fessenden contended, "the company will raise the balance, and promptly and efficiently complete the work; or the Government will have its remedy in its own hands by foreclosing on the company and taking all its property." Lovejoy's substitute bill would, in the Maine legislator's view, simply authorize a contract "between one company and the Government" for the construction of the railroad and telegraph line to the Pacific.[56]

In the end the New England group of capitalists did not win with Lovejoy's bill. Yet the final bill reflected the influence of his questions and criticism.

Commenting on the debate that began on April 17, the Washington correspondent of the *Bureau County Republican* said: "Mr. Lovejoy made a strong speech against the bill in its present shape; and it is now conceded that it cannot pass until some important modifications and improvements are made." [57]

President Lincoln signed the Pacific railway bill on July 1, 1862. The Union Pacific company was chartered, and empowered to build from Omaha to the eastern boundary of California; and the Central Pacific was to build eastward from the coast to make a junction with the Union Pacific. Both lines were joined in 1869 at Promontory Point, near Ogden, Utah, overcoming awesome engineering obstacles. The construction was also attended by frauds of tremendous proportions. The financial hocus-pocus practiced by the Union Pacific company and its fiscal ally, Credit Mobilier of America, resulted in one of the most staggering scandals in the country's history. The commendable ambition of the railroad builders was in the end reduced to a sordid reputation, at least, by their greed and corruption.

Lovejoy's impeccable record of honesty came dangerously close to compromise in his advocacy of the People's Pacific Railroad Company of Maine. Yet he kept the record unmarred by his insistence on a strict accountability of the railroad builders. In the last analysis, his role in the railroad bill debates must be considered an honest effort to serve the national interests above all else. In similar fashion Lovejoy's fight for the Homestead Act, the Department of Agriculture, the Illinois ship canal, and sound money must be seen as arising from his honest concern with the best development of his section and the nation. Successful or not, he established himself not only as the able ally of the Negro people but of the farmers as well. And on the basis of his actions in the 37th Congress none could say he had not diligently upheld the Republican party platform of 1860 nor that he did not deserve to be reelected in 1862.

18

The Bitter Campaign of 1862

"The sentiment, like the handle of a jug, is all one way."
—*Peoria* Daily Transcript

". . . a most graceless fight with pro-slavery democracy. . . ."
—*Owen Lovejoy*

Straight from his appearances at the war rallies in Chicago and Milwaukee at the end of July and the beginning of August, 1862, Lovejoy plunged into the campaign for his reelection. He was now contending for a seat from a newly organized congressional district, the Fifth. It embraced "one of the richest and loveliest regions of the West," and comprised Peoria, Knox, Marshall, Henry, Stark, Putnam, and Bureau counties. Since only one of his old Third District counties was left to him, Lovejoy had to establish rapport with a different set of voters. This would have been necessary to some extent without the redistricting, for in his preoccupation with the demanding duties of Congress, and with the necessity to promote the war effort before large city gatherings, he was out of touch with his constituents. Moreover, lingering resentments by "sorehead" Republicans were promising to arise during the campaign.[1]

Nor were the fortunes of the Republican party running high on a national basis. The party was entering its first wartime election campaign and found that it was contending against feelings of war weariness and impatience with the failures of the war. Instead, the party should have been running on the basis of the positive achievements in the 37th Congress. But the complicating realities were high prices, high taxes, military failures, and demagogic racist propaganda intended to set white people against free Negroes. In the summer of 1862 the failure in the Virginia Peninsula campaign in July and the Union defeat at the second battle of Bull Run in August depressed the people and alienated large numbers of them from the Lincoln Administration and the Republican party. Further disappointment came when Confederate General Robert E. Lee crossed the Potomac on September 7, moved into Frederick, Maryland, and appeared to be on his way to an invasion of Pennsylvania. At the same time Confederate Generals Braxton Bragg and E. Kirby-Smith had succeeded in fighting their way into Kentucky and were threatening Cincinnati and Louisville.

Peace Democrats in a number of Northern states played on the people's frustration over the military failures and half-victories. This wing of the opposition proposed an armistice and a return to the Union and the Constitution as they were before secession, with nothing done to the slave system. On the other hand, War Democrats, who supported the Administration, attempted to form coalitions with Republicans wherever possible.

In Illinois, as in other Northern states, Democrats appealed to race prejudice and seized on the charge that the war was being conducted as an abolition war. In Pennsylvania, New York, and Illinois these prejudicial appeals were especially blatant. In Lovejoy's new district he faced not only the bitter opposition of unreconstructed Whigs in the Republican party but the distorted propagandizing of Democrats in Princeton and in the Peoria

362

area. This was not unlike the 1856 and 1858 campaigns, when T. Lyle Dickey and David Davis had opposed him. In the 1862 campaign the Joliet *Republican* charged that there was a plan afoot for the Democrats to have no candidate but to get a "conservative Republican" to run against Lovejoy. The newspaper further maintained that the opposition to Lovejoy came mainly from "men now in revolt against the government." [2] Lyman Trumbull expressed fears in September that if the Democrats gained control in Illinois, they would cripple the state's war effort.

In the new Fifth District Lovejoy was forced to adopt a line that would appeal to the broadest sections of the voters. When he began touring the towns and cities of western Illinois early in September, the issue, as he presented it, was the suppression of the rebellion and the preservation of the Union under the leadership of Abraham Lincoln. On this basis there was truly little damage the opposition in both parties could inflict on him. Proof of the wisdom of Lovejoy's platform came in the first week of September when conservative Senator Orville H. Browning was wheeled into Princeton as one of the opposition's biggest guns against Lovejoy. Browning made an antislavery speech, quite to the discomfort of his sponsors. When impatient opposition spectators demanded raucously that he "hit Lovejoy," Browning replied, "I don't want to hit Mr. Lovejoy. We are working to the same end." To appease the crowd he did pitch into the *Bureau County Republican* and its editor, J. G. Hewitt. Later, in private, the foes of Lovejoy complained to Browning that he failed to provide them with an issue. Still Browning declined to attack Lovejoy. Had he done so, he would have been attacking Lincoln and the Administration as well. [3]

Lovejoy's reputation was strong across the northern sections of the state, so strong that several newspapers supported him just because he had given the Lincoln Administration "a vigorous and hearty" backing. The Joliet *Republican*, not in his district, hammered away at this point, and the influential Peoria *Daily Transcript* underscored it. The Pontiac *Sentinel* played upon the fact that "the relations existing between President Lincoln and Mr. Lovejoy are of the most friendly and confidential; and that the opinion of Owen Lovejoy is deferred to with more alacrity and cheerfulness by the Executive head of the nation than of any other man in Congress." [4]

This was a large claim for Lovejoy, yet it was not without a considerable germ of truth. For example, Lincoln probably gave a cordial hearing to Lovejoy when he conferred with him in Washington on patronage matters on August 27. This happened to be the day on which began the second battle of Bull Run. Only a week earlier Horace Greeley in an open letter in the *Tribune* had called on the President to carry out the emancipation provisions of the Confiscation Act. Lincoln's reply was the famous one: "My paramount object in this struggle *is* to save the Union, and is *not* either to save or to destroy slavery." Lincoln's letter appeared in the *Tribune* on August 25, followed by Greeley's reiterated question, "Do you propose [to reestablish the authority of the federal government] by recognizing, obeying, and enforcing the laws, or by ignoring, disregarding, and in effect denying them?" Following this exchange Lovejoy appeared at the President's office on August 27. One writer suggested that Lincoln and Lovejoy spoke about deeper matters than political patronage. Robert H. Browne, in his *Abraham Lincoln and the Men of His Time*, reported what he said was Lovejoy's version of this interview. Browne was careful to point out that he was telling *"in substance"* a story that "always fascinated and held in deep attention all who heard Mr. Lovejoy's relation of it." [5] Briefly this was the heart of Browne's (and Lovejoy's) story:

The President requested Lovejoy to call on him. Lincoln welcomed Lovejoy and expressed his perplexity over the military situation. While they talked a bit about the early days of the war when Lovejoy recruited regiments in Illinois, the President walked across the room several times in "deep and profound study." Then the two men went to a large window, presumably open in the close August evening, and conversed for about half an hour. Lincoln spoke "in a soft, easy voice, mingled with feeling too pathetic for any description." At one point, as he handed Lovejoy a copy of Greeley's protest of August 19, the President said, "Tell me how you would proceed in my place, and with due respect for the thousands of loyal people who differ with you. I have given it thought and concern, the best I could. . . ."

Lovejoy replied, according to Browne, "Is not Mr. Greeley right in asking you to promulgate the law known as the Confiscation Act, which you have approved, liberating every slave whose owner is in the rebellion, or who gives it aid and comfort?"

At the close of the talk Lincoln said he was glad Lovejoy had come.[6]

Without doubt the President was perplexed, for he had received very scant reports from the Virginia front, where McClellan's army was regrouping nearer to Washington. Pursuing the Union forces of seventy-five thousand men under General John Pope was a Confederate army of fifty-four thousand under Robert E. Lee, Thomas J. (Stonewall) Jackson, and James Longstreet. In three days of bloody and sharp engagements, August 28–30, the rebel army outmaneuvered and outfought Pope's forces, which on August 30 were sent into battle no more than twenty thousand at once against the whole of Lee's army. The Union defeat was crushing. It distressed Lincoln, angered abolitionists and radical Republicans like Lovejoy, and made the war feel "like a dead weight," as Robert Collyer, a Chicago Unitarian minister and abolitionist, expressed the mood of the North.[7] Lovejoy's response may be inferred from his determined campaign to support Lincoln, and to call for Negro troops and for confiscation measures.

Upon his return to Illinois Lovejoy made an appearance at Galesburg on September 3. This was the center of radical abolitionism that had been an important Underground Railroad station and that supported the antislavery faculty and students of Knox College. Lovejoy had been on the college board of examiners and in 1846 was chosen by the Adelphi society there to be the speaker that year. "Mr. Lovejoy has lost none of his prestige in our section," a Galesburg writer noted in the Chicago Tribune.[8]

A few days later Lovejoy made three major appearances in Peoria. The first was before the soldiers at Camp Peoria. He appealed there to the common sense of the men in uniform on the Negro question. He exposed the "miserable claptrap of those who did not hesitate to sacrifice the dearest rights and even the lives of white men to their prejudices against the blacks." Lovejoy advocated confiscation measures against the rebels, but denounced indiscriminate plunder by the troops of the Union. He endorsed Lincoln's reply to Greeley's demands for a proclamation of emancipation, but explained that adoption of an emancipation policy would be but a means to the preservation of the Union and the Constitution. He proclaimed himself for the Union first, last, and all the time, and professed that hostile though he was to slavery he would place saving the republic before abolishing that hated institution, if he must.[9]

On the same evening he spoke in the courthouse to the citizens of Peoria. The Transcript was certain there could be no other candidate and no other winner in the contest than Lovejoy. "The sentiment," said the editor, "like the handle of a jug, is all one way." The main question now, he wrote, was "not who shall administer the government, but shall we have a government to be administered." [10]

366

Lovejoy made his third appearance in Peoria on a Saturday afternoon, September 13, in the open air of the courthouse square. A large crowd gathered and was swelled with numbers and enthusiasm and noise by soldiers of the 77th Illinois Regiment, who marched down to the city from Camp Peoria. Once again Lovejoy placed suppression of the rebellion at the head of the tasks facing all loyal men. He hardly mentioned the slavery question and when a heckler demanded, "What about the n-----r?" Lovejoy put him off. Instead he made his second point support of Lincoln: Old Abe is captain and I am prepared to pull the ropes just as he orders.[11]

When he came to the emancipation question, Lovejoy said he had stopped agitating the question long ago. The wagon had got to the top of the hill, he was reported to have said, and it will go down fast enough without any further aid. The antislavery measures of the second session of the 37th Congress, and his knowledge of a preliminary emancipation proclamation, although he expressly did not refer to it, gave him reason to see such a future.[12]

Only a few days later, on September 22, the President issued his preliminary Emancipation Proclamation giving notice that on January 1, 1863, he would declare "forever free" all slaves in the rebellious states; he also would exempt from the terms of the proclamation the loyal slave states and any in rebellion that returned to the Union before that date. President Lincoln had informed his Cabinet on July 22 that he intended to issue an emancipation proclamation. Postmaster General Montgomery Blair thought such a move would lose the fall elections for the Administration. Secretary of War Stanton favored immediate issuance, and Bates and Chase approved the President's intentions. Seward approved but preferred that the proclamation be issued only after a Union military victory, lest the move be interpreted as a sign of weakness and despair. The President, accepting these opinions, continued to think seriously about issuing the proclamation. In August, Greeley had pressed for it, and so had a delegation of Chicago clergymen. Finally, in September, the military victory came at Antietam.

McClellan pursued Lee, after the Confederates withdrew toward Virginia. The bloodiest battle of the war took place at Antietam on September 17. McClellan was credited with a victory, but he failed to prevent the rebel army from escaping across the Potomac. Although an expensive victory in men and materials, Antietam provided Lincoln with that military success for which Seward had counseled waiting before issuing the emancipation proclamation. On September 21, Lincoln called in the Cabinet and told the members that he had made up his mind to issue the preliminary proclamation.

Abolitionists hailed the Proclamation as a triumph. Frederick Douglass welcomed it as a repudiation of border state influences and as a force removing the danger of European intervention in favor of the rebels. Above all, Douglass declared, the Proclamation "recognizes and declares the real nature of the contest, and places the North on the side of justice and civilization, and the rebels on the side of robbery and barbarism." [13]

Exciting and momentous as the Proclamation was, at that particular time Lovejoy seemed to sail casually past it and concentrated his oratory on winning support for the Administration and the war, and citing his record in Congress on homesteads, railroads, and the Department of Agriculture bill. The Quincy *Whig*, however, did say a month later that "Lovejoy supports the proclamation, but has never been officious in urging it." [14] Probably this approach was Lovejoy's way of driving easy blows into the "cross grained or frozen wood" of anti-Administration sentiment.

In all, Lovejoy's prestige seemed not to have suffered in Peoria, even though the city contained an appreciable number of Democratic and other opposition elements. After speaking there on September 13, he embarked on a tour of almost daily speech-making for the following six weeks. He was confident that if the voters of the country saw him and heard him, they would vote for him. It was an old story he had lived through in past campaigns. So heavy was the tide of opposition that his friend B. C. Cook feared that "in this contest he would be overborne." In Knox County a few Republicans were believed to be trying to form a "Union party" against Lovejoy. In Peoria a delegation of Bureau County "soreheads" had gathered to attempt a division of Republican ranks. In Stark County Lovejoy's foes hoped to nominate Colonel T. J. Henderson, but in Henry and Marshall counties "things are working all O.K.," one observer reported. The Copperhead Chicago *Times* threw in its objection to Lovejoy's nomination, denouncing him as one of "the most objectionable men of the present Congress." On the other hand the Peoria *Transcript* assured its readers that Henderson was a sorehead Republican—he would have to be, said the newspaper, since not even a regular Democrat would run against Owen Lovejoy.[15]

In October, when the campaign was blowing up as stormily as the autumn winds, the *Transcript* became quite excited by reports that Senator Browning and Judge William Kellogg planned to stump against Lovejoy in the district and "in favor of some one on whom the Vallandigham and other opposition may unite." If Browning is for supporting the Union and the President, the editor lectured him, he should support men like Lovejoy and E. C. Ingersoll, the lifelong Democrat who now threw in his fortune with the pro-Union men as candidate for congressman-at-large. Moreover, the *Transcript* asserted, it is useless to charge Lovejoy with being radical—"The President of the United States has issued a proclamation as radical as anything Mr. Lovejoy has uttered." The newspaper scolded Henderson. The opposition candidate said he was for Lincoln but opposed the Emancipation Proclamation. How then could Vallandigham Democrats support Henderson, asked the *Transcript*, when they opposed Lincoln *and* the Proclamation? How could Henderson consort with these deadly enemies of Lincoln? [16]

The Chicago *Tribune* also entered the fray with the warning, "The schemers will do well to let Mr. Lovejoy alone and devote their spare time to fighting the common enemy. . . ." The campaign's heat burned away the trappings of the opposition and showed their plan against Lovejoy to be a branch of a larger one for the state. The same tactics used against him in the Fifth District were tried in the Fourth against the pro-Union nominee, and in the Third against E. B. Washburne. One week before the election the *Bureau County Republican* charged that W. C. Goudy of the Democratic state committee was telling his friends that " 'the defeat of Mr. Lovejoy will be regarded as great a victory as the success of the Democratic state ticket.' " [17]

In a final swing around the district Lovejoy reappeared in Peoria, this time to receive the applause of his numerous German friends. In the preceding six weeks he had spoken daily, often twice a day. Before coming to Peoria he had kept an appointment and then ridden twelve miles through blinding dust billowing off the roads to meet the Germans and to give a rousing speech in Parmely's Hall on October 30.[18]

The election on November 4 found Illinois following the national trend toward the Democrats. That party won a majority of House seats in Pennsylvania, Ohio, and Indiana in October elections. In November Democrats took the governorship of New York and seventeen House seats to the Administration's fourteen; and in New Jersey they won four out of five places in the House. The Republicans retained control of the House of Representatives but the increase of Democrats to seventy-seven was cause for concern. The Democrats carried Illinois by a popular vote of 136,662 to 120,116. Of the state's fourteen congressional seats they took nine. Lovejoy was one of the five successful Republicans, while Leonard Swett lost in a district that had gone Republican in the two preceding elections. Washburne was returned from the northwest corner of the state. The Democrats captured a majority in the state legislature to seal their control of the state.

Lovejoy's election was a special triumph for his principles, editorialized the Peoria *Transcript*. He whipped all his opposition, "Tory, Copperhead, butternut, partisan Democrat, 'conservative,' sore-head, sap-head, and the personal friends of his opponent. . . . Radical though he is, he beat them." [19] The dirty campaign against Lovejoy was of no avail, wrote the editor. Why did he win? "We ask because there is an answer and a deep moral that all men should ponder. . . . Owen Lovejoy has triumphed through his principle." He had always been true to that principle, had never compromised it, nor bartered it away. "The people have sustained and endorsed him because of principle." This was what the editor wished the reader to ponder: that Lovejoy was not alone in his devotion to principle, there were others like him at the head of the government. The radical tendencies of the *Transcript*'s editor gave him the right, it seemed, to claim for his wing of the party the success of the Republicans. "Who made the republican party that won the last Presidential election," he demanded to know, "men of the stamp of Browning, Kellogg, Tom Henderson, Sam Galloway or men like Lovejoy, Giddings, Chase, Hale, Sumner and Wilson?" The heroes were a roster of the antislavery stalwarts of three decades. [20]

In Princeton the *Republican* continued the postelection commentaries with a similar claim for the Lovejoy sector of the party: "The Republican party represents the antislavery feeling of the country," was the editor's opinion. As long as slavery divided the country, Bureau County could be counted on to vote

371

Republican, he claimed. Yet Bureau gave Lovejoy a majority of only 192 votes over Henderson; among the voters in Henry County Lovejoy received better treatment. There his majority was 1,020. In all, his net majority in the new Fifth Congressional District was a slim 641. On the basis of this vote he would be entitled to take his seat in the 38th Congress due to convene in December, 1863. So close, however, was the contest that three days after the elections the Washington Letter of the *Republican* reported that there was still doubt there on the Illinois results. The announcement of Lovejoy's victory "produced much rejoicing among the friends of the Administration, and none expressed greater satisfaction than Lincoln himself." [21]

Lovejoy's satisfaction with the results was cogently stated in his speech of November 14. Some fifty or sixty men traveled through the brisk November air from all parts of the district to attend a victory dinner given by Lovejoy at the American House in Princeton. Following a "magnificent" repast, the diners marched in a body across the square to the courthouse to listen to Lovejoy's analysis of the election.[22]

He was first of all grateful, as a knowing politician should be, to the voters for returning him to Congress for the fourth time. He had passed through a contest "without parallel in the bitterness of its animosity . . . and the unscrupulousness of the means put in requisition to ensure my defeat." In view of the sordid facts of the campaign, Lovejoy wondered not so much that his majority was only six or seven hundred but "that I should have any at all." If his opponents felicitated themselves on the meagerness of his majority, all Lovejoy could say was, "If they can stand it, I can."

He had indeed faced a motley coalition, including hard-bitten proslavery Democrats out for the kill and a conglomeration of disgruntled Republicans, many of whom, in Lovejoy's words, "have always been restive under the anti-slavery element." He recognized that many honest voters had marked their ballots for Lovejoy's opponent because they were "uneasy and restive under the state of our national affairs, and under the influence of misstatements—misapprehensions—thought they were doing their country a service in not voting for me."

The so-called Union party in the Fifth District, made up of the two opposition elements, "was really the same as the Democratic party of the state." It was really a union of proslavery men with the immediate purpose of defeating Lovejoy and "the ultimate design of throttling the Administration in its policy of emancipation, and the reconstruction of the Buchanan Democracy, and its restoration to power in '64." Summing up, Lovejoy said, "The Democrats played a sharp game. . . . They played their cards very well, but they did not win. They will never have so good a hand again."

"The truth is," he said, "overlooking the eddies of personal interest and personal hostility, the whole contest resolves itself into a struggle of slavery and freedom, liberty and despotism, and the intense and envenomed opposition to me is because I am supposed to embody and represent an intensified opposition to slavery, from which spell some of the Republicans seem not yet to have been disenchanted. I look upon the recent contest as one of those steps in the progress of freedom towards a final triumph."

He now rallied his supporters to go on with the fight.

"Let those who favor a vigorous prosecution of the war and who mean to give the administration an unconditional support, who are for 'Union and Liberty one and inseparable,' keep up their organization and move forward. . . . Slavery is doomed and so is the party based upon it."

Privately, he told Jesse Fell that he had "a most graceless fight with pro-slavery democracy and pro-slavery conservatism, but the Lord helped me through." [23]

The congratulatory meeting in the Princeton courthouse was

in effect a farewell gathering, for on Monday, November 17, Lovejoy departed for New England and New York en route to the Capital. At Boston he received a warm reception from the leading antislavery people there. On Saturday afternoon, November 22, he was the honored guest at a testimonial dinner in the Parker House attended by Governor John A. Andrew; Senators Sumner and Wilson, his comrades of the 37th Congress; and other prominent Bostonians. Lovejoy and Governor Andrew spoke, but their speeches have gone unrecorded. Several nights later, on Tuesday, November 25, Lovejoy was the speaker in the eighth of a series of thirteen lectures sponsored by the Fraternity of the Twenty-Eighth Congregational Society. Such antislavery luminaries as Henry Wilson, Robert Collyer, Theodore Tilton, Moncure Conway, and Anna E. Dickinson had lectured on successive Tuesdays in Tremont Temple. When Lovejoy spoke the hall was "better filled than on any previous occasion." On the platform were Senator Wilson, Wendell Phillips, and other antislavery leaders during Lovejoy's lecture on "The Death of Slavery the Salvation of the Republic." He said that he had long urged the inherent right of slaves to their freedom; he now wished to pose the question from a different point of view, that is, that the emancipation of the slave is essential to the perpetuity of the republic. He went on to show that Britain and other countries had abolished slavery in deference to the demands of advancing civilization. The United States, ostensibly the land of the free, could not afford to do less. Phillips and Wilson followed Lovejoy with brief speeches.[24]

From Boston Lovejoy traveled to New York for a brief stop, and then went to Washington for the commencement of the third session of the 37th Congress on December 1. Vigorous prosecution of the war, emancipation, and the arming of the Negroes were questions still unresolved and still on Lovejoy's agenda.

374

19

Victories at Last: 1863

> *"The President should be sustained in any measure he might deem it necessary to employ."*
>
> —*Owen Lovejoy*

As soon as the 1862 congressional elections were over, Lincoln felt free to carry out his long-contemplated plan to dismiss General McClellan. On November 5 the President appointed General Ambrose E. Burnside to replace him, and his departure naturally was cheered by Republican newspapers and denounced by Democratic organs. Antislavery people and other proponents of all-out war against the Confederacy had reason to feel gratified. However, many of them felt uneasy with doubts that Lincoln would really issue the Emancipation Proclamation on January 1, 1863. Their fears seemed to be borne out when the President, in his annual message to Congress on December 1. 1862, again proposed gradual, compensated emancipation. He recommended a constitutional amendment that would provide compensation for states abolishing slavery before 1900. Slaves who had won freedom during the war were to be guaranteed their freedom and loyal slaveowners were to be compensated;

and Congress was to have the power to colonize freedmen abroad.

Neither in the North nor in the South did the plan have a chance of acceptance. Confederate successes on the battlefields made the South's leaders confident enough to reject the plan. Northern Republicans, conservative and radical, dismissed the plan as hallucinatory, futile, and tending to weaken the struggle against slavery. Radical Republicans in particular were in no mood in December, 1862, to entertain anything less than the vigorous prosecution of the war that Lovejoy and other Administration supporters had expressed militantly for almost two years. Rather than make concessions to slaveowners and rest content with Democratic electoral gains in November, or be discouraged by rebel victories on the fighting front, Republicans pushed the policies of confiscation, emancipation, and the arming of Negroes to fight against the rebellion. They were further spurred on to such measures by the Confederate defeat of General Burnside's army at Fredericksburg, Virginia, in mid-December. At this time the struggle against slavery in the third session of the 37th Congress took on importance, for in the legislature the important campaigns for policy were resumed.

When Kentucky's Wickliffe arose on December 8, 1862, to introduce a bill to "protect and grant relief" to the citizens of the loyal states whose "property and slaves have wrongfully been taken, seduced, and abstracted by the officers and soldiers of the Army of the United States," he came into immediate collision with Lovejoy. Wickliffe complained that slaves were being abducted by Union army men and sold at Louisville, where the price, he said, was from fifteen dollars to fifty dollars. The old Kentuckian was considerably irked by the army's refusal to turn back to their "owners" those Negroes who had entered the army camps for refuge. Lovejoy chided his foe for raising the question of payment for Negroes when "the very life of the nation is flickering in the socket." The laughter in the House was quick recognition that Lovejoy had turned the tables, for the pro-slavery congressman had used this very argument on him in the tumultuous meetings early in 1862. Lovejoy asserted again his conviction that "every slave has a right to run away, and I am glad for every one that escapes." He was immovably opposed to legislation that would make slave catchers of the army. Wickliffe wanted the bill to go to a select committee, but the House upheld Lovejoy when the bill was referred instead to the Judiciary Committee. When it was reported out on December 18 by Bingham of Ohio, Wickliffe made a lengthy, pleading speech for the measure. Lovejoy labeled it a "shameless attempt" on the part of the slaveholders to divert the United States Army into "the base business of chasing and capturing fugitive slaves." [1]

On the day before this exchange with Wickliffe, Lovejoy had written that he hoped "this Congress may virtually secure freedom to all." This, the goal of men like Lovejoy who had been a band of outcasts in the 1830's, was now well in sight.[2]

The New Year brought the promulgation of the President's anxiously awaited Emancipation Proclamation. Having made up his mind to act, Lincoln did not go back on his resolve, despite his offer of December 1. When he signed the document he said, "I never, in my life, felt more certain that I was doing right than I do in signing this paper." Negroes and whites meeting on January 1 in Boston and New York greeted the act with jubilation. Throughout the North and in some areas of the South occupied by federal troops, similar ecstatic demonstrations were held. The Proclamation was hailed as the climax of the abolitionist crusade. But some of the crusaders looked to further assaults on slavery until it was abolished in the loyal states as well as in the rebel states, where Lincoln had proclaimed freedom. *Universal emancipation* would come when no place under the United States flag contained a single slave.

377

In Congress, Stevens and Lovejoy and their radical colleagues hastened the offensive against slavery. Stevens was preparing to introduce a bill to raise regiments of Negro troops, and other Republicans were working out a general conscription bill. Although Lovejoy and Stevens collaborated toward the same goals, a deep rift opened up between them on the ultimate disposition of the rebellious states. In their clash of opinions on January 8, 1863, the two abolitionists prefigured the struggle that would occupy those who agreed with Lincoln's reconstruction plans and those who were led by Stevens in his "conquered provinces" theory, and Sumner in his "state suicide" theory. In the debate that day on the legislative appropriation bill, Stevens argued that Kentucky as a typical border state had been kept in the Union only by force or fear, that the Southern states in rebellion were no longer members of the Union, and that the Constitution had no "binding influence" over them. Therefore, Stevens asserted, those rebellious states became belligerent nations, and when overcome by the United States became "conquered provinces." They were therefore to be taxed as a necessary war measure; indeed, any action to suppress the rebellion must be justified on the grounds of military necessity.[3]

Olin of New York took strenuous exception to Stevens's theories. Lovejoy attempted several times to get the floor, but Stevens refused to yield. Finally he did so somewhat reluctantly. Lovejoy said he regretted that there was so much excitement upon the grave subject "which calls for such cool and calm deliberation." Lovejoy repudiated for himself "and the Republican party, and the Administration" (at which point there was some laughter in the House), the ideas advanced by Stevens. Lovejoy agreed with Stevens that it was necessary to annihilate the rebels, "extirpate them and repeople those States with a loyal population," but he disagreed as forcefully as he could that such actions were beyond the scope of the Constitution. Lovejoy believed rather that "this is precisely if necessary, just what the Constitution imperatively requires of us." Again there was derisive laughter, but Lovejoy plunged on to develop his thought. He defended the sacred duty to destroy the rebels, exterminate them "in order to restore as a matter of fact, what still exists as a matter of right." [4]

Stevens protested he had been misunderstood by Olin and Lovejoy. He replied that there was "a great difference between a whole community—a nation in arms—and individuals." Stevens believed that "where a nation comes to fight against a nation, a belligerent against a belligerent, there is no arbitrament but the laws of war." [5]

Lovejoy rejoined the debate to assert, "we are not fighting a nation but a horde of traitors and rebels. . . . We are not fighting to obtain redress from a nation, but to subdue a rebellion." The Lincoln plan of reconstruction was obviously in Lovejoy's mind when he made these remarks: "If all the citizens of a state are rebels, and will not repent and return to their allegiance, then I would kill or exile them, if I had the power. But this is not a question of power, but one of theoretical right. I hold that if one third of the citizens of Kentucky are loyal, the State belongs to that third; that if one fourth of the citizens of Tennessee are loyal, the State belongs to that fourth; and that just as soon as the Government can enforce their rights, it is bound to enforce them; and the whole machinery of the state government can be set going by those who remain, who are loyal whether one half, one fourth, one tenth or one hundredth. The right of the Federal Government never was invalidated, and never ceased for a moment." [6]

The irrepressible Illinois man could not allow the Administration to be responsible for the "idiosyncrasies of my very able and accommodating friend from Pennsylvania." He could not resist tossing a barb at Stevens: "The gentleman is like an ocean of wisdom with a little island of folly." [7] Yet Stevens and Lovejoy remained firmly united in support of other measures designed to win the war, notably the Negro regiment bill.

H. 675 would authorize corps of Negroes and would provide for their protection and punishment on an equal basis with white soldiers. One of its more far-reaching intentions was to prevent brutal maltreatment and shooting of Negro prisoners by Confederate forces, and probably to prevent throwing captured Negroes back into slavery.

Wickliffe began with a bitter complaint about General David Hunter's use of Negro troops, and about General Benjamin Butler's use of "contrabands" in breaking the Confederacy's hold on New Orleans. Dunn of Indiana had made a report on the subject and interrupted Wickliffe to reprove him for misinterpreting and distorting his report. The old man resumed in a rage that led him into futile digressions. The Chair was forced to call him to order.[8]

Shortly afterward Lovejoy obtained the floor to make a scathing attack on the "almost revolutionary organization known as the Democratic party" for "threatening the Federal Government with violent resistance to a draft for the purpose of recruiting an army for the Union." He charged the Democratic side of the House with obstructing efforts of the government to send recruiting agents out into the loyal states. "We turn to the free man of African descent," he said, "and to the poor slave held in the grasp of the rebel, and propose to ask and require of him to help fight the battles of the country, and to give him that freedom for himself and family of which he ought never to have been deprived," and the rebel sympathizers, Lovejoy complained, "insist that shall not be done."

Roused to a red-faced ire, Lovejoy answered his foes and defended his position. The Republicans were not in favor of carrying on the war as an antislavery or abolition war, he said, but *he* was for doing away with slavery "because in suppressing the rebellion and preserving the Union it is necessary as a means, and not as an end; although God knows the means are just such as I desire to be used. . . ."

Wickliffe had earlier derided putting white troops under the command of "general Sambo," "colonel Sambo," or "captain Sambo." Lovejoy hurled the insults back into his teeth—he denied that anyone proposed "putting white men under black officers," but as for himself, he said, "I would rather follow the black man than a slaveholder as an officer, for I would expect that the one would betray me, whatever his ability, while I am sure the other would be loyal and true, and fight it out."

Another objection to Negro regiments was that proponents of the measure were said to claim "that the black man shall be enlisted on his own account." Lovejoy flatly denied this was their claim. "The black man is of no consequence, and neither is the white man," he asserted, "in comparison with the life of the nation."

Would he arm Negroes? he was asked. He most certainly would "employ the lowest and feeblest agency in this war with the highest and mightiest." Later he cited the testimony of navy Captain Woodhull that the twenty-six Negroes on board the *Cimerone* were among the best sailors and fighters of his ship. There was really nothing new in this, said Lovejoy, "the world is full of instances to justify the course we propose to take." Crittenden followed with a speech of opposition for an hour, and others also took up sides in the debate. When the measure came to a vote on February 3, it was passed 83 to 54.[9]

Hewitt reported that the fracas in the House on January 29 was quelled by Lovejoy and exulted that "he is acknowledged the great political general of the House." He also reported that before the debate ended Thaddeus Stevens had made the closing speech—"one of his most remarkable productions." The vote in the House served to remind the correspondent of the time nearly two years earlier when Lovejoy in a speech at Princeton had advocated arming the slaves. The congressman had been denounced then, Hewitt wrote, but now his advocacy was being adopted by this branch of the government at least.[10]

The enlistment of Negro troops was permitted on a very limited basis early in the war, and it was left to the discretion of field generals. In October, 1861, General Thomas W. Sherman was authorized to organize Negro "squads, companies, or otherwise," in the Port Royal, South Carolina, coastal area, but Sherman did not wish to interfere with slavery nor to arm Negroes. On December 1, 1861, Secretary of War Cameron had attempted to release his departmental report in which authority was given for the enlistment of Negro soldiers, but Lincoln ordered a revision of the order. David Hunter tried to organize the 1st South Carolina Volunteer Regiment in April, 1862, but he received no support from Washington and on August 10 disbanded the outfit except for one company. Beginning in August, 1862, General James Lane tried to raise Negro troops under the terms of the Second Confiscation Act, and by the end of October he organized two regiments of Kansas Colored Volunteers. When New Orleans was threatened by Confederate attack in August, 1862, Ben Butler reversed himself and authorized enlistments of free Negroes to form the First Regiment Louisiana Native Guards. Meanwhile, in South Carolina General Rufus Saxton replaced David Hunter, and he brought with him authority from the War Department to accept up to five thousand Negro volunteers. On November 7 the 1st South Carolina Volunteers were mustered in. General Saxton invited a young Bostonian and militant abolitionist, Thomas Wentworth Higginson, to accept the colonelcy of the regiment, the first regiment of slaves enlisted in the service of the United States Army during the Civil War.[11]

Higginson was surprised by the offer but accepted it, for, as he said, "I had been an abolitionist too long, and had known and loved John Brown too well, not to feel a thrill of joy at last on finding myself in the position where he only wished to be." Later Higginson wrote that there was no guarantee of freedom for the black men until they were armed. "It was their demeanor under arms that shamed the nation into recognizing them as men," he said.[12]

The Emancipation Proclamation also provided for receiving Negroes in the armed forces. Within a few days after its issuance Governor Andrew of Massachusetts requested and received authorization from War Secretary Edwin M. Stanton to raise a regiment of Negro volunteers to serve for three years. A recruiting campaign was led by George L. Stearns, a white abolitionist and manufacturer, and carried out by Negro leaders Frederick Douglass, William Wells Brown, Charles Lenox Remond, Henry Highland Garnet, Martin R. Delany, J. Mercer Langston, J. W. Loguen, George T. Downing, and Stephen Meyers. The Fifty-Fourth Massachusetts Regiment was organized and ordered to South Carolina on May 18, 1863. So many volunteers had come forward that a second regiment, the Fifty-Fifth, was also organized.

The Negro regiment bill that passed in the House of Representatives in February, 1863, was intended to authorize large-scale enlistments of Negroes. By the time it was sent to the Senate, the Administration had already approved Governor Andrew's request and had authorized General Saxton's action. However, the Senate refused to go along with the lower house on the ground that the President already had the power to use volunteers to suppress the rebellion. Instead, the Senate voted 18 to 7 to prohibit Negroes from becoming commissioned officers in the army. But events moved so swiftly that Negro regiments were organized in Pennsylvania and New York, despite the Senate's negative attitude and the anti-Negro and anti-draft riots in the summer of 1863 in New York City.

By the end of the war, about 200,000 Negro troops had been enlisted in at least 154 regiments, 140 of them infantry, the remainder in artillery, cavalry, and separate companies and batteries. The Massachusetts Fifty-Fourth played a heroic part in the assault on Fort Wagner near Charleston harbor in July, 1863. The men proved decisively that the Negro would fight, despite those who persisted in characterizing him as a weak and inferior being. Negroes proved their valor in at least five important engagements during 1863. By the end of the war Negro losses were more than 38,000 men.[13]

Although the Negro regiment bill for which Stevens and Lovejoy fought never became law, their efforts may have served as additional leverage for the Administration's policy of arming Negroes, slave and free.

The fight for the bill turned out to be Lovejoy's last major effort in this short session, which adjourned in March. It was also his last major effort for many months to come, for he was stricken by illness in the last week of February during the smallpox epidemic that raged in Washington and he was ordered by his physician not to speak in public for six months. While Congress adjourned and its members departed for their homes, Lovejoy lay quite ill in his boardinghouse, which was operated by the widow of Dr. Gamaliel Bailey, the highly respected editor of the *National Era*. But while Lovejoy convalesced he enjoyed a visit from President Lincoln, which cheered him, and Chase was another well-wisher who sat with him in his rooms. By April 3 he was reported to be recovering after being "dangerously sick for 8 weeks." In mid-April a very feeble Owen Lovejoy was taken home by Mrs. Lovejoy and two relatives. Toward the end of the month he said jocularly that "he supposed he felt like some man who said he was '*might* weak but *terrible* comfortable.' " [14]

Lovejoy was recovering nicely in the bright Midwest May when he received a warm letter from a Philadelphia friend, who said firmly, "you must get well because you are needed. It is a great thing to be a good fighting man, & I hope you may be able to fight as good battles in Washington for this coming season as ever were fought in the field." The same writer was perplexed and wondered, if Lovejoy were forbidden to work, what was the congressman "going to do in Cleveland?" This was a reference to the coming National Convention of the Union League of America. The ailing congressman's response was to show up with John H. Bryant, Joseph Medill, and others as a delegation from Illinois on May 20 and 21, 1863. His old comrade Codding, who now lived in Baraboo, Wisconsin, was sent as a delegate from that state, along with William E. Wheeler of Beloit. Old-time abolitionist General James H. Lane was one of the three Kansas delegates present.[15]

The Union League was the outgrowth of several distantly separated efforts in Illinois, in Maryland, and in other Northeastern and Midwestern states to form bands of patriotic and loyal citizens behind the banner of the Union Army and the Lincoln Administration. The militant tone of its resolutions and objectives revealed a healthy core of staunch old abolitionists now joined to combat Copperhead secret orders. Having finally resolved the many differences over approach and tactics that beset young radical organizations with a cause, the Union Leaguers were able to rally their forces for the Cleveland meeting. A prime mover and the man credited with being one of the chief organizers of the League was Enoch Emery, editor of the Peoria *Transcript.* The clear radical Republican tone of his editorials had shown him to be an ardent Lovejoy man. He had participated in forming the first known Union League in the country at a June, 1862, meeting at Pekin, Illinois, in Lovejoy's Fifth Congressional District. In September, 1862, Emery had joined with Medill and twenty-three other delegates from twelve northern and central Illinois counties at Bloomington to set up a state organization.[16]

Now at the national convention in Cleveland in May, 1863,

Lovejoy found himself stemming a powerful abolitionist attack against Brigadier General John Schofield, who was about to be appointed by Lincoln as commander of the army's Department of the West. To General Jim Lane and some of the old-line anti-slavery men, Schofield appeared a milk-and-water protector of the emancipation policy. They felt he was no friend of their policies. Lane proposed a resolution on May 21 calling on the President not to appoint Schofield and requesting the appointment of General Ben Butler instead. Beneath the resolution Lovejoy saw an attack on Lincoln in the making. Indeed this was his principal line of resistance to the resolution of his old friend Jim Lane. Lovejoy now took a middle position between Lincoln and scores of his old comrades who would probably not hate him but whose love for him would cool a bit. Lovejoy "vindicated the transparent honesty of the President, to which we as patriots can anchor as to 'a hope sure and steadfast.' " He deprecated attacks on the Administration by its friends and asserted that the patriots and friends of the government should end all their minor differences and that "the President should be sustained in any measure he might deem it necessary to employ." For the time Lovejoy quelled the outbreak.[17]

Bryant and Lovejoy traveled together from Cleveland to Washington, where they spent a few days. The President and some of his Cabinet members received them warmly, and Lincoln congratulated Lovejoy on his recovery from his long illness. But no more was heard of Lovejoy until August, when a personal letter written by him from Skaneateles, New York, turned up in the pages of the *Bureau County Republican*. While visiting his sister Elizabeth he had learned that her son Lieutenant Edward Wiswall had died in action somewhere in the South. Lovejoy's public appearances were obviously still restricted, for he absented himself from just such a meeting in Springfield, Illinois, as he would have loved to attend.[18]

Illinois patriots and political friends of the government had organized an "unconditional Union" rally in the state capital for September 3. Lovejoy's physicians had advised him that public speaking at this time would so impair his health as to make him unfit for his duties in Congress in the coming winter. Yet he hoped despite this warning that he would be well enough to attend the rally and to speak. So he delayed his letter of acceptance and reply to the invitation. Finally on August 31, only three days before the event, Lovejoy confessed that his inability to participate was "a greater disappointment" to him "than it can possibly be to those who may wish to hear me." He contented himself with a letter to the meeting expressing his conviction that to sustain the Union was the same thing as to sustain the Administration. He called for the "undivided and earnest support of all loyalists" for the Chief Executive. He asserted that the victorious achievements of the army in July, 1863, "must be credited to the Administration." Then he recalled that Aaron Burr had once denounced George Washington as a bad general and "an honest weak man." Comparing Lincoln to the first President, Lovejoy said, "honest, but weak and imbecile, is the language" contemporary opponents apply to Lincoln. He was certain history would correct this mendacious estimate of the Springfield lawyer in the White House. Lovejoy therefore urged the Unionists to give "three hearty deeptoned cheers" for Abe Lincoln "while shouts of acclaim are ascending for the Union." [19]

Lincoln sent a letter of greeting to the rally in his home town. The President upheld his war-for-the-Union policy, his Emancipation Proclamation, and the necessity for organizing Negro regiments.[20] The President and his faithful supporters felt justified in those policies, and, moreover, were encouraged by the Union military victories in 1863. In the West General Grant had scored a decisive and brilliant one in the capture of Vicksburg, Mississippi, on July 4. In the East Lee's invasion of Pennsylvania had come to grief in the defeat of Confederate forces by General George Meade at Gettysburg on the same day. These two successes for Union arms came after a dismal six months for the Union. They not only boosted Northern morale, but caused the British Parliament to withdraw a motion before it for recognition of the Confederacy as an independent belligerent nation. Napoleon III of France was also persuaded to give up schemes for intervention on the side of the South.

Lovejoy apparently was well enough to make a trip to Washington a few days later ostensibly to look after the interests of disabled Illinois soldiers. The weather there was unhealthily dry and hot, with the city in a cloud of dust—"everybody looks as if they had been feeding a threshing machine or a clover mill," one reporter wrote. Sickness prevailed in the Capital, which was full of filth, dust, and mud, "and 3 times the population of before the war." Hotels and boardinghouses were jammed with army officers. When a friend asked Lovejoy why he was in the city, he replied, "To thank the President for his letter to the Springfield Convention." He was adulatory and claimed for Lincoln "the highest place among living statesmen—a claim which history will triumphantly vindicate." [21]

About a month later Lovejoy made a powerful speech in Princeton that drove the Democratic *Patriot* of that city to despair. The editor labeled Lovejoy a "miserable demagogue," but to his consternation stimulated an additional reprint of two thousand copies of the congressman's speech.[22]

The occasion had been a rip-roaring celebration in Princeton of pro-Union off-year election victories in Pennsylvania—which had felt the lash of war that year—and in Ohio, Maine, California, and Iowa. After a display of fireworks, illuminations, and bonfires, the streets were taken over by a torchlight procession to the courthouse. Inside, every spot was soon occupied, and Lovejoy stepped up to break his retirement from public speaking. He acclaimed the election results as "a heavier blow to the armed treason and traitors of this country than has been dealt to them since the opening of the war." Indeed, he said, the enemy would feel it more—"will feel greater discouragement than they did at Gettysburg, Vicksburg, New Orleans, or any other place, where victory has crowned our arms." Lovejoy considered the political victories as a mortal blow to the conspiratorial plans of the rebels and their Northern allies. As he saw the situation, the rebels could not hope for ultimate victory on their arms alone; they had to hope for—and plan for—"fires in the rear," for division and disunion in the North. He thanked God that "this last and only hope has been swept away." He pointed to the "conspiracy of the Northern Democrats with Lee to invade Pennsylvania and—in case of his success—of their arrangements for a counterrevolution in the North." He was grateful to the people for having crushed that conspiracy, and for the patriotic action of the people of Ohio in blasting the hopes of the Copperhead Democrats clustered around Vallandigham. In the last analysis, Lovejoy said, the people had spoken from deep in their hearts in favor of "a vigorous prosecution of the war, in favor of the Proclamation of Emancipation, in favor of arming the Negroes, in favor of confiscation and all the measures of the administration for the suppression of the rebellion." [23]

From this he urged the people of Illinois to take heart and vote in their local elections on November 3, "overwhelmingly for the Union." Although the contests were to be minor ones, Lovejoy counseled that it was a sacred duty "due to the country that even in our county elections we elect avowed representatives of the friends of the Union." The ballot box was the "potent engine of war" and the basis of "all our military operations." In the end he urged all to vote for the soldier, for the country, and for the right and liberty. He sat down "amidst a perfect storm of applause." [24]

389

Lovejoy thus made a dynamic return to public life after his long convalescence. He followed the Princeton speech with an appearance in Chicago early in November, at the Northwestern Fair for the benefit of sick and wounded soldiers. After heaping praise on the ladies who planned and carried forward the fair, Lovejoy hoped he would be forgiven if he occupied most of his time on the platform with a few words on the "necessity and obligation of our giving a cordial, unselfish, and unstinted support of the Administration." He meant to criticize the critics, to find fault with the fault-finders. He was particularly concerned with leading articles in "certain widely circulated and influential journals in the East as well as in the West—journals which are very able, very loyal and sometimes—(*cum pace dixerim*) very dogmatic." Lovejoy was referring to the antislavery and radical abolitionist *Independent* of New York, which had sharply criticized the President for "misstating" the letter sent him by a group of Missouri radical Republicans.[25]

Without becoming entangled in the bitter struggle in that state between radical and conservative factions of the Republican party, Lovejoy made only one point. He deplored the tendency on the part of the radicals to air "unjust and pernicious" criticisms of the Chief Executive that could hurt him and the Administration. "Let us have faith in the President," Lovejoy proposed. He reviewed for his radical friends the procession of antislavery actions already taken by the President and warned them: "Do not let any power from earth or from beneath the earth alienate your attachment or weaken your confidence in the President." He summoned them and the people to the next tasks: "And now let the people in their sovereignty and power, through their chosen Representatives in Congress, complete what has so auspiciously begun, and pass an act of universal emancipation, and thus make 'Union and Liberty now and forever one and inseparable.' "[26]

Despite this heavily laden plea, Lovejoy was met with a continuing argument by the new editor of the *Bureau County Republican*. No longer did Lovejoy enjoy the unqualified agreement and acquiescence of that newspaper, as he had when Hewitt was one of its leading lights. The young editor had contracted a fatal (but unknown) disease in Washington, and he and his seven-year-old son had died in the summer of 1863. J. W. Bailey, now at the head of the paper, took a more independent radical position, expressing open dissatisfaction with some of Lincoln's actions regarding emancipation. He confessed as much confidence as Lovejoy, "our worthy Representative," in the President's honesty and was as much opposed to fault-finding. Nevertheless he called attention to the wrong of the President in failing to heed the pleas of the Missouri radicals led by B. Gratz Brown for the removal of General Schofield. The radicals regarded the general as "detrimental to the best interests of the Union." The New York *Independent* went so far as to charge that Schofield had permitted fugitive slaves to be "hunted from our forts and from beneath our flag." However, there is good evidence that Schofield was caught in the crossfire of Missouri politics and that he was acting under instructions from Lincoln to remain neutral in that embittered struggle. Bailey persisted in believing that the President was at fault in retaining Schofield. The argument in the *Republican* seemed to have ended there, for there is no record of a rejoinder from Lovejoy.[27]

Far more weighty matters were on his mind now. He had hinted at them in his speech at the great Northwestern Fair: the need for a measure declaring *universal* emancipation; and the proper reconstruction of the rebellious states in the Union were the chief points in his agenda.

Lovejoy made his last public appearance in Princeton on Thanksgiving Day. Speaking in the Congregational Church, he opened with Leviticus 25:10—"And ye shall hallow the fiftieth

391

year, and proclaim Liberty throughout all the land unto all the inhabitants thereof." The subject of his speech had been well advertised in the *Republican* as "The Question of 'State Suicide' and the Reconstruction of the Union." Before advancing to the topic Lovejoy spent some time proposing that a law be passed by Congress making slavery a crime punishable by fine and imprisonment. On the announced subject he said there were insuperable objections to the theory that the rebel states had committed suicide and were no longer states, and therefore to be considered as territories.[28]

He did not believe that even the majority of the people of Tennessee, for example, could transfer their allegiance from the United States to the "so-called Confederate government." If they could, he maintained, then we are not fighting to subdue a rebellion but to re-annex a foreign nation. But this was not the case, he asserted. We are fighting to "compel them to remain in the Union and return to their allegiance," he said, "and we have no right to punish the loyal men for the crimes of the disloyal." Lovejoy was for punishing traitors for their crimes, wherever they might be found; rebels should be deprived of the "elective franchise" and the privilege of holding office. He would give the loyal men representation in Congress, but under no circumstances would he consent "that a star be taken from the national ensign." [29]

This was only the commencement of a new fight he hoped to take on when he resumed his place in the House of Representatives. When he left Princeton on Monday, November 30, 1863, neither he nor his constituents knew that they would never again hear his powerful voice or see him indignantly shaking his fist high over his head.

20

On Pisgah

The thirtieth anniversary of the American Anti-Slavery Society was celebrated in Philadelphia. December 3 and 4, 1863, had been set aside for the rejoicing of the old abolitionists, and every star in the antislavery firmament was invited. Garrison addressed an invitation to Lovejoy, and Lovejoy answered just after the Chicago Northwestern Fair, in November, saying that he had some hope of attending, but that in the event that he could not, "Will you allow me to say that I am in favor of an act of Congress abolishing slavery throughout the entire limits of the United States, & making it a penal offense to hold or to claim to hold a slave." He was aware that "the dogma, or fiction (for it is nothing more) of State sovereignty will be opposed to this legislation." Nevertheless, Lovejoy asserted, the Constitution was supreme and the laws passed under it were supreme over the laws of any state. He would chance a test before the Supreme Court as another mode of reaching the same end. "I have never had a doubt that a bench of honest judges would liberate a slave if once in court," he wrote Garrison. He bade the abolitionists Godspeed in their efforts in Philadelphia, where he would be with them in spirit if not in person.[1]

The doctrine on reconstruction that Lovejoy had advocated in his Thanksgiving Day speech in Princeton, and debated with Thaddeus Stevens in the House in January, was now vigorously contested by some of his constituents. A long-time supporter of Lovejoy since Liberty party days, signing himself "Henry" and taking a lead from the *Bureau County Republican*'s editorial of December 10, said he felt that Lovejoy's plan for a federal law abolishing slavery was impractical without a change in the Constitution. Editor Bailey had wondered if Congress could make slavery a penal offense in any state. The federal legislature could make laws for a territory, but could not exercise the same power for a state's "domestic institution," such as slavery. Bailey questioned whether, if such an act proposed by Lovejoy were passed, it would stand once the rebellious states were permitted to resume their authority. Such a law could be passed only as a military necessity and be binding on the states only "so long as the rebellion lasts." Bailey feared that even if an act like Lovejoy's were constitutional, it would not meet the requirements, "for the reason that the Secessionists of the South, with the aid of their Northern allies, would repeal it the very moment they came into power." A constitutional amendment abolishing slavery, Bailey said, would be "the most practicable way to sever the gordon [sic] knot of our difficulties." [2]

By the time these views appeared in his home town newspaper, Lovejoy had already become immersed in the duties of the first session of the 38th Congress. He had hinted in a letter to his nineteen-year-old daughter Sallie (Sarah Moody) that if he had started out to win the Speakership of the House away from Schuyler Colfax, he could have beat Colfax but he preferred to bide his time.[3] He balanced this disappointment with joy that he had been instrumental in blocking the distasteful scheme of Emerson Etheridge to sabotage the seating of Republicans in the House.

Etheridge was Clerk of the House and, true to his Copperhead sympathies, had informed congressional Democrats he hoped to disqualify members whose certificates of election did not bear the exact wording required by an act rushed through the previous Congress on its last day. The key phrase of the certificate was a statement that the member had been elected "according to the laws of the State or of the United States." Etheridge was counting on omissions of the phrase by some who might have lost sight of the requirement. Lincoln got wind of the scheme and rallied the leading Republican congressmen. Lovejoy spent a good part of Sunday morning, December 6, in John Hay's office, where he avowed his faith in Lincoln "and the firmest adherence, though there is nothing subservient about it," Hay recorded. Lovejoy squared himself and said he was going into the House the next day and vote. If it came "to a question of muscle," Lovejoy felt he could whip Etheridge. Lincoln had urged, according to Nicolay, that if Etheridge persisted in his unsavory plan, "let him be carried out on a chip, and let our men organize the House." [4]

Hay went up to the House on Monday morning "expecting a taste of a scrimmage," but was disappointed. Etheridge seemed quiet and reasonable. Lovejoy was prepared for the scrap but took time to give notice he intended to introduce a bill at an early day "providing for the punishment of slaveholding in the United States and throughout the Territories thereof." The showdown with Etheridge did not come that day. On Tuesday, after Lovejoy introduced the usual motion to inform the Senate that "the House has organized and is ready to proceed with transaction of public business," the clerkship came up for a vote. Edward McPherson of Pennsylvania was nominated as the

Administration's choice, and Mallory of Kentucky offered Etheridge's name. The Kentuckian asked the withdrawal of McPherson and stated, "I give them [the Republicans] this last chance to be magnanimous, perhaps the last one they will have." Lovejoy, almost breathless with anger, said "it required a good deal of brass" to make the appeal. Stevens asked coolly, "Is this levity on the part of the gentleman from Kentucky allowable according to the rules of the House?" On the vote McPherson won 102 to 69.[5] When the committees were organized, Lovejoy was named chairman of the House Committee for the District of Columbia.

The President's message was read on Wednesday, December 9, and evoked outraged condemnation from his opponents and ecstatic praise from his friends. Hay wrote in his diary that "Men acted as if the millennium had come. . . ." Lovejoy said the message was "glorious" and exclaimed, "I shall live to see slavery ended in America." The President had announced a plan to issue a proclamation of amnesty and reconstruction that would help reunite the nation, and in it he erased all speculation that the emancipation order of January 1 would be revoked. A tremendous burst of applause broke the tense silence in the House after these words were read: "While I remain in my present position I shall not attempt to retract or modify the Emancipation Proclamation; nor shall I return to slavery any person who is free by the terms of that proclamation, or by any of the acts of Congress." [6]

Republican congressmen speedily moved to implement the President's intentions and to press on their own offensive against slavery. On December 14 Lovejoy introduced a bill "to give effect to the Declaration of Independence, and to certain provisions of the Constitution of the United States"—a universal emancipation bill. Holman of Indiana read the bill, after which it was referred to the Committee on the Judiciary. It was essentially the bill Lovejoy had promised in November that he would introduce. The enacting clauses provided freedom forever to slaves in the states or territories of the United States; protection of freedmen from unlawful search and seizure and the right to sue and be sued and to testify in United States courts. Furthermore, any person convicted of an attempt to re-enslave any person was made punishable by imprisonment of from one to five years and by fine of from one thousand to five thousand dollars.[7]

Lovejoy's bill was one of several moves in Congress for universal emancipation. James Ashley of Ohio introduced a thirteenth amendment to the Constitution abolishing slavery, on December 14, and James F. Wilson of Iowa proposed a similar one. Also, on that date, Isaac N. Arnold of Illinois introduced a bill to aid the President in executing immediately his proposed proclamation, that is, giving him the power to free slaves in loyal territory as well as in the rebel states. This measure was referred to the Judiciary Committee. In the Senate John B. Henderson of Missouri submitted a joint resolution on January 11, 1864, proposing a constitutional amendment banning slavery anywhere in the United States; and it was sent to the Senate Judiciary Committee. Charles Sumner wrote his own version of a thirteenth amendment, stating, "everywhere within the limits of the United States . . . all persons are equal before the law, so that no person can hold another as a slave." Senator Lyman Trumbull, chairman of the Senate Judiciary Committee, reported a substitute for Henderson's and Sumner's proposals, and on April 8 it was passed by a vote of 36 to 6. This version was introduced in the House by Ashley and Wilson and when it came up for a vote in June it failed to receive a necessary two-thirds majority. However, the next Congress approved this amendment on January 31, 1865, in the language in which it emerged from Trumbull's committee, and this became the Thirteenth Amendment to the Constitution when finally adopted on December 18, 1865, almost a year after

Lovejoy's death. Yet it was his cherished bill for universal emancipation in essence.[8]

On December 14, 1863, Lovejoy moved another attack on mistreatment of Negroes. He introduced a resolution calling for equal pay for enlisted soldiers "without distinction of color." Negro military men having served at this time for half the pay of white soldiers, Frederick Douglass and other abolitionists, Negro and white, demanded an end to such discrimination, and Lovejoy responded. George W. Julian of Indiana on the same date introduced a long-awaited bill to repeal sections of the Fugitive Slave Laws of 1793 and 1850. The stage was thus set on that busy day for the final acts to rid the country of slavery in 1865.[9]

A few days later Lovejoy received an urgent message from Israel Washburn, governor of Maine and brother of Lovejoy's colleague from Galena. The governor wanted Lovejoy to fill an announced speaking engagement in Portland, in the state of his birth. "Congress or no Congress you must come," Washburn wrote. "It would play the deuce with us if you should not." It is not clear why the governor was so perplexed. At any rate, in some consternation, Lovejoy passed the message across his desk to a fellow member suggesting he go along to the Maine engagement. Christmas adjournment would be in a few days and he thought he "must go to Portland." But the note Lovejoy wrote seemed to be cut short when the work of the House demanded his attention.[10]

Lovejoy surprised the crowded New City Hall audience in Portland when he spoke there on Saturday evening, December 26. At least one among the crowd had expected to see "a rather bilious looking, bitter toned radical, with few of the graces and none of the suavity of a *popular* speaker." This rather supercilious opinion was changed rapidly for the editor of the literary tabloid *Transcript*, E. H. Elwell, for he found Lovejoy's "personal appearance decidedly prepossessing." The editor confessed that he was indeed impressed with the congressman's broad shoulders, strong build, and genial face and pleasant voice. "His hair," Elwell wrote of Lovejoy, "originally light, is silvered a little by the fifty winters he has seen." [11]

Arguing principally against Charles Sumner's State Suicide theory, that is, that the rebellious states had not seceded but had committed suicide and returned to territorial status, Lovejoy spoke nearly two hours "in an extemporaneous, discursive manner." He seasoned his arguments with witty illustrations and allusions that kept the audience in a gale of laughter, according to Elwell. His gesture of bringing a high-raised right hand "down towards, but not hitting his left hand outstretched to receive it," was especially impressive to Elwell. Lovejoy used this gesture repeatedly when he spoke, but when fully incensed he raised his right hand, sometimes both hands, directly over his head, quivering for a long time, and Elwell was moved to note that this was "a very remarkable gesture." [12]

Lovejoy said he was about to introduce in Congress "a decree freeing every slave in the land." He also stated that he thought Lincoln would be reelected next year. In the end the Maine homecoming was a triumph that "called out an enthusiasm such as is rarely seen in a Portland audience." [13]

On his way back to Washington Lovejoy stopped in New York City and was introduced to a young artist who proposed the idea of painting the President reading the Emancipation Proclamation to his Cabinet. Lovejoy visited Francis B. Carpenter in his studio at 653 Broadway and was so impressed with the artist and his work that he agreed to introduce him to President Lincoln.[14]

When Carpenter arrived in the Capital on February 5, 1864, Lovejoy was very ill but insisted on seeing him in his rooms on Fifteenth Street and writing a note of introduction for the artist to President Lincoln. The painting, which Carpenter completed during the next six months at the White House, now hangs in the Capitol and has often been reprinted.

"I am gaining very slowly," Lovejoy told Carpenter. "It is hard work drawing the sled up-hill," he said from his sickbed. Only then did Carpenter realize why he had not heard from Lovejoy during January. Lovejoy was fast losing his capacity to resist debilitating attacks of his liver and kidneys. The President called repeatedly on Lovejoy during his illness and, moved by the saddening sight of a staunch friend slipping away, said, "The war is eating my life out; I have a strong impression that I shall not live to see the end." [15]

Lovejoy's correspondence was now written in the hand of another person, and the congressman apologized for this to several friends. His physician had positively forbidden him to go out. He cancelled a visit to Seward at the State Department, for example, on February 19. Only two weeks earlier Lovejoy had written "Friend Nicolay," Lincoln's secretary, that "I hope to be on my pegs again shortly." But even his great heart was not strong enough to fulfill his hope so quickly.[16]

He rallied, however, and on Washington's birthday was well enough to dictate a lengthy letter to William Lloyd Garrison. Lovejoy assured him that in the presidential elections that year Lincoln deserved to be reelected. "I am satisfied," he told the Boston abolitionist, "as the old theologians used to say in regard to the world, that if he is not the best conceivable President, he is the best possible." As for Henry Winter Davis's recent insertion of the word "white" as a qualification for voting in Arkansas, Lovejoy told Garrison he would "bring the House to a vote on it, and let them confront the question face to face." He would move to amend the offending clause by striking out the word "white"—"if I am ever able to be in my seat again." [17]

Toward the end of February the artist Carpenter and a friend "W——" called on Lovejoy, who thought he was well again

and in "fine spirits." The conversation naturally touched on reports that Frémont would be brought out as an opposition candidate to Lincoln. Lovejoy said, "Any attempt to divide the
party at such a time was criminal in the last degree."

Carpenter observed that many antislavery men did not trust
Lincoln.

Lovejoy indignantly knocked this sectarianism on the head.
"I tell you Mr. Lincoln is at heart as strong an anti-slavery man as
any of them," Carpenter reported Lovejoy's words, "but he is
compelled to *feel* his way. He has a responsibility in this matter
which many men do not seem to be able to comprehend."

Rousing himself, Lovejoy pursued the matter in these words:
"I say to you, frankly, that I believe his course to be right. His
mind acts slowly, but when he moves, it is *forward*. You will
never find him receding from a position once taken. He is going
to be the candidate of the Baltimore convention, and is sure to be
re-elected." Lovejoy said he had no patience or sympathy with
those "who are trying to manufacture issues against him." Those
opponents would not succeed, Lovejoy said, because Lincoln is
"too strong with the masses." For his own part, Lovejoy was not
only willing to take Lincoln for another term, "but the same
cabinet right straight through." [18]

Lovejoy came out of his rooms for a signal honor on March 9
when at one o'clock in the afternoon he was one of the privileged
witnesses to Ulysses S. Grant's commissioning as lieutenant general in the army of the United States, and as commander of all the
armies of the United States. Present at the ceremony in the Cabinet Room at the White House were the President; Generals Halleck and John A. Rawlins; Lovejoy; John Nicolay; Grant's four-
teen-year-old son Fred; and the members of the Cabinet. [19]

Lincoln summoned Grant from the battlefield to give him this
unique commission, held only by Washington and Winfield
Scott, after Congress revived the office and awarded Grant a

401

medal in recognition and thanks for his victories at Vicksburg, Fort Henry, and Fort Donelson. During 1864 and early 1865 the country watched gratefully as Grant led the armies to a stunning victory over Lee's formidable forces. Grant demonstrated his superior strategical abilities by refusing first to accept a psychologically inferior position even after the Union failure in the Wilderness battle of May, 1864, and second by retaining his initiative and pursuing Lee as no other Union general had, as T. Harry Williams has pointed out. Such a general was the kind Lovejoy and his antislavery colleagues had hoped for in 1861. Had Lovejoy lived to April, 1865, he would have rejoiced in Grant's total victory.

He would have rejoiced as well in the major Union offensives that led to Lee's surrender at Appomattox Courthouse. Strategically the most valuable of these offensives was General William T. Sherman's march from Chattanooga beginning May 4, 1864, and continuing to Atlanta and then to Savannah. He thus cut the Confederacy in two and helped to tighten the ring of steel around the Confederate armies. Lovejoy undoubtedly would have hailed these generals for their part in suppressing the rebellion begun by and in the interest of the slaveowners and their "peculiar institution."

Ailing though he was at the time of Grant's commissioning in 1864, Lovejoy braved a trip to New York on March 15. "I feel so mean to be sick," he wrote his daughter Sarah. "I never wanted to be in the House so much," he confessed. "I do not know as I shall get beyond Pisgah. . . ." [20]

He stayed at the Brooklyn Heights home of J. N. Ely, a New York drygoods merchant. On March 16 Lovejoy stepped out of the house at 106 Henry Street for a brief saunter in the gracious Brooklyn streets, where once Walt Whitman and other beloved allies of the slave had passed. It proved to be his last walk outdoors. He suffered a relapse of "an ailment of liver and kidneys" (diagnosed after a postmortem examination as Bright's disease) and was confined to bed until his death at fifty-three years of age on Friday night, March 25, 1864. His wife, Eunice Conant Storrs Denham Lovejoy, and a daughter were at his bedside when he breathed his last.[21]

Funeral services were held in Plymouth Church on Hicks Street around the corner from the Ely residence, on Monday, March 28. Henry Ward Beecher spoke the invocation and the Reverend George B. Cheever delivered the eulogy. The pallbearers were William Cullen Bryant, "E." Tappan, John H. Bryant, a former slave known only as Mr. Davis, Dr. Dexter Fairbanks, a Dr. Ritter, a Mr. Carpenter, and the Reverend Simeon S. Jocelyn.[22]

A letter from A. G. Benson, a New York friend of Francis Carpenter's, had informed the artist of how near to death Lovejoy was. When Carpenter went to tell the President the sad news, he met Lincoln in the vestibule of the White House preparing to go over to the War Department. The President was deeply affected but said only, "Lovejoy was the *best* friend I had in Congress." [23]

21

"Such Men Should Never Die"

To the black men and women who hungered for their freedom, Lovejoy was a symbol of their struggles. Indeed among the throng at his funeral in Brooklyn, one Negro woman poignantly expressed the love of her people for Lovejoy. With her small child in her arms she stepped up to the bier, kissed Lovejoy's hand, and lifted her child so that he could see the man's features and remember this friend of the Negro.[1]

In the House of Representatives that day, and in the Senate on the following day, members delivered eulogies of Lovejoy's integrity, courage, and nobility of character. They constituted "the most remarkable demonstration of admiration, respect and love," said the New York *Tribune*, on the death of a member since the passing of John Quincy Adams.[2]

The Speaker of the House recognized E. B. Washburne as the first of several colleagues who wished to record their esteem for Lovejoy. Washburne stressed the fact that Lovejoy had been elected four times to Congress and that he had served for a longer period, with four exceptions, than any other man elected from Illinois. He recalled that Lovejoy had displayed "undaunted courage and matchless bearing" in the mêlée of April 5, 1860. Lovejoy's eloquence was compared to that of Mirabeau in the National Assembly and of Danton in the National Convention. It was in his home state, Washburne asserted, that Lovejoy made his greatest impact. "In the presence of the people he was invincible," Washburne proclaimed.

Thaddeus Stevens spoke briefly of the powerful younger man who had stood shoulder to shoulder with him in their common fight. "If his hatred of slavery sometimes seemed too intense," Stevens said, "it must be remembered that early in life he saw a beloved brother murdered by the northern minions of that infamous institution." The old commander of the House regretted that Lovejoy could not have lived to see "the salvation of his country; to see peace and Union restored, and universal emancipation given to his native land." But such were the ways of Providence. "Moses was not permitted to enter the promised land with those he had led out of bondage. . . ."

Jesse Norton of Illinois recalled that Lovejoy was ever welcome "in the social circle. . . . Frank, generous, genial, full of wit and humor, he could always 'set the table in a roar.' . . ." Perhaps he was thinking of Lovejoy's stinging witticisms in the House, too. Only a few days before he died, Lovejoy, pallid and wan, listened to Henry W. Harrington of Indiana offer a resolution declaring that Congress had no power to delegate to the President the authority to suspend the writ of habeas corpus. Such a presidential power, deemed by the Copperheads to be a dictatorial power, was designed to suppress treasonous activity behind the lines of the armies. Such a suspension violated the spirit at least of constitutional civil liberties, but the Administration defended the action as a necessary wartime measure, overriding all other considerations. The Speaker ruled debate out of order, but Lovejoy asked, "Would it be in order to refer these resolutions to the Committee on Buncombe when it shall be appointed?" [3]

Justin S. Morrill, the slim, solemn Vermonter, had visited with the Lovejoys and their sparkling brood of girls and boys in Princeton. He reminded his fellow legislators that Lovejoy's family life was graced with "the perpetual sunshine of his own genial humor."

Moses Odell, the handsome representative of the Brooklyn district in which Lovejoy had died, rose now to say of Lovejoy, "I am authorized to say that the Executive had in our departed associate at all times a warm supporter of every measure which had for its aim the restoration of the Government."

The hard-working congressman from Iowa, Josiah B. Grinnell, had long been a close friend of Lovejoy's and had visited him in his sick room on Fifteenth Street. "I saw the tears course down his manly cheeks," Grinnell related, as Lovejoy said, "Ah! God's will be done, but I have been laboring, voting, and praying for twenty years that I might see the great day of freedom which is so near and which I hope God will let me live to rejoice in. I want a vote on my bill for the destruction of slavery root and branch."

Others had remarked on their fears that Lovejoy would not live through the winter of 1863–64. In December, when Lovejoy took his seat, Washburne said, "there was something in his altered look . . . which told of disease and death, creating in the minds of his friends the gravest apprehensions." After the Christmas recess Lovejoy had been stricken again and confined for some weeks. When he reappeared in the House on February 29, 1864, it was plain to see that "his eye had lost its brightness." Ashley confessed that for more than two years, in committee meetings, he had witnessed with anxiety "month by month and week by week, the fire of his eye grow dim and the vitality of his organization gradually yield to the approaching destroyer." J. C. Allen had walked over to Lovejoy when he last appeared in the House and told his associate he hoped he would again participate actively. Lovejoy replied despondently, "I have been very near to the portals of death and eternity; I feel that I must soon enter there." But Charles Sumner, who also sat by Lovejoy's bedside in those last days, found a less somber man. The senator observed that Mrs. Lovejoy, "the beloved partner of his life," was within call to comfort him. Lovejoy "was cheerful," Sumner recalled, "but his thoughts were mainly turned toward his country. . . . He longed to be at his post again."

At this juncture, the House approved Washburne's resolution of condolence. John F. Farnsworth was named to head a committee of representatives to attend the funeral in Princeton on Friday, April 1.

On Tuesday, March 29, Trumbull, Pomeroy, and Sumner spoke for the upper house in praise of Lovejoy. Trumbull linked him to Thomas L. Harris and Stephen A. Douglas as one among the three great Illinois legislators who had died in the last six years. He said Lovejoy had "acquired and maintained his popularity by appealing directly to the masses. He had nothing to do with, and knew little about, the appliances sometimes resorted to by politicians to acquire position."

Not that he was politically naïve. Lovejoy had amply shown he knew a corrupt deal when it came to the Utah actions of 1857–58. He had a kind of honesty that is a rare novelty today and that seemed almost naïveté then. When one hopeful promoter attempted to get him to vote for a bill that favored a claim the man was interested in, Lovejoy replied, "If I am present [in the House of Representatives] I shall vote against it." The man persisted and offered Lovejoy two thousand dollars. The irate congressman turned on the promoter and said, "When I said no, I meant no! I never took a bribe. I shall not begin now. I mean to leave a public record of which my children shall never be ashamed." [4]

Sumner's eulogy revealed his own sensitivity to the slavery question: Lovejoy, he said, "was gifted to see that slavery—unlike the tariff or bank—did not come within the range of compromise any more than the decalogue or multiplication table." Lovejoy had never been a judge, and not even a lawyer, "so that the technicalities and subtleties of the profession had no chance of enslaving him." To an independent spirit like Lovejoy's, "what were the sophisms of learning and skill when employed in the support of wrong?" Sumner asked.

Against the generosity of these eulogies there is a haunting irony in Lovejoy's confession of weariness after seven years in Congress. To an old friend in Princeton he said, "If I had my life to live over again, I do not believe I would forsake the pulpit. Politics is simply a dog's existence." [5]

Lovejoy's funeral train reached Princeton on March 31, and the next day that town of mourners turned out in a throng to mark "a sad, great day for Princeton." The Chicago *Tribune* writer mingled with the crowds and felt "how deep his [Lovejoy's] hold of the hearts of the people." It was much like the reaction Lincoln had experienced on July 4, 1856, when he faced a Princeton crowd and felt the powerful love of the people for the living Lovejoy.[6]

Following private funeral services, conducted in the Lovejoy farmhouse by the Reverend Edward Beecher, former president of Illinois College and now a resident of Galesburg, public services were held in the Congregational Church. Heading the funeral procession were the Sergeant at Arms of the House and the congressional delegation and the clergy in carriages. Alongside the hearse, drawn by four cream-colored horses, walked eight prominent Princeton citizens, who served as pallbearers.

Behind came judges and members of the bar, county officers, soldiers, the town council, and private citizens.

A long line of carriages followed the cortège as it passed slowly down Main Street to the Oakland cemetery half a mile west of the village. Up and down the street merchants had draped their stores with flags and mourning, and people came out into the street and marched behind the funeral carriages and wagons.

Bryant and other Princetonians and Codding in Baraboo, Wisconsin, began a movement shortly after Lovejoy's funeral to erect a marble grave monument in Princeton. Among the messages and contributions, a letter from the Quaker businessman of Bloomington, Jesse Fell, said that his religious faith did not prevent him from supporting the erection of the monument to "our dear friend, the brave and lamented Lovejoy. I concur with you. *Lovejoy was the real hero of the antislavery cause.* . . ." Later, at a meeting in Princeton of the Lovejoy Monument Association, Codding praised Lovejoy when he said, "He saw from the beginning as in the very light of heaven that the Negro possessed our *common human nature,* and that in his rights were involved the rights of man, the principle of popular government. . . . It mattered not to him, whether the cold oblique rays of the North paled a man's face to the standard of Anglo-Saxon fairness, or whether the vertical rays of the south should give it the hue of a raven's wing. 'A man's a man for a' that.' " [7]

Codding, who died on June 17, 1866, gave the last year of his life to the building of the Lovejoy monument. It was made up of four large blocks of stone, its marble obelisk of three and a half tons then being one of the largest in the Midwest. Among the many who sent messages to the monument association were Abraham Lincoln; William Cullen Bryant; Joshua R. Giddings, now aged and frail and "lingering on the verge of life" at his post in the United States consulate in Montreal; Gerrit Smith; Governor John A. Andrew of Massachusetts; and Brigadier General

Neal Dow, his health broken by imprisonment in Confederate prisons.

Along with the inscriptions of family birth and death dates the base of the obelisk might well have borne Lincoln's words: ". . . My personal acquaintance with him commenced only about ten years ago, since when it has been quite intimate; and every step in it has been one of increasing respect and esteem, ending, with his life, in no less than affection on my part. It can be truly said of him that while he was personally ambitious he bravely endured the obscurity which the unpopularity of his principles imposed, and never accepted official honors, until those honors were ready to admit his principles with him. Throughout my heavy, and perplexing responsibilities here, to the day of his death, it would scarcely wrong any other to say, he was my most generous friend. Let him have the marble monument, along with the well-assured and more enduring one in the hearts of those who love liberty, unselfishly, for all men." [8]

One last memorial was a Negro woman's. She was on a train traveling from the West on the day Lovejoy's body arrived in Princeton. When she heard other passengers say that Lovejoy was being brought to his home town, she asked why, and was told that they were bringing his body back for burial.

"Dead!" she murmured, with grief in her eyes and voice. "Lovejoy dead! Such men should never die." [9]

410

Epilogue

By 1864 the abolitionist crusade was drawing to a close. Universal emancipation was already on the agenda. The Thirteenth Amendment, prohibiting slavery forever in the United States, was to be introduced in Congress only two weeks after Lovejoy's death. That act of universal emancipation had been the specific goal set by the American Anti-Slavery Society in 1833, and in 1864 Lovejoy could have rendered substantial aid in carrying the amendment to passage against some late obstacles.

A year after his death the war ended, and soon the Freedmen's Bureau was established to aid the former slaves in their transition into a life legally free. The Thirteenth Amendment became part of the Constitution in December, 1865, and it was followed by passage on April 9, 1866, of the Civil Rights Act, giving citizenship and equal rights to the freedmen. Lest the act be overturned in the courts, the radical Republicans almost immediately embodied its salient features in the Fourteenth Amendment. A draft was brought out on April 30, 1866, by the Joint Committee of Fifteen on Reconstruction under the chairmanship of Thaddeus Stevens.

It is obvious from the record of Lovejoy's activities that had he lived he would have been in the forefront of the campaigns to extend citizenship and equal rights to the Negro freedmen. In doing so he would have been performing as he had for sixteen years, as a radical and dynamic member of the antislavery united front. It is especially for his role in the coalition that he is memorable.

Lovejoy might have been an effective force in other advances for the unity movement in 1864. For example, having already signified his confidence in and support of Lincoln for the Presidency in 1864, Lovejoy would have joined William Lloyd Garrison when he opposed their good friend Wendell Phillips that summer. Phillips had taken the independent position of rejecting Lincoln and backing Frémont. For Phillips and a group of sincere but politically shortsighted abolitionists Lincoln seemed too slow and cautious in supplying an effective emancipation policy. Lovejoy, in his ceaseless efforts to maintain the united front with Lincoln, had lectured against this impatience in 1861 and 1862, and had argued with fellow abolitionists over it in 1863. In the few months of his life in 1864 he had contended that Lincoln was the best possible candidate. Phillips little realized that he was splitting the antislavery united front. His separatism opened the way for a victory by McClellan and the Democrats, who would restore the union "as it was," without touching slavery in the states coming back. Understanding the predicament, radicals led by Theodore Tilton energetically threw themselves into the campaign for Lincoln and persuaded Frémont to withdraw from the campaign.

Garrison's plunge into politics is notable, for it was an implicit admission that Lovejoy, Giddings, Myron Holley, and other

412

pioneer political abolitionists had followed a sure path to power. The militant editor of *The Liberator* was now urging abolitionists to get into politics and into the united front with moderates like Lincoln. Moreover, by praising Lincoln in 1865 for passage of the Thirteenth Amendment, Garrison reversed his position of the 1840's and 1850's. Now he accepted the Constitution and the need to amend it.

Phillips belatedly saw the error of his support for Frémont against Lincoln. That he should have failed to see it before taking the independent position underscores the lesson in political science taught by Lovejoy's pursuit of antislavery unity. Phillips did in the end welcome the Republican victory with Lincoln in 1864 as a victory for universal emancipation. That, after all, was the most important reason for party and antislavery unity.

Lovejoy had seen this as early as 1848, when he had been the Liberty party's candidate for Congress in the Illinois Fourth District. He had especially intensified his efforts for such unity when Fort Sumter fell and the country was threatened with permanent dismemberment. At that point, unity became necessary if the country were to continue according to the ideas embodied in the Declaration of Independence and the Constitution.

Those ideas had been applied to the slavery question by Giddings and John Quincy Adams as leading spokesmen in Congress for the antislavery and civil rights viewpoints. With a reputation for militancy established in Illinois, Lovejoy had inherited the role from them when he became a Member of Congress. In the Civil War days he had increasingly attacked slavery and slave-owning and pressed for the use of abolitionist policies in order to uphold the government. He had said that he preferred not to fight an antislavery war as such, but overwhelming realities took that choice away from him and from the nation. The logical policy, as Lovejoy and other radicals demonstrated despite their protestations, was to destroy the rebellion with "radical and ex-

413

treme" measures. In turn, the success of such a policy depended upon unity in the antislavery coalition, specifically and primarily with Lincoln.

When Lovejoy elected to enter the united front on the basis of a nonextensionist policy, he was forced to give up some of the more far-reaching measures and policies proposed by the Liberty party. Lovejoy insisted that such a modification of the political antislavery movement would lead to the desired end of universal emancipation. On the other hand, he continued to work in the Underground Railroad and when war came he worked hard for repeal of the Fugitive Slave Law. In support of the antislavery coalition he lectured his comrades to support Lincoln (he is traveling in the right direction) and to uphold the Administration (it was committed to limiting slavery's domain and was fighting a war against the interests of the slaveowners).

His careful concern for the united front did not prevent Lovejoy from running against Lincoln's warnings to avoid extreme and revolutionary measures. Nor did his careful concern for the Republican party prevent him from taking independent positions on a number of economic questions. He nevertheless played a unique role in supporting Lincoln and the coalition, for he counted on its power to abolish slavery. There is therefore much to be said in favor of Lovejoy's skill in advancing the cause of universal emancipation while maintaining a position of militancy and radicalness in the united front with Lincoln.

Owen Lovejoy was indeed that mixture of caution and extreme doctrine that Louis Filler has discerned. Lovejoy held some mixed notions about the economic affairs of his time. On the one hand he seemed to be speaking for the creditor class when he made his proposals against the greenbacks. On the other hand he was certainly defying all the basic precepts of propertied classes when he offered his land sequestration measure on January 8, 1862. He supported strict confiscation measures against the leaders of the rebellion while professing to be willing to pay compensation to slaveowners.

He attacked the army's kid-glove approach to the war, but he praised McClellan when he won a victory. Lovejoy wanted to speed up the war and the use of antislavery enactments but he never goaded the President in public, however impatient he may have been with the chief executive's cautiousness. Paradoxically, Lovejoy aligned himself with the President when he suppressed General Frémont's emancipation order in Missouri. That was a strange position for a man who had only a few months earlier, in July, 1861, attempted to ease the way for *de facto* emancipation by preventing the army from turning back fugitives. Radical abolitionists might well have wondered about the price Lovejoy seemed to be paying for unity with Lincoln. But Lovejoy was not dissuaded by such a consideration. He hastened to attack the problem facing the antislavery cause at its decisive point, and that was the army's slowness and timidity and its practice of turning back or surrendering fugitive slaves.

Emancipation orders and proclamations were important and Lovejoy fought for them, but until they could be promulgated and applied, the void in policy had to be filled by immediate on-the-ground measures. When thousands of Negroes were flocking into Union camps and offering to fight and offering information about the enemy, that was the time to welcome them, protect them and their families, and give them arms with which to fight if they chose to. This was the Underground Railroad en masse, and the Union could only benefit from its successes. In acting along those lines Lovejoy was not surrendering old abolitionist principles but furthering them, and from within the united front.

Rather than surrender abolitionist principles Lovejoy advanced them by constantly urging Congress and the people in his district to sustain the Administration, to back any measures the President proposed to win the war and abolish slavery. At the same time

415

Lovejoy struck out on his own path and advanced the antislavery movement by attacking the army's slowness, and Halleck's Order No. 3; by pressing for the enrollment of Negro troops and for the equal pay and equal rights measures that followed. He pushed the bill abolishing slavery in the territories and heartily supported the District of Columbia abolition of slavery bill. Finally, Lovejoy was prepared to fight for universal emancipation through his bill of December 14, 1863, signifying a farther reach than the admirable but partial Emancipation Proclamation.

Sometimes the focus of Lovejoy's contemporaries and the focus of later observers may shift to the disunity of the antislavery coalition. Obviously, Lincoln was opposed to the radicals, and vice versa; and radicals were opposed to one another on different questions, even on antislavery aims and tactics. The coalition was alive with sects and factions, parties and caucuses, representing innumerable differences. But the light is wasted if it does not focus on the unity of these conflicting forces working for the ultimate antislavery goal. Such a narrow focus omits the clear and memorable and far more significant pictures of the united front in its developing stages and in its forward motion.

The abolitionists never could have gained their objectives by going it alone or by remaining a one-idea party in the political realm. The Negro people could not have gained their freedom from slavery in separatist movements alone but rather through that unity of forces and with that variety of tactics in which their spokesman was the incisive Frederick Douglass and their allies were the white antislavery people. The Union could not have been preserved without the force and spirit of the antislavery coalition, and foremost in it the marching Negro population. In grasping the significance of the united front and in maintaining it over the years, even though it led him through the valley of apparent compromise, Lovejoy stands out with other political

416

abolitionists as a true leader of the people, and he merits a niche in history.

Conservative antislavery Republicans, moderates like Lincoln, the Negro people, and radicals of different hues from Garrison and Phillips through Thaddeus Stevens, George W. Julian, Joshua R. Giddings, Zebina Eastman, Ichabod Codding, and Owen Lovejoy—all of them united to change America for the better. All of them should be remembered as America keeps faith with Jefferson and the Bill of Rights, with Elijah Lovejoy and the promises of the revolution begun in the 37th Congress, and with the hopes and needs of the Negro people.

Notes

1. See Arthur C. Cole, "President Lincoln and the Illinois Radical Republicans," *Mississippi Valley Historical Review*, IV (1918), 417–36; T. Harry Williams, *Lincoln and the Radicals* (Madison, 1941). These writers saw a hard hostility between Lincoln and the radicals—"Lincoln *versus* the radicals." On the opposite side is David Donald's essay "The Radicals and Lincoln," in his *Lincoln Reconsidered* (New York, 1955). Donald saw Lincoln, "not in constant conflict with the Radical members of his own party." Eric L. McKitrick entered the debate with his *Andrew Johnson and Reconstruction* (Chicago, 1960), in which he supports Donald's view, at least with respect to radicals in 1865 and 1866, by asserting, "one must be governed by the fluid side, rather than the rigid side, of the 'radical' concept" (p. 54). The argument over Lincoln and the Radicals and over the meaning of "radical" found expression again in two essays, "Devils Facing Zionwards," by David Donald, and "Lincoln and the Radicals: An Essay in Civil War History and Historiography," by T. Harry Williams, both published in Grady McWhiney (ed.), *Grant, Lee, Lincoln and the Radicals* (Evanston, 1964). In this connection, two recent works that delineate the differences among abolitionists are Martin Duberman (ed.), *The Antislavery Vanguard: New Essays on the Abolitionists* (Princeton, New Jersey, 1965), and James M. McPherson, *The Struggle for Equality: Abolitionists and the Negro*

in the Civil War and Reconstruction (Princeton, New Jersey, 1964).

2. Louis Ruchames, "The Historian as Special Pleader," *The Nation*, November 24, 1962, p. 356; *Bureau County Republican*, May 19, 1864.

3. Larry Gara, *The Liberty Line: The Legend of the Underground Railroad* (Lexington, 1961); Wilbur H. Siebert, *The Underground Railroad from Slavery to Freedom* (New York, 1898). Also see Hermann R. Muelder, *Fighters for Freedom: The History of Anti-slavery Activities of Men and Women Associated with Knox College* (New York, 1959), which makes the Underground Railroad in Illinois significant and widespread, and buttresses Siebert's early research with careful new scholarship. Despite Gara's skeptical appraisal of the accomplishments of the Underground Railroad, he does point out that the story of the institution has come down to us with far too little of the role played in it by the Negroes.

1 · THE MURDER OF ELIJAH P. LOVEJOY

The description of the events leading up to the murder and the deed of violence itself is based on Joseph C. and Owen Lovejoy, *Memoir of the Rev. Elijah P. Lovejoy; Who Was Murdered in Defence of the Liberty of the Press at Alton, Illinois, Nov. 7, 1837* (New York, 1838); William S. Lincoln, *The Alton Trials* (New York, 1838); Edward Beecher, *Narrative of the Riots at Alton* (Alton, 1838); Henry Tanner, *The Martyrdom of Lovejoy* (Chicago, 1881); the files of the St. Louis *Observer* and the Alton *Observer*. Recent biographies of Elijah Lovejoy also furnished new insights into the problem he faced; they are John Gill, *Tide Without Turning: Elijah P. Lovejoy and Freedom of the Press* (Boston, 1958), and Merton L. Dillon, *Elijah P. Lovejoy, Abolitionist Editor* (Urbana, 1961).

Professor Dillon maintains that Elijah Lovejoy became an abolitionist rather early in his career. I, on the other hand, believe that he did not become one until rather late, after events had moved him to change his position. Only in June, 1837, did Lovejoy identify himself with the American Anti-Slavery Society, which had been in existence since 1833. He delayed issuing a call for the state society until late in the summer of 1837. It was organized in the last few days of October, and he was murdered on November 7.

1. "Elijah P. Lovejoy as an Anti-Catholic," *Records of the American Catholic Historical Society of Philadelphia*, LXII (September, 1951), 172, cited by Dillon, p. 40.

As Lovejoy advanced into abolitionism he gave less and less emphasis to Catholicism, and more and more he linked the cause of freedom for the Negro slaves to freedom of speech and press for all Americans. Concerning the inseparability of the two questions see Russel B. Nye, *Fettered Freedom: Civil Liberties and the Slavery Controversy, 1830-1860* (East Lansing, 1949), and Gill's biography. Finally, as Lovejoy grew in understanding of the abolitionist movement he began to extricate himself from the trap of bigotry and xenophobia.

2. Elijah P. Lovejoy to Joseph C. Lovejoy, November 21, 1834, Wickett-Wiswall Collection of Lovejoy Papers, Texas Technological College, Lubbock; Calvin M. Clark, *American Slavery and Maine Congregationalists* (Bangor, 1940), pp. 49, 72–73.

3. Elijah P. Lovejoy to Owen Lovejoy, November 2, 1835, in *Memoir*, p. 56; Owen Lovejoy to (?), April 28, 1860, Boston Public Library. In the latter Owen explained that his brother "was always antislavery, though at first he sought to make a distinction between *that* & *abolition*, but the distinction gradually faded away & he advocated the principles in the usual mode."

4. St. Louis *Observer*, November 5, 1835.

5. N. Dwight Harris, *The History of Negro Servitude in Illinois* (Chicago, 1904), p. 74; *Shepherd of the Valley*, cited in Dillon, p. 11.

6. Harris, p. 75; Elijah P. Lovejoy to Brother, January, 1836, in *Memoir*, p. 65

7. Elijah P. Lovejoy to Mother, November 23, 1835, in *Memoir*, p. 159.

8. Elijah P. Lovejoy to Brother, January, 1836, in *Memoir*, p. 165.

9. This account is based on John F. Darby, *Personal Recollections of Men and Events in St. Louis* (St. Louis, 1880), pp. 239–41. Darby was mayor of St. Louis and active in its early political history.

10. "Judge Lawless vs. Law," *Quarterly Anti-Slavery Magazine*, I (1836), 406. Wright asserted, "McIntosh owed the mode of his death not to his crime but to his *complexion*."

11. St. Louis *Observer*, July 21, 1836; Harris, p. 76

12. Elijah P. Lovejoy to Joseph C. Lovejoy, July 30, 1836, in *Memoir*, p. 182; Elijah P. Lovejoy to Mother, August 31, 1836, in *Memoir*, p. 186 (the original is at the Chicago Historical Society).

13. Alton *Observer*, August 10, 1837.

14. *Ibid.*, February 2, June 29, 1837.

15. A. B. Hart, *Slavery and Abolition, 1831–1841* (New York, 1906), p. 184; Harris, *passim*.

16. Madison County, Illinois, *Gazeteer* (Alton, 1866), pp. 83–84.

17. Tanner, p. 22.

18. Elijah P. Lovejoy to Joshua Leavitt, October 3, 1837, in *Memoir*,

p. 258; Dillon, p. 126; Hermann R. Muelder, *Fighters for Freedom: The History of Anti-slavery Activities of Men and Women Associated with Knox College* (New York, 1959), p. 127.

19. Dillon, p. 130; Dwight L. Dumond (ed.), *Letters of James Gillespie Birney, 1831–1857* (New York, 1938), I, 414, 416.

20. Dr. Samuel Willard in Tanner, p. 220.

21. Nye, p. 117.

22. *Memoir*, p. 261; Dillon, p. 120.

23. Beecher, pp. 85–91.

24. Based on Beecher, Lincoln, and Tanner.

25. *The Liberator*, December 28, 1837, quoted in Herbert Aptheker (ed.), *A Documentary History of the Negro People in the United States* (New York, 1951), p. 175.

26. Chicago *Tribune*, June 12, 1874.

27. *Ibid.*

2 · "WAS I TO BEWRAY THE WANDERER?"

1. Clarence E. Lovejoy, *Lovejoy Genealogy* (New York, 1930), pp. 122f.; Joseph C. and Owen Lovejoy, *Memoir of the Rev. Elijah P. Lovejoy; Who Was Murdered in Defence of the Liberty of the Press at Alton, Illinois, Nov. 7, 1837* (New York, 1838), pp.13–17.

2. *Memoir*, p. 18.

3. *Ibid.*, p. 261; Clarence E. Lovejoy, *Genealogy*, p. 172; Dumas Malone (ed.), *Dictionary of American Biography* (New York, 1933), XI, 435; Calvin M. Clark, *American Slavery and Maine Congregationalists* (Bangor, 1940), pp. 113–14.

4. Clarence E. Lovejoy, *Genealogy*, 122.

5. Owen Lovejoy to James G. Birney, December 9, 1837, Illinois State Historical Library.

6. Owen Lovejoy to H. G. Chapman, December 9, 1837, Garrison Collection, Boston Public Library; Dillon, p. 178.

7. Owen Lovejoy to "My Dear Mother," January 25, 1838; February 10, 1838, Wickett-Wiswall Collection of Lovejoy Papers, Texas Technological College (Lubbock).

8. Owen Lovejoy to Mother, February 10, 1838; Owen Lovejoy to Joseph C. Lovejoy, April 16, 1838, Lovejoy Papers, Texas Technological College; New York *Tribune*, March 29, 1864.

9. Owen Lovejoy to Mother, March 22, 1838, Chicago Historical Society.

10. *Ibid.*

11. Letters cited in notes 8 and 9; C. L. Kelsey, speech of June 1, 1864, reprinted in *Bureau County Republican*, June 16, 1864.

12. Julian M. Sturtevant, speech of June 1, 1864, reprinted in *Bureau County Republican*, June 9, 1864; Owen to John E. Lovejoy, June 15, 1838, Lovejoy Papers, Texas Technological College; Guy Study, *History of St. Paul's Church, Alton* (St. Louis, 1943), p. 37

13. Sturtevant, *Bureau County Republican*, June 9, 1864

14. Kelsey, *Bureau County Republican*, June 16, 1864; Henry A. Ford, *The History of Putnam and Marshall Counties . . . and Formation of Bureau and Stark Counties* (Lacon, Illinois, 1860), p. 66.

15. Ella W. Harrison, "A History of the First Congregational Church of Princeton, Illinois, 1831–1924," *Journal of the Illinois State Historical Society*, XX (April, 1927), 106; Owen Lovejoy to Joseph C. Lovejoy, November 12, 1838, Lovejoy Papers, Texas Technological College.

16. Thomas Pope, "Manuscript History of the Quincy Church,' *Transactions of the Illinois State Historical Society*, X (1905), 317.

17. George Owen Smith, "The Lovejoy Shrine, the Lovejoy Station on the Underground Railroad" (Princeton, Illinois, 1949), p. 31.

18. Joseph H. Simpson, Handwritten Journal, I, 92, cited in George Owen Smith, "The Lovejoy Shrine," p. 13

19. *Ibid.*

20. Pope, p. 321.

21. Ruth E. Haberkorn, "Owen Lovejoy in Princeton, Illinois," *Journal of the Illinois State Historical Society*, XXXVI (1943), 284–315.

22. *Ibid.*

23. *Bureau County Republican*, January 11, 1912.

24. Ida Lovejoy to William Lloyd Garrison (1889), Sophia Smith Collection, Smith College Library, Northampton, Massachusetts.

25. *Ibid.*

26. *Western Citizen*, July 26, 1842.

27. *Ibid.*, August 3, 1843. The Agnes–Nancy cases were reported from the *Western Citizen's* antislavery point of view on July 13, August 3, October 19, and October 26, 1843. Another account of the trial was told half a century later by John D. Caton, the judge in the case, in his *Early Bench and Bar in Illinois* (Chicago, 1893). See also N. Dwight Harris, *The History of Negro Servitude in Illinois* (Chicago, 1904), pp. 110–12, where the legal question is clarified.

28. Haberkorn, p. 295.

29. R. S. Bergen to Owen Lovejoy, November 12, 1843, Lovejoy Papers, Texas Technological College.

30. *National Anti-Slavery Standard*, April 14, 1843, disclosed the intent of those who pressed charges against Lovejoy. See also Harris, p. 114.

31. *Western Citizen*, February 17, 1845; Alton *Telegraph*, February 3, 1844; Chicago *Express*, February 20, 1844; all quoted in Harris, p. 115.

32. *Western Citizen*, August 17, 1843.

33. *Ibid.*

34. *Ibid.*, August 24, 1843.

35. John Buckner's rescue was described in the *Western Citizen*, July 7, 1849, and in a letter of Justin H. Olds to Sarah Lovejoy, May 17, 1874, Owen Lovejoy Collection, Bureau County Historical Society, Princeton, Illinois; P. Atkinson, "A Reminiscence of the Late Hon. Owen Lovejoy," New York *Independent*, May 5, 1864.

36. *Weekly Democrat*, Somonauk, Illinois (December, 1854), quoted in *Journal of the Illinois State Historical Society*, XVIII (1925), 715–16; *Congressional Globe*, 35 Congress, 2 Session, Appendix, pp. 199–203.

3 · RENOVATE THE STATE! —1840–1844

1. Quoted in Russel B. Nye, *Fettered Freedom: Civil Liberties and the Slavery Controversy, 1830–1860* (East Lansing, 1949), p. 38. In addition, the reader who wishes to understand slavery as an institution may consult Herbert Aptheker, *Negro Slave Revolts* (New York, 1943), Dwight L. Dumond, *Antislavery: The Crusade for Freedom in America* (Ann Arbor, 1961), Louis Filler, *The Crusade Against Slavery, 1830–1860* (New York, 1960), Eugene D. Genovese, *The Political Economy of Slavery* (New York, 1965), and Kenneth M. Stampp, *The Peculiar Institution* (New York, 1956). Also see Leon F. Litwack, *North of Slavery: The Negro in the Free States, 1790–1860* (Chicago, 1961).

2. Benjamin P. Thomas, *Theodore Weld, Crusader for Freedom* (New Brunswick, 1950), p. 179.

3. Ralph V. Harlow, *Gerrit Smith, Philanthropist and Reformer* (New York, 1939), pp. 132–62; Dwight L. Dumond, *Antislavery Origins of the Civil War in the United States* (Ann Arbor, 1939), p. 89.

4. *The Philanthropist*, November 26, 1839, quoted in T. C. Smith, *The Liberty and Free-Soil Parties in the North West* (New York, 1897), p. 33; Owen Lovejoy to John E. Lovejoy, February 1, 1840, Lovejoy Papers, Texas Technological College (Lubbock); Hermann R. Muelder, *Fighters for Freedom: The History of Anti-slavery Activities of Men and Women Associated with Knox College* (New York, 1959), pp. 158–59.

5. William Birney, *James G. Birney and His Times* (New York, 1890), pp. 340–42; Lewis Tappan to Benjamin Tappan, November 4, 1837, quoted in Thomas, p. 180; Dumond, *Antislavery Origins*, pp. 89–90.

6. T. C. Smith, p. 42.

7. *Ibid.*, pp. 42, 46–47; N. Dwight Harris, *The History of Negro Servitude in Illinois* (Chicago, 1904), p. 267, records 160 votes for the antislavery ticket of 1840.

8. John Cross to *Emancipator*, June 10, 1841, quoted in T. C. Smith, pp. 45–46.

9. *Ibid.*

10. *Ibid.*

11. Harris, p. 148.

12. *Western Citizen*, July 26, 1842.

13. *Ibid.*

14. *Ibid.*, January 20, 1843; T. C. Smith, p. 57; Harris, p. 150. Harris cited 931 votes for governor, from "official returns" in *Western Citizen*, October 12, 1843.

15. Dumond, *Antislavery Origins*, p. 90.

16. *Western Citizen*, October 5, 1843; Charles H. Wesley, "The Participation of Negroes in Anti-Slavery Political Parties," *Journal of Negro History*, XXIX (January, 1944), 37–69.

17. *Ibid.*, September 14, 1843.

18. C. L. Kelsey in *Bureau County Republican*, June 16, 1864; Theodore C. Pease, *Illinois Election Returns, 1818–1848* (Springfield, 1923), p. 138.

19. Matthew Spinka (ed.), *A History of Illinois Congregational and Christian Churches* (Chicago, 1944), p. 86.

20. *Ibid.*, p. 91; *Western Citizen*, September 21, 1843.

21. Owen Lovejoy to Lewis Tappan, December 21, 1841, American Missionary Association Archives, Fisk University, Nashville, Tennessee; Louis Filler, *The Crusade Against Slavery, 1830–1860* (New York, 1960), pp. 167–69.

22. *Ibid.*

23. *Ibid.*

24. Owen Lovejoy to Lewis Tappan, August 17, 1847, AMA Archives, Fisk.

25. Owen Lovejoy to Lewis Tappan, November 21, 1847, February 4, March 5, June 17, 1850; Owen Lovejoy to Wm. Harned, Esq., May 21, 1850, January 26, 1851; Owen Lovejoy to Bro. Whipple, August 20, 1853; Owen Lovejoy to Lewis Tappan, August 18, 1853, April 3, 1854, August 27, 1854; all in AMA Archives, Fisk.

26. Frederick I. Kuhns, *The American Home Missionary Society in Relation to the Antislavery Controversy in the Old Northwest* (Billings, 1959), p. 17.

27. *Western Citizen*, January 24, 1844; Harris, Appendix IV, p. 267

4 · FROM A ONE-IDEA PARTY TO FREE-SOILISM

1. C. D. Cleveland (ed.), *Anti-Slavery Addresses of 1844 and 1845* (Philadelphia, 1867), Appendix, p. 1; T. C. Smith, *The Liberty and Free-Soil Parties in the North West* (New York, 1897), pp. 88–89.

2. *Bureau County Republican*, June 16, 1864.

3. *Ibid.*

4. Dwight L. Dumond, *Antislavery Origins of the Civil War in the United States* (Ann Arbor, 1939), p. 95; *Western Citizen*, March 11, 1846.

5. *Western Citizen*, July 7, 1846.

6. *Ibid.*

7. John Farnsworth, *Congressional Globe*, 38 Congress, 1 Session, p. 1327; Kelsey in *Bureau County Republican*, June 16, 1864.

8. *Western Citizen*, May 6, 1846.

9. *Ibid.*, June 10, 1846.

10. *Ibid.*

11. *Ibid.*, June 23, 1846.

12. Theodore C. Pease, *Illinois Election Returns, 1818–1848* (Springfield, 1923), p. 156, gives Wentworth 12,026, Kerr, 6,168, and Lovejoy, 3,531; *Western Citizen*, November 14, 1846.

13. *Ibid.*

14. *Ibid.*, October 13, November 14, 1846.

15. *Ibid.*, December 1, 1846.

16. James H. Collins to Owen Lovejoy, March 17, 1847, Owen Lovejoy Collection, Bureau County Historical Society, Princeton, Illinois.

17. *Western Citizen*, April 20, May 4, 1847.

18. *Ibid.*, December 14, 1847.

19. *Ibid.*, May 4, 1847.

20. N. Dwight Harris, *The History of Negro Servitude in Illinois* (Chicago, 1904), p. 164; *Western Citizen*, July 11, 1848.

21. *Western Citizen*, May 2, 1848.

22. *Ibid.*, June 20, 1848.

23. *Ibid.*, June 27, 1848.

24. John H. Bryant to William Cullen Byrant, January 14, 1848, William Cullen Bryant Papers, New York Public Library.

25. Harris, p. 164; *Western Citizen*, July 11, 1848.

26. T. C. Smith, p. 142.

27. Richard Sewell, "John P. Hale and the Liberty Party, 1847–48," *New England Quarterly* (June, 1964), 221.

28. *Western Citizen*, August 22, 1848.

29. Don E. Fehrenbacher, *Chicago Giant, a Biography of "Long John" Wentworth* (Madison, 1957), p. 83.

30. *Bureau County Republican*, June 16, 1864.

5 · A MORE CERTAIN SOUND IN ANTISLAVERY POLITICS

1. T. C. Smith, *The Liberty and Free-Soil Parties in the North West* (New York, 1897), pp. 193ff.
2. *Western Citizen*, December 11, 1849.
3. Roy F. Nicholas, *The Stakes of Power, 1845–1877* (New York, 1961), p. 29.
4. *Western Citizen*, April 23, 1850.
5. *Ibid.*, June 11, 1850.
6. *Ibid.*, September 3, 1850.
7. *Ibid.*, October 8, 1850; N. Dwight Harris, *The History of Negro Servitude in Illinois* (Chicago, 1904), p. 179.
8. *Western Citizen*, October 15, 1850; Harris, p. 180; T. C. Smith, pp. 195–96.
9. *Western Citizen*, October 15, 1850; October 29, 1850.
10. *Ibid.*, December 31, 1850; T. C. Smith, pp. 196–97; Harris, p. 180.
11. Albert J. Beveridge, *Abraham Lincoln, 1809–1858* (Boston and New York, 1928), II, 125; Harris, p. 180.
12. *Frederick Douglass' Paper*, quoted in *Western Citizen*, March 9, 1852.
13. Frederick Douglass to Gerrit Smith, July 15, 1852, quoted in Philip S. Foner (ed.), *The Life and Writings of Frederick Douglass* (New York, 1950–1955), II, 75–76; 206.
14. *Western Citizen*, August 17, 1852; T. C. Smith, p. 247; Beveridge, II, 156–57; New York *Tribune*, August 12, 1852; Eric Foner, "Politics and Prejudice: The Free Soil Party and the Negro, 1849–1852," *Journal of Negro History* (October, 1965), 251–53.
15. Philip S. Foner (ed.), p. 76.
16. *Western Citizen*, August 17, 1852.
17. *Ibid.*, August 31, 1852.
18. *Ibid.*; Harris, Appendix IV, p. 267.
19. T. C. Smith, p. 323.
20. *Free West*, December 1, 1853.
21. *Ibid.*, June 2, 1854.
22. Arthur C. Cole, *The Era of the Civil War, 1848–1870* (Chicago, 1922), p. 123; Herman Schlueter, *Lincoln, Labor and Slavery* (New York, 1913), p. 76; Karl Obermann, *Joseph Weydemeyer, Pioneer of American Socialism* (New York, 1947), p. 79.
23. Allan Nevins, *Ordeal of the Union* (New York, 1947), II, 123; Obermann, p. 80.
24. Francis Curtis, *The Republican Party* (New York, 1904), pp. 178–79.
25. *Ibid.*, pp. 181ff.; Beveridge, II, 264.

26. *Free West*, August 10, 1854.
27. *Ibid.*, September 7, 1854; Harris, p. 190; Cole, p. 123.
28. *Free West*, September 7, 1854; Cole, p. 123.
29. *Free West*, September 7, 1854.

6 · ANTI-NEBRASKA BREAKTHROUGH: 1854

1. *Free West*, September 7, 1854; Paul Selby, "Genesis of the Republican Party in Illinois," *Transactions of the Illinois State Historical Society*, XI (1906), 270–83; Paul Selby, "Republican State Convention, Springfield, Illinois, October 4–5, 1854," *Transactions of the McLean County Historical Society*, III (1900), 43.
2. Selby, "Republican State Convention," p. 44.
3. Horace White, "Abraham Lincoln in 1854" (Springfield, Illinois, 1908), p. 10; Paul M. Angle (ed.), *Herndon's Life of Lincoln* (New York, 1949), p. 296; Dwight L. Dumond, *Antislavery Origins of the Civil War in the United States* (Ann Arbor, 1939), p. 107.
4. Roy P. Basler, Marion Dolores Pratt, and Lloyd A. Dunlap (eds.), *The Collected Works of Abraham Lincoln* (New Brunswick, New Jersey, 1953), II, 255, 266. These statements are extracted from the text of Lincoln's Peoria speech of October 16. The editors point out that the speech of October 4 was essentially the same.
5. White, p. 11; Selby, "Genesis of the Republican Party," p. 272; Angle, (ed.), *Herndon's Life of Lincoln*, pp. 298–99; Albert J. Beveridge, *Abraham Lincoln, 1809–1858* (Boston and New York, 1928), II, 266.
6. Angle (ed.), *Herndon's Life of Lincoln*, p. 299; Basler *et al.* (eds.), III, 13.
7. Selby, "Republican State Convention," pp. 44–45; Selby, "Genesis of the Republican Party," pp. 272, 277.
8. *Ibid.;* Selby, a participant of the convention, recalled, "I remember it was Owen Lovejoy who responded with an earnest endorsement of Lincoln's position on the slavery question—showing that the real attitude of the future emancipator of a race was understood, however much he may have misunderstood the actual sentiments of the convention."
9. A. Lincoln to Ichabod Codding, November 27, 1854, Basler *et al.* (eds.), II, 288; Selby, "Genesis of the Republican Party," p. 277.
10. White, p. 16.
11. Angle (ed.), *Herndon's Life of Lincoln*, pp. 300–301; John H. Bryant to William H. Herndon, March 15, 1866, in Angle (ed.), p. 301.
12. N. Dwight Harris, *The History of Negro Servitude in Illinois* (Chicago, 1904), p. 192; *Free West*, October and November, 1854.
13. *Free West*, November 23, 1854.

14. *Ibid.*

15. Owen Lovejoy to Joshua R. Giddings, November 10, 1854, Ohio Historical Society, Columbus.

16. *Ibid.;* Peoria Weekly Democratic Press, August 26, 1854, in Ameda Ruth King, "The Last Years of the Whig Party in Illinois, 1847–1856," *Transactions of the Illinois State Historical Society,* XXXII (1925), 141

17. Harris, p. 194.

18. *Free West,* January 11, 1855.

19. *Ibid.,* December 14, 1854.

20. Harris, p. 195; Jay Monaghan, *The Man Who Elected Lincoln* (Indianapolis and New York, 1956), p. 39.

21. *House Journal* (Springfield, 1855), pp. 348–61; Lanphier Mss., January 14, 1855, quoted in Beveridge, II, 282; Willard L. King, *David Davis, Lincoln's Manager* (Cambridge, 1960), p. 106. A total of ten ballots was taken in the joint session of the House and Senate. On ballots four through seven Lovejoy voted for William Ogden, and on the last three ballots for Lyman Trumbull.

22. *Free West,* January 11, 1855.

23. *Ibid.,* February 1, 1855.

24. *Ibid.,* February 15, 1855, which copied from the *Princeton Post,* February 6.

25. *Ibid.*

26. *Ibid.,* March 15, 1855.

27. *Ibid.,* April 12, 1855.

28. *House Journal,* p. 306; *Free West,* February 15, 1855.

7 · THE ILLINOIS REPUBLICAN PARTY IS ORGANIZED

1. Lincoln to Joshua Speed, August 24, 1855, in Roy P. Basler, Marion Dolores Pratt, and Lloyd A. Dunlap (eds.), *The Collected Works of Abraham Lincoln* (New Brunswick, 1953), II, 322–23.

2. Joliet *Signal,* September 18, 1855, in Albert J. Beveridge, *Abraham Lincoln 1809–1858* (Boston and New York, 1928), II, 353; Philip S. Foner (ed.), *Life and Writings of Frederick Douglass* (New York, 1950–55), II, 383.

3. Horace White, *Abraham Lincoln in 1854* (Springfield, Illinois, 1908), p. 6.

4. Lincoln to Owen Lovejoy, August 11, 1855, Henry Huntington Library, San Marino, California.

5. *Ibid.*

6. Zebina Eastman, "History of the Anti-Slavery Agitation, and the Growth of the Liberty and Republican Parties in the State of Illinois"

(undated pamphlet, Eastman Collection, Chicago Historical Society), p. 671.

7. *Ibid.*

8. *Ibid.*

9. Lincoln to Speed, August 24, 1855; Lincoln to Robertson, August 15, 1855, Basler *et al.* (eds.), II, 317–18, 322–23.

10. Lyman Trumbull to Owen Lovejoy, August 20, 1855, Brown University Library.

11. Paul Selby, "The Editorial Convention of 1856," *Journal of the Illinois State Historical Society*, V (1912), 343–49; Paul Selby, "The Editorial Convention, February 22, 1856," *Transactions of the McLean County Historical Society*, III (1900), 30–43; George W. Julian, "The First Republican National Convention," *American Historical Review*, IV (1899), 312–22.

12. Chicago *Journal*, February 25, 1856.

13. John M. Palmer, *Personal Recollections: The Story of an Earnest Life* (Cincinnati, 1901), p. 72; Selby, "The Editorial Convention, February 22, 1856," *Transactions of the McLean County Historical Society*, III, 25; Beveridge, II, 359.

14. Julian, pp. 313–14; New York *Times*, February 22, 1856.

15. New York *Times*, February 23, 1856.

16. William E. Smith, *Francis Preston Blair Family in Politics* (New York, 1933), pp. 327–28.

17. Julian, *passim;* New York *Times*, February 22, 23, 1856, tell the story of the convention first-hand.

18. *Ibid.*

19. Julian, p. 317.

20. New York *Times*, February 26, 1856.

21. Julian, p. 320.

22. Foner (ed.), II, 392.

23. Julian, p. 315.

24. Beveridge, II, 360.

25. David Donald, *Lincoln's Herndon* (New York, 1948), pp. 86–87.

26. *Ibid.*, p. 87; Paul M. Angle (ed.), *Herndon's Life of Lincoln* (New York, 1949), p. 312.

27. J. O. Cunningham, "The Bloomington Convention of 1856 and Those Who Participated in It," *Transactions of the Illinois State Historical Society*, X (1905), 105; Angle (ed.), pp. 312–13; Eastman, *op. cit.*

28. Henry C. Whitney, *Life on the Circuit with Lincoln* (Boston, 1892), I, 76; Willard L. King, *David Davis, Lincoln's Manager* (Cambridge, 1960), p. 104.

29. "Official Record of Convention" [Bloomington, May 30, 1856], in *Transactions of the McLean County Historical Society,* III, 148–66.

30. Cunningham, p. 105.

31. *Ibid.;* "Address by Honorable George Schneider," in *Transactions of the McLean County Historical Society,* III, 93–94.

32. Cunningham, p. 106.

33. *Ibid.,* p. 107.

34. *Ibid.; Transactions of the McLean County Historical Society,* III, 174; Angle (ed.), *Herndon's Life of Lincoln,* p. 312.

35. Ward Hill Lamon, *Life of Abraham Lincoln* (Boston, 1872), pp. 210, 376.

36. Alton *Courier,* June 5, 1856, in Angle (ed.), *Herndon's Life of Lincoln,* p. 313; General Thomas J. Henderson of Princeton, Illinois, made these remarks in May, 1900. See *Transactions of the McLean County Historical Society,* III, 81.

37. Angle (ed.), *Herndon's Life of Lincoln,* p. 313.

38. *Transaction of the McLean County Historical Society,* III, 160–61.

39. Eastman, p. 671.

40. Basler *et al.* (eds.), II, 366.

8 · LOVEJOY IS ELECTED TO CONGRESS: 1856

1. Philip S. Foner (ed.), *The Life and Writings of Frederick Douglass,* (New York, 1950), II, 398.

2. William E. Smith, *Francis Preston Blair Family in Politics* (New York, 1933), p. 359; New York *Tribune,* June 18, 1856. These are the principal sources used here in the discussion of the Philadelphia Republican Convention. See also Green B. Raum, *History of Illinois Republicanism* (Chicago, 1900), p. 30; Roy F. Nichols, *The Disruption of American Democracy* (New York, 1948), *passim;* and Allan Nevins, *Ordeal of the Union* (New York, 1947), II.

3. *Proceedings of the First Three Republican National Conventions of 1856, 1860, and 1864* (Minneapolis, 1893), p. 30; New York *Tribune,* June 18, 1856.

4. *Proceedings . . . First Three . . . Conventions,* p. 57.

5. Albert J. Beveridge, *Abraham Lincoln, 1809–1858* (Boston and New York, 1928), II, 431; Nevins, pp. 488–89.

6. *Ibid.*

7. *The Liberator,* September 5, 1856, quoted in Herbert Aptheker (ed.), *A Documentary History of the Negro People in the United States* (New York, 1951), p. 388; Foner (ed.), II, 400.

8. Charles L. Kelsey in *Bureau County Republican*, June 16, 1864; Bloomington *Daily Pantagraph*, July 16, 1856.

9. Ottawa *Republican*, July 5, 1856, Urbana *Union*, July 10, 1856, in David Davis Papers, Chicago Historical Society; Willard L. King, *David Davis, Lincoln's Manager* (Cambridge, 1960), pp. 113–14.

10. A. Lincoln to David Davis, July 7, 1856, David Davis Papers; A. Lincoln to H. C. Whitney, July 9, 1856, in Roy P. Basler, Marion Dolores Pratt, and Lloyd A. Dunlap (eds.), *The Collected Works of Abraham Lincoln* (New Brunswick, 1953), II, 347.

11. Bloomington *Daily Pantagraph*, June 4, 11, July 9, 16, 1856; Cyrus Aldrich to David Davis, July 14, 1856, David Davis Papers.

12. T. Lyle Dickey to John Dickey, July 29, 1856, in Isabel Wallace, *Life and Letters of General W. H. L. Wallace* (Chicago, 1909), pp. 73–74.

13. *Ibid.*, Bloomington *Daily Pantagraph*, July 23, 1856.

14. *Ibid.*

15. *Ibid.*, July 23, 1856, November 17, 1906.

16. *Ibid.*, July 16, 23, 1856.

17. David Davis to T. Lyle Dickey, July 18, 1856, in Wallace, pp. 74–76.

18. *Ibid.*

19. *Ibid.*

20. *Ibid.*, p. 76.

21. J. E. McClun to A. Lincoln, July 21, 1856, David Davis Papers.

22. *Ibid.*

23. Thomas Knox to Owen Lovejoy, July 29, 1856, Owen Lovejoy Collection, Bureau County Historical Society, Princeton, Illinois. A typewritten copy is at the society's museum and it may be in error in using the name Thomas Knox. A better known name was that of Joseph Knox of Rock Island, an attorney and Republican politician, who spoke in Princeton on July 4, 1856. See also Clark E. Carr, *My Day and Generation* (Chicago, 1908), p. 273, for a personal recollection of the July 4 meeting, where he heard "Joe" Knox speaking. T. Lyle Dickey to Owen Lovejoy, July 30, 1856, Owen Lovejoy Collection.

24. Owen Lovejoy to T. Lyle Dickey, no date, Owen Lovejoy Collection.

25. Wallace, p. 80; Bloomington *Daily Pantagraph*, August 13, 1856.

26. Paul M. Angle, *Lincoln, 1854–1861; Being the Day-By-Day Activities of Abraham Lincoln* (Springfield, 1933), pp. 142, 144, 145; Bloomington *Daily Pantagraph*, October 1, 1856.

27. Bloomington *Daily Pantagraph*, October 1, 1856.

28. Angle, *Lincoln, 1854–1861*, pp. 144, 145; Bloomington *Daily Pantagraph*, October 15, 1856.

29. Bloomington *Daily Pantagraph*, October 29, 1856.

30. October 31, 1856, in David Davis Papers.

31. *Ibid.*

32. C. H. Moore to David Davis, November 3, 1856, David Davis Papers.

33. Bloomington *Daily Pantagraph*, November 17, 1858.

34. Owen Lovejoy to Gerrit Smith, November 18, 1856, Gerrit Smith Papers, Syracuse University Library; *Bureau County Republican*, June 16, 1864; *Western Citizen*, May 6, 1846.

35. *Bureau County Republican*, June 16, 1864; January 11, 1912.

9 · IN THE THIRTY-FIFTH CONGRESS

1. John B. McMaster, *A History of the People of the United States, from the Revolution to the Civil War* (New York, 1915), VIII, 291; New York *Tribune*, April 4, 1857; D. W. Mitchell, *Ten Years in the United States*, p. 328, cited in Allan Nevins, *The Emergence of Lincoln* (New York, 1950), II, 179.

2. Owen Lovejoy to Gerrit Smith, November 15, 1856, December 21, 1856, January 20, 1857, Gerrit Smith Papers, Syracuse University Library; Ruth E. Haberkorn, "Owen Lovejoy in Princeton, Illinois," *Journal of the Illinois State Historical Society*, XXXVI (1943), 307.

3. Owen Lovejoy to Gerrit Smith, January 20, 1857, Gerrit Smith Papers.

4. Owen Lovejoy to Lucy Lovejoy, December 8, 1857, Owen Lovejoy Papers, William L. Clements Library, University of Michigan (Ann Arbor).

5. Owen Lovejoy to Sarah Lovejoy, December 8, 1857, Owen Lovejoy Papers.

6. Owen Lovejoy to Gerrit Smith, January 20, 1857, Gerrit Smith Papers.

7. "The House of Representatives," *The Nation*, April 4, 1879.

8. *Congressional Globe*, 35 Congress, 1 Session, p. 131.

9. *Ibid.*, pp. 130–32.

10. *Ibid.*, p. 132.

11. *Ibid.*, p. 201

12. *Ibid.*, p. 392.

13. *Ibid.*, p. 580.

14. *Ibid.*, pp. 752–54.

15. *Bureau County Republican*, March 4, 1858; Pontiac *Sentinel* quoted *ibid.*, March 25, 1858; Owen Lovejoy to Lewis Tappan, March 12, 1858, American Missionary Association Archives, Fisk University, Nashville, Tennessee; New York *Tribune*, February 19, 1858; Urbana *Union* and

Danville *Independent,* cited in *Bureau County Republican,* April 1, 1858.

16. Roy F. Nichols, *The Disruption of American Democracy* (New York, 1948), makes quite clear the nature of the Administration's close dealings with the contractors; and its use of the Utah War to win votes that would help bring Kansas into the Union as a slave state. It seems no accident, as Nichols notes, that on the same day, May 4, 1858, President Buchanan signed (1) the Lecompton bill and (2) the deficiency appropriation bill, against which Lovejoy had taken a leading part in the House.

17. Albert C. Browne, "The Utah Expedition," *Atlantic Monthly* (April, 1859), 478.

18. Nichols, pp. 100–102.

19. *Cong. Globe,* 35, 1, pp. 1256, 1477, 1516–17.

20. *Ibid.,* pp. 1451–52.

21. *Ibid.*

22. *Ibid.,* pp. 1452–53.

23. *Ibid.,* p. 1524.

24. *Ibid.,* p. 1526.

25. *Ibid.,* 38, 1, p. 373

26. *Ibid.,* 35, 1, p. 2861

10 · CAMPAIGN FOR REELECTION IN 1858

1. A. Lincoln to Hon. O. Lovejoy, March 8, 1858, Roy P. Basler, Marion Dolores Pratt, and Lloyd A. Dunlap (eds.), *The Collected Works of Abraham Lincoln* (New Brunswick, 1953), II, 435; Willard L. King, *David Davis, Lincoln's Manager* (Cambridge, 1960), p. 117.

2. O. Lovejoy to "Dear Sir," March 15, April 20, 1858, Illinois State Historical Library, Springfield; *Bureau County Republican,* March 11, April 1, 1858.

3. A. Wardlow to W. H. L. Wallace, May 5, 1858; C. H. Moore to T. Lyle Dickey, June 5, 1858, in Isabel Wallace, *Life and Letters of General W. H. L. Wallace* (Chicago, 1909), pp. 81–84; *Bureau County Republican,* June 1, 1858; the Bloomington *Daily Pantagraph,* June 1, 1858, preferred to wait for the decision of the 3rd Congressional District convention on June 30 before throwing the weight of the press either to Davis or to Lovejoy.

4. David Davis to Ward Hill Lamon, May 25, 1858, David Davis Papers, Chicago Historical Society; *Bureau County Republican,* June 10, 1858; Henry C. Whitney, *Life on the Circuit with Lincoln* (Boston, 1892), p. 81.

5. Davis to Lamon, May 25, 1858, David Davis Papers.

6. Wallace, p. 82; *Bureau County Republican,* June 10, 1858. Jesse Fell, however, was opposed to Davis for Congress in 1858. "I told him [Davis] frankly," Fell wrote, "he was not sufficiently identified with the anti-slavery movement of the times." Bloomington *Daily Pantagraph,* April 11, 1868.

7. Urbana *Union,* May 31, 1858; Chicago *Tribune,* June 4, 1858; David Davis to A. Lincoln, June 14, 1858, Robert Todd Lincoln Papers, Library of Congress, copies in David Davis Papers, Chicago Historical Society.

8. Josh Whitmore to T. Lyle Dickey, June 5, 1858, in Wallace, pp. 83–84; Ward Hill Lamon to A. Lincoln, June 9, 1858, Library of Congress; C. H. Moore to T. Lyle Dickey, June 5, 1858, in Wallace, p. 81; Robert H. Browne, *Abraham Lincoln and the Men of His Time* (Cincinnati, 1901; rev. ed. Chicago, 1907), II, 171; Bloomington *Daily Pantagraph,* June 9, 1858, provided the breakdown of votes by counties.

9. Robert H. Browne, pp. 170–76. The shrewd Lincoln scholar William E. Baringer observed that Browne's works were "pious, ponderous, erratic, yet containing much interesting reminiscence." See Baringer, *Lincoln's Rise to Power* (Boston, 1937)

10. Whitmore to Dickey, June 5, 1858; Davis to Wallace, June 7, 1858, in Wallace, pp. 83–84; Ottawa *Republican,* June 9, 1858; Lamon to Lincoln, June 9, 1858; David Davis to A. Lincoln, June 14, 1858, Library of Congress, copy in David Davis Papers. The Bloomington *Daily Pantagraph,* June 7, 1858, said that the vote and the sentiment for Lovejoy at the June 5 meeting was large; and that Fell's resolution endorsing Lovejoy was adopted.

11. Davis to Lincoln, June 14, 1858, David Davis Papers.

12. James W. Somers to A. Lincoln, June 22, 1858, Library of Congress, copy in David Davis Papers.

13. Lamon to Lincoln, June 9, 1858, David Davis Papers.

14. Lincoln to Lamon, June 11, 1858, in Basler *et al.* (eds.), II, 458; Davis to Lincoln, June 14, 1858.

15. Lincoln to Lamon, June 11, 1858, in Basler *et al.* (eds.), II, 458–59; Edward Magdol, "Owen Lovejoy's Role in the Campaign of 1858," *Journal of the Illinois State Historical Society,* LI (1958), 403–16.

16. *Bureau County Republican,* June 17, 1858; Albert J. Beveridge, *Abraham Lincoln, 1809–1858* (Boston and New York, 1928), II, 572.

17. Basler *et al.* (eds.), II, 461–69.

18. Robert H. Browne, II, 210.

19. Basler *et al.* (eds.), II, 461.

20. Robert H. Browne, II, 210.

21. *Bureau County Republican,* July 8, 1858; Bloomington *Daily Pantagraph,* July 2, 1858. It is also interesting to note that the resolutions

committee included two pro-Lovejoy editors: Edward J. Lewis of the *Pantagraph* and Philip Cook of the Pontiac *Sentinel* in Livingston County

22. *Bureau County Republican* (no date) "Extra," containing "Remarks of Mr. Lovejoy on receiving the Nomination at the Convention Held at Joliet, June 30th."

23. *Ibid.*, July 22, 29, 1858.

24. *Ibid.*, August 12, 1858; Willard L. King, p. 120; Joliet *Signal*, July 27, 1858, in Beveridge, II, 566.

25. H. C. Whitney to A. Lincoln, July 31, 1858, Library of Congress.

26. *Ibid.*

27. *Ibid.*

28. David Davis to A. Lincoln, August 2, 1858, David Davis Papers.

29. A. Lincoln to Henry C. Whitney, August 2, 1858; A. Lincoln to Burton C. Cook, same date; A. Lincoln to Joseph O. Glover, August 9, 1858; all in Basler *et al.* (eds.), II, 534, 532, 537.

30. Owen Lovejoy to A. Lincoln, August 4, 1858, Library of Congress.

31. *Bureau County Republican*, August 26, 1858; Charles W. Marsh, *Recollections, 1837–1910* (Chicago, 1910), pp. 74–75; Chicago *Press and Tribune*, August 26, 1858, in Paul M. Angle (ed.), *Created Equal?; The Complete Lincoln-Douglas Debates of 1858* (Chicago, 1958), p. 102; Allan Nevins, *The Emergence of Lincoln*, (New York, 1950), II, 376.

32. Angle (ed.), *Created Equal?*, pp. 103–137; Marsh, p. 75.

33. *Bureau County Republican*, August 26, 1858; Chicago *Daily Journal*, in Paul M. Angle, *Lincoln, 1854–1861; Being the Day-By-Day Activities of Abraham Lincoln* (Springfield, 1933), p. 242.

34. Robert H. Browne, II, 227–30; Angle (ed.), *Created Equal?*, p. 138; Angle says that Lincoln spent the night of August 26 at Amboy, which is about twenty-five miles away

35. *Bureau County Republican*, August 26, 1858. In the Ottawa debate, Douglas attributed these resolutions to the radical abolitionists' convention in Springfield on October 5, 1854. Lincoln denied knowing of the resolutions or attending the meeting; he also pointed out, in the Freeport debate, that the resolutions read by Douglas were not passed at Springfield but at "some convention or public meeting in Kane County." Douglas admitted the error in regard to the place where the resolutions originated and in his "correction" attributed them to a convention at Rockford on August 30, 1854, that also nominated Elihu B. Washburne for Congress; Paul Selby, "Genesis of the Republican Party in Illinois," *Transactions of the Illinois State Historical Society*, XI (1906), 270–83.

36. Benjamin Shaw, "Owen Lovejoy, Constitutional Abolitionists and the Republican Party," *Transactions of the McLean County Historical Society*, III (1900), 72.

37. Angle, *Created Equal?*, p. 178.
38. *Ibid.*, pp. 178–79.
39. *Bureau County Republican*, September 9, 1858.
40. *Ibid.*
41. *Ibid.*, September 16, 1858; Angle, *Created Equal?*, pp. 186–87.
42. Wallace, p. 85.
43. Bloomington *Daily Pantagraph*, November 17, 1858.
44. Henry C. Whitney, p. 411. Robert H. Browne, II, 241, offered his version of a different appraisal by Lincoln. He wrote that after the election Lincoln said to him, "You are young and ambitious and partial to me. I appreciate the good wishes of young men, independent enough to have stood the slang against Abolitionists, as you have for years, and I admire your courageous work for Mr. Lovejoy. I am glad that your judgment has been sustained." In the same work, pp. 252–53, Browne wrote that Lincoln later came "to the Urbana court, and was there a day or two. He congratulated us on our thousand majority for Lovejoy We had a pleasant day with him, and he was in the best of humor."

Whitney was no doubt pressing his own prejudice *against* Lovejoy, while Browne was revealing his *for* the abolitionist congressman. His memory of a "thousand majority" does not agree with the vote for Lovejoy in Champaign County. Rather, a thousand was the figure for the De Witt, Champaign, and McLean counties' combined majority for Lovejoy.

11 · HIS REPUTATION IS NATIONAL

1. *Congressional Globe*, 35 Congress, 2 Session, Part 1, p. 547.
2. *Ibid.*, p. 1070.
3. *Ibid.*, p. 1132.
4. *Ibid.*, p. 1127.
5. *Bureau County Republican*, May 26, 1859.
6. *Free West*, June 7, 1855; the pamphlet "Letter from J. C. Lovejoy, Esq., to His Brother, Hon. Owen Lovejoy, M. C. " (Boston, 1859).
7. Chicago *Press and Tribune*, July 2, 1858; Ruth E. Haberkorn, "Owen Lovejoy in Princeton, Illinois," *Journal of the Illinois State Historical Society*, XXXVI (1943), 288; Owen Lovejoy, " An Agricultural Poem . . . delivered before the Bureau County Agricultural Society, October 1859, Princeton, Illinois" (Princeton, 1862).
8. Owen Lovejoy to Charles Sumner, November 23, 1859, Harvard University Library; Edward L. Pierce (ed.), *Memoirs and Letters of Charles Sumner* (Boston, 1877–1893), III, 602.
9. Richard B. Morris, *Fair Trial* (New York, 1953), pp. 259–60, quoted

in Louis Ruchames (ed.), *A John Brown Reader* (London and New York, 1959), p. 29.

10. Ruchames, p. 159; Allan Nevins, *The Emergence of Lincoln* (New York, 1950), II, 98–101.

11. *Cong. Globe,* 36, 1, p. 16.

12. Owen Lovejoy to Henry Asbury, January 30, 1860, Illinois State Historical Library.

13. *Cong. Globe,* 36, 1, Appendix, p. 174.

14. Roy M. Robbins, *Our Landed Heritage; the Public Domain, 1776–1936* (Princeton, New Jersey, 1942), pp. 178–82; James T. Du Bois and Gertrude S. Mathews, *Galusha A. Grow, Father of the Homestead Law* (New York, 1917), pp. 204, 220ff.; *Bureau County Republican,* April 5, 1860.

15. Nevins, p. 124; Owen Lovejoy to Eunice Lovejoy, April 6, 1860, Owen Lovejoy Papers, William L. Clements Library, University of Michigan (Ann Arbor).

16. *Ibid.*

17. Owen Lovejoy to Joshua Reed Giddings, May 7, 1860, Giddings Collection, Ohio Historical Society, Columbus.

18. *Cong. Globe,* 36, 1, Appendix, pp. 202–07; New York *Tribune,* April 6 and 7, 1860; Washington *National Intelligencer,* April 6, 1860; Henry B. Stanton, *Random Recollections* (New York, 1886), p. 104.

19. Owen Lovejoy to Joshua Reed Giddings, May 7, 1860, Giddings Collection.

20. Owen Lovejoy to Eunice Lovejoy, April 6, 1860; Owen Lovejoy to "My Dear Sir," April 9, 1860, Owen Lovejoy Collection, Bureau County Historical Society, Princeton, Illinois.

21. George V. Bohman, "Owen Lovejoy on 'The Barbarism of Slavery,' April 5, 1860," in J. Jeffrey Auer (ed.), *Antislavery and Disunion, 1858–1861: Studies in the Rhetoric of Compromise and Conflict* (New York and Evanston, 1963), p. 121; Washington *National Intelligencer,* April 6, 1860; Peoria *Daily Transcript,* April 20, 1860; James S. Pike, *First Blows of the Civil War* (New York, 1879), pp. 506–07.

22. Bloomington *Daily Pantagraph,* May 28, 1900; *Bureau County Republican,* April 19, 1860; *Central Illinois Gazette,* April 25, 1860. The New York *Tribune* proposed that a printing of two million copies should be circulated throughout the country. Today, a number of libraries have copies of the English version as well as of a German translation, in pamphlet form.

12 · THE ELECTION OF 1860

1. *Central Illinois Gazette,* April 25, 1860; Lovejoy's letter to Peoria *Daily Transcript,* March 5, 1860, in Frank I. Herriott, "The Conference of the German Republicans in the Deutsches Haus, Chicago, May 14–15, 1860," *Transactions of the Illinois State Historical Society,* XXXV (1928), 120–21.

2. Owen Lovejoy to Jesse Fell, May 28, 1860, Bloomington *Daily Pantagraph,* May 28, 1900.

3. Owen Lovejoy to Hon. A. Lincoln, June 10, 1860, Abraham Lincoln Collection, Library of Congress.

4. Owen Lovejoy to Jesse Fell, June 16, 1860, Bloomington *Daily Pantagraph,* May 28, 1900.

5. [William W.] Orme to Ward Hill Lamon, April 23, 1860, David Davis Papers, Chicago Historical Society.

6. Owen Lovejoy to Jesse Fell, June 27, 1860, Bloomington *Daily Pantagraph,* May 28, 1900.

7. *Bureau County Republican,* July 5, 1860; *Central Illinois Gazette,* July 11, 1860; Owen Lovejoy to Jesse Fell, June 27, 1860.

8. *Bureau County Republican,* July 19, 1860.

9. *Ibid.,* July 26, 1860; Racine *Daily Journal,* August 15, 1860; Owen Lovejoy to Jesse Fell, July 21, 1860, Bloomington *Daily Pantagraph,* May 28, 1900.

10. *Bureau County Republican,* August 2, 9, 1860; *Central Illinois Gazette,* August 1, 8, 1860; Ezra M. Prince, "Reminiscences of Owen Lovejoy," Bloomington *Daily Pantagraph,* November 17, 1906; Owen Lovejoy to Thurlow Weed, July 24, 1860, Thurlow Weed Collection, University of Rochester.

11. Owen Lovejoy to Hon. W. H. Seward, July 24, 1860, William Henry Seward Collection, University of Rochester.

12. Owen Lovejoy to W. H. Seward, August 14, 1860, Seward Collection.

13. O. Lovejoy to Gov. Seward, September 18, 1860, Seward Collection.

14. Owen Lovejoy to Charles Sumner, September 21, 1860, Harvard University.

15. Benjamin Shaw, "Owen Lovejoy, Constitutional Abolitionists and the Republican Party," *Transactions of the McLean County Historical Society,* III (1900), 71.

16. *Bureau County Republican,* October 4, 1860.

17. Chicago *Press and Tribune,* October 3, 1860.

18. *Ibid.*

19. *Ibid.;* Racine *Advocate,* October 10, 17, 1860; Racine *Daily Journal,* October 19, 1860.

20. Chicago *Press and Tribune,* October 18, 1860.

21. *Bureau County Republican,* November 1, 1860.

22. *Ibid.*

23. *Ibid.,* November 8, 15, 1860; D. W. Lusk, *Eighty Years of Illinois; Anecdotes and Incidents; Politics and Politicians: A Succinct History of the State, 1809–1889* (Springfield, 1889), p. 103.

24. *Bureau County Republican,* November 15, 1860.

25. Two complementary interpretations of the success of the Republican party in the 1860 elections are by Glyndon G. Van Deusen, "Why the Republican Party Came to Power," in George H. Knoles (ed.), *The Crisis of the Union, 1860–1861* (Baton Rouge, 1965), pp. 3–20; and by Don Fehrenbacher in the same volume, p. 29. Essentially, they say, the party won because it was an antislavery party. Van Deusen also attributes success to the Free Soil planks. Another view supporting the Free Soil but especially the free labor aspect of the party platform is in Philip S. Foner, *History of the Labor Movement in the United States* (New York, 1947), I, 289–96.

13 · THE SECESSION CRISIS

1. J. H. Hammond to Maj. M. C. M. Hammond, April 23, 1860, in John B. McMaster, *A History of the People of the United States, from the Revolution to the Civil War* (New York, 1915), VIII, 445–46; Ashmore's statement in Roy F. Nichols, *The Disruption of American Democracy* (New York, 1962 ed.), p. 369.

2. Philip S. Foner, *Business and Slavery: The New York Merchants and the Irrepressible Conflict* (Chapel Hill, 1941), p. 230; David M. Potter, *Lincoln and His Party in the Secession Crisis* (New Haven, 1942), chapter 5. The pro-Breckenridge Washington, D. C., *Constitution* (September 6, 1860) complained that moderate Republicans "occupy back seats in the synagogue, and play second fiddle to Lovejoy and Sumner," quoted in Howard C. Perkins (ed.), *Northern Editorials on Secession* (New York, 1942), p. 32; Kenneth M. Stampp, *And the War Came* (Baton Rouge, 1950), p. 22.

3. Philip S. Foner, *History of the Labor Movement in the United States from Colonial Times to the Founding of the American Federation of Labor* (New York, 1947), pp. 298–303.

4. A. Lincoln to Lyman Trumbull, December 10, 1860; A. Lincoln to William P. Kellogg, December 11, 1860; A. Lincoln to E. B. Washburne, December 13, 1860; all in Roy P. Basler, Marion Dolores Pratt and Lloyd

A. Dunlap (eds.), *The Collected Works of Abraham Lincoln* (New Brunswick, 1953), IV, 149–51.

5. Owen Lovejoy to Bronson Murray, December 11, 1860, New York Historical Society; Potter, p. 16.

6. *Congessional Globe*, 36 Congress, 2 Session, p. 109.

7. *Ibid.*, pp. 279, 281.

8. *Ibid.*, p. 457.

9. *Ibid.*, Appendix, pp. 84–87.

10. *Bureau County Republican*, February 7, 1861.

11. *Cong. Globe*, 36, 2, pp. 621–22.

12. Stampp, pp. 137, 148.

13. Potter, p. 39.

14. Foner, *Business and Slavery*, pp. 227–32; Potter, pp. 121–22, 185–86; Stampp, p. 221.

15. Emily V. Mason to Thomas Rowland, February 15, 1861, John T Mason Papers, Detroit Public Library.

16. *Cong. Globe*, 36, 2, p. 1236.

17. Thomas M. Eddy, *The Patriotism of Illinois* (Chicago, 1865), pp. 48–49.

18. *Bureau County Republican*, January 24, 1861.

19. A. Lincoln to James T. Hale, January 11, 1861, in Basler *et al.* (eds.), IV, 172.

20. Owen Lovejoy to Abraham Lincoln, March 27, 1861, Abraham Lincoln Collection, Library of Congress; *Bureau County Republican*, April 25, 1861.

21. *Bureau County Republican*, May 2, 9, 1861.

22. *Central Illinois Gazette*, May 22, 1861.

14 · FOR A VIGOROUS PROSECUTION OF THE WAR

1. Owen Lovejoy to Hon. J. R. Giddings, November 23, 1860, Ohio Historical Society, Columbus.

2. Owen Lovejoy, John F. Farnsworth, and E. B. Washburne to A. Lincoln, January 18, 1861, Abraham Lincoln Collection, Library of Congress.

3. Francis Milton I. Morehouse, *The Life of Jesse Fell* (Urbana, 1916), p. 66.

4. *Bureau County Republican*, June 13, 1861.

5. Ralph Korngold, *Two Friends of Man: The Story of William Lloyd Garrison and Wendell Phillips and Their Relationship with Abraham Lincoln* (Boston, 1950), p. 289; Philip S. Foner (ed.), *The Life and Writings of Frederick Douglass* (New York, 1950–1955), III, 94.

6. New York *Tribune*, July 7, 1861.

7. Richard S. West, Jr., *Lincoln's Scapegoat General: A Life of Benjamin F. Butler, 1818–1893* (Boston, 1965), p. 83.

8. Benjamin Quarles, *The Negro in the Civil War* (Boston, 1953), pp. 56–66.

9. Foner (ed.), III, 125.

10. *Congressional Globe*, 37 Congress, 1 Session, pp. 24, 32; Owen Lovejoy to Charles Sumner, July 11, 1861, Harvard University Library.

11. Foner (ed.), III, 126, 149.

12. New York *Tribune*, July 7, 28, 1861; Allan Nevins, *The War for the Union* (New York, 1960), I, 339.

13. New York *Tribune*, July 28, 1861.

14. Nevins, *War for the Union*, p. 190; Albert G. Riddle, *Recollections of War Times: Reminiscences of Men and Events in Washington, 1860–1865* (New York, 1895), p. 41.

15. James G. Blaine, *Twenty Years of Congress from Lincoln to Garfield* (Norwich, Connecticut, 1884), I, 337.

16. *Cong. Globe*, 37, 1, pp. 248, 269, 287, 304, 323, 325; New York *Tribune*, July 26, 1861.

17. *Bureau County Republican*, August 8, 1861, quotes Waukegan *Gazette*.

15 · ON THE BATTLEFIELDS: SUMMER, 1861

1. *Bureau County Republican*, August 29, 1861.

2. *Ibid.*, August 15, 1861. Lovejoy's own account was in a speech on August 24 at Princeton and was reported, without quoting him, in the August 29 issue of the *Republican*; Jay Monaghan, *The Man Who Elected Lincoln* (Indianapolis and New York, 1956), pp. 234ff.

3. Monaghan, p. 249; Lovejoy in *Bureau County Republican*, August 29, 1861.

4. *Ibid.*

5. James Sesley, Jr., Chief Clerk, War Department, to Col. Owen Lovejoy, July 31, 1861, Owen Lovejoy Collection, Bureau County Historical Society, Princeton, Illinois; Simon Cameron to Owen Lovejoy (telegram), August 17, 1861, Illinois State Historical Society, Springfield.

6. Owen Lovejoy to *Bureau County Republican*, September 5, 1861 (his letter was dated September 3).

7. Richard Yates to O. Lovejoy, September 25, 1861, Owen Lovejoy Collection; Owen Lovejoy to *Bureau County Republican*, September 28, 1861.

8. Allan Nevins, *The War for the Union* (New York, 1960), I, 309.

9. Owen Lovejoy to *Bureau County Republican,* October 12, 1861; Lovejoy to "My Dear Bess" (probably his sister Elizabeth), October 2, 1861, Owen Lovejoy Papers, William L. Clements Library, University of Michigan (Ann Arbor).

10. *Bureau County Republican,* October 12, 1861.

11. *Ibid.;* John Raymond Howard, *Remembrance of Things Past* (New York, 1925), p. 157.

12. Owen Lovejoy to *Bureau County Republican,* October 12, 1861.

13. *Ibid.* (letter of October 31), November 14, 1861.

14. *Ibid.;* Owen Lovejoy to Sarah Lovejoy, October 28, 1861, Owen Lovejoy Papers.

15. Owen Lovejoy to "My Dear Mary," October 1, 1861, Owen Lovejoy Papers; Thomas J. McCormack (ed.), *Memoirs of Gustave Koerner, 1809–1896* (Cedar Rapids, 1909), II, 182.

16. Owen Lovejoy to *Bureau County Republican,* November 14, 1861 (letter of October 31).

17. Owen Lovejoy to his sons, October 6, 1861; Owen Lovejoy, to Lucy Lovejoy, October 22, 1861; both in Owen Lovejoy Papers.

18. Owen Lovejoy to *Bureau County Republican,* November 21, 1861 (letter of November 7); Dudley T. Cornish, *The Sable Arm: Negro Troops in the Union Army, 1861–1865* (New York, 1956), p. 13.

19. *Bureau County Republican,* December 5, 1861.

20. Lovejoy to *Bureau County Republican,* November 21, 1861.

16 · THE REVOLUTIONARY THIRTY-SEVENTH CONGRESS

1. Rev. D. Heagle, "The Great Anti-Slavery Agitator, Hon. Owen Lovejoy" (Princeton, Illinois, 1885), p. 35.

2. *Bureau County Republican,* December 5, 1861.

3. New York *Tribune,* December 3, 1861; *Bureau County Republican,* December 12, 1861.

4. Allan Nevins, *The War for the Union* (New York, 1959), I, 401.

5. W. H. Russell, *My Diary North and South* (Boston, 1863), p. 582; *Bureau County Republican,* December 19, 1861; New York *Tribune,* December 12, 1861.

6. *Bureau County Republican,* December 12, 1861.

7. Lincoln's Message to Congress, in Roy P. Basler, Marion Dolores Pratt, and Lloyd A. Dunlap (eds.), *The Collected Works of Abraham Lincoln* (New Brunswick, 1953), V, 35–53.

8. Albert G. Riddle, *Recollections of War Times: Reminiscences of Men and Events in Washington, 1860–1865* (New York, 1895), p. 41; *Congressional Globe,* 37 Congress, 2 Session, p. 5.

9. Carl Sandburg, *Abraham Lincoln: The War Years* (New York, 1939), I, 358–69; Nevins, *War for the Union*, I, 387–94; *Cong. Globe*, 37, 2, p. 333.

10. *Cong. Globe*, 37, 2, p. 333.

11. *Bureau County Republican*, February 27, 1862.

12 *Cong. Globe*, 37, 2, pp. 16, 33, 35; New York *Tribune*, December 6, 10, 12, 21, 1861.

13. New York *Tribune*, December 12 and 13, 1861; *Cong. Globe*, 37, 2, p. 57.

14. *Cong. Globe*, 37, 2, pp. 58–59.

15. *Ibid.*

16. *Ibid.*

17. James G. Blaine, *Twenty Years of Congress, from Lincoln to Garfield* (Norwich, Connecticut, 1884), I, 380; George W. Julian, *Political Recollections 1840–1872* (Chicago, 1884), p.366; *Cong. Globe*, 37, 2, p. 194.

18. *Cong. Globe*, 37, 2, p. 194.

19. *Ibid.*, pp. 102–04.

20. Chicago *Tribune*, January 9, 1862; *Bureau County Republican*, January 16, 1862.

21. William A. Crofutt, *An American Procession, 1855–1914* (Boston, 1931), pp. 58–59, 71.

22. Chicago *Tribune*, January 13, 1862; *Cong. Globe.*, 37, 2, p. 229.

23. *Bureau County Republican*, April 3, 1862.

17 · THE FIGHT FOR EMANCIPATION POLICIES

1. John B. McMaster, *Our House Divided* (New York, 1961), p. 200. (originally published in 1927 as *A History of the People of the United States During Lincoln's Administration*).

2. James M. McPherson, *The Struggle for Equality, Abolitionists and the Negro in the Civil War and Reconstruction* (Princeton, New Jersey, 1964), pp. 85, 95–96.

3. *Congressional Globe*, 37 Congress, 2 Session, p. 1170.

4. New York *Tribune*, December 21, 1861; *Cong. Globe*, 37, 2, p. 158; Henry Wilson, *History of the Antislavery Measures of the Thirty-Seventh and Thirty-Eighth Congresses, 1861–64* (Boston, 1864), p. 173.

5. New York *Tribune*, December 12, 1861.

6. Owen Lovejoy to "My Dear Children," February 23, 1862, Owen Lovejoy Papers, William L. Clements Library, University of Michigan (Ann Arbor).

7. James G. Blaine, *Twenty Years of Congress, from Lincoln to Garfield* (Norwich, Connecticut, 1884), I, 372.

8. *Ibid.*, Isaac Newton Arnold, *The Life of Abraham Lincoln* (Chicago, 1885), p. 229.

9. *Cong. Globe*, 37, 2, pp. 1367–68; McMaster, p. 200.

10. *Cong. Globe*, 37, 2, p. 1645.

11. *Ibid.*, p. 1646.

12. Blaine, I, 369–70.

13. *Bureau County Republican*, April 14, 1862.

14. *Ibid.*

15. *Ibid.;* Benjamin Quarles, *The Negro in the Civil War* (Boston, 1953), p. 141; Philip S. Foner (ed.), *The Life and Writings of Frederick Douglass* (New York, 1950–55), III, 233–34.

16. *Cong. Globe*, 37, 2, p. 1805; *Bureau County Republican*, May 1, 1862; Chicago *Tribune*, April 25, 1862.

17. *Cong. Globe*, 37, 2, p. 1818.

18. Wilson, p. 93.

19. *Ibid.*, p. 94; Chicago *Tribune*, May 2, 9, 1862; New York *Times*, May 9, 1862; *Cong. Globe*, 37, 2, pp. 1906, 2030, 2041.

20. New York *Times*, May 10, 1862; George B. McClellan, *McClellan's Own Story; the War for the Union* (New York, 1887), p. 355.

21. *Cong. Globe*, 37, 2, pp. 2041–46; Chicago *Tribune*, May 10, 11, 1862; Wilson, pp. 96–97.

22. *Cong. Globe*, 37, 2, pp. 2052, 2054; Wilson, p. 106; Chicago *Tribune*, May 13, 1862.

23. *Cong. Globe*, 37, 2, p. 2769; Wilson, pp. 105–06.

24. Chicago *Tribune*, May 14, June 21, 1862.

25. New York *Tribune*, May 14, 1862.

26. Quarles, pp. 27, 29.

27. Ellis P. Oberholtzer, *Jay Cooke, Financier of the Civil War* (Philadelphia, 1907), I, 197; Allan Nevins, *The War for the Union* (New York, 1960), II, 9.

28. Arnold, pp. 251–56; A. Lincoln to A. G. Hodges, April 4, 1864, in Roy P. Basler, Marion Dolores Pratt, and Lloyd A. Dunlap (eds.), *The Collected Works of Abraham Lincoln* (New Brunswick, 1953), VII, 281–82.

29. Owen Lovejoy to William Lloyd Garrison, February 22, 1864, in Wendell P. and Francis J. Garrison, *William Lloyd Garrison, 1805–1879: The Story of His Life Told by His Children* (New York, 1886–1889), IV, 97–99; Eckert's story in Paul M. Angle (ed.), *The Lincoln Reader* (New Brunswick, 1947), p. 405.

30. Allen Thorndike Rice (ed.), *Reminiscences of Abraham Lincoln by Distinguished Men of His Time* (New York, 1886), pp. 530–31.

31. New York *Times* and New York *Tribune*, June 13, 1862.

32. New York *Times,* same date.
33. Owen Lovejoy to Lucy and Mary Lovejoy, June 15, 1862, Owen Lovejoy Papers; Peter Cooper to Hon. Owen Lovejoy, June 24, 1862, Owen Lovejoy Collection, Bureau County Historical Society, Princeton, Illinois; New York *Independent,* June 19, 1862.
34. John H. Bryant to Owen Lovejoy, June 30, 1862, Owen Lovejoy Collection.
35. Edward L. Pierce (ed.), *Memoir and Letters of Charles Sumner* (Boston, 1877–1893), IV, 83; Ralph Korngold, *Thaddeus Stevens, a Being Darkly Wise and Rudely Great* (New York, 1955), p. 185.
36. New York *Tribune,* July 19, 1862.
37. *Daily Milwaukee News,* August 2, 1862; Chicago *Tribune,* August 2, 1862; Thomas M. Eddy, *The Patriotism of Illinois* (Chicago, 1865), I, 521ff.; D. W. Lusk, *Eighty Years of Illinois; Anecdotes and Incidents; Politics and Politicians: A Succinct History of the State, 1809–1889* (Springfield, 1889), p. 127.
38. E. G. Spaulding, *History of the Legal Tender Paper Money Issued During the Great Rebellion* (Buffalo, 1869), *passim;* Robert P. Sharkey, *Money, Class and Party: An Economic Study of Civil War and Reconstruction* (Baltimore, 1959), pp. 24, 28, 34; Wesley C. Mitchell, *A History of the Greenbacks* (Chicago, 1903), *passim;* Blaine, I, 399, 407ff.
39. *Ibid.;* Fawn M. Brodie, *Thaddeus Stevens, Scourge of the South* (New York, 1959), chapter 14 *passim.*
40. *Cong. Globe,* 37, 2, p. 691; Chicago *Tribune,* February 14, 1862.
41. Hewitt wrote in the *Bureau County Republican* of February 10, 1862, that Lovejoy believed the people would rather pay a heavy tax than hazard the experiment of flooding the country with irredeemable paper currency.
42. Blaine, I, pp. 415–16, 421.
43. *Cong. Globe,* 37, 2, p. 2885.
44. *Cong. Globe,* 37, 3, pp. 344–45.
45. *Ibid.*
46. *Ibid.,* p. 346.
47. *Ibid.,* p. 347.
48. *Ibid.,* p. 346.
49. *Ibid.,* pp. 346, 830–31; *Bureau County Republican,* February 20, 1863.
50. United States Department of Agriculture, *Yearbook, 1940* (Washington, D. C., 1940), pp. 246ff.
51. Basler *et al.* (eds.), V, p. 46; Joseph F. McGuire, "Owen Lovejoy, Congressman from the Prairie" (thesis for Master of Science in Education), Illinois State Normal University, Studies in Education, No. 137 (Normal, 1950), p. 78; *Cong. Globe,* 37, 2, pp. 629, 856; *Bureau County*

Republican, February 20, 1862; United States Department of Agriculture, *Yearbook, 1940,* p. 246.

52. *Bureau County Republican,* May 15, 1862.

53. *Cong. Globe,* 37, 2, p. 14.

54. *Bureau County Republican,* June 12, 1862; Roy M. Robbins, *Our Landed Heritage; the Public Domain, 1776–1936* (Princeton, New Jersey, 1942), pp. 178–82.

55. *Cong. Globe,* 37, 2, pp. 1698–1700; *Bureau County Republican,* April 24, 1862.

56. *Cong. Globe,* 37, 2, p. 1708; Robert R. Russel, *Improvement of Communications with the Pacific Coast as an Issue in American Politics* (Cedar Rapids, 1948), p. 301.

57. *Ibid.,* pp. 1950, 1971; *Bureau County Republican,* April 24, 1862.

18 · THE BITTER CAMPAIGN OF 1862

1. *Bureau County Republican,* August 28, 1862.

2. *Ibid.;* B. C. Cook in Chicago *Tribune,* June 12, 1874; Allan Nevins, *The War for the Union* (New York, 1960), II, 308.

3. *Bureau County Republican,* September 11, 1862.

4. Peoria *Daily Transcript,* August 27, 1862; *Bureau County Republican,* August 28, 1862.

5. New York *Tribune,* August 22, 25, 1862; Roy P. Basler, Marion Dolores Pratt, and Lloyd A. Dunlap (eds.), *The Collected Works of Abraham Lincoln* (New Brunswick, 1953), V, 388–89.

6. Robert H. Browne, *Abraham Lincoln and the Men of His Time* (Cincinnati, rev. ed., 1907), II, 675–79.

7. James M. McPherson, *The Struggle for Equality: Abolitionists and the Negro in the Civil War and Reconstruction* (Princeton, New Jersey, 1964), p. 117.

8. Chicago *Tribune,* September 3, 1862; Hermann R. Muelder, *Fighters for Freedom: The History of Anti-slavery Activities of Men and Women Associated with Knox College* (New York, 1959), p. 340.

9. Peoria *Daily Transcript,* September 12, 1862.

10. *Ibid.,* September 15, 1862.

11. *Ibid.*

12. *Ibid.*

13. Philip S. Foner (ed.), *The Life and Writings of Frederick Douglass* (New York, 1950–55), III, 275.

14. Quincy *Whig* quoted in Peoria *Daily Transcript,* October 28, 1862.

15. *Bureau County Republican,* September 25, 1862; B. C. Cook in Chicago *Tribune,* June 12, 1874.

16. Peoria *Daily Transcript,* October 1, 6, 1862

17. Chicago *Tribune*, October 6, 1862; *Bureau County Republican*, October 16, 1862; Peoria *Daily Transcript*, October 13, 1862.

18. Peoria *Daily Transcript*, November 1, 1862.

19. *Ibid.*, November 12, 1862.

20. *Ibid.*

21. *Ibid.; Bureau County Republican*, November 13, 1862.

22. *Bureau County Republican*, November 27, 1862.

23. Owen Lovejoy to Jesse Fell, December 7, 1862. Fell Manuscripts, Illinois Historical Survey, University of Illinois, Urbana. Copy furnished by Dr. Helen E. Marshall.

24. Boston *Daily Evening Transcript*, November 24, 26, 1862; Boston *Evening Journal*, November 26, 1862; Boston *Commonwealth*, September 27, 1862.

19 · VICTORIES AT LAST: 1863

1. *Congressional Globe*, 37 Congress, 3 Session, pp. 23–24.

2. Owen Lovejoy to Rev. Edwin A. Park, December 17, 1862, Yale University Library.

3. *Cong. Globe*, 37, 3, p. 243.

4. *Ibid.*

5. *Ibid.*

6. *Ibid.*

7. *Ibid.*

8. *Ibid.*, p. 602.

9. *Ibid.*, pp. 598ff.; pp. 689–90.

10. *Bureau County Republican*, February 5, 12, 1863.

11. Benjamin Quarles, *The Negro in the Civil War* (Boston, 1953), *passim.*

12. Thomas Wentworth Higginson, *Army Life in a Black Regiment* (reprint ed., New York, 1962 [original edition, Boston, 1869]), pp. 29, 251.

13. Quarles, 3–10; W. E. B. Du Bois, *Black Reconstruction* (New York, 1935), pp. 110–12; John Hope Franklin, *From Slavery to Freedom, a History of American Negroes* (New York, 1956), pp. 273–74.

14. *Bureau County Republican*, March 12, 19, April 9, 16, 1863; Peoria *Daily Transcript*, March 17, April 8, 1863.

15. Elijah S. Randolph to Owen Lovejoy, May 17, 1863, Owen Lovejoy Papers, William L. Clements Library, University of Michigan (Ann Arbor); Union League of America (U.L.A.), *Proceedings of National Convention, May 20, 21, 1863, at Cleveland, Ohio*.

16. Guy James Gibson, *Lincoln's League: The Union League Movement During the Civil War* (Ann Arbor, 1958), *passim.*

17. U.L.A. *Proceedings,* pp. 31–32.

18. *Bureau County Republican,* June 4, August 13, 1863.

19. Peoria *Daily Transcript,* September 12, 1863; *Bureau County Republican,* October 1, 1863.

20. Chicago *Tribune,* September 7, 1863.

21. *Ibid.*

22. *Bureau County Republican,* October 22, 1863.

23. *Ibid.*

24. *Ibid.*

25. *Ibid.,* November 19, 1863.

26. *Ibid.*

27. *Ibid.;* New York *Independent,* September 10, 1863; Carl Sandburg, *Abraham Lincoln: The War Years* (New York, 1939), II, 396–410.

28. *Bureau County Republican,* December 3, 1863.

29. *Ibid.*

20 · ON PISGAH

1. Owen Lovejoy to William Lloyd Garrison, November 22, 1863, Garrison Collection, Boston Public Library.

2. *Bureau County Republican,* December 10, 17, 1863.

3. Owen Lovejoy to "My Dear Sallie," December 6, 1863, Owen Lovejoy Papers, William L. Clements Library, University of Michigan (Ann Arbor).

4. Tyler Dennett (ed.), *Lincoln and the Civil War in the Diaries and Letters of John Hay* (New York, 1939), p. 131; Carl Sandburg, *Abraham Lincoln: The War Years* (New York, 1939), II, 502.

5. *Congressional Globe,* 38 Congress, 1 Session, pp. 10–11

6. Sandburg, II, 484; Dennett (ed.), p. 132.

7. *Cong. Globe,* 38, 1, p. 20.

8. *Ibid.;* Sandburg, II, 504; IV, 6; W. E. B. Du Bois, *Black Reconstruction* (New York, 1935), p. 207.

9. *Cong. Globe,* 38, 1, pp. 20, 23.

10. Israel Washburn to Owen Lovejoy, December 19, 1863, Owen Lovejoy Collection, Bureau County Historical Society, Princeton, Illinois.

11. Portland *Transcript,* January 2, 1864.

12. *Ibid.*

13. *Ibid.*

14. Francis B. Carpenter, *Six Months at the White House with Abraham Lincoln* (Boston, 1866), pp. 14–15.

15. *Ibid.,* p. 17; Francis B. Carpenter to Hon. Owen Lovejoy, January 15, 1864, Owen Lovejoy Collection.

16. Owen Lovejoy to William Seward, February 18, 1864, William Henry Seward Collection, University of Rochester Library; Owen Lovejoy to John G. Nicolay, February 2, 1864, Abraham Lincoln Collection, Library of Congress.

17. Owen Lovejoy to William Lloyd Garrison, February 22, 1864.

18. Carpenter, pp. 47–48.

19. *Ibid.*, p. 56.

20. Owen Lovejoy to Sarah Lovejoy, March 15, 1864, Owen Lovejoy Papers.

21. New York *Times*, March 25, 27, 1864; Brooklyn *Eagle*, March 25, 1864; Chicago *Tribune*, April 3, 1864.

22. Brooklyn *Daily Union*, March 28, 1864. The "E." Tappan listed by the *Daily Union* seems to be an error. More likely it should have been "A." for Arthur Tappan or "L." for his brother Lewis. They had been active abolitionists for more than thirty years and had known Lovejoy.

23. Carpenter, p. 18; Francis B. Carpenter to Mrs. Owen Lovejoy, May 18, 1865, Owen Lovejoy Collection. In this letter Carpenter reports that Lincoln said, "Lovejoy was the *best* friend I had in Congress." The letter was copied and deposited with the Bureau County Historical Society.

21 · "SUCH MEN SHOULD NEVER DIE"

1. C. L. Kelsey in *Bureau County Republican*, June 16, 1864.

2. This and the following eulogistic remarks in the House of Representatives are recorded in *Congressional Globe*, 38 Congress, 1 Session, pp. 1326–31; those made in the Senate are on pp. 1333–35.

3. Carl Sandburg, *Abraham Lincoln: The War Years* (New York, 1939), II, 555.

4. Chicago *Tribune*, April 4, 1864.

5. Rev. D. Heagle, "The Great Anti-Slavery Agitator, Hon. Owen Lovejoy" (Princeton, Illinois, 1885), p. 16.

6. The funeral description is based on Chicago *Tribune*, April 4, 1864.

7. *Bureau County Republican*, June 9, 1864.

8. Baraboo (Wisconsin) *Republic*, July 11, 1866; A. Lincoln to John H. Bryant, May 30, 1864, in *Bureau County Republican*, June 9, 1864.

9. C. L. Kelsey in *Bureau County Republican*, June 16, 1864.

EPILOGUE

In considering what Lovejoy might have done had he lived beyond 1864, I have called particularly upon the following sources: the letter from Owen Lovejoy to William Lloyd Garrison, February 22, 1864, in Wendell P. Garrison and Francis J. Garrison, *William Lloyd Garrison, 1805–1879: The Story of His Life Told by His Children* (New York, 1886–1889), IV, 97–99; Carl Sandburg, *Abraham Lincoln: The War Years* (New York, 1939); James M. McPherson, *The Struggle for Equality: Abolitionists and the Negro in the Civil War and Reconstruction* (Princeton, New Jersey, 1964), pp. 124–27, and his chapters on the ballot for the freedmen and on the reelection of Lincoln; W. E. B. Du Bois, *Black Reconstruction* (New York, 1935).

Bibliography

MANUSCRIPTS

These are the principal manuscript collections used in the preparation of this book. Scattered items are not included here, but their locations are supplied in the notes.

Owen Lovejoy Collection, Bureau County Historical Society, Princeton, Illinois

Owen Lovejoy Papers, William L. Clements Library, University of Michigan, Ann Arbor

Wickett-Wiswall Collection of Lovejoy Papers, Texas Technological College, Lubbock. (Many of the papers in this collection are those of Elijah P. Lovejoy, but a fair number are those of Owen Lovejoy.)

American Missionary Association Archives, Fisk University, Nashville, Tennessee

William Cullen Bryant Papers, New York Public Library

David Davis Papers, Chicago Historical Society

Zebina Eastman Collection, Chicago Historical Society

Jesse Fell Papers, McLean County Historical Society, Bloomington, Illinois

Garrison Collection, Boston Public Library
Abraham Lincoln Collection, Library of Congress
William Henry Seward Collection, University of Rochester
Gerrit Smith Papers, Syracuse University
Thurlow Weed Collection, University of Rochester

GOVERNMENT DOCUMENTS

The *Congressional Globe*, 35th through 38th Congresses (1857–1865), was an indispensable primary source of information.

OWEN LOVEJOY SPEECHES

Lovejoy's only published works were the *Memoir of Elijah P. Lovejoy*, which he and his brother Joseph C. Lovejoy prepared in 1838, and a lengthy poem published in 1862 (a reprint of the agricultural poem delivered before the Bureau County Agricultural Society in 1859). However, a number of his major speeches were printed in pamphlet form or were reproduced in newspapers, if not in the *Congressional Globe*. The principal ones are:

Acceptance Speech, on renomination for Congress, at Republican Third Congressional District Convention, June 30, 1858, Joliet, Illinois (*Extra, Bureau County Republican*, Princeton, July 8, 1858).

The Barbarism of Slavery. Delivered in the United States House of Representatives, April 5, 1860 (Washington, Buell & Blanchard, 1860).

Conduct of the War. Delivered in the United States House of Representatives, January 6, 1862 (Washington, Scammell & Co., 1862).

Confiscation of Rebel Property. In reply to Messrs. [John J.] Crittenden and [Charles] Wickliffe of Kentucky, in the House of Representatives, April 24, 1862 (Washington, Scammell & Co., 1862).

The Fanaticism of the Democratic Party. Delivered in the United States House of Representatives, February 21, 1859 (Washington, Buell & Blanchard, 1860).

Freedom the Shekina of America, Address at Cooper Institute, June 12, 1862 (New York *Tribune*, June 13, 1862).

The Great Struggle (over Kansas), in House of Representatives,

February 17, 1858 (*Congressional Globe*, 35 Congress, 1 Session, pp. 752–54).

BOOKS AND PAMPHLETS

Angle, Paul M., ed., *Created Equal?; The Complete Lincoln-Douglas Debates of 1858;* Chicago, 1958.

——, *Herndon's Life of Lincoln*, New York, 1949.

——, *Lincoln, 1854–1861; Being the Day-By-Day Activities of Abraham Lincoln*, Springfield, 1933.

——, *The Lincoln Reader*, New Brunswick, 1947.

Aptheker, Herbert, ed., *A Documentary History of the Negro People in the United States*, New York, 1951.

——, *American Negro Slave Revolts*, New York, 1943.

Arnold, Isaac Newton, *The Life of Abraham Lincoln*, Chicago, 1885.

Baringer, William E., *Lincoln's Rise to Power*, Boston, 1937.

Barton, W. E., *The Life of Abraham Lincoln*, vol. II, Indianapolis, 1925.

Basler, Roy P., Marion Dolores Pratt, and Lloyd A. Dunlap, eds., *The Collected Works of Abraham Lincoln*, 9 vols., New Brunswick, 1953.

Beecher, Edward, *Narrative of the Riots at Alton*, Alton, 1838.

Beveridge, Albert J., *Abraham Lincoln, 1809–1858*, 2 vols., Boston and New York, 1928.

Birney, William, *James G. Birney and His Times*, New York, 1890.

Blaine, James G., *Twenty Years of Congress, from Lincoln to Garfield*, 2 vols., Norwich, Connecticut, 1884.

Bohmann, George V., "Owen Lovejoy on 'The Barbarism of Slavery,' April 5, 1860," in J. Jeffrey Auer, ed., *Antislavery and Disunion, 1858–1861: Studies in the Rhetoric of Compromise and Conflict*, New York and Evanston, 1963.

Bradsby, H. C., *History of Bureau County* (Illinois), Chicago, 1885.

Brodie, Fawn M., *Thaddeus Stevens, Scourge of the South*, New York, 1959.

Browne, Robert H., *Abraham Lincoln and the Men of His Time*, 2 vols., Cincinnati, 1901; rev. ed., Chicago, 1907.

Carpenter, Francis B., *Six Months at the White House with Abraham Lincoln*, Boston, 1866.

Carr, Clark E., *My Day and Generation*, Chicago, 1908.

Caton, John D., *Early Bench and Bar in Illinois*, Chicago, 1893.

Church, Charles A., *History of the Republican Party in Illinois*, Rockford, 1912.

Clark, Calvin M., *American Slavery and Maine Congregationalists*, Bangor, 1940.

Cleveland, C. D., *Anti-Slavery Addresses of 1844 and 1845*, Philadelphia, 1867.

Cole, Arthur C., *The Era of the Civil War, 1848–1870*, Chicago, 1922.

Cornish, Dudley T., *The Sable Arm; Negro Troops in the Union Army, 1861–1865*, New York, 1956.

Cox, Samuel S., *Eight Years in Congress from 1857–1865*, New York, 1865.

Crofutt, William A., *An American Procession, 1855–1914*, Boston, 1931.

Curtis, Francis, *The Republican Party*, New York, 1904.

Darby, John F., *Personal Recollections of Men and Events in St. Louis*, St. Louis, 1880.

Dennett, Tyler, ed., *Lincoln and the Civil War in the Diaries and Letters of John Hay*, New York, 1939.

Dillon, Merton L., *Elijah P. Lovejoy, Abolitionist Editor*, Urbana, 1961.

Donald, David, *Lincoln's Herndon*, New York, 1948.

———, *Lincoln Reconsidered*, New York, 1955.

Duberman, Martin, ed., *The Antislavery Vanguard: New Essays on the Abolitionists*, Princeton, New Jersey, 1965.

DuBois, James T., and Gertrude S. Mathews, *Galusha A. Grow, Father of the Homestead Law*, New York, 1917.

Du Bois, W. E. B., *Black Reconstruction*, New York, 1935.

Dumond, Dwight L., *Antislavery: The Crusade for Freedom in America*, Ann Arbor, 1961.

———, *Antislavery Origins of the Civil War in the United States*, Ann Arbor, 1939.

———, ed., *Letters of James Gillespie Birney, 1831–1857*, 2 vols., New York, 1938.

Eastman, Zebina, "History of the Anti-Slavery Agitation, and the Growth of the Liberty and Republican Parties in the State of Illinois," undated pamphlet, Eastman Collection, Chicago Historical Society, Autograph Letters, vol. 40.

Eddy, Thomas M., *The Patriotism of Illinois*, 2 vols., Chicago, 1865

Fehrenbacher, Don E., *Chicago Giant, Biography of "Long John" Wentworth*, Madison, 1957.

Filler, Louis, *The Crusade Against Slavery, 1830–1860*, New York, 1960.

Fladeland, Betty, *James Gillespie Birney: Slaveholder to Abolitionist*, Ithaca, 1955.

Flower, Frank A., *History of the Republican Party*, Springfield, 1884.

Fogel, Robert W., *The Union Pacific Railroad; A Case in Premature Enterprise*, Baltimore, 1960.

Foner, Philip S., *Business and Slavery: The New York Merchants and the Irrepressible Conflict*, Chapel Hill, 1941

———, *History of the Labor Movement in the United States from Colonial Times to the Founding of the American Federation of Labor*, New York, 1947.

———, ed., *The Life and Writings of Frederick Douglass*, 4 vols., New York, 1950–1955.

Ford, Henry A., *The History of Putnam and Marshall Counties . . . and Formation of Bureau and Stark Counties*, Lacon, Illinois, 1860.

Franklin, John Hope, *From Slavery to Freedom, a History of American Negroes*, New York, 1956.

Gara, Larry, *The Liberty Line: The Legend of the Underground Railroad*, Lexington, 1961.

Garrison, Wendell P. and Francis J., *William Lloyd Garrison, 1805–1879: The Story of His Life Told by His Children*, 4 vols., New York, 1886–1889.

Genovese, Eugene D., *The Political Economy of Slavery*, New York, 1965.

Gill, John, *Tide Without Turning: Elijah P. Lovejoy and Freedom of the Press*, Boston, 1958.

Harlow, Ralph V., *Gerrit Smith, Philanthropist and Reformer*, New York, 1939.

Harris, N. Dwight, *The History of Negro Servitude in Illinois*, Chicago, 1904.

Hart, A. B., *Slavery and Abolition, 1831–1841*, New York, 1906.

Heagle, Rev. D., "The Great Anti-Slavery Agitator, Hon. Owen Lovejoy," Princeton, Illinois, 1885.

Hesseltine, William B., *Lincoln and the War Governors*, New York, 1948.

Higginson, Thomas Wentworth, *Army Life in a Black Regiment*, Boston, 1869; New York, 1962.

Howard, John Raymond, *Remembrance of Things Past*, New York, 1925.

Julian, George W., *Political Recollections, 1840–1872*, Chicago, 1884.

King, Willard L., *David Davis, Lincoln's Manager*, Cambridge, 1960.

Knoles, George H., ed., *The Crisis of the Union, 1860–1861*, Baton Rouge, 1965.

Korngold, Ralph, *Thaddeus Stevens, a Being Darkly Wise and Rudely Great*, New York, 1955

———, *Two Friends of Man: The Story of William Lloyd Garrison and Wendell Phillips and Their Relationship with Abraham Lincoln*, Boston, 1950.

Kuhns, Frederick I., *The American Home Missionary Society in Relation to the Antislavery Controversy in the Old Northwest*, Billings, 1959.

Lamon, Ward Hill, *Life of Abraham Lincoln*, Boston, 1872.

Lincoln, William S., *The Alton Trials*, New York, 1838.

Litwack, Leon F., *North of Slavery: The Negro in the Free States, 1790–1860*, Chicago, 1961.

Lovejoy, Clarence E., *Lovejoy Genealogy*, New York, 1930.

Lovejoy, Joseph C., "Letter from J. C. Lovejoy, Esq., to His Brother, Hon. Owen Lovejoy, M. C.," Boston, 1859.

Lovejoy, Joseph C. and Owen, *Memoir of the Rev. Elijah P. Lovejoy; Who Was Murdered in Defence of the Liberty of the Press at Alton, Illinois, Nov. 7, 1837*, New York, 1838.

Lusk, D. W., *Eighty Years of Illinois; Anecdotes and Incidents; Politics and Politicians: A Succinct History of the State, 1809–1889*, Springfield, 1889.

McClellan, George B., *McClellan's Own Story, the War for the Union*, New York, 1887.

McCormack, Thomas J., ed., *Memoirs of Gustave Koerner, 1809–1896*, 2 vols., Cedar Rapids, 1909.

McKitrick, Eric L., *Andrew Johnson and Reconstruction*, Chicago, 1960.

McMaster, John B., *A History of the People of the United States, from the Revolution to the Civil War*, vol. VIII, New York, 1915.

———, *Our House Divided*, New York, 1961, originally published as *A History of the People of the United States During Lincoln's Administration*, New York, 1927.

McPherson, James M., *The Struggle for Equality: Abolitionists and the Negro in the Civil War and Reconstruction*, Princeton, New Jersey, 1964.

McWhiney, Grady, ed., *Grant, Lee, Lincoln and the Radicals*, Evanston, 1964.

Madison County, Illinois, *Gazetteer* (Alton, Illinois, 1866).

Marsh, Charles W., *Recollections, 1837–1910*, Chicago, 1910.

Matson, Nehemiah, *Reminiscences of Bureau County*, Princeton, Illinois, 1872.

Mitchell, Wesley C., *A History of the Greenbacks*, Chicago, 1903.

Monaghan, Jay, *The Man Who Elected Lincoln*, Indianapolis and New York, 1956.

Morehouse, Frances Milton I., *The Life of Jesse Fell*, Urbana, 1916.

Muelder, Hermann R., *Fighters for Freedom: The History of Antislavery Activities of Men and Women Associated with Knox College*, New York, 1959.

Nevins, Allan, *The Emergence of Lincoln*, vol. II, New York, 1950.

———, *Ordeal of the Union*, vol. II, New York, 1947.

———, *The War for the Union*, 2 vols., New York, 1959 and 1960.

Nichols, Roy F., *The Disruption of American Democracy*, New York, 1948, 1962.

———, *The Stakes of Power, 1845–1877*, New York, 1961.

Nye, Russel B., *Fettered Freedom: Civil Liberties and the Slavery Controversy, 1830–1860*, East Lansing, 1949.

Oberholtzer, Ellis P., *Jay Cooke, Financier of the Civil War*, 2 vols., Philadelphia, 1907.

Obermann, Karl, *Joseph Weydemeyer, Pioneer of American Socialism*, New York, 1947.

Palmer, John M., *Personal Recollections: The Story of an Earnest Life*, Cincinnati, 1901.

Pease, Theodore C., *Illinois Election Returns, 1818–1848*, Springfield, 1923.

Perkins, Howard C., ed., *Northern Editorials on Secession,* New York, 1942.

Pierce, Edward L., ed., *Memoirs and Letters of Charles Sumner,* 4 vols., Boston, 1877–1893.

Pike, James S., *First Blows of the Civil War,* New York, 1879.

Potter, David M., *Lincoln and His Party in the Secession Crisis,* New Haven, 1942.

Prince, Ezra M., ed., *Historical Encyclopedia of Illinois and History of McClean County,* 2 vols., Chicago, 1908.

———, ed., *Transactions of the McLean County Historical Society . . . Meeting of May 29, 1900, Commemorative of the Convention of May 29, 1856,* vol. III, Bloomington, Illinois, 1900.

Proceedings of the First Three Republican National Conventions of 1856, 1860, and 1864, Minneapolis, 1893.

Quarles, Benjamin, *The Negro in the Civil War,* Boston, 1953.

Raum, Green B., *History of Illinois Republicanism,* Chicago, 1900.

Rice, Allen Thorndike, ed., *Reminiscences of Abraham Lincoln by Distinguished Men of His Time,* New York, 1886.

Riddle, Albert G., *Recollections of War Times: Reminiscences of Men and Events in Washington, 1860–1865,* New York, 1895.

Robbins, Roy M., *Our Landed Heritage; the Public Domain, 1776–1936,* Princeton, New Jersey, 1942.

Ruchames, Louis, ed., *A John Brown Reader,* London and New York, 1959.

Russel, Robert R., *Improvement of Communications with the Pacific Coast as an Issue in American Politics,* Cedar Rapids, 1948.

Russell, W. H., *My Diary North and South,* Boston, 1863.

Sandburg, Carl, *Abraham Lincoln: The War Years,* 4 vols., New York, 1939.

Schlueter, Herman, *Lincoln, Labor, and Slavery,* New York, 1913.

Sharkey, Robert P., *Money, Class and Party: An Economic Study of Civil War and Reconstruction,* Baltimore, 1959.

Siebert, W. A., *The Underground Railroad from Slavery to Freedom,* New York, 1898.

Smith, George Owen, "The Lovejoy Shrine, the Lovejoy Station on the Underground Railroad," Princeton, Illinois, 1949.

Smith, T. C., *The Liberty and Free-Soil Parties in the North West,* New York, 1897.

Smith, William E., *Francis Preston Blair Family in Politics*, New York, 1933.
Spaulding, E. G., *History of the Legal Tender Paper Money Issued During the Great Rebellion*, Buffalo, 1869.
Spinka, Matthew, ed., *A History of Illinois Congregational and Christian Churches*, Chicago, 1944.
Stampp, Kenneth M., *And the War Came*, Baton Rouge, 1950.
———, *The Peculiar Institution*, New York, 1956.
Stanton, Henry B., *Random Recollections*, New York, 1886.
Study, Guy, *History of St. Paul's Church, Alton, Illinois*, St. Louis, 1943.
Tanner, Henry, *The Martyrdom of Lovejoy*, Chicago, 1881.
Thomas, Benjamin P., *Theodore Weld, Crusader for Freedom*, New Brunswick, 1950.
Union League of America (U.L.A.), *Proceedings of National Convention, May 20, 21, 1863, at Cleveland, Ohio.*
United States Department of Agriculture *Yearbook 1940*, Washington, D.C., 1940.
Vallandigham, James L., *A Life of Clement L. Vallandigham, by His Brother*, Baltimore, 1872.
Wallace, Isabel, *Life and Letters of General W. H. L. Wallace*, Chicago, 1909.
Wentworth, John, *Congressional Reminiscences*, Chicago, 1882.
West, Richard S., Jr., *Lincoln's Scapegoat General: A Life of Benjamin F. Butler, 1818–1893*, Boston, 1965.
White, Horace, "Abraham Lincoln in 1854," Springfield, 1908.
———, *Life of Lyman Trumbull*, New York, 1913.
Whitney, Henry C., *Life on the Circuit with Lincoln*, Boston, 1892.
Williams, T. Harry, *Lincoln and the Radicals*, Madison, 1940.
———, *McClellan, Sherman and Grant*, New Brunswick, 1962.
Wilson, Henry, *History of the Antislavery Measures of the Thirty-Seventh and Thirty-Eighth Congresses, 1861–1864*, Boston, 1864.

UNPUBLISHED THESES

Brush, Elizabeth P., "The Political Career of Owen Lovejoy," Master's thesis, University of Illinois, 1912.
Gibson, Guy James, "Lincoln's League: The Union League Move-

ment During the Civil War," Ph.D. thesis, University of
Illinois, University Microfilms, Ann Arbor, 1958.

McGuire, Joseph F., "Owen Lovejoy, Congressman from the
Prairie," thesis for Master of Science in Education, Illinois
State Normal University, Studies in Education, No. 137,
Normal, 1950.

ARTICLES

Angle, Paul M., "The Peoria Truce," *Journal of the Illinois State
Historical Society*, January, 1929, 500–05.

Atkinson, P., "A Reminiscence of the Late Hon. Owen Lovejoy,"
New York *Independent*, May 5, 1864.

Baringer, William E., "Campaign Techniques in Illinois—1860,"
Transactions of the Illinois State Historical Society, XXXIX
(1932), 202–81.

Browne, Albert C., "The Utah Expedition," *Atlantic Monthly*, April,
1859, 474–91.

Cole, Arthur C., "President Lincoln and the Illinois Radical Republicans," *Mississippi Valley Historical Review*, IV (1918), 417–
36.

Cunningham, J. O., "The Bloomington Convention of 1856 and
Those Who Participated in It," *Transactions of the Illinois
State Historical Society*, X (1905).

Foner, Eric, "Politics and Prejudice: The Free Soil Party and the
Negro, 1849–1852," *Journal of Negro History*, L (1965),
239–56.

Haberkorn, Ruth E., "Owen Lovejoy in Princeton, Illinois," *Journal of the Illinois State Historical Society*, XXXVI (1943),
284–315.

Harrison, Ella W., "A History of the First Congregational Church
of Princeton, Illinois, 1831–1924," *Journal of the Illinois State
Historical Society*, XX (1927), 106.

Heinl, Frank J., "Congregationalism in Jacksonville and Early Illinois," *Journal of the Illinois State Historical Society*, XXVII
(1935), 441–46.

Herriot, Frank I., "The Conference of the German Republicans in
the Deutsches Haus, Chicago, May 14–15, 1860," *Transactions
of the Illinois State Historical Society*, XXXV (1928), 101–91.

Julian, George W., "The First Republican National Convention," *American Historical Review*, IV (1899), 312–22.

King, Ameda Ruth, "The Last Years of the Whig Party in Illinois, 1847–1856," *Transactions of the Illinois State Historical Society*, XXXII (1925), 108–55.

Kyle, Otto R., "Mr. Lincoln Steps Out: The Anti-Nebraska Editors Convention," *Abraham Lincoln Quarterly*, V (March, 1948), 25–37.

Luthin, Reinhard, "Lincoln Becomes a Republican," *Political Science Quarterly*, LIX (1944), 420–38.

Magdol, Edward, "Owen Lovejoy's Role in the Campaign of 1858," *Journal of the Illinois State Historical Society*, LI (1958), 403–16.

Pope, Thomas, "Manuscript History of the Quincy Church," *Transactions of the Illinois State Historical Society*, X (1903), 317–21.

Prince, Ezra M., "Reminiscences of Owen Lovejoy," Bloomington *Daily Pantagraph*, November 17, 1906.

Ruchames, Louis, "The Historian as Special Pleader," *The Nation*, November 24, 1962.

Selby, Paul, "The Editorial Convention, February 22, 1856," *Transactions of the McLean County Historical Society*, III (1900), 30–43.

———, "The Editorial Convention of 1856." *Journal of the Illinois State Historical Society*, V (1912), 343–49.

———, "Genesis of the Republican Party in Illinois," *Tranactions of the Illinois State Historical Society*, XI (1906), 270–83.

———, "Republican State Convention, Springfield, Illinois, October 4–5, 1854," *Transactions of the McLean County Historical Society*, III (1900), 43–47.

Sellers, James L., "The Make-Up of the Early Republican Party," *Transactions of the Illinois State Historical Society*, XXXVII (1930), 39–51.

Sewell, Richard, "John P. Hale and the Liberty Party, 1847–48," *New England Quarterly* (June, 1964).

Shaw, Benjamin, "Owen Lovejoy, Constitutional Abolitionists and the Republican Party," *Transactions of the McLean County Historical Society*, III (1900), 59–73.

Stoler, Mildred, "Democratic Element in the Republican Party in Illinois," *Illinois State Historical Society Papers* (1942), 32–71.

Wesley, Charles H., "The Participation of Negroes in Anti-Slavery Political Parties," *Journal of Negro History*, XXIX (January, 1944), 37–69.

Wright, Elizur, "Judge Lawless vs. Law," *Quarterly Anti-Slavery Magazine*, I, 4 (1836), 400–09.

anon., "The House of Representatives," *The Nation*, April 4, 1879.

NEWSPAPERS

Alton (Illinois) *Observer*
Bloomington (Illinois) *Daily Pantagraph*
Boston *Commonwealth*
Boston *Daily Evening Transcript*
Boston *Evening Journal*
Brooklyn *Daily Union*
Brooklyn *Eagle*
Bureau County (Illinois) *Republican*
Central Illinois Gazette (Champaign)
Chicago *Journal*
Chicago *Press and Tribune*
Chicago *Tribune*
Daily Milwaukee News
Free West (Chicago)
National Anti-Slavery Standard
New York *Independent*
New York *Times*
New York *Tribune*
Peoria *Daily Transcript*
Portland (Maine) *Transcript*
Racine *Advocate*
Racine *Daily Journal*
St. Louis *Observer*
Washington *National Intelligencer*
Western Citizen (Lowell and Chicago, Illinois)

Index

Abolitionism, 62, 101, 126, 282, 283, 397; antislavery and, 7, 11, 12, 29, 53–54, 411, 414, 416–17; churches and, 6, 33, 36, 65, 68; in Congress, 54, 55, 59, 121, 128, 165, 166–67, 170, 175, 205, 260, 275, 336, 433; conservatism and, 14, 129, 206–207, 208, 209, 217, 337; free speech and, 8, 9, 15, 16–17, 22–23, 35; fund-raising, 18, 19, 28, 29–30, 32, 68, 180; fusion of forces of, 106, 117–19, 120, 128, 130, 131–133, 134, 139–40, 146; immigrants and, 96–97, 105, 108; law and, 78, 102–103, 104, 135–36, 203, 266; Lincoln and, 110, 111, 114, 130, 133, 134, 147, 149, 201, 202, 259, 301, 302, 328, 329–30, 339, 386, 412; Lovejoy (Owen) commitment to, 24, 27–28, 30, 32, 51, 177; political action use in, 55, 56–57, 58, 59, 60, 61, 96–97; radicalism and, 81, 82, 114, 154, 157, 158, 162, 172, 198, 210, 217, 253, 321, 337, 366; secessionism and, 260, 262, 269, 285,

316–17; war and, 75, 278–80, 300, 311, 325
Adams, Charles Francis, 151
Adams, John Quincy, 30, 66, 404; slavery and, 54, 300, 413
Adams County, Illinois, 13, 58, 60
Additional Revenue Bill (1861), 285
"Address of the Liberty Party to the Voters of Illinois" (Lovejoy, Cross and Collins), 60–62
"Address of the Republican Members of Congress" (1862), 344
Adrain, Garnett B., 235, 240
Africa, 6, 12, 18, 53, 66, 179
"Agnes-Nancy" case, 40–46, 64, 81, 85, 170
Agriculture, 13, 109, 168, 171, 184, 233, 352–54; Lovejoy farm and, 25, 38, 227; plantation system, 230, 262, 335; tariffs and, 246; western expansion and, 104, 105
Aldrich, Cyrus, 151, 317; quoted, 156
Allen, J. C., 407

About the Author

Edward Magdol's interest in the antislavery movement began during his undergraduate days at the University of Michigan, and his search for information about Owen Lovejoy has been carried out over a number of years in libraries and manuscript collections in Illinois, Michigan, Wisconsin, Texas, Maine, New York City, and Washington, D.C. Mr. Magdol holds a Master's degree from Teachers College, Columbia University, and taught for several years in New York City high schools; however, at other times in his career he has been a copy editor, a proofreader, even a compositor, for New York City printers and publishers. In 1959 he moved to Madison, Wisconsin, to become a feature writer for credit union publications. He is now the editor of *Everybody's Money* magazine.